Contents

Acknowledgements

The idea for this book was suggested to me several years ago by John Murray, with whom I have had a long and happy association for some quarter of a century. It could not have been written without the help and advice of a number of specialists and institutions. I should like to thank in particular Carol Michaelson of the Oriental Department of the British Museum, an expert on Chinese history and art; also the departmental librarians of the School of Oriental and African Studies of London University for their guidance on the great resources of that library. I am also grateful to Susan Leiper for many valuable comments and for casting a very sharp eye over the proofs. It goes without saying that any outstanding errors are my sole responsibility. I should like to thank Chris Puleston for his excellent drawings that reflect so accurately the art of other ages and cultures. To Stella I remain, as always, grateful for taking on an even larger share than usual of the work in all its stages.

How to Use this Book

THE main dictionary is divided into six sections, according to subject: Abstract signs, Animals (including birds and insects), Artefacts, Earth and Sky, Human Body and Dress, Plants. This should make reference quicker and easier, but if in doubt turn to the index where the main entry is in bold type. Cross-references will be found in the index. In the dictionary itself they are shown in small capitals.

There is a final section (unillustrated) which contains what I call 'Collectives'. These are subjects such as the Four Seasons, Seven Liberal Arts and Twelve Ornaments that comprise numerous symbols and to which reference is made many times in the main dictionary. Gods and others who have multiple attributes will also be found here. This avoids the need for tiresomely repetitive explanations whenever they are mentioned elsewhere.

In choosing the illustrations with Chris Puleston, we usually preferred their less familiar aspects, particularly in the case of well-known, everyday objects.

Transliteration

There are often alternative systems for transcribing foreign alphabets into Roman. This can sometimes be puzzling, especially when using an index. I decided, after much thought, to stick to the older systems when there is a choice, because they are the ones used in most of the older-established reference books mentioned in the bibliography. For Chinese words I have kept to Wade-Giles instead of the more recent Pinyin (e.g., Chou and Ch'ing dynasties, not Zhou, Qing). See also the Appendix, p.216. For Sanskrit I have used the older, more familiar forms that have no diacritical marks (Krishna, Shiva; not Kṛṣṇa, Śiva). Mesopotamian gods are usually referred to by their Akkadian (Semitic) names without accents, though the Sumerian name is used when appropriate (Ea, not Enki; Adad, not Ishkur). Classical deities are given in both Greek and Latin forms (Aphrodite/Venus; Zeus/Jupiter).

About Symbols in Art

A SYMBOL is simply 'something that stands for, represents, or denotes something else' (*OED*). We seem to have a natural tendency to create symbols in the way we think and in our art, which must reflect a deep-seated trait of the human spirit. Take the lion, for instance. In all essentials it is just 'a large, fierce, tawny, loud-roaring animal of the cat family'. Once we begin to call it the 'King of Beasts' or 'Lord of the Jungle' it is on its way to becoming a symbol. In fact, of all creatures it is one of the most richly endowed with symbolism, much of it religious, even among people where it has never been known in the wild state.

Symbols in art function at many different levels according to the beliefs and social customs that inspire the artist. Among the Chinese they may sometimes express no more than a graceful compliment. A painted vase or dish offered as a gift by a visitor to his host might, by its choice of decorative images, wish the recipient a long life, many children, or even success in the state examinations. This symbolic language was once widely understood among educated Chinese.

On another level are those images – and they form the great majority – that are related to worship. Let us consider for a moment the human body, when the artist uses it to represent a god or goddess. By itself a body is impersonal and anonymous. It must first be clothed and accoutred in a distinctive fashion in order to make a recognizable deity. We put it in armour to represent, say, Mars, the god of war. If we then add a pair of wings it becomes the Archangel Michael, Commander of the Heavenly Host. In thus giving substance and identity to beings whose form is, in reality, unknowable the artist is making a symbolic image. The Stoic philosopher, Zeno, who lived around 300 BC, put it this way. The Greek gods, with their distinctive, readily identifiable forms, were, he said, not anthropomorphic at all; they were all symbols, the different aspects of a single divine being whose true nature was wholly impersonal. When we come to oriental art we find it thronging with deities in human form, most of whom represent abstract, metaphysical concepts that have no counterpart in real life. They, too, are symbols.

But even the sacred figures of history may be treated as symbols. We can only guess how the Buddha or Jesus looked in life. The Buddha, with his tight, curly hair and top-knot, tuft between the brows, pendent ear-lobes and mystic signs on hands and feet, bears little or no physical resemblance, we may assume, to the historical founder of Buddhism. Jesus, when crowned and enthroned in the style of an East Roman emperor, is immediately recognizable as the sovereign King of Heaven, the Almighty. Yet when clad in a peasant's tunic, girded at the waist, and carrying a lamb round his shoulders, he becomes the Good Shepherd of the gospels. These are symbolic images of the religious leaders.

Zeno lived in an age when the Olympian gods were in decline. Athens had been conquered by Sparta, a defeat her guardian deity, Pallas Athena, had been powerless to prevent. An element of chance now appeared to govern people's fate. Soon Chance, or Fortune, was deified and became, like the Olympians, a personalized goddess, known in Greece as Tyche. The idea of deifying and giving human form to abstract concepts was taken up in Rome where, from the time of Augustus, Peace, Health and Providence looked after the welfare of the emperors. Medieval and Renaissance Europe created a huge family of symbolic figures of this kind, which still populate our cathedrals, palaces and public gardens. There we find numberless virtues and vices, the seasons of the year, parts of the world, ages of man and much more besides.

But the gods were not always portrayed as human beings. People once believed that natural phenomena – the course of the sun across the sky, rainfall, the fertility of beasts and crops, pregnancy and childbirth – were all controlled by unseen powers. Since one's very existence depended on their favourable behaviour they were propitiated with sacrifice and prayer. These mysterious forces were not at first thought of as having human form, so when an artist made an image of the sun, the moon, or a thunderbolt, it was the god himself that he was portraying. In a sense, therefore, this kind of image goes beyond symbolism: it is a literal representation of a deity.

Animals, too, were endowed with the same mysterious power, or *mana*, that pervaded the natural world. Birds not merely foretold the weather, they somehow created it. They were worshipped as bringers of sunshine and storm. The leader of the primitive tribe, its priest, or 'medicine-man', dressed in the masks and skins of animals to acquire their *mana* for himself and gain control over nature. The half-human, half-animal gods we see in the art of Egypt, Mesopotamia and India are the 'medicine-man's' descendants.

When gods and goddesses began to assume the shapes of men and women the old, primordial images were not abandoned. The human deity was depicted standing above, or seated on, his older animal form, as if it were his mount, or 'vehicle'. The solar disk and crescent moon became part of his crown or head-dress. Finally, having fully evolved into human form, as they did so splendidly in ancient Greece, they retained their previous, non-figurative selves as attributes. We may note, in passing, a similar, though unrelated evolution that took place in early Christian art when Christ and the apostles are initially represented as sheep. When they become men they retain the sheep as attributes. This extremely useful convention, the attribute, which gives identity to an otherwise anonymous figure, later permeated western Christian art and was widely adopted in Hindu and Buddhist art. Indeed, the gods of esoteric, Tantric Buddhism have so many and share them so readily that they are sometimes not much help in identification.

There are many instances when an object is both symbol and attribute. Thus, two keys identify St Peter and at the same time symbolize the founding of the Christian Church. A thunderbolt, the attribute of numerous sky-gods, became for some Buddhists a symbol of the very heart of their philosophy, the state of Enlightenment. On the other hand a swan beside a bishop tells us he is St Hugh of Lincoln, for the simple reason that he kept a tame swan as a pet.

Finally, another word about art and magic. We have seen how they were closely related from very early times, and it is strange to observe that civilized peoples retained beliefs similar to their primitive ancestors. Inert matter, whether clay, metal, stone, or pigment, once it has been shaped by the artist's imagination, seems to vibrate with a numinous power that can influence people and events. Thus, a god's image would be carried into battle in the expectation that it would bring victory. In the city it received oblations in order to protect the citizens from harm. Some, it is claimed, have even been known to nod their head or shed tears. Similarly, snakes, scorpions and suchlike creatures that in real life are dangerous and to be avoided acquired beneficial, magical properties as images. As sculptures or paintings they functioned as symbolic guardians at the gates of temples, palaces and tombs. The lion, which is unlikely to guard anything except its cubs or the next meal, was an especially popular choice. The magical influence emanating from the stone kept evil spirits at bay. Much of Tantric Buddhist art works at this mystical level. The painted *mandala*, an elaborate symbol of the universe, is felt to have the power to conjure the very presence of a god, when subjected to intense, concentrated meditation. Other Tantric images, either purely abstract or consisting of a written word or even a single character, are felt to produce the same effect.

In geographical scope this book takes in the art of Christian and classical Europe, Egypt, the ancient Near East, India and the Far East – not exhaustively, it need hardly be said, but, I hope, in its more important and more widely depicted aspects. It is a region that I think can be shown to have acquired over the course of very many centuries many points of contact (perhaps network is not too strong a word) connecting its different cultures. It was a process that was unhindered (except in Indonesia and Japan) by the 'estranging sea'.

Some five thousand years ago this great region was the birthplace of the world's first civilizations, centred on four river valleys: the Nile, Euphrates/Tigris, Indus and Huang-Ho. From the beginning each had some kind of representational art, much of it consisting of religious symbols that reflected very varied forms of worship. The diffusion of their cultures came about in several ways: invading armies who brought their gods with them; growth of trade (which first brought China into contact with the West) and the accompanying exchange of coinage, a rich and varied source of imagery; and the expansion of religion through missions and pilgrimage, especially Buddhism and Christianity.

Buddhist art travelled from India through South-East Asia, Indonesia, Tibet, China and Japan, taking in local cults on the way and adapting their imagery to its own ends. Christianity, born in the Near East, absorbed some of the religious imagery of the region through the Old Testament. Persian textiles, which found their way to the West, have motifs that reappear in Byzantine church art. Others came from as far away as China. In the West the Church absorbed imagery from the pagan cults it replaced and gave it a fresh, Christian meaning.

We see how easily symbolic images can mean different things to different peoples; how seldom, at least in art, are they endowed with a fixed, immutable core of meaning that transcends different social and religious milieus. This is not to deny the existence of unconscious archetypes as a source of symbolism, but simply to keep them in perspective and be aware of their limited importance in relation to the visual arts.

THE DICTIONARY

1. Abstract Signs

[i]

A. The first letter of Sanskrit, Greek and Roman alphabets. Vishnu, one of the supreme Hindu gods, said 'I am the beginning, the middle, the end of all creation; of letters I am the A.'[1] The letter A is one of a series of usually five mystical characters (Sk. *siddham*) uttered as syllables by Vajrayana Buddhists, especially the Shingon sect of Japan, in their devotions. Its magical power will conjure up the deity. Each letter denotes one of the five Dhyani-Buddhas, 'A', denoting the supreme Adi-Buddha, VAIROCANA [i]. The written character, on a lotus throne, is also an object of contemplation. On Roman funerary monuments the letter A indicates that the deceased was an only child. See also WORD; BUDDHA.

[ii]

A and ω (or Ω). The first and last letters of the Greek alphabet are a Christian symbol of God as the beginning and end of all things. It is found in early funerary inscriptions in the Roman catacombs and occasionally in Renaissance and later painting, where the letters may be inscribed on the facing pages of an open book held by God the Father,[2] particularly in representations of the TRINITY [ii].

[iii]

Ankh. Egyptian hieroglyph for life, possibly originally a representation of a sandal strap [iii]. As a symbol it denotes eternal life and when held to the nose of a dead pharaoh ensures his everlasting existence. It is held by many deities, in particular Atum, the sun-god of Heliopolis, and (when seated) Sekhmet, the lion-headed war-goddess of Memphis. A *was* SCEPTRE combining the *djed* column and ankh is the attribute of PTAH. On the walls of temples it gives divine protection to the deceased. The Coptic Church adopted it as a form of the cross, called ansate (having a handle).

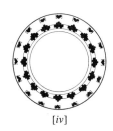

[iv]

Circle (the pure form; see also RING for the annular form). Like the sphere, a symbol of the cosmos, the heavens, and the supreme deity, in East and West. Renaissance humanists likened it to God from its perfect shape. It formed the ground-plan of churches, especially from the 16th cent. [iv: dome, St Peter's, Rome]. Choirs of angels, representing heaven, may have a circular or hemispherical configuration. As a Taoist and Buddhist symbol, heaven and earth may be represented respectively by a circle enclosed in a square. Taoism also taught that the circle, divided into two in a certain way, symbolized the creative principle of the universe, the two parts being its female and male elements (see YIN AND YANG). Having no end or beginning a circle may denote eternity, sometimes depicted in the West as a

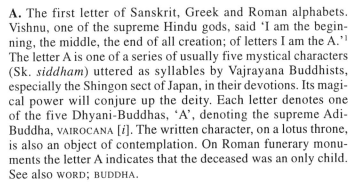

SNAKE biting its own tail, an image of Egyptian origin where it represented the boundlessness of the ocean. For the circle as a Buddhist symbol, see MANDALA. See also COINS; DISK; HALO; SUN; WHEEL.

[*i*]

Cross. The familiar Christian symbol has other, older associations. The equilateral cross [*i*] was once widely used to denote the four cardinal directions, or winds, that brought rain. It therefore became a symbol of sky- and weather-gods like the Mesopotamian sun-god, SHAMASH, and the sky-god, ANU. The cross of the latter may have a solar disk in the centre. See also ANKH; SWASTIKA; T (tau); THUNDERBOLT.

[*ii*]

The earliest Christian cross was the *chi-rho* monogram (see LABARUM). From the 4th cent. when Christians were first allowed to worship freely in the Roman Empire the cross itself began, slowly, to be represented on sarcophagi and other artefacts as a symbol of their religion and of Christ himself. In the Middle Ages it was used on church vestments as a symbol of priestly authority and was borne by orders of chivalry and on banners of guilds. It formed the ground-plan of churches: the Greek, or equilateral, cross for the Byzantine cross-in-square church; the Latin cross [*ii*] typically for western churches and cathedrals (see MAN). The Christian cross has other forms: the saltire, or St Andrew's cross [*iii*], on which the saint was said to have been crucified; the double cross, or cross of Lorraine [*iv*], carried before the bishops, or patriarchs, of the five principal sees of medieval Christendom; with a triple transom it is reserved exclusively for the Pope, e.g. the APOSTLE Peter, and Gregory the Great, one of the FOUR LATIN FATHERS. A cross is the attribute of many Christian saints, too numerous to help identify them. Of the apostles a cross or cross-staff is the attribute of Philip; the saltire, of Andrew. JOHN THE BAPTIST has a reed cross. In Renaissance allegory a cross is an attribute of FAITH personified, who also holds a chalice; of Jeremiah, one of the FOUR PROPHETS; and of three SIBYLS (Hellespontic, Phrygian, Cimmerian). It is one of the INSTRUMENTS OF THE PASSION.

[*iii*]

[*iv*]

Cube. Symbol of stability. In western art FAITH personified rests her foot on it, in contrast to the unstable sphere of Fortune. It is also the foot-rest of History. It is occasionally represented as a polyhedron with more than six sides, as in Dürer's *Melancolia* [*v*] where it symbolizes the Pythagorean doctrine that number and form are the basis of the universe.

[*v*]

Fu. One of the TWELVE ORNAMENTS embroidered on Chinese imperial robes [*vi: Chinese silk, 17th cent.*]. Its origin is uncertain. The two signs were anciently called 'symbols of the discernment we ought to have of good and evil', and may have been intended to represent the upper garment hanging down back to front, or archers' bows. See also DRESS.

[*vi*]

Fungus (Ch. *ling-chih*; Jap. *reishi*). According to a popular su-

[vii]

[viii]

[ix]

[x]

[xi]

[xii]

perstition dating from the Han dynasty there existed a sacred fungus which bestowed immortality when eaten. It was said to flourish in the 'three isles of the blest' in the Western Sea (Japan?) and was especially sought by Taoists whose philosophy held out the promise of eternal life. It is generally represented as the fungus *polyporus lucidus* [vii]. In ceramic decoration it can take a highly stylized form [viii] which is sometimes difficult to distinguish from the CLOUD pattern. It may accompany the BAT of Longevity or the THREE FRIENDS. It is seen in the mouth of a DEER, reputed to be long lived and the only creature able to find it. It is sometimes seen in the hand of Taoist EIGHT IMMORTALS and Lao-tzu himself. See also JU-I sceptre.

IHS. The contraction of the name Jesus in Greek. Other forms are IHC and IC. It is widely seen in the decoration of Greek and Latin churches, on tombs [*ix: Roncevaux, 13th cent.*], vestments and in heraldry. It is the attribute of Bernardino of Siena, of Ansanus when inscribed on a heart, and of the Society of Jesus.

Labarum. Roman military standard emblazoned with the *chi-rho* monogram by Constantine the Great. It is a combination of the Greek letters *chi* and *rho* (X and P). As an abbreviation of *chrestos*, 'auspicious', it had previously been in use as a symbol of good omen, and it is not certain whether the emperor intended it in this sense or as a Christian symbol. A similar motif occurs in Mesopotamia as an Assyrian military ensign and the symbol of a Chaldean sun-god, either of which could be its prototype. As an abbreviation of Christ's name it appears in Roman catacomb art of the 4th cent. or possibly earlier. As a Christian symbol it is often combined with the letters *alpha* and *omega* (see A AND Ω) [*x: Ravenna, 5th cent.*].

Lozenge, Rhomb. A Mesopotamian motif, seen at all periods until the fall of the Assyrian Empire, particularly on 9th – 8th cent. BC cylinder seals and, earlier, on gaming boards from Ur. Its meaning is uncertain but most likely to be an 'all-seeing eye', an apotropaic talisman to ward off the evil eye. In Chinese ceramic decoration a lozenge (*ling ching*) entwined with a red fillet is one of the EIGHT TREASURES [xi]. It is thought to be a symbol of victory. A pair of lozenges, joined end to end or interlocking (*fang cheng*), sometimes seen on the walls of houses, are believed to ward off evil spirits.

Mandala, from the Sanskrit, meaning CIRCLE. A complex image, generally painted on a banner, or *tanka*, the object of meditation by Tantric Buddhists. It is found in India, China, Indonesia and Japan but made its true home among Tibetan Lamaists. Its essential feature is a circle, which usually encloses a square with four 'doors' in the middle of each side facing the four cardinal points [xii]. The ground-plan of the STUPA or pagoda may follow the same geometric pattern. At the centre of the mandala there is usually a sacred figure, a BUDDHA or BODHISATTVA, typically the Adi-Buddha VAIROCANA who may be surrounded by the four Dhyani-Buddhas, each enclosed in his own circle. Alternatively, the central figure may be a demonic 'tutelary deity' embracing his *shakti*. The image probably originated in early Hindu devotional practice. Its characteristic form is a visual metaphor for the structure of the universe as it would be perceived in the act of meditation. It therefore became, magically, the literal dwelling-place of the deity whom the worshipper is invoking in his quest for Enlightenment. There is a 12th cent. record[3] of mandalas having been produced in large numbers between the 6th and 12th cents., an artistic tradition that has continued to the present day. The term is also used of Japanese art to denote a devotional image of a Buddhist deity surrounded by lesser figures, not necessarily embodying the circle (see BODHISATTVA; Kshitigarbha: see also A).

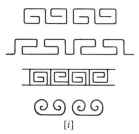

[i]

Meander. A repetitive pattern, having more than one form [*i*], found on sacred bronze vessels of the Chou dynasty in China (*c.* 1050–221 BC). It was derived from pictographs of the previous Shang period representing clouds and rolling thunder and was hence called the 'cloud and thunder pattern' (*yun wen* and *lei-wen*). The pattern symbolized life-giving rain and the abundance it brought to farming peoples. It reached the West and was the prototype of the Greek fret or key-pattern which decorates classical architecture. It has survived, together with more complicated variants, to the present day. As a continuous border it may frame Chinese symbols of longevity.

Mirror (Ch. *ching*; Jap. *kagami*). It was widely believed, especially in the Far East, that a mirror had magical properties and this is borne out by the motifs and inscriptions on its back. In a mirror one could glimpse all knowledge and see into one's own soul; it warded off evil in this life and the next and was therefore buried with the dead. To protect its owner a Chinese bronze mirror could be decorated with dragons and tigresses. In China the art of decorating mirrors underwent great developments in the Han dynasty. They began to replicate the designs on parasols and canopies that were used ritually. These designs represented the 'canopy of heaven', a system of cosmology with appropriate symbols. The 'TLV' mirror, so-called from the decorative motifs on its back, was introduced in the middle of the 2nd cent. BC, and was widely popular. The example shown is only one of several decorative schemes that came to include animals, immortals and other spirits, besides abstract signs [*ii*]. The small bosses inside the square represent the twelve 'earthly branches' of the Chinese CALENDAR. Outside the square there may be animals denoting the FIVE ELEMENTS, four quadrants of the heavens, the seasons, etc. From the 3rd or 4th cents. AD mirrors increasingly depict Taoist and Buddhist motifs, and flora and fauna that symbolize good fortune, marital happiness, and so on. A mirror en-

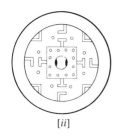

[*ii*]

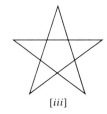

[iii]

[iv]

[v]

[vi]

[vii]

twined with ribbon is one of the Chinese EIGHT TREASURES. See also MAGPIE.

A mirror is one of the THREE SACRED RELICS of the Japanese imperial regalia. It is the repository of the spirit, or *shintai*, of the sun-goddess AMATERASU, ancestress of the imperial family, and features widely in the rites of Shintoism. Since a mirror can reveal the innermost soul of the living and the dead, it is therefore an attribute of Emma-O, the Judge of the Dead (see YAMA). Mirrors, often of Chinese origin, have been found in many Japanese tombs.

In Christian art a 'flawless mirror', *speculum sine macula*,[4] is an attribute of the VIRGIN MARY of the Immaculate Conception. The Virgin's reflection in a mirror held by a bishop identifies Geminianus of Modena (d. ? 348). In Renaissance allegory a mirror is an attribute of Prudence, one of the CARDINAL VIRTUES, and Truth; of the vices Pride, Vanity and Lust (the latter derived from the classical Venus) (see SEVEN DEADLY SINS); and of Sight, one of the FIVE SENSES. See also CIRCLE.

Pentacle, Pentagram. Five-pointed figure first seen in Sumerian royal inscriptions of the late 4th–early 3rd mill. BC, where it appears to symbolize the extent of the king's authority, reaching to the farthest corners of the earth. It was used as a mystic symbol of the Pythagoreans and, later, by medieval astrologers and necromancers. As a good luck charm it was placed at doorways to keep off harmful spirits. As a Christian symbol it stands for the five wounds of Christ [iii].

Shou. Chinese character denoting longevity or immortality, ideals that were popularized by Taoist philosophy and very widely represented as a result of Taoist influence. Over 100 variants are known [iv], [v]. They are seen on ceramics, textiles, medals and elsewhere. The *shou* character is often associated with other symbols of longevity such as the BAT, CRANE, sacred FUNGUS, PINE, TORTOISE, etc. Two together on a wedding gift signify 'May you have many years of married life.' See also PEACH.

Spiral. Mainly associated with fertility and birth. The walls of the entrance to megalithic burial chambers in many parts of Europe are covered with so-called spiral patterns, probably denoting the journey of the soul into the chamber itself [vi]. Religion was then devoted to the cult of the Mother-Goddess, and the tomb chamber is thought to have symbolized her womb wherein the soul was reborn. Early votive figurines of the goddess have similar spirals in the genital area. Well-defined spiral patterns occur on Chinese funerary vases of the Neolithic period. (See also VASE as a symbol of the womb.) A double spiral, known to represent a bovine womb, is an attribute of the Egyptian goddess of childbirth, Meskhenet, and of an unnamed female thought to be her Syrian counterpart [vii]. The spiral also denoted WATER as an agent of fertility. It is a very common mo-

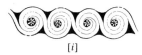

[i]

tif on pottery, especially water vessels. It became the principal motif on Cretan jars (1700–1400 BC), often in the form of a 'running spiral' [i], which is also found on drinking vessels from Byblos, Mycenae and, intermittently, in Egypt. See also OCTO-PUS.

Swastika (Sk. 'well-being'). An ancient and very widespread symbol, believed by many authorities to have been originally a representation of the SUN, indicating its course through the heavens. According to some it represents a wheel of the sun-god's chariot. Hence it shares some of the sun's symbolism: light, fertility and, particularly, good fortune. It was found at Troy, and was a popular motif on Greek coinage, which contributed to its wide circulation. It was virtually unknown in Assyria and Babylon and appeared in Egypt only from the Ptolemaic period. In India the swastika was known to the Indus Valley peoples and was subsequently associated with VISHNU and SHIVA. It is seen in the sculpture of Jain temples, dating from 2nd–1st cents. BC, and is an attribute of Suparshva, one of the twenty-four founding teachers of the sect. In China the swastika (*wan*) was originally a Taoist emblem and may be seen in the hand of Lao-tzu, founder of Taoism, and of other Taoist immortals, symbolizing their divine power. A swastika is one of the 'auspicious signs' on the Buddha's FOOT and, when represented on the breast of Shakyamuni, symbolizes his heart, which holds all his thinking. It was introduced into Japan probably through Buddhism and is seen on numerous Chinese and Japanese deities, as well as those of Tibetan Lamaism. As an auspicious sign swastikas are used for ornamental borders on eastern carpets, silks and woodwork. On Chinese ceramics, with a JU-I sceptre it expresses the wish for a long and happy life. The Chinese character *wan* later denoted the number 10,000.

[ii]

The swastika has two forms. The end-stroke may turn either clockwise, like the Greek *gamma* (Γ), when it is called a *gammadion*, or anticlockwise [ii]. They can denote respectively male and female, *yang* and *yin*, sun and moon. The anticlockwise version is the Buddhist and Taoist form and was sometimes associated with the Greek goddesses Artemis, Demeter and Hera. The same form sometimes accompanies early Christian inscriptions, as a version of the cross.

[iii]

T. Ancient symbol of life, called *tau* (Greek T). For Teutonic peoples it represented the double mallet or hammer of Thor and symbolized the lightning that heralded fertilizing rain. In the Christian catacombs it symbolized the promise of eternal life. The 'mark' put on the foreheads of the righteous Israelites of Jerusalem to save them from destruction was a *tau* (Vulg. *signa thau*).[5] It was adopted by Christians in Egypt as a form of the cross of Christ and is an attribute of Antony the Great, the Egyptian hermit. [*iii: after Grünewald*]. When given a handle it becomes an ANKH, the Egyptian symbol of life.

[iv]

Triangle. The symbol of a three-fold nature. The Christian TRIN-ITY may be represented as a triangle, sometimes framing an eye, the symbol of God the Father. His halo is sometimes triangular. The equilateral triangle is a Hindu symbol of gender: with apex up, it is male, the *lingam*, which is Shiva; apex down is female, *yoni*, his *shakti*. (For the Greeks, the delta (apex up) was a female symbol, *eidolon gynaikeion*, the image of woman.) The combination of male and female symbols, called *Shri yantra*, is an object of contemplation in Tantric Buddhism [iv]. It is intended to release psychic energy and heighten consciousness. As a musical instrument the triangle is sometimes an attribute of Erato, Greek MUSE of love poetry. See also LOTUS.

[v]

Trigram (Ch. *pa kua*). The origin of the eight ancient Chinese divinatory trigrams is unknown. It is said they were revealed to a legendary emperor, Fu Hsi (*c.* 2852 BC), while he was contemplating the patterns on the shell of a tortoise.[6] Each trigram consists of a different combination of three lines. The line may be broken in the middle (*yin*) or unbroken (*yang*). Later interpreters attributed to each sign a natural element, quality of mind, compass point, etc, which became the basis of a philosophical and divinatory system that had universal application. When used for divination the trigrams are arranged in a circle with the YIN AND YANG motif in the centre [v]. The trigrams were formerly found on the garments of military and religious leaders and were worn as an amulet to ensure good fortune. They are frequently seen in ceramic decoration.

[vi]

Triskele. A disk enclosing three legs, joined at the hip and bent, as if running, or three radiating crescents or ogees [vi: *Italian, 1st mill.* BC]. The former was originally a solar symbol, the latter lunar, and was meant to portray the movement of sun and moon across the heavens. The solar symbol, like the SWASTIKA, also came to mean good fortune. It is found frequently on early coinage of Asia Minor and on the shield of the Greek hero, Achilles. It may be seen in conjunction with a solar animal such as the lion, eagle, dragon or cock. This may indicate a connection with the three-legged raven in a solar disk, one of the TWELVE ORNAMENTS on Chinese imperial robes. The triskele when seen on Celtic crosses may symbolize the Christian Trinity. It is the emblem of the isles of Man and Sicily.

Word. Primitive peoples worldwide once believed in the magical power of the spoken word. A person's name was an intrinsic part of his being and must therefore be kept secret lest his enemies use it to cause him harm. The power of the word entered the religious beliefs of ancient civilizations where it had more than symbolic force. The Egyptians inscribed the names of enemies on clay tablets, which they then smashed to pieces. (See also WATER.) The word was also creative. The Egyptian creator-god, PTAH, brought everything to life 'through his heart and

[i]

tongue', in other words, spoke the universe into existence.[7] In the *Rig-Veda*, the oldest of Hindu scriptures, *brahman* denoted the creative power of the spoken word (see BRAHMA). Greeks and Romans believed in the magical power of names. Thus it was an offence to pronounce the names of priests who celebrated the Eleusinian mysteries, while priests in Rome kept secret the name of the city's guardian deity for fear that enemies might lure him away. The ritual of pronouncing magical formulae, or *mantras* [i: 'om mani padme hum', 'Ranja characters', 7th cent. AD], by followers of the Vajrayana sect of Buddhism, was intended to force the gods to comply with the devotee's will and grant his desires. (See further JEWEL; A.) The Hebrew name of God, Yahveh, 'I am that I am', became the symbol of monotheism for the Israelites and is so sacred it is not uttered (is 'ineffable') except on the Day of Atonement. The word of the Hebrews' God had, like Ptah's, the power to create: 'The Lord's word made the heavens ... Let the whole world fear the Lord ... for he spoke and it was'.[8] In Christian theology the 'Word' (Gk. *logos*) is a metaphysical concept developed from Greek speculative thought and only remotely descended from primitive magic. It came to denote the Second Person of the Trinity, the Holy Ghost, which is generally represented in Christian art as a DOVE.

Yin and Yang (Jap. *In, Yo*). Ancient Chinese cosmology, later transmitted to Japan, postulated a dualistic universe based on negative and positive principles, *yin* and *yang*, which pervade all things. The words originally meant the contrasting shaded and sunlit slopes of mountain or valley. *Yin* is female, the earth, darkness, the moon, passivity; *yang* is male, heaven, light, the sun, the active principle in nature, etc. *Yin* and *yang* feature in two of the oldest Chinese classics, the *I Ching* (*Book of Changes, c.* 10th cent. BC, with later accretions)[9] and the *Shih Ching* (*Book of Songs,* or *Book of Odes, c.* 6th cent. BC).[10] They are represented by the *T'ai chi*, a diagram of an egg in which dark and light stand for yolk and white [ii]. It symbolizes the origin of all creation. From the egg was hatched the first man, P'an Ku (Jap. Hanko). For more about him, see HAMMER. See also TRIGRAM.

[ii]

2. Animals

Ant. Symbol of industry and an example to the sluggard.[1] When contrasted with a large animal, especially a camel, it has since antiquity symbolized the inequality of the human condition. It also illustrates a classical saying, 'Through concord small things may grow greater, through discord the greatest are destroyed'[2] which was made into a rebus in the Renaissance that depicted an ant devouring an elephant and vice versa [iii].[3]

[iii]

Antelope. A typical attribute of SHIVA, held in one of his left hands

[iv]

[v]

[vi]

[*iv*], possibly derived from an Indus Valley god of beasts. A black antelope's pelt often serves as a loin cloth for the Hindu ascetic, which is one of Shiva's roles. In Egypt, the antelope, together with other desert animals, was a form of SETH. The Egyptian goddess Satis, who was associated with the annual Nile flooding, wears the CROWN of Upper Egypt adorned with antelope's horns, probably having been originally worshipped as an antelope. See also DEER; GAZELLE.

Antlers. A hunter confronted by a stag with a crucifix between its antlers is St Eustace or St Hubert [*v: Italian, 18th cent.*]. It is also their attribute. The cult of the stag, pre-eminently the sacred beast among Central Asian tribes, reached Hittite Anatolia probably *c.* 1800 BC. Overtaken by Greek cultural influences it acquired (? 6th cent. BC) the eagle of Zeus between the antlers. With the coming of Christianity under the early Byzantine emperors a cross or crucifix was substituted for the eagle. The scene, with Eustace, is first represented in 7th cent. churches of Cappadocia and was revived in Europe in the late Middle Ages.

Ape. In Egypt the baboon was worshipped in archaic times and, by the 1st Dynasty, had merged with THOTH, the patron of scribes and a moon-god [*vi*]. It was also sacred to the moon-god, KHONSU. Baboons were also associated with the sun. Eight baboons raising their forepaws to the rising sun symbolize the creation of the world by the Ogdoad, eight primeval gods of creation. The screeching of apes at daybreak was regarded as homage to the sun-god, RE. One of the four Canopic JARS has an ape-headed stopper.

The Hindu ape-god Hanuman epitomizes loyalty and devotion to duty and his tribe became part of the retinue of the Buddha. A well-known episode in the *Ramayana* tells how Hanuman's followers rescued Sita, the consort of King Rama, from captivity in Sri Lanka[4] (see also BRIDGE; VISHNU, 7). Hanuman has human form with ape-like features. His hands may be in the *anjali* position (see MUDRA).

The ape (Ch. *hou*) is one of the animals of the Chinese zodiac (see CALENDAR). It was believed to have magical powers and could control demons that harmed mankind. It worshipped the moon and may hold the PEACH of longevity, stolen from the garden of HSI WANG MU. The ape is the hero of a popular 16th cent. romance, *The Pilgrim to the West (Hsi Yuchi)*, based on a T'ang dynasty legend. Many types of ape are represented in Chinese painting, ceramics and wood-carving. In Japan the ape (*saru*) is associated with several Shinto deities. Its image guards the gate of the temple of San No Gongen in Tokyo and also stands on the altar. Holding GOHEI banners apes are the attendants of mountain deities. The three 'mystic apes' (*Sambiki saru*) that neither see, hear nor speak evil are the attendants of Saruta-hiko, the Shinto god of roads who has a monkey face. There are many Japanese legends and fairy-tales about monkeys which are popular subjects in *netsuke*.

In the West, medieval and Renaissance man saw in the ape an image of his baser self. Thus it came to symbolize Lust, one of the SEVEN DEADLY SINS, idolatry and vice in general (see FAITH). In Christian art, with an apple in its mouth, it stood for the Fall of Man. Northern European painters, especially 17th cent. Flemish, satirized man's vanities by depicting monkeys performing everyday human activities. The artist represented himself as an ape, illustrating the saying *Ars simia Naturae*, art is the ape of nature. It is an attribute of the Sanguine person, one of the FOUR TEMPERAMENTS; with fruit in its mouth, of Taste, one of the FIVE SENSES.

[i]

Ass. Beast of burden of the poor, hence a symbol of poverty; also of humility, patience, obedience, stupidity, sloth, etc. Present at Christ's Nativity, it bore him on the Flight into Egypt and the Entry into Jerusalem. Kneeling before a chalice, it is the attribute of St Anthony of Padua. Balaam's ass [*i: Spanish, 11th cent.*] found speech and rebuked the spiritual blindness of its master, who therefore prefigures doubting Thomas.[5] An ass is the mount of the satyr Silenus; hence it is associated with sexual licence. Chang Kuo, one of the Taoist EIGHT IMMORTALS, rides an ass. It is one of the several animal forms of the Egyptian SETH. An ass playing a lyre (Ur, 1st half, 3rd mill. BC) also appears in French Romanesque sculpture personifying Pride (see also MILL, MILLSTONE).

[ii]

Badger (Ch. *huan*; Jap. *tanuki*). The subject of many legends in Japan, where it transforms itself magically into human form in order to make mischief. Most remarkably, it can distend its scrotum to smother its pursuers and thereby escape them. In China its name is a homonym of the word meaning 'to be glad'; hence, together with a magpie, the pair denote 'May you experience joy from heaven and on earth'. It is a popular subject in *netsuke* [*ii*].

[iii]

Basilisk. Winged serpent with the head and claws of a cock and a second head at the end of its tail. Instant death came to all on whom it fixed its gaze. A symbol of Satan in medieval Christian art [*iii: heraldic*].

Bat (Ch. *pien-fu*). Believed by the Chinese to reach a great age, hence a symbol of longevity, also of joy [*v*]. It is a homonym for 'good fortune'. In ceramic decoration it may be painted red, the colour of joy. It is an attribute of Fu Hsing, one of the GODS OF HAPPINESS. Five bats are the Five Blessings (also Japanese): longevity, ease, riches, honours, joy. They are a widely depicted motif and are embroidered on the robes of Tibetan high lamas. In Italian Renaissance allegory it is an attribute of Night personified. See also DRAGON.

[iv]

[v]

Bear (Ch. *hsiung*). According to the bestiaries bear cubs are born formless and 'licked into shape' by their mother, symbolizing Christianity converting the heathen. The bear is an attribute of St Euphemia, and of Gluttony, Lust and Anger personified (see SEVEN DEADLY SINS). The nymph Callisto was turned into a bear by ARTEMIS/DIANA for losing her chastity. In China it symbolizes strength and bravery. Its image [v] is a protection against thieves. The great panda was an emblem of rank, embroidered on the robes of certain court officials.

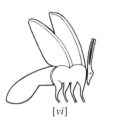

[vi]

Bee, Beehive (Ch. *mi-feng*). A popular symbol of industry, purity, immortality. Associated with the Greek corn-goddess, DEMETER/CERES; with the moon-goddess, ARTEMIS/DIANA, and the emblem of the latter's city, Ephesus. Symbol of the pharaoh of Lower Egypt [vi]. In Chinese art a bee on a PEONY denotes a young man in love, the peony representing the girl. A bee or hive is the attribute of SS. Ambrose (see FOUR LATIN FATHERS), John Chrysostom, and Bernard of Clairvaux, all known for mellifluous eloquence. See also AGES OF THE WORLD – Golden age; HONEYCOMB; SEVEN DEADLY SINS – Sloth.

[vii]

Bird. Widespread symbol of the soul, especially as it rises to heaven after death. The Egyptian *ba*, a bird, hovers above the mummy in tomb painting (New Kingdom), symbolizing the divine power of gods and pharaohs [vii: Egyptian, c. 1250 BC]. Later, it came to denote the soul of the deceased and was identified with the Greek Psyche. Many ancient peoples associated the larger birds with solar and sky deities. The common image of a bird and snake fighting symbolized the conflict between solar and earthly powers (see EAGLE). The Hindu god GARUDA took the form of a bird and is the vehicle of VISHNU. Birds are an attribute of Air personified, one of the FOUR ELEMENTS. See also BLACKBIRD; COCK; CRANE; CROW; DOVE; DUCK; FALCON; GOLDFINCH; IBIS; MAGPIE; OWL; PEACOCK; PELICAN; PHEASANT; PHOENIX; QUAIL; SPARROW; SWALLOW; SWAN; VULTURE; WOODPECKER.

[viii]

Blackbird. St Benedict may be represented standing in a thorn bush in an attempt to extinguish the desires of the flesh. A blackbird perched nearby symbolizes the devil [viii].

Boar. The wild boar has tusks, unlike the domestic pig. In some European and Asiatic cultures it is a sacred animal with magical powers. In Hindu myth VISHNU took the form of a boar in his role as creator of the universe. He is represented with a boar's head or fully zoomorphic. The same role was attributed to BRAHMA. The boar is one of the twelve animals of the Chinese CALENDAR diametrically opposite the SNAKE which makes a symbolic balance [ix: netsuke, 19th cent.]. In Greek myth the Cale- Boar Hunt symbolizes the slaying of Winter to make way for Spring. In Christian art a boar symbolizes Lust, one of the SEVEN DEADLY SINS, and is trodden under the feet of Chastity, one of the THREE MONASTIC VOWS.

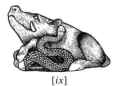

[ix]

Buffalo. The Indian water-buffalo is the mount of YAMA, Hindu and Buddhist lord and judge of the dead. The buffalo-demon, Mahisha [*i*], and his army were overcome by the goddess Durga (DEVI) after an epic struggle.[6] Lao-tzu, the legendary founder of Taoism, is often depicted in Chinese painting and sculpture riding away to the west on a buffalo (see EIGHT IMMORTALS).

[*i*]

Bull. The most representative symbol of the masculine principle in nature, that is, strength and procreative power. It was associated with sun- and sky-gods, the ultimate sources of fertility, and with gods of creation. Bull worship was a major cult in Egypt, the ancient Near East and eastern Mediterranean, and India. From Greece and Rome it extended through parts of Europe. In many places worship of the bull was linked to the Mother-Goddess.

Some bull cults in the Nile Valley are of great antiquity. AMUN, supreme deity of the Egyptian pantheon and worshipped in the Old Kingdom, was called 'bull of his mother' (probably meaning that as creator he had no father). In that role he has an erect phallus. The bull-god, Apis, was worshipped at Memphis in the First Dynasty. He was called son, or messenger, of the creator-god PTAH of the same city. Nun, the creator-god of Heliopolis, sometimes has a bull's head (see WATER). The pharaoh's epithet, 'victorious bull', implied royal strength and virility and was linked to Apis. Yearly rites at Memphis involving the pharaoh and a living sacred bull were meant to renew these vital powers. Apis has a solar DISK and URAEUS between his horns and a vulture's WINGS on his back. Other sacred Egyptian bulls were the war-god MONTU of Thebes, and Mnevis, messenger of Atum, the sun-god and creator of Heliopolis. The latter also has a solar disk and uraeus.

In Mesopotamia and neighbouring regions images of bulls are also related to solar- and sky-gods and to water, as a source of fertility and life. In very early times a bull was the usual symbol of a city's tutelary deity and was often the consort of the Mother-Goddess. Its identification with known deities begins with the Hittite storm-god, Teshub, who holds a lightning bolt and stands above a bull (*c.* 1000 BC). A similar image represents the Akkadian storm-god, ADAD, or Hadad, in the neo-Assyrian period (see also SIN). A hybrid bull-man appears intermittently, first on cylinder seals of the early Dynastic period (mid-3rd mill. BC). He has a human head with horns and is a bull from the waist down. He may be ithyphallic. He is seen again in the neo-Assyrian period (883–612 BC), when he holds up a solar disk or WINGED DISK of the sun-god, SHAMASH. On the early seals he fights a lion-headed eagle and other foes. The latter probably symbolizes some cosmic contest of deities, where the bull's role is beneficent. The bull, human-headed and winged, had the important role of guardian, notably in neo-Assyrian monumental sculpture (see further, WINGS).

Animal sacrifice was a deeply symbolic rite. For the Hebrews and, later, the Romans it was a covenant with a god. Originally it was performed at New Year and spring festivals in Meso-potamia and elsewhere with a bull, ram or goat to ensure a plentiful harvest. The cult image of MITHRAS slaying a bull shows ears of corn sprouting from its blood. In the Dionysiac rites the Bacchantes, female devotees of DIONYSUS/BACCHUS, frenziedly tore the beast apart and ate its raw flesh. This had a more mystical symbolism: they were consuming the god himself, just as they drank his blood in the form of wine. The bull's death released the god's power which passed to the worshippers (see also DE-MON). The animal was closely identified with ZEUS/JUPITER to whom it was sacrificed in a more restrained manner, garlanded, stunned and its throat cut (see TRIUMPH). Evidence of bull sacri-fice in Minoan Crete survives in the bull's horns that surmounted the sacrificial altar and a libation vessel, the *rhyton*, fashioned in the form of a bull's head, to hold the blood. The *taurobolium*, a sacrifice to the Mother-Goddess as the source of fertility and life, was a dramatic ritual. The bull was slaughtered above a pit in which a worshipper stood, to be drenched by a stream of blood flowing over him. The rite seems to have originated in Persia and reached Rome with the cult of the Mother-Goddess, Cybele (204 BC). It spread to the Roman provinces especially Gaul, where many altars to Cybele have been found. They de-pict, in relief, a bull's head, or *bucranium*, somewhat resembling a skull [*ii*].

[*ii*]

The myth of the Rape of Europa, who was abducted by Zeus in the form of a white bull,[7] is of Cretan origin and is probably derived from a rite of sacred marriage. There are examples in early Greek vase painting and relief sculpture. As a medieval Christian allegory it symbolizes Christ carrying a soul to heaven, and features in the TWELVE MONTHS – April.

The likelihood of an early common cultural link between In-dia and her Near-Eastern neighbours is supported by images on seals and other artefacts from the Indus Valley (3rd mill. BC). They indicate worship of a Mother-Goddess associated with a bull. The later Aryan settlers worshipped a male pantheon which included Rudra, the 'Howler'. One of his roles was storm-god and he was sometimes referred to as bull. Rudra was the ante-cedent of SHIVA, whose mount, or *alter ego*, was a white bull, Nandin [*iii: S. Indian, c. 16th–17th cent.*]. Its image stands be-fore Shivaite temples and women entering may touch its testi-cles to make themselves fertile. A black bull is the mount of YAMA, the Hindu/Buddhist ruler of hell. He is widely represented in Tibetan Tantric painting and bronzes. He is opposed by Yaman-taka, conqueror of death, who has nine heads, one of them a bull's (see MANJUSHRI).

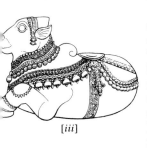

[*iii*]

A bull is the attribute of the Christian saints Thecla, who died tied to a pair of bulls, and Sernin (or Saturninus), first bishop of Toulouse, who met a similar end. Eustace was martyred inside a brass bull. Their legends may well reflect the conflict between the early Church and local pagan, taurine cults. Taurus, the Bull, is a spring sign of the ZODIAC. See also BLOOD; BUFFALO; COMBAT; HORN; MINOTAUR; OX; SEVEN DEADLY SINS – Lust; ZODIAC.

Butterfly (Ch. *hu-tie*; Jap. *cho*). Greek symbol of the SOUL and its personification, Psyche. A butterfly emerging from a chrysalis symbolizes the soul leaving the body. In Christian allegory, especially VANITAS still-life, a caterpillar, chrysalis and butterfly symbolize life, death and resurrection. It is a Chinese symbol for the age of seventy (*tie* is a homonym); with plum blossom it denotes beauty allied to longevity. Sipping nectar from a flower, it represents a lover tasting the joys of love. It is a Japanese symbol of the soul, and of womanhood [*i: costume for the Japanese 'Butterfly Dance'*]; two butterflies symbolize a happy marriage.

[i]

Camel. Popular medieval example of Temperance, from its ability to go several days without drinking; also of Humility, because, according to the bestiaries, it kneels to be loaded (see also THREE MONASTIC VOWS). It is a symbol of Arabia on Roman coinage and, in Renaissance allegory, an attribute of Asia personified, one of the FOUR PARTS OF THE WORLD [*ii: neo-Assyrian, 9th cent.* BC].

[ii]

Carp (Ch. *li*; Jap. *koi*). A Chinese and Japanese symbol of perseverance: fish, traditionally carp, annually leap cataracts in the Huang-Ho to spawn and, on passing the Dragon-gate rapids, are said to be transformed into dragons — a metaphor for success in state examinations. (*Li* also denotes profit or advantage.) The carp's armour-like scales made it a symbol of martial valour for the Japanese warrior-caste, the Samurai. The famous Japanese warrior Yoshitsune (1159–89) is represented carrying a carp. Its 'beard' indicates supernatural powers. A Chinese sage riding on a carp is K'in Kao (Jap. *Kinko*), who befriended the King of Fishes and was persuaded, together with his disciples, to give up ichthyophagy [*iii: after Hiroshige, 19th cent.*].

[iii]

Cat (Ch. *mao*; Jap. *neko*). Widely believed to have occult powers and sometimes deified. The Egyptian cat-goddess, Bastet, who evolved from a lioness deity, was worshipped mainly in Lower Egypt, especially from *c.* 1000 BC. She holds a SISTRUM, sometimes the semi-circular AEGIS, or a basket. Many votive images have been found in her sanctuaries. Cats were consecrated to Bastet and their bodies mummified. Bastet was the daughter of the sun-god, RE, and therefore the enemy of the snake-god of the Underworld, Apophis, whom she beheaded [*iv: Funerary papyrus, 19th Dyn.*]. In China and Japan the cat has demonic powers, released especially after its death, and was therefore propitiated. Like the fox in Japan, it could assume human form. *Mao*, Chinese for cat, is a near homonym for 'eighty years old', thus a cat with bamboo and plum-blossom

[iv]

[v]

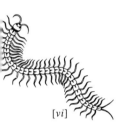

[vi]

[vii]

[viii]

[ix]

illustrated the saying: 'May we always wish you a happy old age'. With a BUTTERFLY, it expresses a similar wish. See also KNIFE.

Centaur. Mythical creature, half horse, half man; one of Homer's race of 'wild beasts', lecherous and usually drunk. Symbol of barbarism in Greek myth and art. Personification of man's lower, bestial nature in Renaissance humanist allegory; in Christian art a symbol of adultery, sometimes heresy. However, Chiron, the centaur-teacher of Achilles, was noted for wisdom.[8] Lion-centaurs guarded the gates of the palace and temple at Nimrud [v].

Centipede (Ch. *wu-kung*). Enemy of the snake in Chinese folklore and once carried by the traveller to warn against its proximity [vi]. See also FIVE POISONS.

Chameleon. In Renaissance allegory an attribute of Air personified, one of the FOUR ELEMENTS. Ripa,[9] following Pliny,[10] says it is 'an animal that eats nothing nor drinks but only feeds on air, and yet lives' [vii].

Chimaera. In Greek myth a monster, sometimes having several heads and with the fore-parts of a lion, its middle a goat and its rear a dragon [viii: Etruscan, 5th cent. BC]. It ravaged Lycia until slain by Bellerophon.[11] It was a popular decorative motif on Greek vases, which occasionally depict the fight with Bellerophon.

Cicada (Ch. *ch'an*). Ancient Chinese symbol of resurrection and immortality derived from its life-cycle, beginning as a larva underground, then a terrestrial pupa, finally a flying insect. In the larval form it is first seen on Shang dynasty bronzes, 2nd mill. BC [ix]. In funerary rites from the very late Chou dynasty until Han times a jade cicada was placed in the mouth of the dead for protection and to ensure immortality. It was also a symbol of purity since it was believed to feed only on dew.

Cock. The male domestic fowl has a rich and varied symbolism in the West and East. In Christian art it is one of the INSTRUMENTS OF PASSION, an attribute of the apostle PETER and hence a symbol of penitence.[12] It greets the rising sun and was therefore sacred to MITHRAS, APOLLO and other solar gods. It is associated with several Graeco-Roman deities, especially ATHENA/MINERVA and HERMES/MERCURY and in Renaissance painting draws the latter's chariot. In ancient Greece it was a traditional love gift. It is an attribute of Vigilance personified; of Lust and Gluttony (SEVEN DEADLY SINS). It is a courageous fighter and is an attribute of the six-headed Hindu war-god KARTTIKEYA, and Skanda, son of SHIVA. In the Chinese CALENDAR it is the tenth of twelve Terrestrial Branches. It represents the male principle, *yang*. Cock-crow drives away the spirit of the night, and a white cock placed on a coffin keeps demons at bay. A painting of a cock on the wall

[i]

of a Chinese house protects it against fire. The cock's comb (Ch. *kuan*) is a homophone of 'official', so the gift of a finely crested bird denotes: 'May you soon attain public office (or promotion)'. Cocks are sacred to the Shinto sun-goddess AMATERASU and are kept in the grounds of her principal temple at Ise. A cock on a war-drum, a popular subject in Japanese *netsuke*, symbolizes Peace, from a Chinese legend concerning such a drum that had long fallen into disuse [i].[13] A cock in the solar disk, see TRISKELE.

Compass. Ancient Chinese astronomy recognized 28 constellations, seven in each of the four quadrants that comprised the vault of the heavens. Each quadrant was guarded by one of four supernatural creatures with mystical powers (Ch. *ssu shen* or *su ling*) who were also associated with the FOUR SEASONS: *East*, the green (or blue) dragon, spring; *South*, the scarlet bird (a pheasant or phoenix), summer; *West*, the white tiger, or a kind of hybrid UNICORN, autumn; *North*, a snake coiled round a tortoise, called the 'dark warrior', winter. They are commonly represented on Han dynasty bronze MIRRORS [ii] and subsequently reached Japan. The Buddhist STUPA and pagoda were oriented to the four points of the compass, sometimes having an image of one of the four Dhyani-Buddhas on each face (see VAIROCANA), as at Borobodur, Java (*c.* 750–800). Buddhist temples from earliest times have also been guarded by the FOUR CELESTIAL KINGS, one assigned to each of the four quarters. They are frequently of ferocious aspect, especially Japanese and Tibetan. The entrance to Egyptian pyramids is on the north face towards the Pole Star and its neighbours, from where the Great God governed the universe. Egyptian temples and tombs usually have an east–west axis. Necropolises usually lie to the west of a city, the sunset land of the dead.

[ii]

Cow. Identified with the great Mother-Goddess, especially in Egypt, the Near East and India. HATHOR wears a head-dress of cow's horns framing a solar disk, or she is entirely bovine [iii: *26th Dynasty*]. This head-dress is also one of the forms of ISIS, who took it from Hathor (New Kingdom). The curious overarching sky-cow of Heliopolis is the sky-goddess, Nut, her belly dotted with stars (see ARCH). The Sumerian Mother-Goddess Ninhursag (also known as Nintu) was represented throughout Mesopotamia until the fall of the Assyrian Empire (612 BC), as a cow suckling its calf, an image that may sometimes denote ISHTAR. For Hindus the cow is of all animals the most sacred, yet it is not identified with any deity. In the *Rig-Veda* it is the rain cloud, which nourishes the earth.[14] According to the *Yajur-Veda* (before 800 BC) the killing of a cow is punishable with death. The Greek goddess Hera is called 'cow-eyed' (or 'ox-eyed') in the *Iliad*, pointing to her origin as Mother-Goddess. Io, changed into a heifer by Zeus, is represented on Greek vases and wall-paintings as a woman with small horns.

[iii]

Crab (Ch. *hsia*; Jap. *kani*). Cancer is the fourth sign of the Graeco-Roman ZODIAC. In the Labours of the Months (see TWELVE MONTHS) it is allotted to June when the sun begins its backward course, reflecting the crab's ability to move backwards. The Chinese describe western handwriting as 'crab-wise', from the creature's sideways gait. Buddhists in northern China and Tibet adopted the crab as a symbol of the cosmic night between the *kalpas* of Brahma, from the belief that it hibernated. It is sometimes the vehicle of Li T'ieh-kuai and, more rarely, Ts'ao Kuo-chiu, two of the EIGHT IMMORTALS. A species found in Japanese waters, having markings on its shell resembling an anguished human face [*iv*], was the subject of several legends: the famous warrior Yoshitsune (1159–89) and his aide Benkei fought a phantom army of such crab-like ghosts at sea off Akamagaseki.[15]

[*iv*]

Crane (Ch. *ho* or *hao*; Jap. *tsuru*). Believed to be very long-lived, hence a symbol of Longevity and an attribute of Shou Hsing, the Taoist god of long life, one of the GODS OF HAPPINESS and of his Japanese counterpart Fuku-roku-jiu; also of HSI WANG MU, Queen Mother of the West. It is the messenger of the gods and carries the tablets of human fate (sometimes a scroll, or twig) to earth. It is seen thus, typically on Ming ceramics [*v*]. It bears the souls of the dead to heaven in Chinese funerary art. It may stand under a PINE TREE or on a TORTOISE both associated with long life. The Shinto spirits of pine trees, Jo and Uba, an old wrinkled couple, have a crane and tortoise for attributes, a popular subject in *netsuke*.[16] Wasobioye, a Gulliver-like hero of Japanese romance (1744), rides on a crane.[17] The crane is an attribute of Vigilance in Renaissance and later allegory: it holds a stone in its claw because, if the bird fell asleep, it would fall and reawaken it.

[*v*]

Crocodile. Sobek, or Suchos, the Egyptian crocodile-god, may be wholly animal or an animal-headed human [*vi: Kom Ombo, Ptolemaic*]. He symbolized the power of the pharaohs, this relationship being indicated when he wears the royal crown of double feathers. His chief cult centres were at Kom Ombo and in the Fayyum. The Underworld goddess, Ammut, 'Devourer of the Dead', is present at the weighing of souls (see SCALES). She has a crocodile's head, the forepart of a lion and rear of a hippopotamus. She devours the heart of the deceased if it is found wanting in the scales. The crocodile was also the embodiment of SETH, and was accordingly destroyed in effigy in certain rites of Osiris and Horus. In Christian art a crocodile or dragon is the attribute of St Theodore, whose legend is similar to St George and the dragon.

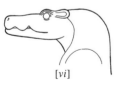

[*vi*]

Crow (Ch. *ya,* or *wuya*; Jap. *karasu*). In Taoist lore a red or golden crow with three legs inhabits the SUN, and is also its symbol (see TRISKELE). This belief reached Japan at an early period, where the

[i]

three-legged crow became the messenger of the Shinto sun-goddess AMATERASU. It also became an emblem of the shrines of the Kumano sect of Shinto. Its solar connection and its uneven number of legs make it *yang*. It is some-times a bird of ill-omen, contrasted with the white heron (*yin*) [*i: after Koryusai*]. In Greece the crow was worshipped for its supposed oracular powers and was sacred to APOLLO and HERA/JUNO. In Christian art it is an attribute of HOPE personified.

Cuckoo (Jap. *hototo gisu*). A sacred bird among primitive peoples and in parts of ancient Greece. Its reputation as a secret lover may explain the myth of ZEUS/JUPITER who transformed himself into a cuckoo in order to ravish HERA/JUNO.[18] It became her attribute. Among the Japanese it was a symbol of unrequited love [*ii*].

[ii]

Deer (Ch. *lu*; Jap. *shika*). Taoist symbol of long life and the only animal able to find the sacred FUNGUS. It sometimes carried Shou Hsing, god of Longevity, one of the GODS OF HAPPINESS; also his Japanese counterpart, Jurojin. It may also symbolize Wealth, as 'deer' and 'official salary' are homophones in Chinese. The deer is sacred to the Kasuga sect of Shinto, which had its origins in primitive agricultural deities dwelling on Mt Kasuga, and is the gods' messenger. Many of them roam wild in the grounds of the Kasuga shrine. Deer are prominent in Kasuga art [*iii*], saddled and sometimes carrying the tutelary deity of the sect, Kasuga Myojin. An alternative devotional image shows a branch of *sakaki*, an evergreen tree, springing from the saddle and surmounted by a mirror on which the sect's five principal deities may be depicted.[19] See also ANTELOPE, ANTLERS, GAZELLE, STAG.

[iii]

Dog (Ch. *kou*; Jap. *inu*). Watchful guardian, symbol of faithfulness and companion and messenger of numerous deities in the art of many civilizations. The early Assyrian Mother-Goddess, Gula, wife of NINURTA, is represented as a dog on cylinder seals and suckles her pups in small, votive sculpture. When in human form she has a dog for attribute. The so-called jackal, the form of the Egyptian god Anubis, was probably the desert pye-dog [*iv*]. The god is wholly animal or a dog-headed human. His role was funerary, guarding the mummy at night and weighing the heart in the Hall of Judgement. A jackal's head forms the stopper of one of the four Canopic JARS (see also WOLF). The Hindu god Bhairava, a Tantric aspect of SHIVA, is a guardian of doors and has a dog for a mount. A dog is the companion of MITHRAS. It is the eleventh creature in the Chinese and Japanese zodiac (see CALENDAR). A pair of 'lion-dogs' guard the entrance to temples of various cults and to palaces throughout the Far East (see LION). In Japan dogs can dispel the evil influences possessed by a FOX, BADGER or CAT.

[iv]

In Greek myth Sirius was the dog who accompanied the hunter Orion; a hunting dog accompanies ARTEMIS/DIANA; a black dog is an attribute of HECATE. Three-headed Cerberus guards the entrance to Hades. It sometimes has a serpent's tail and lion's claws. One of HERCULES' labours was to drag it back to the upper world, a scene depicted on vase paintings and temple metopes. In Christian art black-and-white dogs are *Domini canes*, the dogs of the Lord, a pun on St Dominic's name and an emblem of his Order which has a black-and-white habit. St Roch is accompanied by a dog, with a loaf of bread in its mouth, which fed him as he lay sick with the plague. A dog is the attribute of St Margaret of Cortona. The cynocephalus, one of a race of dog-headed people, is occasionally seen in medieval Christian art (Vézelay, 12th cent.). They were believed to live on the distant fringes of the world, along with other fantastic peoples, and appear to symbolize the furthest reaches of the apostles' evangelizing missions. A dog is an attribute of Smell, one of the FIVE SENSES; Melancholy, one of the FOUR TEMPERAMENTS; and Envy, one of the SEVEN DEADLY SINS.

Dolphin. Seen mainly in the art of Mediterranean peoples [*v*]. It is a symbol of APOLLO. On coins and seals of cities like Carthage and Syracuse dolphins are a symbol of their maritime power. It is an attribute of Poseidon/Neptune from the Hellenistic era onwards, especially popular on Roman mosaics. It is also associated with other deities in a maritime context: APHRODITE/ VENUS; DIONYSUS/BACCHUS; Nereids in general, but especially Galatea and Thetis; Arion, a poet rescued by a dolphin which was attracted by his singing. On Roman sarcophagi dolphins are psychopomps, bearing the soul to the Isles of the Blessed. The Christian symbol of the FISH is often represented as a dolphin. A dolphin entwining an anchor illustrates the Latin motto, *Festina lente*, 'make haste slowly', first seen on the coinage of early imperial Rome and revived in the Renaissance. In Renaissance allegory it is an attribute of FORTUNE. See also FOUR ELEMENTS – Water.

[*v*]

Dove (Ch. *ke*; Jap. *hato*). Sacred to ISHTAR, Astarte and other Mother-Goddesses of the Near East, having a part in their rites. Doves face each other on either side of a sacred stone personifying the goddess, and the OMPHALOS. They were sacred to APHRODITE/VENUS; and to Zeus, to whom they brought ambrosia.[20] A dove, sometimes with an OLIVE branch, is a very early Christian symbol [*vi: Roman catacombs, 3rd cent.*] meaning 'May you rest in peace'. It is also an attribute of PEACE personified. Later, as a symbol of the Holy Ghost,[21] it is ever present in Christian art, especially in the Annunciation, Baptism of Christ, Pentecost, TRINITY. It is the attribute of many saints and hovers at the ear of writers like Gregory the Great (see FOUR LATIN FATHERS), the evangelists and Thomas Aquinas. Seven doves are the 'seven gifts of the Holy Ghost'.[22] In early Christian art the twelve APOSTLES are occasionally represented as doves (see also COLUMBINE). A pair of doves is a widely recognized symbol of love and con-

[*vi*]

cord (see also THREE MONASTIC VOWS – Chastity; SEVEN DEADLY SINS – Lust). In China and Japan it is an emblem of long life and fidelity. Jade batons topped with a dove were given to the aged in the Han dynasty to wish them continued well-being and a good digestion. A dove was associated with the Japanese god of war, Hachiman, symbolizing the expectation of peace to follow.

Dragon. In the West, a symbol of Satan and of evil in general (except in heraldry). In the East, especially in China where it has an ancient lineage, it was a beneficent creature. Its earliest form, on Chinese bronze ritual vessels of the Shang and Chou dynasties (2nd to mid-1st mill. BC) but not widely represented thereafter, is the *k'uei* dragon [*i*]. It was said by an eleventh-century writer to 'exert a restraining influence against the sin of greed'.[23] It seems to have had no connection with the traditional dragon, the *lung* [*ii*], which is one of the most familiar motifs in Chinese art of all periods. The *lung* dragon is thought by some to have originated in the alligators that formerly lived in the Yangtse and other Chinese rivers. Certainly, like the alligator, it was associated with water – it was once worshipped as a bringer of rain and good harvests. It usually has horns, long teeth and long whiskers, a mane and a long scaly body. Originally it was more often three-clawed but since the Sung dynasty (from AD 960) it has usually had four or five. Near its mouth there may be a flaming ball, described as a pearl, probably a symbol of thunder. A green or blue dragon was guardian of the eastern quarter of the universe (COMPASS) and a symbol of spring that brought the fertilizing rain (FOUR SEASONS). Dragon and TIGER (guardian of the West) together symbolize life and death, the principal forces controlling the universe, the dragon appearing among rain clouds, the tiger eyeing it from below. The dragon is one of the twelve Terrestrial Branches of the Chinese CALENDAR. Some have said that it hides in caves or in the depths of the sea. Its legendary appearances, rare and always fleeting, are a portent of some great event such as the birth of a future emperor. For Taoists its appearance is the *Tao* itself, a force suffusing the universe that they may momentarily glimpse. For Zen Buddhists the dragon was also a cosmic spirit, symbolizing their all-too-elusive visions of Enlightenment. From the 2nd cent. BC the dragon was a symbol of the emperor's might and sovereignty, and was the principal motif on imperial robes (see DRESS). From the 14th cent., on the robes of the emperor and princes, it had five claws, distinguishing it from those of courtiers and officials where it had only four or three. A pair of dragons, facing each other head to tail, is one of the TWELVE ORNAMENTS on the imperial robes. Dragon and PHOENIX together, a common motif in ceramic decoration, symbolize the emperor and empress.

Dragon lore reached Japan from China probably soon after the arrival of Buddhism in the 6th cent. AD and was gradually

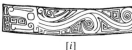

[*i*]

[*ii*]

absorbed into its culture. The earliest written legends appeared about AD 720, though it was not much represented in Japanese art before the later 14th cent.[24] The *lung* dragon (Jap. *ryu*) retained most of its Chinese characteristics and much of its symbolism, especially as a rain spirit. It usually has three claws and may have the mystic pearl. It was the form taken by the King of the Sea, Ryu-jin, who is the subject of numerous legends. In art, he is an old man with a dragon entwining his head and may hold magical jewels that govern the tides. The ancient Shinto god, Susano-O (see MOON), is widely depicted destroying an eight-headed dragon (described in the legend as a serpent), having first made it drunk with eight bowls of saké.[25] In one of its tails he discovered a divine sword, which became one of the THREE SACRED RELICS of the Japanese imperial regalia. A dragon is the vehicle of several Japanese immortal sages, the *sennins*.

In the art of Mahayana Buddhism, the sect of the Great Vehicle, a dragon is the mount of the supreme Adi-Buddha, VAIROCANA. In his fierce Tantric form he is known as Acala and holds a sword entwined by a dragon (see further, DEMON). In Tibetan painting, especially on Lamaist prayer-flags, there is a composite animal with dragon's head and tail and a scaly horse's body. It carries the Buddhist scrolls of the Law on its back. In appearance it is a close relation of the *ch'i-lin*, or kylin (UNICORN).

In Christian art the dragon is one of the forms of Satan (see also DEMON). Since the Latin *draco* means either dragon or snake (as in Greek) Satan is represented in either form. As a dragon, of the kind vanquished by St George and St Michael in late medieval and Renaissance art, he is in essentials human but typically has a bird's beak, claws and, his most characteristic feature, bat's wings [*iii: French, 15th cent.*]. The image originated in China where similar creatures were used to represent the followers of demoness Hariti (see POMEGRANATE). They reached the West with the expansion of the Mongol empire into eastern Europe in the 13th cent. Trade with the East followed and brought with it Chinese ceramics and figured textiles on which such dragons were featured.

In Christian art a dragon is trodden underfoot by the VIRGIN MARY in her role as the Immaculate Conception. Among the saints a chained dragon beside Bernard of Clairvaux symbolizes heresy; beside Pope Sylvester it is paganism. The 'serpent of old'[26] is also chained. Margaret of Antioch treads on a dragon. Legends have connected it with Theodore and Martha. In Renaissance allegory it is an attribute of Vigilance. Dragons draw the chariot of DEMETER/CERES and Cybele. The dragon slain by the greek hero, Perseus, was originally (6th cent. BC) a sea-serpent or whale. See also ADAD; COMBAT; MONSTER; SNAKE; TREE (Yggdrasil); TRISKELE.

[*iii*]

Dragonfly (Jap. *tombo*). One of the emblems of Japan, which is known as 'dragonfly island', Akitsu-shima, because its shape is

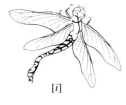

[i]

[ii]

[iii]

[iv]

supposed to resemble the insect [*i*]. Its apparently aimless, darting flight has made it a symbol of instability in Japan and China. It is a Chinese symbol of summer.

Duck. Wild ducks and geese are the subject of numerous Chinese and Japanese legends and are a popular subject in ceramic decoration. A pair of mandarin ducks (Ch. *yuan-yang*; Jap. *oshidori*) symbolizes faithfulness in marriage because they are said to keep the same partners for life. The Chinese lotus (*lien*) is a homophone for partnership, so duck and lotus are typically depicted together. An amulet of a duck resting on a lotus [*ii*], known as the Sacred Duck, protects the wearer against accidents.

Eagle. Associated with solar and sky deities from earliest times. A lion-headed eagle, usually known by its Sumerian name, Imdugud [*iii: Sumerian, c. 2900–2460 BC*], was a symbol of a god of agriculture, Ningirsu, and was bringer of rain (see PLOUGH). Eagle and snake in combat, symbolizing the conflict of sky- and earth-gods, was also of Sumerian origin. It entered Greek and Hindu myth in various contexts: Greek vase painting depicts the sky-god ZEUS/JUPITER (to whom the eagle was sacred) attacking a serpentine monster, Typhon, with a thunderbolt.[27] In Indian art GARUDA, the solar eagle and vehicle of VISHNU, fought the evil snake Kaliya.[28] In Roman funerary art the eagle is a common psychopomp, carrying the soul to heaven, sometimes with the crown of immortality in its beak. The myth of Ganymede, carried to Olympus by Zeus' eagle, acquired the same symbolism. In the rite of apotheosis of a Roman emperor, an eagle was released which bore his soul to heaven. On the standards of the Roman army it symbolized power and victory. The double-headed eagle, first seen on Hittite reliefs and Indian coinage, which found its way to Europe during the Crusades, is of uncertain meaning. It was probably the result of merging pairs of birds as a decorative motif in jewellery, and not originally symbolic. In Christian art the eagle symbolizes the Ascension (medieval) and is one of the APOCALYPTIC BEASTS, representing John the Evangelist. In Renaissance allegory it is an attribute of Sight, one of the FIVE SENSES, and Pride, one of the SEVEN DEADLY SINS. See also COMBAT.

Egg. In many mythologies the source, or womb, from which all creation emerged. Egyptian Coffin Texts and the *Book of the Dead* make references to the egg as the origin of life. It was laid by the 'great cackler', possibly meaning Geb, the earth-god, or AMUN. Alternatively, it was fashioned by PTAH on a potter's wheel [*iv*]. RE, the sun-god, was born from it. In Hindu myth BRAHMA, the creator, was born from a golden egg.[29] The dome of the STUPA symbolizes the same cosmic egg. A Chinese creation legend tells how the earth, the sky and the primeval man, P'an ku, were hatched from a great egg.[30] The Taoist YIN AND YANG symbol, the source of existence, was described as an egg.

In Christian art an egg is the symbol of Christ's Resurrection. An ostrich egg symbolizes the virgin birth, from the medieval belief that it hatched of its own accord. In Greek myth Leda, impregnated by Zeus as a swan, laid two eggs from which were hatched the Dioscuri, Helen and Clytemnestra.[31]

Elephant (Sk. *gaja*; Ch. *hsiang*; Jap. *zo*). Very widely represented throughout the East as a religious symbol and in illustrations of folk legends. The oldest images are found on seals from the Indus Valley (Mohenjo-Daro, 3rd–2nd mill. BC), possibly symbolizing royal prerogative because owning elephants was confined to sovereigns. Early Chinese ritual vessels, made of bronze, often take the form of fantastic animals and birds. A vessel of this kind, covered with magical symbols and possibly used to hold wine, is shaped like an elephant.[32] Elephants figure in Hindu and Buddhist art wherever those religions established themselves. In Hindu creation myths the white elephant, Airavata, the mount of INDRA, was born from the churning of the milky ocean[33] (alternatively from a golden egg in the hand of BRAHMA[34]). It was followed by fifteen more who support the universe on their backs at the eight principal compass points (Temple of Shiva, Elura, 8th cent. AD). Pure albino elephants exist and are especially sacred: rain-bearing clouds are imagined to be heavenly white elephants and have wings. They spray Lakshmi, the fertility goddess, with water (see DEVI). The elephant-headed Hindu god, with a broken tusk, is GANESHA. An elephant-demon was slain by SHIVA.

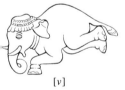

[v]

Elephants are a symbol of sovereignty, royal wisdom and moral and spiritual strength, and therefore came to be identified with the Buddha Shakyamuni. They appear in two scenes from his narrative life-cycle: his mother dreams of a small white elephant entering her womb [*v: Indian, 2nd cent. BC*], whereupon he is conceived;[35] he subdues an elephant made drunk by an enemy who meant to overcome him.[36] A white elephant, usually with six tusks, is the mount of the BODHISATTVA Samantabhadra, one of Shakyamuni's two principal disciples. Elephant and flaming pearl are two of the Buddhist's SEVEN TREASURES. The pearl may be carried on an elephant's back and figures thus especially in Chinese, Tibetan and Japanese art; alternatively it carries the Buddha's begging bowl. An elephant is the mount of the Dyani-Buddha, Akshobhya, guardian of the eastern quadrant (see COMPASS), seen in particular in Tibetan MANDALAS.

In the West the elephant was a symbol of military victory for the Romans (after their near defeat by Hannibal's elephants), and draws the triumphal chariot of Fame personified (see TRIUMPH). In Renaissance allegory the head of an elephant forms a headdress for Africa, one of the FOUR PARTS OF THE WORLD. See also ANT.

Ermine. Its white fur makes it a symbol of purity and hence chastity. In European portraiture it may be held by a female sit-

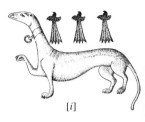

[ii]

[i]

[iii]

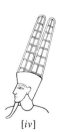

[iv]

ter to denote virginity. Virgin saints of noble families often wear an ermine-lined cloak, in particular Ursula. It is seen in French chateaux of Francis I [*i: Blois*], who married the daughter of Anne of Brittany, whose device it was. Ermine and hedgehog together are attributes of Touch, one of the FIVE SENSES. See also TRIUMPH – Chastity.

Falcon. In common with other large, high-flying birds the falcon is widely associated with sun-gods. The Egyptian falcon-god, Horus, is one of the oldest zoomorphic deities. On monuments of the 1st Dynasty his image is wholly bird-like, a form that recurs later, though the bird's head on a human body became more typical [*ii*]. Horus was king of the gods and therefore the deity with whom the pharaoh was identified. The falcon may therefore wear the double crown of Upper and Lower Egypt. The sun-god RE, who was sometimes identified with Horus, has falcon's head with solar disk. Montu, the Theban war-god, is represented similarly with the addition of the URAEUS and two plumes. The moon-god, KHONSU, has a falcon's head crowned with a CRESCENT and lunar disk. Sokar, the presiding deity of the necropolis at Memphis, also has a hawk's head. One of the four Canopic JARS has a falcon-headed stopper. Falconry was known in China about 2000 BC and in Japan from the mid-4th cent. AD, and the bird has for long been a popular subject in their painting. It symbolizes boldness, power and heroism, as the names for predatory birds (Ch. *ying*; Jap. *taka*) are homophones for 'heroic'. In Christian art a falcon is the attribute of SS. Bavo and Julian the Hospitator. It is an attribute of Touch, one of the FIVE SENSES. Falcons or other raptors draw the chariot of Avarice, one of the SEVEN DEADLY SINS. See also TWELVE MONTHS – May.

Feather. The Egyptian goddess Maat, who embodied truth, justice and morality, wears a single ostrich feather on her head [*iii*]. In the Hall of Judgement the heart of the deceased is weighed against it. Two tall plumes, highly stylized, surmount the crown of AMUN, MIN, MONTU, Nefertum, the lotus-god, and sometimes the king [*iv*]. Four plumes crown the head of Anukis, ancient goddess of the Nile cataracts. In imperial China from the Ming dynasty peacocks' feathers were worn as an insignia of official rank. Three ostrich feathers were first adopted as the device of the Prince of Wales by Edward, the Black Prince (1330–76), for whom they symbolized peace. In Renaissance allegory a headdress of feathers is worn by the personification of America, one of the FOUR PARTS OF THE WORLD.

Fish. In general, a symbol of fertility and procreation originally associated with the Mother-Goddess. It is one of the elements of the sacramental meal in several cults in antiquity, probably including early Christian. The fish-goddess of Lower Egypt, Hatmehit, is crowned with a fish. The Sumerian god of fresh water, EA, takes the form of a fish, or a goat with a fish-tail (the

[v]

[vi]

[vii]

[viii]

[ix]

origin of Capricorn). His priests in the neo-Assyrian period are dressed as fish [v]. VISHNU is represented as a fish (*matsya*), or with a fish-tail in his first incarnation, as are Graeco-Roman marine deities. In China, the fish (*yu*) is an ancient symbol of wealth and abundance, from the phonetic similarity between fish and wealth, hence also of marriage and fertility. A child accompanied by a fish implies the hope for an abundance of sons. The Chinese god of literature, K'UEI HSING, stands on a fish. A pair of fish symbolizes fruitful sexual intercourse. A pair is also apotropaic. They are one of the 'auspicious signs' on the Buddha's FOOT, and are one of the EIGHT LUCKY EMBLEMS [vi]. A gold-fish symbolizes riches. One of the Shinto SEVEN GODS OF HAPPINESS, Ebisu, holds a large fish or catches it with rod and line. In Christian catacomb paintings CHRIST is presented as a fish. Later, the well-known acrostic was devised, which was based on the Greek works for fish *ichthys*: Jesus/Christ/of God/the Son/ Saviour. A fish was an early symbol of baptism, and is the attribute of SS. Antony of Padua, PETER the apostle, Zeno and others. Three fishes symbolize the TRINITY. In Renaissance allegory flowers, fish and stars decorate the robe of PHILOSOPHY. See also CARP; ZODIAC.

Fleece. The Argonaut's quest for the golden fleece[37] belongs to a class of heroic endeavours, like the quest for the holy grail, which was a symbolic search for a magical prize. The order of the Golden Fleece [vii] was instituted in 1429 by Philip the Good, Duke of Burgundy. For the symbolism of Gideon's fleece, see DEW.

Fly. Egyptian symbol of courage, from its persistent behaviour, hence a golden fly was awarded to deserving soldiers. It is sometimes depicted at the edge of a religious painting (especially N. European, mid-15th to early 16th cents.), from the belief that it kept real flies away [viii].

Fox (Ch. *hu-li*; Jap. *kitsune*). Believed by the Chinese to have supernatural powers and therefore the subject of many legends, some of great antiquity. They reached Japan about the 9th cent. AD and are widely represented in Chinese and Japanese art. At the age of fifty the fox can transform itself into a woman and at one hundred into a seductive girl or wizard. At one thousand it grows nine tails and becomes a celestial creature. Foxes are feared for their cunning to make mischief, and so receive placatory offerings. The Shinto god of rice, Inari Sama, whose cult is located around Mt Inari, is accompanied by two foxes or is mounted on one. They are his messengers and guard the door of his temples. A scroll in the fox's mouth [ix] alludes to a legend that the Celestial Fox came to earth bearing a book of knowledge. In the Christian West the fox personifies Satan, especially in medieval sculpture.

Frog, Toad. An Egyptian creation myth names a group of eight deities, or Ogdoad, who personified the primeval chaos, from which they spontaneously created the ordered universe. Four were male frogs, four female snakes. An early frog-goddess was Heket who became, in the Middle Kingdom, the protector of women in childbirth. She is represented in cult images and on amulets usually with a frog's head and a human body.

[i]

There are many Chinese and Japanese folk legends about the frog (Ch. *wa*) and, more particularly, the toad (Ch. *ha-ma*), creatures that are not always easily distinguished in either literature or art. In Han dynasty tomb paintings there are images of the moon's face resembling a toad (like our man in the moon). A popular legend describes it as pure white, three-legged and with the sacred FUNGUS of longevity growing from its head [i]. (See also MOON.) Another legend tells of a three-legged toad that belonged to a tenth-century Chinese court official, Liu Hai, who was subsequently immortalized. He tempted it with a number of gold coins dangling on a string, a popular image symbolizing wealth and prosperity.[38] The same is told of the Japanese Gama Sennin. One of the EIGHT IMMORTALS, Chang Kuo, sometimes rides on a toad. See also FIVE POISONS.

Gazelle. In Egypt worship of the gazelle appears to date from the Pre-dynastic period. From the Old Kingdom it was sacred to Anukis, goddess of the Nile cataracts, who has two gazelles' heads on her crown. The war-god Reshep, worshipped in Egypt from the 18th Dynasty, wears a crown of Upper Egypt with a gazelle's head in front. The BUDDHA is sometimes represented as gazelle, said to be the form he took in a previous incarnation [ii: *N.W. China, 4th–6th cent.* AD]. Two gazelles symbolize his teaching, from the tradition that his first sermon was delivered in the Deer Park at Benares (mod. Varanasi). They kneel on either side of the Wheel of Law, sometimes on the socle of his throne. In Graeco-Roman art the STAG of ARTEMIS/DIANA may be represented as a gazelle. See also ANTELOPE; DEER.

[ii]

Goat. Once worshipped as the embodiment of the fertility of flocks, herds and humans; identified with the Sumerian fertility gods, Tammuz and Ningirsu. In Hindu myth, as a sacrificial animal, it was the mount of AGNI. In Greek myth it was sacred to ZEUS/JUPITER and, more generally, symbolized male sexuality; hence in art it is associated with DIONYSUS/BACCHUS and his followers the Satyrs, also Pan who has goat-like features (see DEMON; and SEVEN DEADLY SINS – Lust). In Christian art goats represent the damned at the Last Judgement.[39] A goat is the eighth Terrestrial Branch of the Chinese CALENDAR. Capricorn, the goatfish, belongs to December in the TWELVE MONTHS and Winter, one of the FOUR SEASONS [iii]. See also FISH; TRIUMPH; ZODIAC.

[iii]

Goldfinch. One of several symbolic objects held by the infant Christ in paintings of the Virgin and Child (see VIRGIN MARY) [iv]. It forecasts his destiny, from the legend that its red marking was

[iv]

a drop of blood that splashed on it as it flew down to draw a thorn from Christ's brow on the road to Calvary.

Goose, Gander (Sk. *hamsa*; Ch. *yen*; Jap. *gan*). The wild goose and its relatives feature widely in religious myths. The egg out of which the world was created was, in Egypt, laid by a goose, the Great Honker (Gengen Wer). AMUN, as god of creation, was identified with it and may be represented as a goose. It is sometimes worn on the head of the earth-god, GEB. In the Ptolemaic period it became a symbol of SETH and embodied the forces of evil. In Hindu myth the 'immortal gander' is first mentioned in the *Mahabharata*.[40] It is associated with BRAHMA, the creator, and is his vehicle. It is at home on land, on water and in the sky and therefore symbolizes two contrasting aspects of the human spirit, the earthbound and the divine. Its name, *hamsa*, is said to echo the sound of the yogi's rhythmic breathing, which contributes to his spiritual enlightenment. It is therefore a symbol of knowledge and intelligence (see also GARUDA). The Chinese take a more mundane view. Since the Chou dynasty two geese have symbolized married bliss and feature together on betrothal gifts. However their migratory habits also make them symbols of separation and home-sickness. The bird is *yang*, signifying maleness, the heavens, the sun. It owes its solar aspect, as in India, to the impression that it follows the sun when migrating. In Japan a goose is the vehicle of Kokuzo, the Japanese version of the Indian BODHISATTVA Akashagarbha (the 'womb of the void'), a figure of indeterminate sex, prominent in the Shingon sect of Buddhism. In Japanese folklore the goose is said to seek the moon, an ever-popular subject in painting showing geese flying across the full moon [v]. Geese were sacred to the Greeks and Romans. They were the guardians of cities, renowned for their watchfulness, like the Capitoline geese who saved Rome, during the night, from the attacking Gauls.[41] In Christian art a goose is the attribute of Martin, bishop of Tours.

[v]

Grasshopper. The general name for cricket, locust, etc. [vi]. The destructive locust is the enemy of Maat, the Egyptian goddess of cosmic law and order, seen on Late Dynastic coffin painting. Athenians wore a golden grasshopper in the hair to denote they were of noble ancestry. In Greek myth the Trojan Tithonus, granted immortality but not eternal youth, eventually turned into a grasshopper.[42] In Chinese painting a grasshopper and chrysanthemums together signify, by a play on words, 'May you remain in high office for a long time.' When held in the hand of the infant Christ it symbolizes the conversion of pagans by recalling the Egyptian plague of locusts.[43]

[vi]

Griffin. Composite beast usually with an eagle's head, sometimes crested, a lion's body, wings and sometimes clawed feet. It is of very ancient lineage and has survived in heraldry until the present day. In the Old Kingdom the pharaoh, as a victorious conqueror,

[i]

was represented somewhat similarly with the falcon's head of HORUS on a lion's body, a symbolic combination of vigilance and strength. This type survived into the Late Period when it symbolized vengeance or retribution and, under the Greeks, was identified with Nemesis. The eagle-lion type may have appeared in the Near East during the great migrations from the north-east in the first half of the second millennium. The crested eagle type flourished in Mesopotamia and Syria in the 14th and 13th cents. BC. It is either at rest, perhaps personifying Death, or, more typically, it attacks other creatures, a motif common on cylinder seals [i: Mid-Assyrian, 14th–13th cent. BC]. It continues to feature among other sacred animals in Near-Eastern art down to Achaemenian Persia. The lion-headed griffin is sacred to the Assyrian moon-god, SIN. The griffin's reputation as a guardian of gold comes from Pliny.[44] In Greece the griffin was sacred to APOLLO and ATHENA/MINERVA.

[ii]

Hare (Ch. k'u; Jap. usagi; Sk. sason). A creature with supernatural powers widely associated with lunar deities. It is the fourth of the twelve Terrestrial Branches of the Chinese CALENDAR. The markings on the moon are said to resemble a hare, a notion probably originating in early lunar cults. Out of this grew a Buddhist legend in which Shakyamuni took the form of a hare in a previous incarnation and was depicted thus on the moon.[45] Chinese legends, at least as early as the Warring States period and later widely known in Japan, told of a white hare that lived on the moon, pounding an elixir of immortality with pestle and mortar [ii]. This image is one of the TWELVE ORNAMENTS on Chinese imperial robes. The elixir was particularly associated with Taoist lore. The Chinese moon-goddess, Ch'ang-O, has a hare for an attribute. Like the fox the hare lives to a great age, some say one thousand years, and is therefore a symbol of longevity. In Egypt the hare was an attribute of the moon-god THOTH at Hermopolis. In the Late Period it was worn as a protective amulet. Like the rabbit, the hare symbolizes fertility and is an attribute of Lust, one of the SEVEN DEADLY SINS. In Christian art a hare at the feet of the Virgin Mary, or in scenes of the Virgin and unicorn, symbolizes victory over lust. Lust personified may have a hare for attribute.

[iii]

Harpies (Gk. harpuiai, snatchers). In Greek myth they were originally beautiful winged maidens who personified the storm-winds.[46] Later they became birds of prey with long claws and hag-like human faces. They caused death by starvation, snatching food from the table and befouling what was left. They were propitiated as messengers of death who bore the soul to the Underworld and are thus represented in funerary art. Dante and Virgil met in the seventh circle of hell.[47] [iii: after Doré]. They reappear in Italian Renaissance painting personifying Avarice.

[iv]

Hedgehog. In Renaissance allegory an attribute of Touch, one

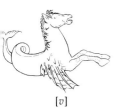

[v]

[vi]

[vii]

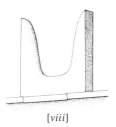

[viii]

[ix]

of the FIVE SENSES; and of Gluttony and Avarice, two of the SEVEN DEADLY SINS [iv].

Hippocampus. Monster with the foreparts of a horse and fish's tail, occasionally with fin-like wings [v: Italian, 15th cent.]. Hippocampi are ridden by Greek marine deities and may draw the chariot of Poseidon/Neptune, ruler of the sea, and of the sea-nymph Galatea. They reappear in Renaissance and Baroque painting, especially French and Italian. See also FOUR ELEMENTS–Water.

Hippopotamus. The ritual slaying of a white hippopotamus by the pharaoh in the Old Kingdom came to symbolize HORUS slaying SETH. A hippopotamus hunt, with this symbolic meaning, is found in tomb paintings of the Old Kingdom and later. The goddess Taweret, who protected women in childbirth, has the head of a hippopotamus and, usually, pendent breasts and enlarged belly [vi: 26th Dynasty]. Her fierce appearance drove off harmful influences. She may have the protective SA symbol beside her. Taweret was widely represented in the Middle and New Kingdoms on amulets worn by pregnant women and on milk vessels shaped in her likeness. See also BES.

Horn. Among many peoples a symbol of power and strength, especially the horns of bull, cow and ram. Therefore it is the attribute of numerous deities, including Mother-Goddesses such as Astarte, and is a feature of the crowns and helmets of kings and warriors. A horn is also phallic. In Mesopotamia from earliest times a cap with one or more pairs of horns was expressly the headgear of a deity and, during the Kassite dynasty (from c. 1600 BC), of ANU and ENLIL in particular. In the neo-Assyrian period (from c. 900 BC) it was the distinctive crown of ADAD, ASSUR, EA, ISHTAR, SHAMASH and perhaps NINURTA [vii]. Stylized bulls' horns on ancient altars from Minoan Crete are a reminder of its bull cult [viii].

Horns are part of the head-dress of many Egyptian deities [ix], often combined with the solar disk and URAEUS, since BULL and COW both have associations with the sun: thus HATHOR and, derived from her, ISIS. The zoomorphic bull-god, Apis, also has a solar disk and URAEUS between his horns. The horns of RAM-headed deities either curl downwards (AMUN, usually) or extend laterally (Khnum; RE; Heryshaf).

The oldest Indian horned deity is seen on a stamp seal from the Indus Valley (3rd mill. BC). He is surrounded by animals and may have been the forerunner of SHIVA, in his role of 'Lord of the Beasts' (Sk. Pashupati). The goddess Durga slew the horned BUFFALO-demon.[48] The lion, the mount of MANJUSHRI, is sometimes horned (Sk. Shardula). See also BULL in Indian art.

The rhinoceros, according to early Taoist texts, was an animal of good omen, its horn having magical properties. The powdered horn was considered to be an aphrodisiac. On Chinese ceramics, silks and amulets a pair of crossed horns symbolizes joy. See EIGHT TREASURES; RHINOCEROS.

A figure with a pair of short horns and fingers terminating in claws is the *oni*, a class of small demons, otherwise of human form, that infest Japanese households and cause mischief. They are exorcized at the New Year. *Oni* are a popular subject in *netsuke*.

In Graeco-Roman art Pan and the Satyrs have horns, also sometimes DIONYSUS/BACCHUS. This pagan attribute is probably the source of the devil's horns in Christian art (see SEVEN DEADLY SINS). The light sometimes seen to radiate from MOSES' brow may be represented as horns.[49] A ram's horn, the *Shofar* of Jewish religion, was represented in synagogues and on certain funerary objects. It stands for the ram sacrificed by Abraham instead of his son Isaac and symbolizes God's sovereignty and mercy.[50] As a musical instrument the horn is an attribute of Melpomene, a MUSE. A horn is a vessel for liquid, typically OIL used for anointing. See also CORNUCOPIA; RHINOCEROS; UNICORN; WINGED DISK.

[*i*]

Horse. Prominent in the myths and religious rites of many civilizations. It is primarily a symbol of the sun, was sacrificed to sun-gods and draws their chariots. It is also associated with marine deities. In funerary art it can symbolize death and bears away the soul of the deceased. The Celtic horse-goddess, Epona, was widely worshipped in Europe as a funerary deity. In primitive funeral rites the horse was prominent among a man's possessions that were buried with him. As the mount of warriors and heroes it is a symbol of courage, strength and swiftness. A white horse is especially prized.

The horse became known in the Near East, Egypt and India following the invasions of Aryan tribesmen from the northern steppes in the 2nd mill. BC, who used a horse-drawn chariot. In northern Mesopotamia the Kassites, who came from the same region about 1800 BC, worshipped a goddess of horse-breeding called Mirizir. The horse on the altar [*i: late 2nd mill.* BC] probably represents her. Horse and chariot appear first in Egyptian and Mycenaean art about 1500 BC in scenes of hunting and warfare . The concept of the sun-god as a charioteer, pursuing the powers of darkness out of the heavens, would have been derived from this imagery. He was SHAMASH in Mesopotamia, Helios/Sol in Etruria, Greece and Rome, MITHRAS in Iran and SURYA in India. Surya is first seen as a charioteer in the 2nd cent. BC, an image probably borrowed from western Asia, though the horse was already associated with him (and AGNI) in earlier religious texts.[51] Also prominent among Hindu solar charioteers were the Ashvins, twins like the Greek Dioscuri with whom they were probably connected (see also INDRA).

The horse as a sacrificial animal was greatly promoted in Brahmanic literature. It reached its peak in the 'royal horse sacrifice' (Sk. *ashvamedha*), a ritual performed by the king to bring prosperity to the state which also enhanced his personal status and divinity. It died out in the later seventh century. In later Hindu myth VISHNU, in his tenth and last incarnation, takes the form of a horse, KALKIN. In his first incarnation, as a fish, he fights the horse-headed demon, Hayagriva, whose identity he later assumes.[52]

On the oldest Buddhist monuments, the Ashoka PILLARS, a horse is one of four sacred animals. In Buddhist legend the horse Kantaka was ridden by Shakyamuni on leaving his father's palace.[53] In early art (before he was depicted in human form) it is riderless. Its hoofs do not touch the ground, thus ensuring that Shakyamuni's departure was silent. A horse is one of the SEVEN TREASURES. The demon Hayagriva reappears in Buddhist art, having been incorporated into the bodhisattva AVALOKITESHVARA. He is known in Japan as Bato-Kannon and in Tibet as Tam-Din. He is a tutelary deity of fierce aspect, the protector of animals, and has a horse's head surmounting his other heads. A horse is the mount of the Dhyani-Buddha, Ratnasambhava.

In China the horse (*ma*) is *yang*, since it has a single (odd-numbered), uncloven hoof. It is therefore a symbol of masculinity. It is the seventh of the twelve Terrestrial Branches of the Chinese CALENDAR. Eight horses, usually loose in a field, drew the chariot of the legendary King Mu (Jap. Boku-O) (10th cent. BC). They are a popular subject with painters. A monkey on horseback illustrates, by a play on words, the saying 'May you swiftly (with the aid of a horse) be rewarded with high rank.'

[ii]

The horse has had an important place in Japanese myths, folk-tales and religious rites. It was once the custom to present a horse to the temple of Shinto gods, a black one to ask the deity for rain, white for fair weather. Subsequently a painting of the animal on wood was substituted (the *ema*). These votive offerings are widely seen in Shinto temples. Sacred white horses are kept in the stables of some temples. At an annual festival at Usakajinja the temple horses were made scapegoats for adulteresses who confessed, and were chased and beaten [ii].

The winged horse of Greek mythology is Pegasus, the offspring of Medusa and Poseidon/Neptune, lord of the sea; alternatively it sprang from the blood of Medusa when she died. Pegasus was ridden by PERSEUS and Bellerophon, and became a symbol of Fame in Renaissance allegory. In a well-known contest with Athene on the Athenian Acropolis Poseidon struck the ground with his trident, whereupon a horse sprang up.[54] A horse is occasionally found in early Christian funerary art in Roman catacombs, probably a borrowing from pagan stelae where it represents a psychopomp. For Christians it alludes to St Paul, who wrote to Timothy: 'the hour for my departure is upon me. I have run the race, I have finished the course . . .'.[55] In medieval and later art the four horsemen of the Apocalypse[56] symbolize war, conquest, famine and death, the agents of divine wrath. A horse is the mount of SS. Eustace, Hubert and Martin.

Hippolytus' martyrdom was to be bound to wild horses and torn to pieces. See also CENTAUR; FOUR PARTS OF THE WORLD–Europe; TRIUMPH–Love; UNICORN.

[i]

Ibex. One of the GOAT family, characterized by long, backward-curving horns. It is first seen on early Mesopotamian cylinder seals (3500–3000 BC) and at that period was probably sacred to the Mother-Goddess. It is widely depicted in the same region during the first half of the first millennium BC, on Assyrian reliefs and wall paintings, as a sacrificial animal. On cylinder seals two ibexes flank the SACRED TREE, or an anonymous 'hero' grapples with them (see COMBAT). The ibex features in Iranian metalwork down to the Achaemenian dynasty [*i: Persian, 5th–4th cent. BC*]. The ibex is destructive to vines and was therefore sacrificed to DIONYSUS/BACCHUS in the Graeco-Roman era.

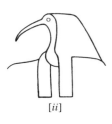

[ii]

Ibis. Genus of wading birds, sacred in Egypt from the Predynastic period. From the Old Kingdom it was worshipped continuously as an incarnation of THOTH, guardian of scribes and learning. He has either the bird's head on a human body [*ii*], sometimes crowned with a lunar crescent and disk, or is entirely aviform. The ibis was embalmed and mummified in very large numbers. Maat and Thoth may both be present in the Hall of Judgement, respectively to determine the truth and record it; hence the FEATHER of Maat sometimes accompanies the ibis.

[iii]

Lamb, Sheep. Sacrificial victim in many ancient religions. It is seen in Jewish funerary art in the Roman catacombs (see also MILK). The Jewish paschal lamb was adopted by the early church as a symbol of CHRIST sacrificed to save mankind. The ram sacrificed instead of Isaac is to be understood in this sense.[57] Hence it may be depicted with a cruciform halo, cross-staff, chalice, or banner of the Resurrection [*iii*]. It has this meaning in scenes of Abel's offering to God and as the shepherds' gift at Christ's nativity. Early Christian art represents the APOSTLES as twelve sheep surrounding the Lamb of God; subsequently, as men, each has a sheep for an attribute. The scene of the Adoration of the Lamb is taken from the Apocalypse.[58] A lamb is the attribute of SS. Agnes, Geneviève and, often with a cruciform halo, of JOHN THE BAPTIST. In Renaissance allegories it accompanies Innocence, Patience, Humility and other personified virtues, also the Phlegmatic person, one of the FOUR TEMPERAMENTS. In Chinese ceramic painting it denotes Filial Piety because it kneels when given suck. See also RAM.

Leopard, Panther. The Egyptian goddess Mafdet, invoked as destroyer of snakes and scorpions, took the form of a leopard. Egyptian priests wore leopard skins when performing funerary rites and the deceased himself may be similarly represented, perhaps a means of ensuring his survival after death. The robes of some Chinese military officials were embroidered with leopards to symbolize bravery in war. Leopards were sacred to

[iv]

DIONYSUS/BACCHUS and, in art, draw his chariot [iv: *Graeco-Roman, Delos*].

Lion. Its appearance in the art of ancient Egypt, Mesopotamia and Persia indicates that it once inhabited those regions. But it is also seen in the art of China and Japan where it was unknown in the wild state. The image was transmitted to the Far East with the spread of Buddhism.

The oldest images of the lion were connected with the worship of sun-gods. They were also symbolic guardians of temples, palaces and tombs, where their ferocity kept harmful influences at bay. In Egypt the lion was identified with the sun-god RE and with the related deity Amun-Re; also with Harakhti, another name for HORUS when he symbolizes the rising sun. Aker, an Underworld deity who protected the sun-god's barque on its nightly return journey to the East, has two lion's heads facing in opposite directions. The lion's ferocity protected the pharaoh: Sakhmet, the lion-headed goddess of Memphis and daughter of Re, breathed fire on his enemies in battle. One of the functions of Mut, the tutelary goddess of Thebes who is sometimes represented with a lion's head, was to protect the pharaoh in war. BES, protector of women in childbirth, may have leonine features or may wear a lion's pelt. Egyptian temples were sometimes guarded by sculptured lions at the entrance. The lion's features were also represented on the bolts of doors.

This magical power, or *mana*, that was believed to be present in the image was also the motive behind much Mesopotamian art, where the lion is often the guardian of temples and palaces. The earliest examples, in clay or bronze, date from the early 3rd mill. BC. In Assyrian sculpture we see a hybrid creature, a lion-headed dragon. Another hybrid, the lion-headed EAGLE, called Imdugud, is first seen on cylinder seals of the 4th mill. BC. A lion is the mount of the Akkadian goddess, ISHTAR, in her warlike aspect. She was worshipped particularly by the Assyrian king, Assurbanipal (668–631 BC), who was a famous lion-hunter. The very widely depicted image of a divine hero holding two lions in his outstretched hands is first seen on early cylinder seals and temple vases. It is so far unexplained, though similar images on Greek and Hindu artefacts are thought to represent a solar deity. The same image occurs in medieval Christian art to represent Daniel in the lions' den (see also COMBAT).

Lion and sun come together in Persia in the image of MITHRAS with a lion's head. He is entwined six times by a snake, symbolizing the path of the sun through the ecliptic, and he holds the globe of the sun. The lion is sometimes represented resting a forepaw on the globe of the sun. Images of this type, probably originating in Persia, reached India and thence were brought to China about the 4th cent. AD in the wake of Buddhism, and to Japan in the early 5th cent. A curious transformation occurred when they were adopted as guardians of Buddhist temples, the

[i]

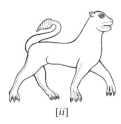

[ii]

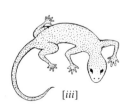

[iii]

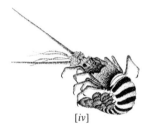

[iv]

lion acquiring some of the features of the Chinese toy dog. His solar globe now represented the *cintamani*, or sacred JEWEL of Buddhism [*i: Japanese, bronze, Fujiwara period*]. They go in pairs, male and female, the male with the globe and, in Japan, a single horn; the female with a lion cub.

In Hindu myth the lion symbolizes the destructive ferocity of a deity. Thus VISHNU in one of his incarnations became a man-lion (Sk. *Narasimha*) in order to destroy a demon king; the goddess DEVI, in her fierce aspect as Durga, rides on a lion, the symbol of her furious energy, when she fights the buffalo-demon. A lion is also sometimes the mount of the elephant-god, GANESHA. Buddhism early on adopted the lion to symbolize Buddha himself and aspects of his doctrine. On an Ashoka PILLAR four lions support the WHEEL of the Law and later appear on the socle of his throne. They may stand in pairs at the entrance to the STUPA. Shakyamuni was also known as Shakya-Simha, 'Lion of the Shakya tribe', his sermons being likened to the power of a lion's roar. Hence the lion became associated with BODHISATTVAS, in particular as the mount of MANJUSHRI, and with certain Dhyani-Buddhas (see VAIROCANA).

In the West we find Cybele, the Phrygian Mother-Goddess, on a throne flanked by lions, which also draw her chariot. HERCULES wears a lion's pelt, first seen on Attic case painting *c.* 650 BC. Later, he is depicted astride the crouching animal, forcing its jaw apart with his hands. The same image is used in Christian art to represent Samson[59] and DAVID, and was probably derived from the well-known cult image of Mithras as bull-slayer. In Christian art the lion symbolizes both Christ, 'the lion from the tribe of Judah',[60] and Satan, who 'like a roaring lion prowls around'.[61] According to medieval bestiaries the lion symbolizes the Resurrection because the cubs are born dead and only come to life on the third day when their father breathes on them. [*ii: Spanish, 11th cent.*]. The lion, usually winged, is one of the APOCALYPTIC BEASTS, standing for the evangelist Mark. It features in the arms and old coinage of Venice, where his supposed remains lie. It is an attribute of SS. Adrian, Euphemia, Jerome (one of the FOUR LATIN FATHERS), Natalia and Thecla; Daniel (one of the FOUR PROPHETS); Renaissance personifications of Fortitude (one of the CARDINAL VIRTUES); Pride and Wrath among the SEVEN DEADLY SINS; Choler (one of the FOUR TEMPERAMENTS) and Africa (one of the FOUR PARTS OF THE WORLD). See also ZODIAC.

Lizard. The gecko, a type of lizard, is one of the FIVE POISONS of Chinese folk medicine. A magical unguent made of pounded gecko and cinnabar was said to be used on ladies of the Chinese court as a test of virginity or marital fidelity [*iii*].

Lobster, Crayfish. In the Far East the lobster, when represented in art, is typically without claws and has long antennae. Known in China as dragon-shrimp (*lung hsia*), it is sometimes seen at the feet of Kuan-yin (see AVALOKITESHVARA) and symbolizes riches,

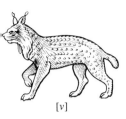

[v]

[vi]

[vii]

[viii]

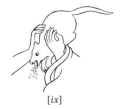

[ix]

married bliss and harmony. In Japan, called *ebi*, it denotes long life, from its bent appearance, and is a common motif on all kinds of gifts at the New Year festival [*iv*].

Lynx. The sharp-sighted 'mountain cat' believed in antiquity to be able to see through a stone wall. A symbol of watchful alertness, especially in heraldry [*v*]. Formerly one of the animals associated with DIONYSUS/BACCHUS. It is an attribute of Sight, one of the FIVE SENSES.

Magpie (Ch. *hsi ch'iao*). The subject of many Chinese popular superstitions and folk-tales. Its name means 'bird of joy', its call foretelling the arrival of a visitor or good news [*vi*]. In paintings and ceramic decoration two magpies symbolize married bliss. Two with bamboo and plum are a play on words meaning 'May you meet each other in happiness.' Three in a tree under a bright sun mean 'One day you will have three joys.' Twelve denote twelve good wishes. The magpie was sacred to the Manchus after a legend that the bird perched on the head of the founder of the dynasty, thereby deceiving enemies who were pursuing him. Magpies decorating a mirror-back refer to a legend that breaking a mirror obliged a man and wife to separate, each taking a piece. If the wife then had a lover her piece turned into a magpie which, tell-tale, flew back to the husband. See also STAR.

Mantis (Ch. *t'ang lang*; Jap, *toro*). In appearance praying, by nature preying [*vii*]. For the Chinese and Japanese it is the embodiment of bravery and the subject of numerous legends. It is a popular motif in Japanese painting, engravings and on articles of lacquer, when it is commonly shown attacking a cicada.

Minotaur (Bull of Minos). In Greek myth a monster with a bull's head and man's body born to Pasiphae, wife of King Minos of Crete, after having sex with a bull. It was kept in the labyrinthine royal palace at Knossos and was ultimately slain by Theseus.[62] (See also LABYRINTH.) The Minotaur appears on Cretan seals and coins from Knossos, and is the symbol of a more ancient bull cult. The fight with Theseus was a popular subject on Greek vases [*viii: Attic, c. 540* BC]. The myth of Pasiphae is thought to be an echo of a fertility rite, the sacred marriage, between the Minoan queen as Mother-Goddess and the King wearing a bull's head mask.

Mongoose, Ichneumon (Sk. *nakula*). The Indian mongoose is an attribute of Vaisravana (Jap. Bishamon), one of the FOUR CELESTIAL KINGS; and, when spitting jewels, of GANESHA and Bakula, one of the sixteen Protectors of the Law (see ARHAT) [*ix*]. Bakula's name is probably a corruption of the Sanskrit for mongoose. Purses were made of the mongoose's skin; hence the animal became the attribute of certain lesser gods of wealth, from whom it probably acquired its jewels. The mongoose's Egyptian relation, the ichneumon, was a deity of the lower world, first seen in tomb paintings of the Middle Kingdom. Wearing a solar disk it was fashioned into a votive offering. At Letopolis in Lower Egypt it was worshipped as a form of HORUS.

Monster. Hybrid creatures, though rare in nature, are commonplace in art. It is significant that many of them embody a human element such as an animal's head on a human body, or vice versa. They are distant echoes from the world of prehistoric man when there was a close identity between man and beast. Members of a tribe felt they were one and the same as their totemic animal. Rituals to promote success in hunting involved wearing animal masks and skins. The priest, or shaman, garbed in this way acquired magical powers. In a well-known prehistoric cave painting[63] he wears antlers, has an owl's face and a horse's tail. We know little of the spiritual condition of man in prehistory though worship of animals as gods already existed with the appearance of the first civilizations. In early historic times priests still wore animal masks and robes, while the gods in animal form gradually gave way to human, or semi-human figures. This sometimes produced hybrids like the Hindu demon Mahisha (a human body with the head of a BUFFALO), GANESHA (elephant's head), the Greek Minotaur (head of a BULL) and much of the Egyptian pantheon.

[i]

The origin of some hybrids, like the Egyptian god, SETH, is still uncertain [i]. The process of syncretism, the merging of different cults, sometimes resulted in creatures such as the Egyptian bull, Apis, which has a vulture's wings. Statuary guarding temples and palaces needed to make an impression of strength and power, which Assyrian sculptors achieved by combining creatures like the lion, eagle and bull that were notably powerful in their own elements.

The stylized creatures represented on early Chinese bronze vessels (Shang and Chou dynasties, 2nd and 1st mill. BC), though not recognizably hybrids, may be classed as monsters. The vessels were used in ritual connected with ancestor worship. The commonest image is the so-called *t'ao-t'ieh* [ii], a bodiless animal mask of fearful aspect, whose meaning is uncertain, probably that of a shaman. Its name means 'glutton', an entirely speculative interpretation dating from the 3rd cent. BC.

[ii]

The old belief that every living thing on earth had its counterpart in the sea created the HIPPOCAMPUS, Capricorn (a GOAT with a fish's tail), Triton, Mermaid and others. Myth, folklore and, in the West, compilations of so-called natural history contributed their share of monsters. See also BASILISK; CENTAUR; CHIMAERA; CROCODILE; DRAGON; GRIFFIN; HARPY; HORSE (Pegasus); SCORPION; SIREN; SPHINX; UNICORN. See also DEMON.

Octopus, Cuttlefish. A popular decoration on late-Minoan and Mycenaean pottery and sometimes on personal ornaments. The eight tentacles often took the form of a spiral [iii], which was a recurrent motif in Cycladic and Cretan art of the period, when it symbolized thunder and rain.

[iii]

Owl. From earliest times a bird of ill-omen and death. A Sumerian cult-relief of early 2nd mill. BC represents a goddess of death, possibly Lilith, with owl-like characteristics. Some Chinese funerary vessels of the Shang dynasty (late 2nd mill. BC) take the form of an owl (*hsiao*). For the Chinese and Japanese the owl (Jap. *fukuro*) was a harbinger of death and, from the belief that it picked out its mother's eyes, a symbol of filial ingratitude. It is an attribute of YAMA, the Hindu Lord of the Underworld. In the West the Etruscans sacrificed slaves and captives to an owl deity. The origin of its association with ATHENA/MINERVA is uncertain, but it was through her that the owl acquired a reputation for wisdom [*iv: Greek coin, 5th cent.* BC]. In Renaissance allegory it is an attribute of Night and Sleep personified.

[*iv*]

Ox (Ch. *niu*; Jap. *ushi*). Of peaceful temperament, being a castrated bull, the ox is therefore a draught animal, beast of burden and symbol of strength and, in the West, of patience. It is one of the twelve Terrestrial Branches of the Chinese CALENDAR, a symbol of agriculture and the spring, and the object of a Chinese spring festival. It is the mount of Lao-tzu, the founder of Taoism, last seen riding away on an ox, and of many Japanese poets and sages. It is the emblem of Japanese Zen Buddhists. As a sacrificial animal the ox symbolizes Christ's sacrifice and in Christian art is an attribute of SS. Thomas Aquinas (called 'dumb ox'); Luke (a winged ox, one of the APOCALYPTIC BEASTS) [*v: Chartres cath., c. 1150*]. Black oxen draw the chariot of Death, at his TRIUMPH. It is an attribute of Sloth, one of the SEVEN DEADLY SINS. See also BULL.

[*v*]

Parrot (Ch. *ying-ko*; *ying-wu*). A decorative motif on Chinese ceramics [*vi*], especially of the *famille rose* type (from 1st half of 18th cent. to 19th cent.). A pearl in its beak alludes to a legend of a pearl merchant who had an unfaithful wife and serves as a warning to married women. A parrot is an attribute of Kama, the Hindu god of love.

[*vi*]

Peacock (Sk. *mayura*; Ch. *k'ung-ch'ueh*; Jap. *kujaku*). A native of India and Sri Lanka, its breeding spread to China, Japan and, in the West, to Persia, Greece and beyond [*vii: Rajput, late 16th cent.*]. The peacock featured in some primitive cults. A pair flank the SACRED TREE, each sometimes having a snake in its beak. It was associated with solar deities perhaps because, like the cock and the Egyptian baboon, its cry greets the dawn. Peacocks were also among the trappings of royalty: Chinese emperors from the Ming dynasty onwards bestowed tail feathers on those they wished to honour; the magnificent jewelled throne of the kings of Persia (looted from India in 1739) was dominated by a golden peacock. The bird was associated with several greater gods, usually as their mount: thus the Hindu god of war, KARRTIKEYA, BRAHMA and his wife SARASVATI; also the heavenly BUDDHA,

[*vii*]

Amitabha. When Amitabha is mounted astride, the tail-feathers
rise fan-like behind him, forming an aureole. It often then has
bit and bridle in its beak. A fan of peacock's feathers is an attribute of several minor Buddhist goddesses of Tibet and is found
among the sacred utensils of Lamaist ritual. It was used by Jains
in India to sweep the way before them to avoid treading on any
living creature. In China the peacock symbolizes beauty and dignity and is often coupled with the PEONY. The Taoist Queen
Mother of the West, HSI WANG MU, sometimes rides on a peacock
but more often on a CRANE. A sage riding a peacock, in Japanese
painting, is Kujaku-Myo-O, a Buddha of healing, thought to be
derived from VAIROCANA.

In the West, it is said that peacocks were kept at the ancient
temple of HERA/JUNO at Samos, perhaps the earliest links between
the goddess and her principal sacred attribute. In Greek myth the
'eyes' in the peacock's tail were put there by HERA who had taken
them from the body of the hundred-eyed giant, Argos, after he
was killed by Hermes.[64] The bird features in Christian art as a
symbol of the Resurrection and immortality, from the old belief
that its flesh never decayed.[65] It was also believed that to eat its
flesh was an antidote to poisons, especially snake-bite, from the
fact that peacocks attack and devour snakes. The symbol of pride
and attribute of Pride personified was a late development (see
SEVEN DEADLY SINS). See also PHOENIX.

[i]

Pelican. The red tip of the pelican's bill pressed against her breast
as she feeds her young is the likely source of the legend that she
pierces her breast to feed them on her blood. It was adopted as a
symbol of CHRIST shedding his blood on the cross and became
known as the 'Pelican in her piety' (*pietas*, filial devotion). The
motif is commonly seen in church decoration [*i*], in allegorical still-life (see VANITAS) and is an attribute of CHARITY personified.

Pheasant (Ch. *chih*, *yeh chi*; Jap. *kiji*, *kigisu*). A combination of
the golden pheasant and peacock provided Chinese artists with
a model for the mythical PHOENIX. The pheasant was a symbol of
beauty and good fortune [*ii*]. It is one of the TWELVE ORNAMENTS
on Chinese imperial robes. Like other long-tailed birds it is often depicted beside the PEONY. In Japan it symbolized mother-
love, because it was observed to save its young when its nest was
threatened by fire.

[*ii*]

Phoenix. Graeco-Roman name for a mythical bird, imagined
to be of gorgeous plumage. The name was used loosely for a
variety of fabulous creatures from Egypt to China. Pliny, seeing
a golden pheasant for the first time, called it a phoenix.[66] According to a well-known legend it was the only bird of its kind;
it inhabited the Arabian desert and had a lifespan of five hundred years, at the end of which time it immolated itself on a funeral pyre and rose again from its own ashes. In imperial Rome

it symbolized the apotheosis of the emperor, and in the Christian catacombs, and later, it stood for Christ's Resurrection (see also THREE MONASTIC VOWS; VANITAS; FOUR ELEMENTS– Fire). Birds associated with fire and the sun's rays tend to be called a phoenix. Thus the Benu, the bird sacred to RE, the sun-god of Heliopolis, was called a phoenix by Herodotus, who visited Egypt in the 5th cent. BC. It was also a manifestation of OSIRIS, when it was represented as a heron. The belief that its birth occurred spontaneously linked it to the sun's daily rising. The Chinese *feng*, or *feng-huang*, another mythical bird with brilliant plumage, is called a phoenix by western writers. It was an emblem of the empress and is represented as a combination of pheasant, peacock and crane [*iii*]. It decorates ceramic ware of all but the earliest periods. As one of the four guardians of the universe the *feng* commands the southern quarter in summer (see COMPASS), when it is known as *chu chieh*, the scarlet bird. The fiery heat of the south in summer may have led to its association with the phoenix. In Japan it is called *Ho-O* and shares many of the Chinese legends and symbolism.

[*iii*]

Pig (Ch. *chu*). The domestic swine has a varied and sometimes contradictory symbolism. The sow, having a large litter, symbolized fertility and therefore was once sacrificed to Mother-Goddesses and, in the early Hellenic era, to DEMETER/CERES [*iv: Attic cup, c. 480* BC]. It is unclean to Jews and Moslems and, in Egypt, being identified with SETH, was taboo in the sacrificial rites of HORUS. ISIS was worshipped as a sow at Heliopolis. It was also sacrificed at Egyptian lunar festivals. Sow and piglets formed a popular amulet, worn to make women fertile. A pig, or boar, is one of the twelve Terrestrial Branches of the Chinese CALENDAR. A popular female BODHISATTVA in Tibetan Lamaism, Marici, sits on a lotus throne drawn by seven pigs. She has three faces, one of which is a boar's. In Christian art a pig is the attribute of Antony the Great. In medieval and Renaissance allegory it is an attribute of Gluttony, Sloth and Lust among the SEVEN DEADLY SINS. It is trodden underfoot by Chastity personified. It is an attribute of Melancholy, one of the FOUR TEMPERAMENTS. It is fattened in November and eaten in December (see TWELVE MONTHS). See also BOAR.

[*iv*]

Quail (Ch. *an-ch'un*). Widely associated with courage, from its pugnacious character, also with the amorous, but rare in art, except Chinese. Here its name (*an*) is a homophone of tranquillity; thus two birds together make a loving couple. Nine quails among autumn flowers, especially chrysanthemums, express the hope that nine generations will live together in peace. Quail and plum together are an expression of general good wishes. Its ragged plumage makes it also a symbol of poverty [*v*].

[*v*]

Rabbit. It shares much of the symbolism of the HARE as a lunar animal; it is a symbol of fecundity and hence of Lust (see SEVEN

[i]

[ii]

[iii]

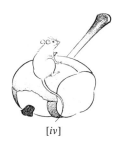

[iv]

DEADLY SINS). It sometimes appears in Renaissance marriage portraits at the feet of the betrothed couple. At the feet of the VIRGIN MARY it symbolizes the victory of chastity [*i: French, late 15th cent.*].

Ram. One of the principal animal forms in which gods of procreation and fertility were worshipped in the ancient Near East, Egypt, Greece and Rome. Images of the ram, dating from 3500–3000 BC, have been found in the temple of the Sumerian Mother-Goddess and also, made of precious metals, in the royal tombs at Ur, *c.* 2500 BC. A ram-headed sceptre is an attribute of the Sumerian god of fresh water, Enki (see EA). Egypt had several ram-gods, each with its own cult centre. Probably the oldest was Khnum, a creator who is depicted with a ram's head fashioning a man on a potter's wheel. His cult at Elephantine, where mummified rams have been found, may be pre-dynastic in origin. Heryshaf, a fertility deity worshipped in Middle Egypt, was another very early ram-headed god. He may also wear the *atef* CROWN of Osiris. The horns of both extend laterally [*ii*]. The sun-god, RE, is represented similarly. AMUN, head of the Egyptian pantheon, may take the total form of a ram, distinguished by its down-turned horns (after the 12th Dynasty) [*iii*]. In the Hellenistic period ZEUS became identified with Amun and acquired the ram as an attribute. For Greeks and Romans it symbolized fertility and was sacrificed to the Mother-Goddess, Cybele, in the rite of the *criobolium*, its blood imparting vital strength and immortality. It was sacred to HERMES/MERCURY (see also LAMB.) In eastern art the ram is comparatively rare. One of the earliest known sculptures of SHIVA (? 1st cent. AD) shows him standing in the *lingam* holding a ram.[67] It is mentioned in the *Rig-Veda* as the mount of AGNI. It doubles with a he-goat as one of the twelve Terrestrial Branches of the Chinese CALENDAR, and is a symbol of happy retirement. In the western ZODIAC the ram is Aries. See also FISH; FLEECE.

Rat (Ch. *shu*; Jap. *nezumi*). In Hindu myth and art a rat (the Indian bandicoot) is the vehicle of the elephant-headed deity GANESHA. A white rat is the messenger, or familiar, of Daikoku, one of the Japanese GODS OF HAPPINESS (see also HAMMER) [*iv*]. A rat is the first of the twelve Terrestrial Branches of the Chinese CALENDAR. In Renaissance allegory rat and mouse symbolize destruction, decay and, hence, the passage of time. A black and a white rat are together an attribute of Night personified. A rat is the attribute of St Fina who lived in a garret infested with them. See also MONGOOSE, which sometimes resembles a rat in Tibetan painting.

Raven. One of the crow family, with which it shares much symbolism. Its black plumage linked it with death and ill-omen. It is the attribute of several Celtic war-goddesses. The Norse god Odin in his warlike aspect has a raven on each shoulder, which

[v]

[vi]

[vii]

[viii]

are his messengers [v]. In the rites of MITHRAS initiates into the first grade of the cult wore raven masks. As the messenger from the sun-god, Sol, to Mithras the bird may have the CADUCEUS of HERMES/MERCURY. The raven was a Christian symbol of Satan because it feeds on carrion (= corruption), yet it succoured desert hermits such as Elijah,[68] SS. Paul the Hermit, Antony the Great and others, bringing them bread.(A three-legged raven in a solar disk: see SUN; TRISKELE.)

Rhinoceros. According to early Taoist texts, an animal of good omen, its horn having magical properties. If used as a drinking vessel, the horn sweated or even dissolved if its contents were poisonous. The powdered horn was considered an aphrodisiac. A pair of crossed horns symbolizes joy in Chinese ceramics, silks and amulets [vi]. They are one of the EIGHT TREASURES.

Salamander. A small lizard-like creature wrongly believed, since antiquity, to be unharmed by fire and even to extinguish flames. It is a Christian symbol of faith tested in the fires of temptation, and in Renaissance and later allegory an attribute of Fire personified, one of the FOUR ELEMENTS. A salamander surrounded by flames was an emblematic device of Francis I, King of France [vii].

Scarab. The sacred dung-beetle of Egypt was identified with the solar-god, Khepri, of Heliopolis. The god's name, 'he who comes into being', that is, is self-created like the sun every morning, seemed to fit the beetle, which was believed to be generated spontaneously from its solar-shaped ball of dung. The beetle, pushing against its ball, represents the god with his solar disk [viii]. Together with other gods he crosses the sky every day in his solar boat, often flanked by APES in attitudes of adoration. The scarab is first represented on amuletic seals of the Middle Kingdom. Amulets of faience, cornelian, etc. were placed on the heart of the deceased in order to win the favour of Khepri when the soul came to judgement. The scarab featured commonly on rings, necklaces and other articles of jewellery to protect the wearer and were subsequently placed in the tomb. Later tomb paintings depict a partly human figure with the head of a scarab, or fully anthropomorphic with a beetle on his head. Scarab amulets dating from the 8th cent. BC have been found in great numbers from Mesopotamia to Sardinia, probably brought by Egyptian armies and Phoenician traders.

Scorpion. It was once believed that images of a harmful creature had the magical power to ward off the living creature itself (and other evils), which may explain the two-sided symbolism of the scorpion. Thus in Tibet a scorpion-image on paper was once eaten as a charm against injurious demons. In Tibetan art it is an attribute of PADMASAMBHAVA, founder of Lamaism, in his 'wrathful' aspect as destroyer of demons (see also FIVE POISONS). Egypt had a scorpion goddess, Serket, who was worshipped from the Early Dynastic period. She has human form and wears a crown of a scorpion with its tail up, as if about to sting. She protected the pharaoh's throne, the contents of one of the Canopic JARS during embalming and was a guardian in the Underworld. Scorpion amulets protected Egyptians against poisonous bites. In Mesopotamia scorpion-deities appear originally to have had a solar connection as guardians of the 'place of sunrise'.[69] They are first represented on early cylinder seals (1st half of 3rd mill. BC). Later, in Assyrian sculpture they feature as partly human guardians of temples and their resident gods (see SHAMASH) [*i: Assyro-Kassite, late 12th cent.* BC]. As guardians of a royal palace (Tell Halaf, 10th–9th cent. BC) they have a god's horns, wings, clawed feet and scorpion's tail. Scorpions were among the agents of Ahriman, the Zoroastrian god of darkness and evil. One of them clasps in its claws the genitals of the bull in the cult image of MITHRAS, the bull-slayer, who was a god of light and enemy of Ahriman.

[*i*]

Christ said that snakes and scorpions were the agents of Satan.[70] In later medieval Christian art the scorpion symbolized the Synagogue personified (see BLINDFOLD) and Jews in general. It is seen on standards raised at the crucifixion, sometimes with the Greek letter sigma (Σ), denoting Synagogue. It is an attribute of Judas, of the allegorical figures of Envy, one of the SEVEN DEADLY SINS, and Hatred; also of Logic, one of the FOUR ELEMENTS, and Africa, one of the FOUR PARTS OF THE WORLD. As a sign of the ZODIAC it belongs to October.

Shell (1) *Conch* (Sk. *shanka*). Ancient war trumpet, also used in Hindu and Buddhist religious rites. It is one of VISHNU's most typical attributes, used by him to terrorize his enemies. As a marine object it is also linked to him because he is co-existent with the primeval WATERS of creation. It is the attribute of his spouse Lakshmi and of KRISHNA, in one of his incarnations; of the river-goddess SARASVATI; of the war-god KARTTIKEYA and of KALKIN; occasionally of the sun-god SURYA and the elephant-headed god, GANESHA. Shells in general symbolize the female principle. The SPIRAL markings on the conch make it a symbol of the womb. Buddhists regard the conch's note as the voice of Buddha. In Hindu and Buddhist Tantric painting it is often highly stylized and gives off flames [*ii: S. India, 16th cent.*]. It is an attribute of AVALOKITESHVARA in some manifestations. It is one of the 'auspicious signs' on the Buddha's FOOT and one of the EIGHT LUCKY EMBLEMS. It is one of the Chinese insignia of royalty. In Graeco-Roman and Renaissance art it is an attribute of Poseidon/Neptune and the Tritons (see WIND). See also VANITAS; FORTUNE.

[*ii*]

(2) *Scallop.* The attribute of APHRODITE/VENUS, born of the sea, and of other marine deities. It is the distinctive badge of the pilgrim to Santiago de Compostela and may feature over the doors of their hostels *en route* [*iii*].

[*iii*]

[iv]

[v]

[vi]

Sirens. In Greek mythology, sea nymphs with the head of a woman and body of a bird who lured sailors to their doom by their songs. Odysseus and his crew escaped that fate by a well-known subterfuge,[71] a scene often depicted on Greek vases [*iv: Attic, 5th–4th cent.* BC]. In early Christian funerary art Odysseus symbolizes the virtuous man not tempted by sensuous pleasures into mortal sin, or the sage undeceived by false doctrine. Other traditions made them vampires that flitted among the tombs, or spirits who attended Hades and Persephone and conducted the souls of the dead to the Underworld. In the latter role they have a place on Roman sarcophagi.

Skin. To wear an animal's pelt was sometimes to acquire its power, or *numen*, as with the lion-skin of HERCULES. Hence it is an attribute of Fortitude personified in Renaissance allegory. In Christian art John the Baptist wears animals' skins, being a desert-dweller. The apostle Bartholomew, who was flayed alive, may carry his skin [*v: Ital., 16th cent.*]. See also GOAT.

Snail. Christian symbol of the sinner since it was once believed to be born from the mud; also of sloth and voluptuousness. The Buddha's head is said to be 'snail-covered', from its typical spiral curls. A snail crawling over broken matter is a Buddhist symbol of the transience of earthly power. It is popular in Japanese *netsuke* [*vi: 19th cent.*]. In Renaissance allegory it is an attribute of Touch, one of the FIVE SENSES, and Sloth, one of the SEVEN DEADLY SINS.

Snake. Very widely venerated from prehistoric times and a religious symbol with many, varied meanings. It was early connected with sun worship. By periodically shedding its skin it appeared to renew itself like the sun and was therefore a symbol of death and rebirth. Yet, being earthbound by nature the snake was also a chthonic deity and enemy of the sun-god (see EAGLE). Like the SCORPION, it could cause injury and death. It was therefore ritually placated with offerings and became the protector of gods and kings. It was an object of ancient fertility rites, partly from its resemblance to a PHALLUS, and it received offerings at harvest-time. It was associated with gods of healing. In the Christian West it was synonymous with Satan.

In Egyptian art the snake has several aspects. It had a part in creating the world. A creation myth from Hermopolis[72] tells of eight deities, the Ogdoad, who personified the primeval chaos that preceded the ordered universe. Four were male frogs, four female cobras, through whom AMUN, in the form of a snake, generated the stable world. Other texts[73] describe the continual threat of a return to chaos from an Underworld monster, the snake-god, Apophis. At dawn and sunset he tries to destroy the sun-god, RE, by attacking his boat, but he is repulsed and sometimes bound. (The boat of RE was protected in the Underworld by the snake-god, Mehen.) The blood from the wound of Apophis

reddens the evening sky. Snake goddesses are typically cobras.
The most important was Wadjet, the ruling goddess of Lower
Egypt and protector of pharaohs (see further URAEUS). There are
others who are widely depicted. The cobra-goddess Meretseger
dwelt on the hill overlooking the Valley of the Kings and protected the region. She is sometimes wound in a coil, or has a
human head with a *uraeus*, or may take the form of a scorpion.
Renenutet, also a cobra-goddess, who guarded the pharaoh, was
a Mother-Goddess. She received sacrificial offerings at harvest-
time and may be depicted suckling a child. She is usually human
with a snake's head. The cults of the last two deities were prominent in the New Kingdom. The *Book of the Dead* mentions a male
snake deity, who guards the world by embracing it with his body.[74]
In art his body forms a circle, with tail in his mouth. The image
is known as an *ouroboros* (Gk. 'tail-devouring'). It had a long
life and was revived in the Renaissance as a symbol of time, eternity and the universe.[75] It is also an attribute of FATHER TIME, Saturn and JANUS [*i*].

[*i*]

What may be the oldest archaeological evidence for a snake-
cult comes from Mesopotamia, where votive figurines of a
snake-headed female (in some cases suckling an infant like the
Egyptian Renenutet) have been found at Ur dating from 4000
to 3500 BC. A 'snake-dragon', having snake's head, a four-
legged, scaly body and tail, lion's forepaws and rear talons, was
the symbol of Marduk [*ii: Babylonian, early 16th cent.* BC] (see
SPADE). Cylinder seals of the later 4th mill. depict a pair of snakes
entwined, apparently to denote copulation (in a stylized, not
naturalistic manner). The image seems to signify that these essentially terrestrial creatures were a divine source of the earth's
fertility. The motif recurs continually in Mesopotamian art and
spreads far beyond, acquiring fresh meanings on the way. In India and Indonesia it formed part of the repertoire of Hindu and
Buddhist art. In the West it was the attribute of Asclepius, god
of healing, and, later, a symbol of western medicine (see CAD-
UCEUS). By the end of the 3rd mill. the snake had already been
identified in Mesopotamia as a male god of healing called Nin-
gizzida. He was especially venerated by Gudea, the ruler of
Lagash (Telloh), who reigned in the 21st cent. BC and was famous
as a patron of the arts and as a temple builder. Sculptures of his
reign depict snakes entwined or flanking the SACRED TREE,
another indication of their power to infuse nature with their
vitality.

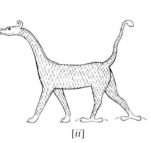

[*ii*]

In India the snake (Sk. *naga*) was worshipped by the Indus
Valley peoples. It seems to have been unknown among the later
Aryan invaders (who came from a climate less friendly to it).
Indeed, their myth of INDRA slaying the serpent-demon, Vritra,
probably refers to the worship of an older, native deity overtaken
by the Vedic god.[76] Even so, many ophidian cults survived at
a local level, especially in the form of genii of springs, lakes
and rivers (since the snake is amphibious). As a remedy for wom-

en's infertility votive images in stone, of a snake, or more often of a pair entwined, were placed in ponds to absorb the *mana* of the water and then set up under a tree. (The entwined pair suggests a Mesopotamian origin.) There are popular Hindu legends about a race of snakes, the Nagas and their wives, the Naginis, whose king and queen rule the earth's waters and guard the treasures lying beneath them. A few of their images are of early date, but they are most widely seen in relief sculpture from about the 6th cent. AD, often in pairs, male and female. They are typically human from the waist up with long, entwined tails. Above them is a hood, or canopy, of multiple cobras' heads. The latter is also sometimes seen over the head of SHIVA and DEVI (in her role of Durga). Such images, together with those of other nature spirits, were introduced into the sculpture of Buddhist stupas, among many other Buddhist borrowings from traditional Hindu art. From the 8th cent. AD, especially in Cambodia, the Buddha is enthroned on a convoluted snake under a canopy of seven (sometimes nine) cobras' heads [*iii*]. This is derived from the iconography of Vishnu, though a later legend sought to explain the image by inventing a fictitious visit by the Buddha to the palace of a snake-king.

[*iii*]

The snake has an important place in the extensive mythology of VISHNU, where it has two contrasting roles. Between each cosmic age Vishnu sleeps on the primeval ocean. He is seen reclining on a couch made of the thousand-headed cobra Ananta, who is curled beneath him.[77] At the same time the god is regarded as Ananta himself in human form; thus he is very often represented, like the Nagas, with a hood of nine cobras' heads. By contrast Vishnu, when incarnated as a BOAR, overcomes a snake-demon living at the bottom of the ocean, which, like the Egyptian Apophis, threatened to bring chaos to the universe.[78] When incarnated as KRISHNA he destroys the evil serpent-king, Kaliya.[79] He is then usually seen with one foot on its upraised head, holding its tail in one hand. The well-known Hindu creation myth of the Churning of the Ocean involved a serpent-king, Vasuki, who formed the cord that went round the churning-stick (see MILK).

In China and Japan, as in India, the snake (Ch. *she*; Jap. *hebi*) was associated with water and was the form taken by river-gods. It is the sixth of the twelve Terrestrial Branches of the Chinese CALENDAR and, when curled round a TORTOISE, forms the 'Dark Warrior' that rules the northern quadrant of the heavens (see COMPASS). In general, its influence is harmful. It is one of the group of noxious reptiles that produces the FIVE POISONS. The snake's venom, its gall, liver and even scales were used in Chinese medicine on the principle that 'like cures like'. Snake amulets, embroidered on pieces of cloth, were worn by children to protect them from illness. In Japan there are many shrines that mark the spot where a snake was killed and where its spirit was afterwards propitiated. It is sacred to the Japanese goddess

Benten, one of the GODS OF HAPPINESS, who is thought to be descended from the Hindu river-goddess, SARASVATI.

Among the animals that played such an important part in Greek religion snakes had a pre-eminent role from the Minoan-Mycenaean period onwards. The Greeks, like many other peoples, regarded them as the reincarnation of the spirits of the dead, in particular the heroic ancestors of clan or family. The sloughing of the snake's skin was evidence of their rebirth and immortality. Shrines, as at Delphi, were erected where live snakes were kept and fed by priestesses, a familiar scene in Attic vase painting (see also APOLLO). Myths gradually evolved around these sacred sites after their original use had lapsed, like the colourful stories associated with the shrine on the Athenian Acropolis. They concern Cecrops, legendary first king of Attica, whose body, like the Nagas', ends in a snake's tail. His daughters were entrusted by the city's tutelary deity, Athena, with the upbringing of an infant, Erichthonius, offspring of the earth-goddess, Gaea. The infant turned out to be a snake, which drove the daughters mad and to suicide.[80] The subject occurs in Greek vase painting and was revived in the Renaissance. With the evolution of anthropomorphic deities from more primitive animal forms the snake became an attribute of ATHENA/MINERVA, the corn-goddess DEMETER/CERES, and HECATE, Queen of the Dead. Snakes had a place in the rites of DIONYSUS/BACCHUS, who was originally a god of fertility; they are held by his votaries the Satyrs and, sometimes, the Bacchantes. The hair of the head of the Gorgon, Medusa, consisted of snakes (see PERSEUS). See also FOUR ELEMENTS—Earth.

Snake and tree together are male and female respectively and formerly symbolized the earth's fertility. The image was first associated with the Near-Eastern fertility goddess, ISHTAR and included the figures of two acolytes flanking the tree (see SACRED TREE). It required little modification to become eventually the model for the Christian scene of the Temptation,[81] first seen in Roman catacomb painting. Thus the snake is a Christian symbol of the Fall of Man and also of Satan. When seen at the foot of the cross it is a reminder of the role of Christ as Redeemer. It is trodden under the foot of the VIRGIN MARY and the Persian SIBYL. In a CHALICE it is a determinative attribute of St John the Evangelist; in a loaf of bread, of St Benedict. In Renaissance allegory a snake is an attribute of Deceit; Earth, one of the FOUR ELEMENTS; Logic, one of the SEVEN LIBERAL ARTS; Prudence, one of the CARDINAL VIRTUES;[82] Africa, one of the FOUR PARTS OF THE WORLD; and Envy and Lust, among the SEVEN DEADLY SINS. The last is opposed to Chastity, one of the THREE MONASTIC VOWS. See also BREAST; DRAGON; HERCULES; SASH; WINGED DISK.

Sparrow. Christian symbol of lowliness and, according to the apocryphal gospels, the object of Christ's first miracle: as a child he fashioned twelve sparrows from clay, which came to life and

[i]

flew away when he clapped his hands.[83] In Japan the sparrow (*suzume*) is a symbol of loyalty and is also the subject of a popular, often depicted fable, the 'tongue-cut sparrow'. The bird, victim of an old woman's spite, obtained revenge by a ruse that appealed to her greed and unleashed a horde of demons on her [*i: Netsuke, 18th–19th cent.*]. A sparrow is an attribute of APHRODITE/VENUS.

[ii]

Sphinx. The oldest sphinxes are Egyptian and date from the mid-3rd mill. BC. They represent the pharaoh with a human, bearded head and the body of a crouching lion, which symbolized his superhuman power. The sphinx is first seen in the Near East on Assyrian cylinder seals (13th–11th cents. BC) and more widely from the 9th cent. as the sculptured guardian of temples and palaces. Its general character is derived from Egypt, but with the addition of wings. In Syria and Asia Minor the sphinx acquired a female head, the form in which it reached Greece. The role of the sphinx in Greek myth and art was malelovent, bringing ruin and misfortune. Its interrogation of Oedipus[84] is first seen on vase painting, 5th cent. BC [*ii: Attic cup, c. 470 BC*].

[iii]

Spider. Associated with deities that spin and weave human destiny, since it was once believed its web was woven. It is an attribute of the Egyptian creator-goddess, Neith, who wove the universe and to whom woven mummy wrappings were sacred; and of the THREE FATES of ancient Greece who spun, measured and cut the thread of life. In Greek myth a Lydian maid, Arachne, a clever weaver, angered ATHENE/MINERVA, patron of spinners and weavers, and was changed into a spider by the goddess.[85] A spider is one of the creatures producing the FIVE POISONS of Chinese folk-medicine [*iii*]. A spider (*chih-chu*) descending on its thread symbolizes good fortune coming from heaven. Its influence is malign in Japan, where medieval legends tell of the evil 'earth spider', Tsuchi-Gumo, invulnerable to sword or arrow, which was eventually captured in its cave and smoked to death.[86] In Renaissance allegory it is an attribute of Touch, one of the FIVE SENSES. See also SPINDLE.

[iv]

Sponge. In Christian art a sponge on the end of a cane is a symbol of the Crucifixion[87] and is one of the INSTRUMENTS OF THE PASSION [*iv*].

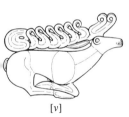

[v]

Stag. Sacred to the Indo-European peoples of Central Asia and often represented in their art [*v: Caucasian, 7th–6th cent. BC*]. It is one form of the Mesopotamian sky-god, ANU; also of the Celtic god, Cerunnos, benefactor of hunters, who is known as Lord of all the Stags. He is usually anthropomorphic with antlers or horns. In Graeco-Roman myth and art a stag is the attribute of ARTEMIS/DIANA, usually in her role of huntress; HERCULES captured the Arcadian stag. In Renaissance allegory it is an attribute of Hearing, one of the FIVE SENSES, and of Prudence, one of the CARDINAL VIRTUES. Stags, being swift, draw the chariot

[i]

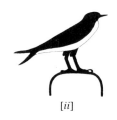

[ii]

[iii]

of FATHER TIME (see TRIUMPH). Among Christian saints Julian the Hospitator is accompanied by a stag; Giles protects a stag or hind, pierced by an arrow. See also ANTLERS; DEER.

Stork. Symbol of piety, especially filial, among many peoples, western and eastern: according to the bestiaries its young, when big enough, care for it in the nest [*i: English bestiary, 12th cent.*]. It heralds the coming of spring and is therefore associated in Christian art with the Annunciation that heralded Christ's Advent. In Chinese ceramic decoration it is a symbol of longevity and is sometimes a substitute for the CRANE. It is occasionally an attribute of HERA/JUNO, the Graeco-Roman goddess of marriage and childbirth.

Swallow (Ch. *yen*; Jap. *tsubame*). A Christian symbol of the Incarnation of Christ, therefore sometimes depicted in the Annunciation and Nativity. Its arrival in spring made it also a symbol of the Resurrection. It was sacred to APHRODITE/VENUS. In Chinese painting swallow and willow together are a popular subject, both being harbingers of spring. To build its nest in the eaves of a house brings joy, marriage, children, etc to the occupants. In Japan, however, the swallow symbolizes unfaithfulness as it is said often to change its mate. In Egyptian funerary painting a swallow expresses the wish of the deceased to be transformed into the bird, in order to pass through the gates of the Underworld and out into the sunlight[88] [*ii: Book of the Dead*].

Swan. Once believed to have magical powers of prophecy, enchantment and, especially, transformation. The *apsarases*, the NYMPHS of Hindu legend, could turn into swans, like their musical companions, the *gandharvas*. The Valkyries of Scandinavian myth became swans when accompanying Odin into battle. In Greek myth ZEUS/JUPITER changed into a swan in order to ravish the unsuspecting Leda.[89] The youth Cygnus, grieving over the death of his friend Phaethon, was changed into a swan while he mourned.[90] The Greeks believed the bird was silent until its death approached, when it sang its only song. Thus it became a symbol of the Christian martyr who welcomed death. A swan is one of the attributes of APHRODITE/VENUS, APOLLO and the MUSES Erato and Clio; in Renaissance allegory, of Music, one of the SEVEN LIBERAL ARTS, and Touch, one of the FIVE SENSES [*iii: Italian, late 15th cent.*]; in Christian art, of St Hugh (Bishop of Lincoln) who kept a swan as a pet. It is sometimes substituted for a GOOSE in Hindu and Buddhist art.

Tiger (Ch. *hu*; Jap. *tora*). Peculiar to Asia and once very common in the wild, the tiger is popular in the myth and fable of India and China and hence in their art, especially the latter's. It is a symbol of physical strength, power and military prowess. When painted on the walls of houses or on soldiers' shields its function was to ward off harm. In spite of being a man-eater its influence was more often beneficent than otherwise.

Its origins in art are remote. A clay tablet from the Indus Valley (3rd mill. BC) shows a tiger among other animals round a deity who is thought to be the antecedent of SHIVA in his role of 'Lord of the Beasts'. Whatever link there may be, Shiva typically wears a tiger-skin or, as an ascetic in a yoga posture, sits on one, as do other ascetics. It is also sometimes the loin-cloth of BRAHMA.

The tiger was adopted by Buddhism as a symbol of the power of the Buddhist faith. A popular legend,[91] depicted on wall-paintings in Central Asian temples, tells how Shakyamuni in a previous incarnation sacrificed himself as food for a starving tigress and her young. A tiger sits at the feet of Po-lo-t'o-she, one of a group of Lohans, the Chinese disciples of Buddha (see ARHAT).

[iv]

The oldest image of the tiger in China is on archaic sacred bronze vessels where it is likely to have been a protector of the contents against evil influences. It was represented in Chinese funerary art for the same reason. Tiger amulets and tallies were carried by Chinese soldiers in the Han dynasty. The amulets were sometimes of JADE, the tallies of precious metal. It is the third of the twelve Terrestrial Branches of the Chinese CALENDAR. In Chinese cosmology a white tiger is the guardian of the western quadrant of the universe (see COMPASS). Tiger and DRAGON, *yang* and *yin* respectively, are the principal animals in the ancient Taoist pseudo-science of geomancy, called *feng-shui*. They symbolize land (tiger) and water, or air (dragon), a combination that symbolizes the two main constituents, or forces, of the universe. This image spread to Japan and, with modified meaning, to Tibet. Tiger and bamboo, another Chinese motif that is found in Japan [*iv: Netsuke, 18th cent.*], symbolize the union of contrasting forces: strength and pliability.

The so-called Red Tiger in pre-Lamaist native Tibetan religion was a feared demon, once propitiated by human sacrifice. It subsequently entered the Lamaist pantheon: a tiger-skin, probably a Shivaite derivation, is worn by several Buddhist deities, such as MANJUSHRI, in their fierce, Tantric aspect. PADMASAMBHAVA, founder of Lamaism, stands on a tiger to symbolize his victory over the demon. The tiger-and-dragon motif reached Tibet from China. It was represented very widely on Lamaist prayer-flags as a contest between good (dragon) and evil (tiger). Five tigers together are thought to represent five elements (water, fire, metal, wood, earth).

In the West tigers sometimes draw the chariot of DIONYSUS/ BACCHUS, probably a sign that his cult had spread to the East.

Tortoise, Turtle (Sk. *kurma*; Ch. *kuei*; Jap. *kame*). Associated with water-gods; a symbol of the universe in the East, where it also denotes long life, endurance and strength. EA, the Akkadian god of fresh water, is represented as a tortoise on monuments of the Kassite dynasty and later (from 2nd half of 2nd mill. BC). The goddesses of Indian RIVERS may be mounted on a tortoise or turtle (from *c.* 6th cent. AD). In his second incarnation VISHNU took the form of a tortoise to help the Churning of the Ocean (see MILK).

[*i*]

In the East the tortoise forms part of the structure of the universe. According to one Hindu tradition it provides the base for eight white elephants, which stand on its back supporting the terrestrial world and the firmament.[92] An alternative cosmology, originally Chinese but widely known in the Far East, describes the sky as the tortoise's shell and the earth as its belly, the two being *yang* and *yin* respectively. Yet again, a tortoise entwined by a snake is the guardian of the northern quadrant of the heavens [*i*] (see COMPASS). This curious composite image represents copulation, some say, all tortoises being female and requiring a snake to inseminate them. More likely, it represents a combat, for it once featured on Chinese military standards, apparently symbolizing a contest in which each side was impregnable against the other. The markings on the shell were used for divination at least as early as the Shang dynasty (ended 1050 BC). Earlier still, the legendary pre-dynastic Emperor Fu Hsi was said to have devised the system of eight TRIGRAMS from studying the shell's markings. The tortoise being long-lived — over 3,000 years according to one Chinese author — symbolized Longevity and is sometimes an attribute of Shou Hsing, god of long life and one of the GODS OF HAPPINESS. In Chinese art tortoise and DRAGON together symbolize winter (*yin*) and spring (*yang*). A CRANE standing on the tortoise's back stands for longevity, its message being 'May you enjoy it.' (See also K'UEI HSING.)

Tortoise and crane may accompany Jo and Uba, the aged Japanese spirits of the PINE TREE. One of the oldest and most popular Japanese legends tells of a fisher-boy, Urashima, who caught a tortoise but, out of kindness, returned it to the sea. It was, in reality, the daughter of the Sea-King in disguise. She offered herself to him provided that her gift, a kind of Pandora's box, was kept unopened. He opened it and lost his bride.

The tortoise is an attribute of HERMES/MERCURY. In Renaissance allegory it symbolizes the slow-moving. With a sail on its back it signifies the popular motto, *Festina lente*, 'Make haste slowly'. It is an attribute of Touch, one of the FIVE SENSES.

Unicorn. According to Greek and Latin writers the unicorn had a long, straight horn and resembled an antelope or an 'Indian ass'. In western art it is usually represented as a small horse. In fable it was associated with a virgin, on account of the phallic aspect of its horn. Only a virgin could capture it, but once caught its lust abated (see also TRIUMPH–Chastity). Its horn purified everything it touched. Such fables were turned into a Christian allegory of somewhat questionable theology in medieval bestiaries: Christ, a 'spiritual unicorn', descended into the womb of the VIRGIN MARY. Therefore the image of a unicorn resting its horn on the Virgin's breast is a symbol of Christ's Incarnation. It is

[ii]

[iii]

[iv]

[v]

seen in Romanesque and Gothic stained glass and in Renaissance tapestries and paintings of northern Europe [*ii*]. It may be accompanied by other symbols of Marian virginity: the 'enclosed garden', 'closed gate' and 'flawless mirror'. The idea of the incarnation is also present in the scene of a unicorn chained to a POMEGRANATE tree in a fenced enclosure; or it dips its horn in a spring, a symbol of the 'fountain in my gardens', another Marian symbol (originally pagan);[93] or it takes refuge at the Virgin's breast when pursued by a huntsman with a horn (he stands for Gabriel, the angel of the Annunciation).

The fabulous one-horned animal of ancient China is the *ch'i-lin* or kylin (known in Japan as *kirin*). It is androgyne, *ch'i* and *lin* denoting male and female respectively. It has a stag's body, the head of a dragon, a long, tufted tail and horse's hooves, but its form may vary [*iii*]. It is first mentioned in the *Book of Odes* (*c.* 800 BC).[94] Its outstanding trait is its benevolence. Its appearance portends some auspicious event such as the birth of a sage or wise ruler; thus it appeared to the mother of Confucius. It also symbolizes longevity, happiness and the prospect of a large family of children. It may replace the dragon as guardian of the eastern quadrant (see COMPASS; FOUR SEASONS). It is often associated with the PHOENIX, both being regarded as harbingers of prosperity and happiness. It is seen in ceramic decoration, bronzes, wood-carving, embroidery and painting. Like its western counterpart its horn has the power to purify water. See also RHINOCEROS; FOUR ELEMENTS.

Uraeus. Symbol of ancient Egyptian kingship, worn on the royal head-dress. It takes the form of a cobra rearing its head in readiness to spit flames at the king's enemies [*iv: Tomb painting, 20th Dyn.*]. It represents the cobra-goddess Wadjet, tutelary deity of Lower Egypt and the king's protector. Her fire-spitting power linked her to the sun so that, when represented in human form, she may have solar emblems: a lion's head and a disk, as well as a *uraeus*. The sun-god RE also may have a *uraeus* encircling the solar disk. It is worn, with solar disk, by Mnevis, sacred bull of Heliopolis and incarnation of RE; by HATHOR and by Apis, the bull-god of Memphis; and, with the addition of two plumes, by MONTU, the war-god of Thebes. As a symbol of kingship it may be worn by the 'royal' gods, HORUS and SETH. See also VULTURE; WINGED DISK.

Vulture. The Egyptian vulture-goddess, Nekhbet, was tutelary deity of Upper Egypt [*v: Temple relief, Ptolemaic period*], the counterpart of Wadjet, the cobra-goddess of Lower Egypt (see URAEUS). She may hold a kind of RING in each claw, a symbol of eternity. The two deities may be represented together in wholly animal form as protectors of the Two Lands. Mut, the principal goddess of Thebes, first depicted in the Middle Kingdom, has a vulture for a head-dress, sometimes surmounted by the *pschent* (CROWN) or a solar disk. In the Late Period vulture and SCARAB together symbolized the male and female principles in the universe. They sometimes denote Neith and Ptah respectively, both gods of creation. (See also WINGS.)

Greeks and Romans made the vulture a symbol of rapacious lust, after the Greek myth of the giant Tityus who was condemned to have his liver (the seat of the passions) eternally torn by two vultures in hell. His crime was the attempted rape of Leto, mother of Apollo.[95] The theme recurs in Renaissance painting with the same symbolism.

Whale. By tradition the fish that swallowed the prophet Jonah,[96] though the Bible is silent as to its species. In Christ's own words the three days and nights Jonah spent in the fish's belly prefigured his own death and resurrection.[97] It is in this sense that it features in Christian art. It is seen in early funerary art and in medieval sculpture [*i: French, 12th cent. relief*].

[*i*]

Winged Disk. The image of a sun- or sky-god in the form of a solar disk with wings occurs widely in the Near East. Its origin was Egyptian. The wings of HORUS, the falcon-god, symbolizing the sky, appear at the beginning of the dynastic period. From the 5th Dynasty the sun's disk was placed between them, forming a solar symbol. Horus, being identified with the king, made it also a royal symbol. By the end of the Old Kingdom the disk had acquired a royal URAEUS on each side [*ii*]. Later it appears above temple doors and in funerary art as a protection against harm.

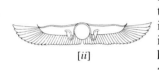

[*ii*]

With various modifications, but still recognizable, it reached the Near East, perhaps about mid-2nd mill. BC. It is seen above the Hittite sky-god, Teshub (who is in human form), in the late 2nd–early 1st mill. BC. It became the symbol of ASSUR, chief god of the Assyrian pantheon, and of their sun-god SHAMASH. It floats above the SACRED TREE on Assyrian cylinder seals. Assur himself, armed with bow and arrow, appears within the disk as it hovers protectively above the king in battle or when hunting. After the Persian conquest of Babylon (538 BC) it was adopted as the symbol of Ahura-Mazda, god of the Achaemenian kings, replacing his earlier personification as an altar FIRE. It is represented widely on Persian buildings.

Wings. Wings on humans or animals are a sign of divinity. They symbolize the power to give protection (see ISIS). They also denote swiftness when associated with messengers of the gods or with the winds, and may signify the swift passage of time. In western art such figures are mainly descended from ancient Mesopotamia. Winged figures are ultimately derived from the representation of sacred birds such as the FALCON and VULTURE in Egypt (see HORUS) and the EAGLE in the Near East. Winged animals are also the outcome of the merging of characteristics of different gods; thus the wings of the Egyptian vulture-goddess, Nekhbet, appear on the back of the bull-god, Apis; a combination of eagle and lion deities, which took place in the Near East about the 18th cent. BC, produced the GRIFFIN. The WINGED DISK is another early example of the merging process.

The winged hybrids that are such a striking feature of neo-Assyrian sculpture (9th–7th cents. BC) seem to be the product not so much of religious syncretism as of the lively creative imagination of artists. Eagle, man, lion and bull had magical power, and each was the lord of his own kingdom. When combined in a single image they made irresistibly powerful guardians of temple and palace. Standing figures composed of the same elements represent genii, the servants of gods, who perform fertility rituals beside a SACRED TREE. These must have been the kind of images, seen in relief sculpture and wall-painting, that inspired the vision of the Hebrew prophet Ezekiel and ultimately became the APOCALYPTIC BEASTS in Christian art.[98] See further ANGEL.

[*iii*]

The long tradition of winged deities reached Greece from the Near East and thence Rome. Among winged figures on Greek vase painting from the 5th cent. BC are EROS/CUPID, Hypnos and Thanatos, gods of sleep and death, and Nike, goddess of VICTORY [*iii: c. 200* BC]. The wings of HERMES/MERCURY sprout from his hat or boots, though he has none in his earliest, 6th cent. images in vase painting. Iris ('rainbow'), the female counterpart of Hermes as messenger of the gods, has wings on her boots, or they grow from her temples or shoulders. Winged hat and boots, derived from Hermes, are an attribute of the hero, Perseus, whose horse, Pegasus, is also winged.

Many of the Greek pantheon, with their attributes, came to life again in the Renaissance. Among winged allegorical figures, old and new, which flourished from this period in painting and sculpture are FAME (see TRIUMPH), History, PEACE, FORTUNE, Nemesis, Night and, occasionally, Melancholy, one of the FOUR TEMPERAMENTS. Wings are an attribute of FATHER TIME, the WINDS and Opportunity, who all pass swiftly. A winged hand belongs to Poverty personified (see THREE MONASTIC VOWS). See also DRAGON.

Gods, whether in human or animal form, are rarely winged. Lakshmi (see DEVI) in her earliest representations has wings, probably a reflection of Near Eastern influence, and the elephant, Airavata, mount of INDRA, may be winged; also, occasionally, the sun-god, SURYA. Lei Kung, the Chinese god of thunder, has wings which, according to some, are derived from the Hindu eagle-god, GARUDA. (See also BES.)

Wolf. An animal of mainly ill-repute. In China the wolf (Ch. *lang*) is a symbol of rapaciousness and cruelty. In western allegory it is an attribute of Gluttony and Anger personified two of the SEVEN DEADLY SINS. In Christian art of the Dominicans it stands for heresy. Francis of Assisi, friend of all living creatures, tamed the wolf of Gubbio, so it is occasionally his attribute. The Ro-

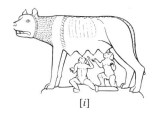

[i]

[ii]

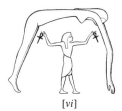

[iii]

[iv]

[v]

[vi]

mans honoured the wolf for having suckled Romulus and Remus, the legendary founders of Rome [99] [*i: Bronze, early 5th cent.* BC]. They were the children of the Roman god of war, Mars, to whom the wolf was sacred. It was depicted on Roman battle-standards (The wolf is not associated with Ares, the Greek antecedent of Mars.) It is occasionally the attribute of APOLLO. The Egyptian god, Wepwawet, who was known in the pre-dynastic period, was, like Anubis, a jackal (see DOG). The Greeks regarded him as a wolf and renamed the city of his cult Lycopolis, or 'wolf-city' (modern Asyut).

Woodpecker. Sacred to several Graeco-Roman gods, especially to the old Italian god of war, Mars, from its supposed aggressive behaviour. It is his attribute. Its probing beak and long tongue made it a Christian symbol of heresy, which undermines the true faith [*ii*].

3. Artefacts

Abacus. Attribute of Arithmetic personified, one of the SEVEN LIBERAL ARTS [*iii: 16th cent.*].

Anchor. One of the oldest Christian symbols, found in funerary inscriptions in the Roman catacombs, possibly then a disguised form of the cross. Later, a symbol of hope, which St Paul compared to an anchor.[1] An attribute of HOPE personified, of Bishop Nicholas of Myra and of Pope Clement I [*iv*]. See also DOLPHIN.

Anvil. Often with a hammer, the attribute of the smith gods, Hephaestus, Vulcan, etc [*v: Roman graffito*]. Also of SS. Eloi, patron saint of metal-workers, and Adrian. See also FOUR ELEMENTS – Fire.

Arch. An Egyptian creation myth from Heliopolis[2] tells how the god of the air, Shu, raised his daughter, the sky-goddess, Nut, into the heavens to form an arch over the earth [*vi: coffin painting, 21st Dynasty*]. The earth-god, GEB, brother/spouse of Nut, is sometimes depicted lying below, face up, with erect PHALLUS. The scene symbolizes the union of earth and sky that produced the pantheon of Egyptian deities. The arch was also a Roman symbol of sky and heavens, which were the abode of Jupiter. (See ZEUS/J.) The garlanded arches under which a Roman triumphal procession passed on its way to the temple of Jupiter on the Capitoline hill had this sacred meaning for the citizens. Christianity borrowed the idea. The architecture of early churches in Rome included an 'arch of triumph' at the east end of the nave beyond which was the sanctuary. To pass through it symbolized the transition from death to eternal life. See also TORI-I.

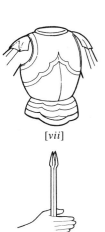

[vii]

[viii]

[ix]

[x]

[xi]

Armour. Identifies a 'warrior saint' in Christian art, e.g. George, Longinus, Maurice, Michael (winged), Theodore, etc., and is their protection against evil [vii]. A soldier in armour is one of the AGES OF MAN. A cuirass mounted on a pole is sometimes an attribute of Minerva (see ATHENA/M.), and thence of Wisdom personified.

Arrow (without bow). Weapon symbolizing the power of a king or god. Assyrian kings held arrows in triumphal processions and when receiving tribute: two in the right hand, pointing up, denoted peace and friendship [viii: neo-Assyrian, 9th cent. BC]; pointing down, enmity and war. The pharaoh on his accession shot an arrow towards each of the four cardinal points to symbolize his boundless sovereignty. Arrows are the attribute of Sakhmet, the war-goddess of Memphis; two, crossed on a shield, of Neith, the warlike tutelary goddess of Sais in Lower Egypt. An arrow (Sk. *bana*) is among the weapons of VISHNU.

Arrows symbolizing the sun's rays are associated with several solar deities, especially AMATERASU, APOLLO, MITHRAS. A bundle of arrows, denoting lightning, is held by INDRA; sometimes by the Dvarapalas, the two guardians of Buddhist temple gates (see DOOR).

The arrow is also phallic. SHIVA's arrow, symbolizing his power, is identified with the *lingam*; similarly phallic are the arrows of the Greek Eros, echoed in Christian art in the angel's flaming arrow that pierces the heart of St Teresa of Avila. Arrows are held by, or pierce the body of, SS. Augustine (one of the FOUR LATIN FATHERS), Ursula, Christina, Sebastian. Giles protects a STAG pierced by an arrow. See also BOW.

Aspergillum. Brush for sprinkling holy water in order to expel evil. In Christian art, the attribute of SS. Antony the Great, Benedict, and Martha who overcame the devil [ix]. See also DEMON.

Axe. The double axe, used for hewing wood, was already sanctified in prehistoric times as a representation of sky- and weather gods, and featured in the cult of the Mother-Goddess. It was a typical symbol in Minoan religious images [x: Mycenaean, 16th–15th cent. BC], probably having come from Caria in Asia Minor, where it survived in the cult of Zeus 'of the Double Axe' (*Labrandeus*). It was an attribute of the Mesopotamian weather-god ADAD and of his Hittite counterpart, Teshub. Axes were buried in the foundations of Adad's temple at Assur, for protection. A single-bladed battle-axe (Sk. *parashu*) [xi: Indian, 18th cent.] is the attribute of SHIVA, GANESHA, AGNI and KRISHNA; and of Parashurama, the sixth incarnation of VISHNU. An axe (Ch. *fu*) is one of the TWELVE ORNAMENTS on Chinese imperial robes and is the attribute of Lu Pan, god of carpenters. In Christian art St Peter Martyr has an axe embedded in his skull; it is the instrument of martyrdom of St Matthew.

[i]

[ii]

[iii]

[iv]

[v]

Bagpipe. Typical instrument of European folk-culture, known in antiquity. Like other piped instruments, a phallic symbol, especially in 17th cent. northern European painting [*i: after Dürer*]. See also PIPE.

Ball. A spherical object held by the child KRISHNA is a ball of butter [*ii*]. Three golden balls are the attribute of St Nicholas, bishop of Myra. In Renaissance allegory, Avarice personified may be accompanied by HARPIES who have golden balls or apples, emblems of the miser's riches. See also PEARL.

Basket. Kings of Mesopotamia may be represented (from 3rd mill. BC) carrying a basket on their head containing building materials for a temple. This untypical aspect of royalty probably symbolized the king's role as builder and his readiness to humble himself before the god.

Nephthys, an Egyptian funerary goddess and protector of coffins and canopic JARS, whose name means Lady of the House, wears on her head the plan of a house surmounted by a basket [*iii: Tomb painting, New Kingdom*]. The Greek goddess, HECATE, sometimes wears a tall basket on her head.

Sacrificial offerings carried in a basket made the receptacle itself sacred and, moreover, a symbol of the salvation that the offering would procure. For Greeks and Romans the sacred basket, or *calathos*, was a symbol of fertility, which is sometimes placed on a deity's head. The regular use of baskets in Jewish sacrificial rite[3] is probably the reason why the bread of the eucharist, the symbol of Christ's sacrifice, is, in early Christian art, nearly always represented in the traditionally shaped wicker *calathos* [*iv*]. Indeed, the bread itself is sometimes invisible so that the symbolism is transferred to the receptacle itself. The Feeding of the Five Thousand, which gives textual authority of the use of baskets,[4] also prefigured the eucharist. In early Christian art a communal meal, with several baskets, symbolizes the Last Supper. In later Christian art, the basket loses its symbolic associations. As an attribute of St Dorothea it contains roses and perhaps apples; of HOPE personified, flowers (see THEOLOGICAL VIRTUES). A basket of fruit is an attribute of Taste, one of the FIVE SENSES. See also BREAD; WAND.

Bell. Widely used in religious ritual. The 'sacring', or Sanctus bell has been used in the Mass since the 12th cent. A bell is rung in Hindu, Buddhist, Lamaist, Confucian and Taoist ritual throughout Asia. Besides marking the stages of worship, its sound disperses evil spirits.[5] Some of the oldest known ritual bells are Chinese, made of bronze and dating from the Chou dynasty [*v: bell of the* chung *type; Warring States period*]. In Tantric Buddhist doctrine, the bell symbolizes the universal womb, complementing the *vajra*, or THUNDERBOLT, which is the PHALLUS; the bell itself may have a *vajra* for a handle. The bells used in Hindu worship (Sk. *ghanta*) are of various types, and are an attribute of the goddesses SARASVATI and Durga (DEVI), probably as a symbol of the womb. A bell sometimes replaces the wheel as one of the Buddhist EIGHT LUCKY EMBLEMS. In Christian art a bell is the attribute of St Antony the Great. In medieval psalters King David strikes a chime of bells, as does Music personified, one of the SEVEN LIBERAL ARTS.

[vi]

Boat, Ship. In many religions a boat has two symbolic functions. It is the vehicle of the sun-god and also carries the soul of the deceased to the after-life. In early Christian funerary art it has a cross for a mast and may be seen heading towards a lighthouse. Egyptian solar deities travelled by day across the celestial ocean in a barque which returned to the east at night through the Underworld [*vi: Egyptian, c. 1400* BC]. It bore the dead to the after-life and so model boats were usually buried with them, especially in tombs of the Middle Kingdom. Mesopotamian sun-gods were also borne in a boat. They are first seen thus on Akkadian cylinder seals (late 3rd mill. BC). The boat of heaven carried the deity to the temple crowning the ZIGGURAT where he performed the sacred marriage. The Japanese 'spirit boat' (*Shoryo-bune*) is a miniature funerary vessel. Made of straw and shaped like a junk, it is dedicated to a deceased relative or ancestor and, containing food and drink, is floated down the river at the conclusion of the Shinto Festival of the Dead. The legendary Shinto Treasure Ship (*Takara-bune*) carries the seven Japanese GODS OF HAPPINESS and their treasures, the TAKARA-MONO. It sails into port on New Year's Eve and its image is commonly seen in celebrations at that season. It is also a popular subject for *netsuke*. A ship is the symbol of the Christian Church, as is Noah's ark and the 'Navicella'.[6] Vessels of various kinds are the attribute of SS. PETER the Apostle, Julian the Hospitator, Erasmus, Ursula; also of the Vestal Virgin Claudia, HOPE personified (who may wear it on her head) and FORTUNE.

Book. The attribute of the learned in many walks of life, especially religious; in Christian art, of the evangelists, several APOSTLES (Paul in particular), Church Fathers, the Sibyls, FAITH personified and many saints known for their writings or learning. It may carry a title or quotation. The book 'sealed with seven seals' held the secrets of human destiny.[7] A book, usually a scroll, is a symbol of wisdom and the attribute of several personified virtues: ATHENA/MINERVA; the MUSES Clio and Calliope; Prudence, one of the CARDINAL VIRTUES; Grammar and Rhetoric, two of the SEVEN LIBERAL ARTS; PHILOSOPHY; Melancholy, one of the FOUR TEMPERAMENTS; History. EROS/CUPID surrounded by books symbolizes Love's victory over Learning.

In Hindu sculpture BRAHMA, and VISHNU in his fifth incarnation, hold a book (Sk. *pustaka*) of the *Vedas*; in older sculpture it is always a palm-leaf book. SARASVATI, the Hindu goddess of learning, also has a book. It is an attribute of the Vedic god, Brihaspati, 'Lord of sacred speech', a semi-mythical sage, seer

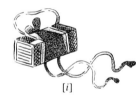

and teacher of other gods. He was identified with the planet
Jupiter and is widely represented among other planetary deities
in Shivaite temples of southern India. He also holds a ROSARY. A
book of Buddhist texts rests on a lotus flower beside PRAJNA-
PARAMITA, goddess of wisdom; also beside MANJUSHRI and AVALO-
KITESHVARA. A book is an attribute of several Buddhist Protectors
of the Law (see ARHAT).

[i] Chinese books are typically represented in sets, in a cover, tied
with a ribbon [i]. Two together form one of the EIGHT TREASURES.
A bound set, sometimes with two brushes, symbolizes Literature,
one of the FOUR ARTS of the Chinese scholar. A book is an attribute of K'UEI HSING, the demon-like Chinese god of literature.
Lao-tzu, founder of Taoism, holds a book or scroll (see EIGHT
IMMORTALS). A Chinese priest carrying books on his back is Hsüan
Tsang, or Yüan Tsang (Jap. *Sanzo Hoshi*) who collected Buddhist
texts in India in the 7th cent. Chinese classics like *I Ching* have
the power to keep evil spirits away.

Bow. To string a great bow was a test of manhood, successfully
accomplished by Odysseus[8] and the Buddha Shakyamuni.[9] Bow
and arrow are the typical attributes of war-gods and heroes of
many peoples and symbols of their unconquerable prowess: thus
the Assyrian war-god, NINURTA; the goddess of love and war,
ISHTAR; and her Syrian-Phoenician counterpart Astarte; also
ASSUR, the tutelary deity of the Assyrians. In a famous Hindu
myth SHIVA's great bow and arrow, formed out of the gods themselves, destroyed the Triple City of the demons.[10] Bow and arrow (Sk. *capa; shara*) are the characteristic weapons of Rama,
the epic hero of the *Ramayana* and the Indian ideal of manhood.
He became an incarnation of VISHNU. Other Hindu deities with
bow and arrow are INDRA; BRAHMA and his spouse SARASVATI;
GANESHA; KARTTIKEYA; ARJUNA.

Bow and arrow are the commonest weapons among many in
the multiple hands of Tibetan Buddhist deities in their wrathful
aspect, such as AVALOKITESHVARA, Ushnisha-Vijaya, the goddess
[ii] of wisdom [ii]. (See also SURYA.)

In China a bow and arrow was a symbol of male domination
and was hung at the door on the birth of a son. To shoot arrows
in the air expressed the wish for many sons, or to drive away evil
spirits, or scare off birds of ill omen. A Japanese woman warrior
holding bow and arrow or writing on a rock with a bow is Jingo
Kogo, who led the emperor's army to conquer Korea (3rd cent.
AD).

In Graeco-Roman and Renaissance art, bow and arrow, or
quiver, are the attributes of APOLLO, EROS/CUPID, ARTEMIS/DIANA,
Orion, and occasionally HERCULES. In Renaissance allegory they
are an attribute of America personified, one of the FOUR PARTS OF
THE WORLD. A man fixing three arrows simultaneously into his
bow is Wrath, one of the SEVEN DEADLY SINS. The archer of the
ZODIAC is Sagittarius.

[iii]

[iv]

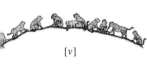

[v]

[vi]

[vii]

[viii]

Bowl, or cup. Attribute of beggars, especially religious mendicants in the East. The bowl of SHIVA, as an ascetic, was originally the top half of a human skull (Sk. *kapala*), which was later depicted simply as an earthenware bowl. In Tibetan art the skull-bowl is held by deities in both their benign and wrathful forms, usually the latter, when it may be filled with blood [*iii*]. (See AVALOKITESHVARA; PRAJNA-PARAMITA; MANJUSHRI; PADMASAM-BHAVA, etc.). Benign figures may hold a more stylized receptacle (Sk. *patra*) [*iv: Tibetan, late 17th–early 18th cents.*]. The bowl of GANESHA in Tibetan art is filled with jewels. A bowl is the attribute of Durga and Pidari (see DEVI), both at one time associated with Shiva. The Buddha Shakyamuni holds a begging bowl in his lap, especially in Tibetan painting, as does the ARHAT, Pindolabharadvaja. A bowl or cup is an attribute of K'UEI HSING, Taoist god of literature, and is used to measure a student's deserts.

In western art, a bowl is the attribute of the Cumaean SIBYL; a broken bowl, of St Benedict; in allegorical still-life painting, an overturned bowl literally denotes VANITAS, emptiness. A jug and bowl of water with which Pilate washed his hands are a symbol of innocence and one of the INSTRUMENTS OF THE PASSION.

Bridge. A link between earth and heaven, like Jacob's LADDER. The Persian *Avesta* describes a symbolic 'bridge of decision' or 'judgement', which all souls must cross at death.[11] Some fall into purifying flames below, i.e. purgatory. In later Pahlevi texts (3rd–7th cents.) they fall into flames of hell with no hope of redemption. The latter passed into Christian imagery via patristic literature. A razor-bridge of judgement, i.e. very narrow, was originally Islamic[12] and also appears in *Pilgrim's Progress*. In medieval romance, especially Arthurian, it is depicted as a sword-blade. A Chinese myth describes the way to the after-life across three bridges, a golden one for the gods, a silver for the virtuous and a third (of iron?) for sinners who fall into a river below, to be torn apart by snakes and iron dogs. For the Chinese bridge of magpies, see STAR. A bridge of monkeys [*v: Punjabi, 17th cent.*] was used to rescue Sita, wife of the Indian hero Rama, from captivity in Sri Lanka (see VISHNU, para. 7).

Bridle. Especially with a bit and reins, in Renaissance allegory is an attribute of Temperance, one of the CARDINAL VIRTUES [*vi: Italian, 17th cent.*], also of Nemesis and FORTUNE.

Brush. The Chinese brush-pen is one of the FOUR TREASURES of the scholar [*vii*]. It is a symbol of the arts of painting and writing and, hence, of learning and wisdom. A scholar of many talents was called 'a brush of five colours', a reference to the various animals whose hair is used to make it. It is an attribute of K'UEI HSING, the demon-like Chinese god of literature. The hairs are set in a long bamboo holder or, exceptionally, in a decorated handle [*viii: Ming, Wan-li period, 1573–1619*].

[i]

[ii]

[iii]

[iv]

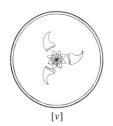

[v]

Bucket. In late Assyrian reliefs winged genii on each side of the sacred tree hold a bucket (*situla*) and the so-called PINE CONE [*i: neo-Assyrian, 8th cent.* BC], fertilizing the tree with the contents of the bucket or collecting the tree's sacred essence to purify the king.

Caduceus. The Roman name for the staff carried by messengers and heralds to ensure their safe passage, hence a symbol of peace. In the form of a rod ending in a circle and crescent it existed among Assyrians, Hittites and Phoenicians as the emblem of messengers of the gods. The Greeks acquired it from the Phoenicians in the course of trade, probably the origin of its use as a symbol of commerce. In early Greek vase painting it is represented as a cleft stick. Later it has intertwined snakes and is tipped with wings, which may have been a modification of the WINGED DISK [*ii*]. It became the wand of HERMES/MERCURY through his role as the gods' messenger. As a psychopomp he used it to revive the dead rescued from Hades, perhaps the source of its association with healing.

Candle. Widely used as a symbol in the ritual, especially funerary, of many religions. It is less often encountered in art, except Christian. Usually carried in the scene of the Presentation in the Temple,[13] which is commemorated in the Feast of Candlemas and which includes, in the West, a procession of lighted candles. Candles in general denote Christ as 'the light of the world'. During the office of Tenebrae (darkness) in Holy Week, a frame holding fifteen lighted candles is placed before the altar. They are extinguished one by one, the last symbolizing the death of Christ. FAITH and CHARITY personified hold a candle. In VANITAS paintings a lighted candle signifies the brevity of life [*iii*]. A candle is the attribute of SS. Bridget of Sweden, Geneviève, Donatian and the Libyan SIBYL; a pair of crossed candles, of Blaise.

Canopy (Ch. *pao kai*). Like the UMBRELLA, a symbol of high rank and sovereignty, especially in the East where it shelters Buddhas, especially MAITREYA. It is one of the Buddhist EIGHT LUCKY EMBLEMS [*iv*]. In greater Christian churches a canopy covers the high altar and major tombs. The underside sometimes depicts the heavens. In Lamaist temples thunder-dragons of the sky may be depicted.

Cards. The original home of playing cards was probably Iran or Central Asia, whence they spread to India. They were introduced into Europe in the late 14th century via Egypt and Italy. Suits and court cards vary in number from place to place and have a rich and very varied symbolism. Court cards may represent gods, goddesses or historical figures. Indian packs [*v: Lion's claws, Jaipur, 19th cent.*] can have eight or ten suits, often named after the incarnations of VISHNU. Chinese packs are of many kinds, some embellished with Taoist gods and symbols.

[vi]

[vii]

[viii]

In the West court cards may represent Graeco-Roman or Egyptian deities. In Renaissance allegory cards are an attribute of Vice personified (see VIRTUES AND VICES) and Sloth, one of the SEVEN DEADLY SINS.

Castanets. The attribute of Ts'ao Kuo-chiu, one of the EIGHT IMMORTALS [vi]. They are played by Maenads, the votaries of DIONYSUS, in Greek vase painting and reliefs.

Censer (Ch. *lu*). Incense has been used symbolically in many cults. For Jews and Christians the smoke denotes their prayers rising to God.[14] A censer is the attribute of the deacons SS. Stephen and Lawrence. In Egypt its use was originally purificatory; in funeral rites the smoke signalled a new arrival to the nether world. In Buddhist art, in China, Tibet and Japan it is an attribute of AVALOKITESHVARA, also of the ARHAT Angaja (Jap. Inkada Sonja) and other Buddhist sages. In Renaissance allegory, it is an attribute of Asia, one of the FOUR PARTS OF THE WORLD.

Types of censer: Christian: usually circular, perforated lid, on chains; Egyptian: bowl with a handle like a human arm, terminating in a god's head; Buddhist: bowl with lid, usually long-handled, or a miniature stupa or pagoda; Taoist: a 'hill-censer' (Ch. *po shan-lu*) representing the fairy mountain on the Isles of the Blest (the home of immortals), with animals, trees, etc. in relief [vii]. Smoke from the hill-censer symbolizes clouds that are exhaled by the mountain.

Chalice. Ritual vessel used in the Christian Eucharist to hold wine, a symbol of Christ's blood.[15] Together with a wafer (his body) they symbolize Christ's redemptive power. The chalice sometimes holds his bleeding heart. Blood flowing from the wounds of Christ on the cross is caught in a chalice held by Adam (medieval) or by an angel (from the 13th cent.). It is an attribute of FAITH personified; of SS. Barbara (with wafer); the Franciscan Bonaventura; the apostle, John the Evangelist (snake emerging, symbolizing Satan) [viii]; the Dominican Thomas Aquinas.

Chariot. The swift horse-drawn chariot of the Aryan invaders from the northern steppes in the first half of the 2nd mill. BC was decisive in their military victories. It was copied first by the peoples of Egypt, the Near East and India and subsequently began to appear in their art, e.g. reliefs of Ramesses II (1304–1237 BC), temple of Amun, Luxor; palace of Ashurnasirpal II (883–859 BC), Nimrud (Br. Mus.). Hence it became a symbol of military triumph. As the horse was a symbol of solar power the chariot also became the vehicle of many sun-gods, such as SURYA (Hindu), MITHRAS (Persian, Roman), APOLLO/Helios/Sol (Graeco-Roman). ISHTAR, as a war-goddess, rides on a chariot (see also INDRA).

SHIVA's great chariot, described in detail in a well-known myth,

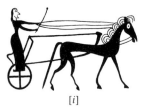

[i]

[ii]

[iii]

[iv]

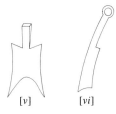

[v]   [vi]

[vii]

was constructed for him by the other gods from parts of the earth and sky. With BRAHMA as his charioteer, he destroyed the 'triple city' of the demons.[16] The scene is depicted in relief at Eluru (Ellora), 8th cent. AD.

A chariot is the vehicle of many Graeco-Roman deities and personifications in antiquity and from the Renaissance onwards [i: Greek vase painting, 6th cent. BC]. It is drawn by a variety of usually appropriate living creatures (gods' names Latinized): Apollo (four horses, white, or of different colours); Jupiter (eagles, bulls); Juno (peacocks); Venus (doves, swans); Mars (horses, wolves); Diana (stags); Luna (one black, one white horse); Aurora (white horses); Cupid (white horses or goats); Mercury (cocks, storks); Ceres (dragons); Bacchus (leopards, tigers, goats); Silenus (ass); Pluto (black horses); Vulcan (dogs); Neptune (Hippocampi or Tritons); Galatea (dolphins); Cybele (lions); Night personified (black horses); Avarice (vultures or falcons). See also TRIUMPH.

Chessboard. Its alternating colours symbolize many aspects of duality, or YIN AND YANG. The game was said to have been devised by a Northern Chou emperor, Wu-ti (560–578). It had several versions, indicated by the varied symbolism of the pieces, especially military and astrological. The game is probably of Indian origin. In China the board symbolizes one of the FOUR ARTS of the scholar [ii]. See also SEVEN DEADLY SINS – Sloth.

Clock. Symbol of fleeting time and a reminder of the brevity of life in VANITAS still-life painting; it is an attribute of Temperance personified (one of the CARDINAL VIRTUES), since time is well regulated; in portraiture a clock implies that the sitter has a temperate disposition [iii: French, 16th cent.].

Club. (Sk. *gada*). Weapon of several Indian gods and heroes, also a phallic symbol [iv]. It is an attribute of VISHNU in several of his incarnations and was said to symbolize his authority and the 'power of knowledge'. From Vishnu it was passed on to KRISHNA. It is the weapon of Bhima, brother of ARJUNA, and of the demons in Shiva's train; also of the BUFFALO demon. The *khatvanga* (Sk.), with its distant echoes of human sacrifice, has a shaft made of a human tibia and is topped by a human SKULL. It is wielded by many Tantric Buddhist deities (male and female) in their demonic aspect. The club of HERCULES is also an attribute of Fortitude, one of the four CARDINAL VIRTUES. SS. Jude and James the Less were clubbed to death (see APOSTLE). See also MACE.

Coins (Ch. *ch'ien*). Images reproduced on coins are often symbolic, though coins themselves are seldom symbols, except in China. Metal coinage was first used in Greece and China about the 7th cent. BC. Early Chinese coins were variously shaped (spade, knife, etc. [v, vi]), all eventually being superseded by the circular disk with a square hole [vii]. Coins in general sym-

[viii]

[ix]

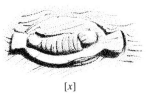

[x]

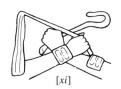

[xi]

bolize riches and prosperity. With a red fillet, a coin is one of the EIGHT TREASURES. Pairs of such coins often decorate blue-and-white porcelain (14th–15th cents.). Coins were engraved with good-luck messages and propitious symbols. By a play on words, a BAT or two MAGPIES with a coin denotes 'May joy be before your eyes'. In Christian art a coin denotes the 'tribute money';[17] it may be drawn from a fish's mouth by St Peter.[18] Judas' thirty pieces of silver symbolize a bribe or blood-money and are one of the INSTRUMENTS OF PASSION.[19]

Coins in VANITAS still-life are earthly possessions abandoned at death. An old man counting coins represents the last of the AGES OF MAN.

Comb. A wool-carder's comb [viii] is the attribute of St Blaise who wears bishop's vestments. According to legend it was the instrument of his martyrdom. He is the patron saint of wool-workers.

Compasses, or dividers, are used to measure, and therefore symbolize restraint or judgement. They are the attribute of God, as architect of the universe; of Urania, MUSE of Astronomy, and of Astronomy and Geometry personified, two of the SEVEN LIBERAL ARTS; of Justice and Prudence, two of the CARDINAL VIRTUES; of Melancholy (one of the FOUR TEMPERAMENTS and Maturity (one of the four AGES OF MAN), in Renaissance and later art [ix]. The legendary Chinese emperor, Fu Hsi (early 3rd mill. BC), inventor and benefactor, is represented in Chinese and Japanese art, holding compasses and a mason's square.

Cradle. Symbol of new life. It complements the cosmic barque (see BOAT), which conveys the dead to the after-life. The infant Christ is sometimes depicted in a cradle at his Nativity, though it has no biblical sanction. The cradle of Moses was made of bulrushes[20] [x: Ivory relief, 4th cent.]. The infant Zeus lies in a cradle in a pastoral setting. A cradle is the attribute of the Samian SIBYL.

Crook. Attribute of shepherds and pastoral deities and, by extension, a symbol of guidance or authority. The Egyptian pharaoh typically holds a crook and FLAIL crossed on his breast, as shepherd of his people and denoting royal authority [xi]. Both are also held by OSIRIS, as the judge of the dead, by HORUS, KHONSU, and, more seldom, by AMUN. A crook is the attribute of Amurru, a Phoenician god associated with the ram, seen first on early Babylonian cylinder seals. The crook alone also symbolizes the god. In Graeco-Roman art it is an attribute of APOLLO, Pan, Orpheus, Argus and Polyphemus, all having pastoral connections; in Christian art, of Christ, the Good Shepherd, and St Geneviève, a shepherdess. A pastoral staff with voluted end is carried by bishops and abbots and is the attribute of SS. Benedict, Bernard, Martin and Clare. A fish hangs from the staff of St Zeno, reputedly an angler.

[i]

[ii]

[iii]

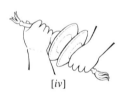

[iv]

[v]

[vi]

Crucible. The alchemist's vessel, a symbol of purification by fire, therefore a test of worth [i]. It is seen in his laboratory, especially in 16th–17th cent. northern European painting, and was used as an emblematic device by Italian Renaissance families.

Crucifix. The model of Christ on the cross is the attribute of too many saints to aid identification [ii: Italian, 5th cent. ivory]. The following are unusual: entwined with lilies, Antony of Padua, Nicholas of Tolentino; with a dove, Scholastica; the head of Christ inclined, as if in movement, Giovanni (or John) Gualberto; between a stag's ANTLERS, Eustace, Hubert. A crucifix may feature in VANITAS paintings as a symbol of the Christian's hope of life after death.

Crutch. Symbol of old age, the cripple and the beggar [iii]. It is an attribute of SS. Antony the Great, Giovanni (John) Gualberto, Romuald; in Graeco-Roman art of Hephaestos/Vulcan, the lame blacksmith of the gods; the aged Saturn and his descendant, FATHER TIME. Li T'ieh-kuai, one of the Taoist EIGHT IMMORTALS, leans on a crutch. See also FOUNTAIN.

Cymbals. Percussion instruments widely used in East and West to accompany orgiastic dancing and other rites, first seen on cylinder seals from Ur (1st half, 3rd mill. BC). They are played by the followers of DIONYSUS/BACCHUS. There are two types: large and flattish, struck horizontally; and smaller and rounder, struck vertically [iv: Italian, 15th cent.]. Both are still in use throughout Asia. In Tibetan Lamaist temples, and probably elsewhere, the former type accompanies the worship of greater heavenly divinities, especially Buddha; the latter, earthly deities. Cymbals are an attribute of the Hindu god Ravana, chief of the demons, and occasionally of VISHNU.

Dagger (Sk. *phurbu*). Sacred weapon of ASSUR, supreme deity of Assyria and symbol of his invincible power. A dagger (or its image) was kept in his temple from c. mid-2nd mill. BC, on which oaths were sworn. A dagger is the weapon of Kali, the destructive aspect of the Hindu/Buddhist Mother-Goddess (see DEVI). In her 'wrathful' Tantric identity in Tibetan painting her weapon (possibly a flaying knife or dart) is topped with peacock feathers [v: Tibetan, 18th cent.]. A dagger is the attribute of MITHRAS, as bull-slayer; occasionally of HECATE; in western art of SS. Thomas and Lucia, and of Melpomene (MUSE of Tragedy) and Wrath, one of the SEVEN DEADLY SINS.

Dice. One of the INSTRUMENTS OF THE PASSION. An attribute of FORTUNE personified; and of the THREE GRACES, attendants of Venus [vi].

Disk (Sk. *chakra*). Originally a primitive weapon, probably thrown [vii]. It is one of the most typical attributes of VISHNU in his several incarnations. It may then resemble a wheel or a lotus

[vii]

[viii]

[ix]

[x]

[xi]

bloom within a rim and is often highly ornamented, with ribbons attached [viii]. It is held by KRISHNA, as an *avatar* of Vishnu, by SURYA, GANESHA, KARTTIKEYA and some manifestations of DEVI. The lotus type of *chakra* is used in Tantric diagrams of the human body to indicate the position of certain nodes, usually four or six, through which vital energy is supposed to pass, and on which the adept focuses his meditations. See SUN, MOON, HALO for solar and lunar disks.

Distaff. From antiquity, the symbol of the activity of women in the home. It is the attribute of Clotho, one of the THREE FATES of Greek mythology who spins the thread of life; of Eve after the Expulsion; of the Virgin of the Annunciation (medieval); of the shepherdess St Geneviève and HERCULES, having been seduced and made effeminate by Omphale [ix].[21]

Door, or gateway, is the entrance to the realm of the dead. On Roman funerary monuments it is typically a double door, one ajar. Figures of the FOUR SEASONS, or winged Victories, around it suggest resurrection. In Egypt the deceased passed through a series of gates on his journey to the next world. Opening the doors of the temple sanctuary symbolized opening the gates of heaven. A false door, carved or painted inside an Egyptian tomb, or inside the coffin, allowed the deceased's spirit to come and go. In medieval Christian art, the entrance to hell may be represented as a door, sometimes ajar like its Roman antecedent [x: Burgos, 13th cent.]. The gates of hell lie broken beneath Christ's feet, crushing Satan, at the Harrowing of Hell. Over the portal of Christian churches, St Michael slays Satan, the dragon, an apotropaic image to prevent him entering. The gates of heaven are of marble or finely wrought gold. A closed door or gate symbolizes virginity (see VIRGIN MARY).

The sun-god, on his chariot, enters through a gate in the east in near-eastern myth and, later, Greek (see SHAMASH). A gate with wings, in reality the sun's rays, was a symbol of the Sumerian sky-god ANU.

Doors and gates of temples, palaces and houses are protected by many kinds of guardian, for example the Mesopotamian SCORPION – man; the Hindu Bhairava mounted on a DOG; Chinese LION – dogs; the FOUR CELESTIAL KINGS, seen throughout India and the Far East. The Buddhist *Dvarapalas* are fierce, armed soldiers of Hindu origin who stand guard in pairs at the entrance to temples. In China they are identified with two historical heroes, Ch'in and Yu.[22] See also TORI-I.

Drum. Has many functions in religious rites, including the dance. The rattle-drum (Sk. *damaru*) is an attribute of SHIVA, especially when dancing, of male and female deities associated with him, of Tibetan Buddhist gods in their 'wrathful' forms and of the war-god KARTTIKEYA [xi]. It may be entwined by a snake, typically in southern India. In the hand of Shiva dancing it symbolizes the

[*i*]

[*ii*]

[*iii*]

[*iv*]

[*v*]

creative process (of music). According to others it heralds the destruction of the universe. It also symbolizes sound, hence the spoken word, incantation, revelation. In China the drum (*ku*) takes many forms. A hollow bamboo beaten with two sticks is the attribute of Chang Kuo, one of the EIGHT IMMORTALS [*i*]. Thunder-gods in general have one or more drums, thus Lui Kung in China and Rai-Jin, or Rai-den, in Japan. The latter is demon-like with claws for hands and feet. See also COCK.

Fan (Ch. *shan* or *shanzi*). The flat, rigid type of fan was first found in a Han dynasty tomb of 186–168 BC, but may have been used in China from the 1st mill. BC. It is the attribute of Chung-li Ch'uan, one of the Taoist EIGHT IMMORTALS; of Fa-she-na-fu-to (Sk. Vajriputra) and Fa-na-p'o-ssu (Sk. Vanavasi), two of the sixteen Lohans (see ARHAT), and of two handmaidens attending HSI WANG MU, Queen Mother of the West. Japanese fans are either the rigid type (*uchiwa*) [*ii*] or folding (*ogi*). The latter, familiar in the West, may have been a Japanese invention. The earliest references to a folding fan in China and Japan are 10th cent. AD. According to one's station in Japanese life, so one used a fan appropriate to it, distinguished by the number of ribs, the material and its decoration. Courtiers, certain ranks of nobles, geishas, actors, partakers of the Tea Ceremony, all had their own style of *ogi*. Military leaders and referees of Sumo wrestling, among others, used the *uchiwa* fan. A fan is the attribute of the Hindu god of fire, AGNI, which he uses as bellows. See also PEACOCK.

Fasces. Bundle of wooden rods enclosing an axe, carried by the attendants of Roman magistrates and symbolizing their authority to scourge and behead. As an attribute of Justice personified (one of the CARDINAL VIRTUES), the fasces may include scales and a sword [*iii*]. In Renaissance allegory they may be held by Cupid as a symbol of conjugal unity.

Fetters and **Manacles.** In Christian art, fetters are one of the INSTRUMENTS OF THE PASSION and the attribute of St Leonard, patron of prisoners of war (6th cent.). In Renaissance allegory a woman manacled to a heavy stone personifies Poverty, while a fettered man, also shouldering a yoke, personifies Matrimony [*iv*].[23] See also VIRTUES AND VICES.

Flag. Symbol of Victory, like the Christian banner of the Resurrection, a long white flag bearing a red cross [*v*]. It is held by Christ at his Resurrection, and Descent into Limbo. It accompanies him when he takes the form of the paschal lamb. It is the attribute of SS. Ansanus and George (warriors), Reparata, Ursula, and the Phrygian SIBYL. In parts of the Far East, banners bearing religious texts invoking the help or protection of the gods are flown in public places or attached to walls of houses. In Tibet such prayer-flags on long poles are a feature of Lamaist temples and monasteries. Besides texts they can portray various symbolic creatures, mainly borrowed from China. The common-est are a horse-headed DRAGON carrying the scrolls of the Bud-dhist Law on its back, and a scene of contest between TIGER and dragon. See also MANDALA.

Flail. In Egypt a symbol of authority and an attribute of MIN [*vi*]. When combined with the CROOK it is the attribute of several other deities and of the pharaohs. In western art the harvest is threshed with a flail in August or September (see TWELVE MONTHS).

[*vi*]

Fly-whisk. (Sk. *chamara*; Ch. *fu-tzu*). Carried by attendants of royalty and gods in the East, therefore a symbol of obeisance or veneration. On reliefs and cylinder seals depicting Assyrian kings, it is made of woven reeds [*vii: 9th–7th cents.* BC]. Indians and Chinese used the tail-hairs of the yak or buffalo, fastened to a handle. This type is held by attendants of SHIVA and of Kubera, the Hindu lord of wealth; by Shatrughna, half-brother of Rama (see VISHNU, 7), especially in late bronzes of S. India; by Lu Tung-pin, one of the Taoist EIGHT IMMORTALS; and by Vajriputra and Vanavasi, two of the sixteen Protectors of the Law (see ARHAT). When carried by a Buddhist priest it denotes obedience to the commandment not to kill any living creature. Hence it is an at-tribute of Buddhist saints, in particular Bato-Kannon, a Japanese and Tibetan manifestation of AVALOKITESHVARA who is a protec-tor of animals. The FLAIL of the Egyptian pharaoh may originally have been a fly-whisk.

[*vii*]

Font. Vessel for baptismal water and in Christian art a symbol of the rite. Romanesque fonts in particular bear a great variety of relief sculpture. Tertullian (*c.* 160–*c.* 225) compared Chris-tians to little fishes swimming in the water of baptism,[24] hence fish in some form are a popular subject for decoration, which may occasionally have pagan overtones [*viii: Norman English*]. A font is an attribute of FAITH personified.

[*viii*]

Fountain. A source of fresh water, such as a spring. It is usually represented in art as the ornamental kind, when it is a symbol of the various regenerative powers of WATER. In the myths of Meso-potamian peoples the source could revive the dead in the Under-world. The biblical water of life[25] that flowed through Paradise from the throne of God gave salvation to the spirit and conferred immortality. (See also RIVER.) A fountain, sometimes sealed, is one of the attributes of the Virgin of the Immaculate Conception (see VIRGIN MARY) [*ix*]. The Fountain of Youth, which the aged enter and emerge made young again, abandoning their crutches, was a popular theme in Renaissance allegory.

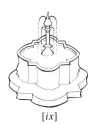

[*ix*]

Goad. The elephant goad (Sk. *ankusha*) is an attribute of SHIVA and his spouse in her manifestation as the demon-slayer DEVI; also GANESHA and sometimes INDRA. It is one of the symbols on the FOOT of Vishnu. It is one of the many weapons in the hands of Tantric Buddhist deities in their wrathful aspect [*x*].

[*x*]

[i]

Gohei. Shinto ritual object made of strips of paper hung on a frame, later often made of metal [i], and found in all Shinto temples. When carried by a priest its purpose is to attract the deity to his temple, the paper representing offerings. It is also carried in procession in times of drought, to bring rain. In a Japanese myth it was one of the devices used to entice the sun-goddess, AMATERASU, from her cave.[26]

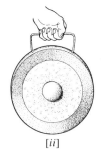

[ii]

Gong. In Buddhist temples used to drive away evil spirits and to mark the stages of the service [ii]. A circular gong hangs from the shoulder of a Japanese Buddhist monk, Kuya-Shonin (903–972). The 'MUSICAL STONE' is a kind of jade gong.

Gridiron. The customary attribute of St Lawrence, deacon and Christian martyr, who was executed at Rome in 258. According to an early tradition he was burned to death on a gridiron [iii]. It is also sometimes the attribute of St Vincent of Saragossa, patron of wine-growers (died Valencia, c. 304).

[iii]

Hammer. With the THUNDERBOLT, an attribute of storm-gods. It is typically double-headed when held by Hadad, the Semitic form of the Akkadian ADAD [iv: Dura-Europos, c. 2nd cent. BC], and by the Scandinavian god, Thor. The Graeco-Roman god of fire, Hephaistus/Vulcan, who forged weapons and armour for gods and heroes, has a hammer among other blacksmith's tools. P'an Ku, the primordial man of a Chinese creation legend (known in Japan as Hanko), was, in one version, born of a great egg and then proceeded to fashion the universe with hammer and chisel. He is seen in Taoist and Buddhist painting. A mallet-shaped hammer, a miner's tool, is the attribute of Daikoku, Japanese god of riches (got from mining) (see GODS OF HAPPINESS). In Christian art hammer and nails are INSTRUMENTS OF THE PASSION and the attributes of Helena, mother of Constantine the Great, from the tradition that she discovered Christ's cross. St Eloi (c. 588–660), a smith who became bishop of Noyon, has a hammer among other tools of his trade. See also T (tau).

[iv]

Harp. Played throughout the ancient world [v: neo-Babylonian, 7th cent. BC] and the principal musical instrument in Egypt (see BES). Harps found at Ur (c. 2500 BC) had an animal's head fixed to the sound-box, perhaps indicating a belief that the source or inspiration of music was an animal deity, possibly bull or goat. In Greece a harp was the instrument of Terpsichore, MUSE of dancing and song. In Christian art it is the attribute of King DAVID and sometimes of the elders of the Apocalypse.[27]

[v]

Hoe. To hoe the ground was an annual ritual dedicated to Osiris in his role as agricultural deity. It symbolized his death and burial [vi: Egyptian, 1st Dyn.]. Sokar, a hawk-headed god of Memphis, was associated with the fertility of crops and became identified with this aspect of Osiris. He is represented in the Old Kingdom hoeing with a mattock. In Christian art, Adam, after the

Expulsion, holds a hoe or spade,[28] as does Christ whom Mary Magdalene mistook for a gardener.[29] A hoe is an attribute of Spring, one of the FOUR SEASONS.

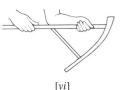

[vi]

Horseshoe. A symbol of protection since the Middle Ages, placed on or over the door of many kinds of buildings, or worn as an amulet. It was also part of the repertoire of graffiti made by Christian pilgrims at their stopping places [vii]. Its origin is uncertain. Its popularity as a symbol of good luck is a modern development.

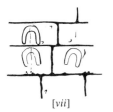

[vii]

Hour-glass. A reminder of the transience of our life on earth in VANITAS still-life paintings [viii], an attribute of Death personified and of FATHER TIME; also of the penitent St Jerome in the desert (see FOUR LATIN FATHERS). The so-called 'hour-glass' throne of Buddha, common in east Asia, consists of a lotus throne which stands on a kind of stepped pyramid representing Mt Meru, the holy MOUNTAIN.

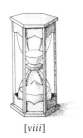

[viii]

Ink, Inkstone. Two of the FOUR TREASURES of the Chinese scholar's study, the other two being BRUSH and PAPER. Ink, in the form of a solid block or stick, is wetted and rubbed on to an inkstone, which has a small well for the water. Inkstones are often finely decorated [ix: Chinese, early 4th cent. AD].

[ix]

Jar, Canopic. In ancient Egypt, probably from the Old Kingdom, the so-called 'Canopic' jars (named after jars found at Canopus, an ancient port near Alexandria) consisted of a set of four that held the internal organs of the deceased during his embalming. The stoppers were in the form of the heads of the four sons of HORUS, symbolic protectors of the contents. The regular arrangement, dating from the New Kingdom, was as follows: Imsety, human-headed, guardian of the southern quarter of the universe, had charge of the liver; Qebsennuef, hawk-headed, the West, the intestines; Duamutef, jackal-headed, the East, the stomach; Hapi, ape-headed, the North, the lungs. During the 18th Dynasty all stoppers tended to assume human heads. This type of funerary urn appeared in Etruria in the first half of the 1st mill. BC to hold the ashes or bones of the dead. The stopper was intended to be a replica of the deceased's features, making it a receptacle for his soul [x: Etruscan, c. 7th–6th cents. BC]. See also VASE.

[x]

Jewels, Jewellery, are one of the distinguishing attributes of royalty and certain deities, especially in the East. In Indian art necklaces, armlets, bracelets, anklets, etc, are typical of SHIVA, in the role of Great Lord, and of Parvati, his *shakti* or spouse; of VISHNU in many roles; and of ARJUNA, KRISHNA, Rama and other heroes of the Indian epics. Ganga, the river goddess of the Ganges is similarly adorned, as are the heavenly nymphs, the *apsarases*. The Nagas, the snake-genii of Hindu myth, inhabit underwater palaces decorated with gems. They are said to carry a jewel in their heads and are guardians of the wealth of the sea, such as pearls. Princely attire, with much jewellery, is characteristic of the BODHISATTVA, in contrast to the Buddha himself who is unadorned, except sometimes in later Far-Eastern images of the Mahayana and Vajrayana sects (see BUDDHA).

'Jewel' is also a metaphor in Hindu and Buddhist writings. It generally stands for the infinitely precious insight received in the act of contemplation. Tantric Hindu paintings depict an Island of Jewels, an image intended as an object of contemplation. It shows an island set in jewels with a jewelled palace in which a goddess, who is Shiva's *shakti*, sits on a jewelled throne. Together with other details the whole image is a symbolic expression of Shivaite metaphysics. For Buddhists, especially of the Mahayana and Vajrayana sects, 'jewel' expresses several ideas which are represented as symbols. A Buddhist trinity (Buddha, the Law and the priesthood) is known as the Three Jewels (Sk. *Tri-ratna*). They may be represented as three Buddhas or, symbolically, as a jewel [*i* and *ii*]. A somewhat similar gem (Sk. *mani*), often called a pearl, is a symbol of purity. A flaming pearl, which can take more than one form, is the 'wish-granting' gem (Sk. *cintamani*) [*iii*]. It is an attribute of AVALOKITESHVARA, Kshitigarbha (see BODHISATTVA) and the Dhyani-Buddha, Ratnasambhava (see VAIROCANA) in their various eastern manifestations. The pearl is one of the Buddhist's SEVEN TREASURES. It may be a single gem, perhaps beribboned, or a group of three or five, when it is usually surrounded by flames. The beribboned pearl is one of the EIGHT TREASURES. It may be spherical or, especially in China and Tibet, egg-shaped, tapering at the bottom, and is sometimes encircled with rings or spirals. A spherical jewel lies under the paw of the male of the pair of lion-dogs that guard the entrance to Chinese and Japanese temples (see LION). A jewel may be seen on the forehead of Chinese and Japanese dragons and in the jaws of the fox. The *magatama*, a precious stone shaped like a COMMA, is a symbol of the sovereignty of the Japanese emperor.

The 'Jewel in the Lotus' is a magical formula, *Om mani padme hum*, which is uttered daily by Tibetans. It can be interpreted in various ways and may denote the creative act of sexual union between certain heavenly Buddhas and bodhisattvas and their Tara, or *shakti*. It also expresses the devotee's hope of eventual rebirth in the Buddhist paradise. Besides being spoken it is written or printed on long ribbons and inserted into prayer-wheels (see WORD).

In the West, the symbolism of jewellery is essentially moralistic. It is an attribute of Vanity personified and symbolizes the worldly possessions taken away by Death (see VANITAS). The earthly, profane Venus of Renaissance philosophers wears jewels (see APHRODITE/VENUS; NUDITY) while the penitent Mary Magdalene casts hers off. See also FOUR PARTS OF THE WORLD – Asia; FOUR TREASURES; MENAT; MONGOOSE.

[*i*]

[*ii*]

[*iii*]

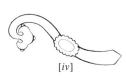

[iv]

Ju-i (Jap. *Nyo-i*). An S-shaped blade, probably once an iron weapon, subsequently made of jade or wood and given by the Chinese, especially to the old, as a token of good wishes. (*Ju-i* = 'as you may desire'.) The tip is decorated with a stylized form of sacred FUNGUS, a Taoist symbol of long life and prosperity [iv]. Thus it may be combined with a BAT or PEACH. It is an attribute of Fu Hsing, one of the Taoist GODS OF HAPPINESS and Lao-tzu, Taoism's founder (see EIGHT IMMORTALS). Held by a child it denotes a wish for a male offspring, and for Confucians symbolizes filial piety. For Buddhists it represents the lotus, symbol of Buddha and his doctrines, and is used by them ceremonially in China and Japan. It may also be decorated with SWASTIKA and PEARL, both Buddhist symbols. It is an attribute of Kuan-yin (AVALOKITESHVARA), Samantabhadra and other BODHISATTVAS.

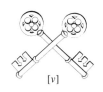

[v]

Key. The old Italian god of doors and gates, JANUS, holds a key. It is an attribute of HECATE, Cybele (the Phrygian Mother Goddess) and the Japanese goddess Benten, one of the GODS OF HAPPINESS. In Christian art the keys of heaven are the principal attribute of the apostle PETER[30] and a symbol of the Church. A pair of crossed keys [v] is a charge in the arms of the Pope and of some English dioceses. The key of hell is held by the angel of the Apocalypse.[31] Martha, personification of the active housekeeper, has a bunch of keys. The key to his cash-box is an attribute of Avarice, one of the SEVEN DEADLY SINS in Renaissance allegory and of Fidelity personified.

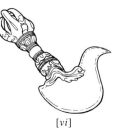

[vi]

Knife. In Egypt a magical weapon, used to destroy evil. Apophis, snake-god of the Underworld and enemy of RE, is beheaded with a knife by Re's CAT. It is sometimes an attribute of Taweret, the HIPPOPOTAMUS deity. A flaying knife (Sk. *karttrika*) with a *vajra* for a handle [vi: Tibetan, 18th cent.] is an attribute of certain Tantric deities in their fierce aspect. They are mainly female, like the Shaktis, Dharmapalas and Dakinis, but YAMA, Lord of the Dead, and AVALOKITESHVARA also have one. As a Christian symbol a knife denotes sacrifice, as in Abraham's sacrifice of Isaac;[32] also martyrdom, being the attribute of the apostle Bartholomew who was flayed alive. It is one of the INSTRUMENTS OF THE PASSION.

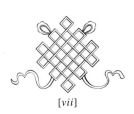

[vii]

Knot (Ch. *pan-chang*). The endless, mystic knot [vii] is one of the Buddhist EIGHT LUCKY EMBLEMS, a symbol of longevity; alternatively a stylized rendering of the bowels of the Buddha, or of a vanquished enemy. Perhaps originally it was a mark on the breast of VISHNU. Egyptian amulets were commonly tied with knotted cords to retain their magic powers. (See also TYET.) Three knots in a Franciscan's girdle denote the three monastic vows of poverty, chastity, obedience; in a whip held by St Ambrose, the persons of the Trinity. Renaissance cupids tie the knot of love that binds Mars and Venus.

[i]

Labyrinth. Originally any large building with a complicated plan, such as the palace of Minos at Knossos where, in Greek myth, Theseus slew the Minotaur[33] [*i: Knossos, 4th cent.* BC].

This theme, popular in ancient and medieval art, acquired symbolic overtones: the hero's steps were guided through a maze by a thread which held him to the true path of life. Ancient burial places sometimes had a labyrinthine plan, perhaps to deter the dead from returning. A labyrinth with a single path is seen on pavements of medieval churches, especially French and Italian. It was known as the 'Chemin de Jérusalem', indicating a connection with pilgrimage. Those unable to visit the Holy Land or other shrines in person made a symbolic, spiritual journey on their knees, tracing the path on the church floor.

[ii]

Ladder. The 'ladder of heaven', joining heaven and earth, is found in more than one religion. It is often mentioned in the Pyramid Texts[34] in association with OSIRIS, as god of resurrection, and was used by the pharaoh to ascend to heaven. In the art of the eastern Christian Church the souls of the dead climb a ladder, sinners falling off into the fiery river of hell below [*ii: Byzantine, 12th cent.*] (see also BRIDGE). Jacob's ladder,[35] with angels going up and down, was made a symbol in the Middle Ages of the VIRGIN MARY, through whom the alliance of heaven and earth was sealed. A ladder is one of the INSTRUMENTS OF THE PASSION.

[iii]

Lamp, Lantern. Shares some of the symbolism of Fire. The Assyrian fire-god, Nusku, personified the sacred fire of the sacrifice and is represented as an oil-lamp, which stands on an altar [*iii: Assyro-Kassite, late 12th cent.* BC]. Lamp-light, like candle-light, when accompanying worship, symbolizes the light of the spirit, divinity, the transience of earthly existence. Among the articles buried with the deceased, a lamp will light his after-life. The lantern held by Diogenes, the Greek philosopher, symbolizes his search for truth and virtue. A lamp is the attribute of the wise and foolish virgins,[36] of St Lucia, the Persian SIBYL and of the personifications of Night and Vigilance. It is one of the INSTRUMENTS OF THE PASSION.

[iv]

Lance. Weapon of cavalrymen, usually with a pennant. The lance of the centurion (later called Longinus) which pierced Christ's side is one of the INSTRUMENTS OF THE PASSION.[37] Pennants on the lances of other centurions at the crucifixion may bear the motto of the Roman legions, S.P.Q.R. (*Senatus Populusque Romanus*, the Senate and People of Rome) [*iv*]. A lance is one of the attributes of the APOSTLES Thaddeus (Jude) and Matthias. See also SPEAR.

Lute. The oldest kind, with a small body, long neck and two strings, is seen on Mesopotamian reliefs and figurines of the early 2nd mill. BC, when it accompanied religious rites. This was the ancestor of later types. The 'short lute', with a tapering body, is

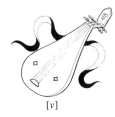

[v]

[vi]

[vii]

[viii]

[ix]

represented on Persian figurines of the 8th cent. BC, and reappears in early Ghandaran sculpture, reaching China about the 3rd cent. AD [v]. This type, with four strings (often wrongly called a guitar), is the distinctive attribute of Mo-li Hai, one of the FOUR CELESTIAL KINGS, and the Japanese goddess, Benten, one of the GODS OF HAPPINESS. Another so-called lute, strictly a long ZITHER, symbolizes Music, one of the FOUR ARTS of the Chinese scholar. All these instruments also symbolized purity and faithfulness. The lute was rare in ancient Greece and Rome. In Europe it achieved its fully developed form with eleven strings in the mid-15th cent. In Renaissance and later painting it often replaces the lyre of classical antiquity in representations of Orpheus, Apollo, and Polyhymnia, one of the MUSES. It is an attribute of Music, one of the SEVEN LIBERAL ARTS, and Hearing, one of the FIVE SENSES. With a broken string it symbolizes Discord in allegorical still-life painting. See also VINA.

Lyre. Several types, dating from the first half of the 3rd mill. BC, have been recovered from the royal tombs at Ur. Mesopotamian lyres of that period are often decorated with a bull's head, suggesting it was used in connection with worship of the animal. In ancient Greece the lyre was the instrument of APOLLO and the legendary Thracian poet, Orpheus. Its strings echoed the harmony of the celestial spheres. The purity of its tone was contrasted with the coarse notes of the flute or *aulos*, symbolizing the contrasting aspects of human nature, Apollonian (enlightened and restrained) and Dionysiac (orgiastic and passionate). The Greek myth of the contest between Apollo and the Satyr Marsyas is a paradigm.[38] The instrument had two forms: the simple lyre with a sound box made of a tortoise shell [*vi: Greek, 5th–4th cent.* BC] and the more solid kithara [*vii: Attic, c. 480* BC], used by the early rhapsodes and known to Homer. The latter is the instrument of the MUSES Erato and sometimes Terpsichore; and of the legendary Greek poets Orpheus and Arion.

Mace. Ancient war-club with a round, metal head [*viii: Assyrian, 9th cent.* BC]. In Mesopotamia in the early dynastic period (first half of the 3rd mill. BC) mace-heads of marble or alabaster were engraved with lions or lion-heads and dedicated in the temple as votive offerings, mainly to Ningirsu, whose roles were agriculture and war (see also NINURTA). The mace was the weapon of ISHTAR, in her role of war-goddess, and other Mesopotamian deities (see SHAMASH). A mace and ogival sceptre were the insignia of Assyrian kings and the attributes of Teshub, the Hittite storm-god (see ADAD). See also CLUB; SURYA; YAMA.

Menat. A wide necklace consisting of several rows of beads with a counterweight that hung at the back of the neck [*ix: Egyptian funerary papyrus, 19th Dynasty*]. It is worn by HATHOR in the reliefs in her temple at Dendera (rebuilt in late Ptolemaic and

[i]

[ii]

[iii]

[iv]

[v]

Roman times). It gave her the power of healing. Priestesses of Hathor shook the menat to provide percussion music during her rites.

Menorah. Seven-branched golden lamp-stand, the prototype of which stood in the Jewish Temple in Jerusalem.[39] In the Roman era its image appears as a cult symbol on Jewish graves, in synagogues and on oil-lamps of all kinds [*i: Arch of Titus, Rome, after* AD *81*]. The seven lamps are thought to have symbolized the planets, hence the heavens and the universe. In a funerary context it may have implied the hope of immortality. Today a menorah in the form of a candelabrum is used in Jewish ritual.

Mill, Millstone. The 'mystic mill' and the 'mystic wine-press' together formed a medieval Christian allegory of the bread and wine of the Eucharist, which was transformed into the body and blood of Christ after passing through a mill and wine-press (see WINE). The oldest example of the former shows the prophet Isaiah pouring corn into a mill and St Paul, below, receiving the flour in a sack [*ii: Vézelay, 12th cent.*]. In German art of the 15th cent. Isaiah is replaced by the four evangelists, and Paul by the Fathers of the Church. A millstone was the instrument of martyrdom of SS. Christina of Tyre, Pope Callistus I, Vincent of Saragossa and Florian. It is usually tied round their neck. An ass carrying a millstone personifies Obedience, one of the THREE MONASTIC VOWS.

Model. The model of a church or city in the hands of a Christian saint or benefactor denotes his or her patronage, or some other association with it, e.g., Bernardino (Siena), Charlemagne (Aix-la-Chapelle), Constantine the Great (Constantinople), Elizabeth of Hungary (Marburg), Fina (San Gimignano), Geminianus (Modena), Helena (Holy Sepulchre), Henry II (H.R.E.) and his wife Cunegunda (Bamberg), Jerome (Rome), Justa and Rufina (Seville), Petronius (Bologna) [*iii: 15th cent.*], Zenobius (Florence).

Musical stone (Ch. *ch'ing*). A stone, roughly L-shaped, the majority carved from JADE, that emits a musical note when struck [*iv*]. It is mentioned by Mencius (372–289 BC).[40] It was compared, symbolically, to a tuning fork and so it was said of a virtuous woman, 'However worthy she would not dare strike the *ch'ing.*' It is one of the EIGHT TREASURES. Its main use is in the temple services of Confucians, either the single stone or a chime of sixteen strung from a frame in two rows (*pien ch'ing*). The notes of the upper row are *yang*, the lower, *yin*. By a play on words the *ch'ing* symbolizes joy and good fortune.

Nail. The nails, usually three, of Christ's cross are one of the INSTRUMENTS OF THE PASSION [*v*]. They are an attribute of St Helena, of the Hellespontic SIBYL and, with other symbols of the crucifixion, of SS. Joseph of Arimathaea, Bernard of Clairvaux and Louis IX. As holy relics they number some twenty or more.

Net. Symbol of the power of a god to bind and hence to overcome enemies; for example, the net of the Sumerian god, Ningirsu, sometimes identified with NINURTA, snares the enemies of the king of Lagash [*vi: Sumerian, c. 2700* BC]. It is an attribute of Hephaestus/Vulcan, blacksmith of the Greek gods, forged by him to trap Mars and Venus in the act of making love.[41] In Christian art a net, sometimes holding a fish, is an attribute of the apostle Andrew, a fisherman.

[*vi*]

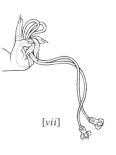

Noose (Sk. *pasha*). One of the many weapons of Hindu gods who use it to bind their enemies or, on the moral plane, to ensnare evildoers and draw them towards the truth. It is the attribute of: GANESHA; SHIVA, as destroyer; KARTTIKEYA; the goddess DEVI in her role as demon slayer; Lakshmi, spouse of VISHNU; KRISHNA, as one of Vishnu's incarnations; YAMA, Lord of the Dead. Varuna, the Jehovah-like god of the *Vedas*, binds sinners with a noose.

A noose is the attribute of several Buddhist deities, such as the bodhisattva Vajrapani, one of the two attendants protecting the Buddha. It identifies Kanatavatsa, among the sixteen ARHATS, who are Protectors of the Law. It is seen especially in the hands of Tantric Buddhist deities in their fierce aspect [*vii: Tibetan, 16th–17th cent.*], for example Amoghapasha, a Tantric form of AVALOKITESHVARA; the female bodhisattva Marici who is enthroned on a PIG; Yamantaka, a form of MANJUSHRI and the conqueror of Yama; and the Japanese Fudo-Myo-O, who is identified with VAIROCANA. They hold it, among other weapons, in one of their many hands. The noose may have a single or double loop and is generally without a knot, particularly in Tibetan art.

[*vii*]

[*viii*]

Oar. An attribute of river-gods in the Renaissance and later; also of the legendary Christian saint, Julian 'the hospitaller', patron of travellers and innkeepers, whose inn was beside a ford. Julian was absolved from the sin of having murdered his parents by his acts of charity towards travellers whom he ferried across the river [*viii*]. He is depicted in later medieval French and Italian painting.

[*ix*]

Obelisk. Of the several functions of the PILLAR among early peoples, the Egyptian obelisk was worshipped as the dwelling-place of the sun-god. The oldest known, from Heliopolis and called *benben* (sun stone), dates from the 5th Dynasty and was dedicated to RE. Many much taller and more slender columns were erected by pharaohs in the 18th and 19th Dynasties to AMUN in his role of sun-god (Amun-Re), in the expectation that he would grant them eternal life after death. [*ix: Thebes, 18th Dynasty*]. At Thebes, and elsewhere, they stood in pairs at the entrance to temples, symbolizing sun and moon. The top was pyramidal in shape and plated with a gold–silver alloy which brilliantly reflected the sun.

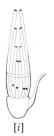

[i]

[ii]

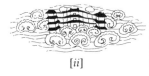

[iii]

[iv]

[v]

[vi]

Organ. The Chinese reed organ (*sheng*) was made of a gourd holding thirteen or more bamboo pipes of varying length, and a mouthpiece [*i*]. It is first mentioned in the *Shih Ching (Book of Odes,* 800–600 BC) but is traditionally much older. It appears first in art in AD 551, by which time it was known in Korea, Japan (*sho*) and Persia (*mustaq sini*). It symbolized the Chinese PHOENIX, from a supposed resemblance, and was played at weddings, funerals and other functions.

The western portative organ, with keyboard, graduated pipes and bellows, is a familiar instrument in late medieval and Renaissance painting. It is seen in the hands of Cecilia, patron saint of music. It is an attribute of Music personified, one of the SEVEN LIBERAL ARTS; Hearing, one of the FIVE SENSES; Polyhymnia, one of the MUSES.

Palace. Heavenly palaces are a feature of paintings of the 'Pure Land of the West.' This is a Buddhist paradise, the abode of the principal divine Buddha of the Mahayana sect, Amitabha, a god of infinite mercy, whose cult was prominent in the Far East (see BUDDHA). The deity surrounded by bodhisattvas and their splendid mansions form a series of images seen widely in central and eastern Asia [*ii: painted scroll, Central Asian, c. 10th cent.* AD]. The founder of Tibetan Lamaism, PADMASAMBHAVA, is likewise seen in *tanka* paintings of a similar character.

Palette. The Egyptian scribe sits before his patron, THOTH, an open scroll on his lap, a palette of pens and red and black ink lying on his left knee [*iii*]. Thoth himself holds pen and palette in the Hall of Judgement to record the verdict. See also INK/INKSTONE.

Paper. One of the FOUR TREASURES, or 'priceless jewels', of the Chinese scholar's study. Its supposed inventor, Ts'ai Lun (d. AD 144), chief eunuch to the emperor, holds a paper scroll [*iv*]. He was subsequently deified and commemorated annually by the burning of paper charms and images. See also GOHEI. In fact, archaeological evidence indicates paper was being made in the 1st or 2nd cent. BC.

Pattens. Thick wooden soles, sometimes mounted on iron rings [*v: Early Netherlandish, 15th cent.*] to raise the feet above the wet and mud, at the same time increasing the wearer's stature. Not uncommon in European art from the Middle Ages onwards, where they are a sign of royal or noble rank. They may be worn by ARJUNA and Bhima, two of the Pandu princes in the *Mahabharata*, to denote their royal status.

Pen. In eastern and western Christian art, pen and inkhorn are attributes of the four evangelists, patristic authors and numerous saints known for their writing [*vi: French, 12th cent.*]. See also BRUSH.

Pestle and Mortar. In Christian art an attribute of the legendary

[*vii*]

[*viii*]

[*ix*]

twins, SS. Cosmas and Damian, who were physicians; also of the alchemist in his workshop [*vii*]. See also HARE.

Pillar. One of the oldest types of cult monument, of prehistoric origin. It was built to support the heavens which would otherwise fall and destroy mankind. The top of the pillar came to be regarded as the dwelling-place of the sky-god and supported his image. Evidence from coins shows that such monuments continued to exist in Greece, Italy and central Europe until the Christian era. In Rome the figure of the deified emperor supplanted the sky-god.

The origin of the Egyptian *djed* pillar [*viii*] is uncertain but may have been connected with prehistoric harvest rites. In funerary painting at Saqqara (3rd Dynasty) they support the heavens, marking the limits of the pharaoh's earthly realm beneath. In the New Kingdom the *djed* became a symbol of Osiris. It was used in his rites and was called his 'backbone'.[42] The columns of the Egyptian temple represent papyrus, lotus and palm, which support the vault of heaven, which is painted with stars and sacred birds.

The concept of the pillar as underpinning the heavens was known in the Near East and India but seems absent from Far-Eastern cosmologies. A 'pillar of heaven' supported the WINGED DISK in the art of the Mitanni, Indo-European settlers in northern Syria (mid-2nd mill. BC). The *Rig-Veda*[43] describes AGNI as a 'cosmic pillar' of fire extending between heaven and earth, an image taken over by early Buddhism as one of the prefigurative ways of representing Shakyamuni. The earliest Buddhist monuments were great monolithic pillars erected in many places throughout India by the Emperor Ashoka (? 273–232 BC). They were inscribed with imperial edicts and surmounted by Buddhist symbols in a style derived from the imperial monuments of Achaemenid Persia. At each of the four entrances to the Buddhist STUPA are five pillars symbolizing the five main events in the life of Shakyamuni. They are sometimes topped with appropriate symbols. See also OBELISK; PHALLUS. In Christian art, the scene of Christ's scourging depicts him bound to a pillar, which is one of the INSTRUMENTS OF THE PASSION. It is an attribute of Fortitude personified, one of the CARDINAL VIRTUES, perhaps an allusion to Samson.[44]

Pincers, Tongs. In Christian art a pair of pincers gripping a tooth is an attribute of St Apollonia (3rd cent. AD) whose teeth were drawn at her martyrdom [*ix*]. Pincers, used to remove the nails from Christ's cross, are one of the INSTRUMENTS OF THE PASSION. Pincers are sometimes an alternative to the shears of St Agatha whose breasts were shorn. The French bishop Eloi, a blacksmith (*c.* 588–660), tweaked the devil's nose with a pair of tongs. Tongs holding a glowing coal are an attribute of Isaiah, one of the FOUR PROPHETS. A seraph touched his lips with it in an act of purification. They are among the attributes of the Graeco-

Roman god of fire and patron of blacksmiths, Hephaestus/Vulcan, and the Teutonic thunder-god, Thor.

[i]

Pipe. The musical instrument, both flute and reed pipe, had a place in primitive fertility rites owing to its phallic appearance. As a symbol of male sexuality it occurs in Graeco-Roman and Renaissance art in representations of the myth of Apollo and Marsyas [45] (see LYRE) and in various amorous contexts from the Renaissance onwards (see VIRTUES AND VICES). Pastoral deities typically play a pipe. KRISHNA, in his pastoral aspect, is often represented thus in southern Indian bronzes.[46] Greek shepherds more often play the pan-pipes, or syrinx, an instrument thought to have particularly erotic overtones. It is the attribute of Pan himself (see DEMON), Daphnis and Polyphemus.

Single and double pipes, among other instruments, are depicted in Mesopotamian art from the 3rd mill. BC, where music accompanied religious rites, as in many civilizations [*i: from a votive relief of Cybele, Roman, 2nd cent.* AD]. A flute-playing monkey on an early 3rd mill. cylinder seal from Ur is the precursor of many animal musicians seen in Mesopotamian art (see also LYRE). They may play together to form an animal orchestra, a tradition, so far unexplained, that was revived in Romanesque sculpture, where it is given a Christian gloss. The flute is among numerous instruments in Egyptian tomb painting where it provides for the deceased's entertainment in the after-life. The Chinese philosopher Han Hsiang-tzu, one of the EIGHT IMMORTALS, plays a flute, as does Euterpe, the MUSE of music and lyric poetry.

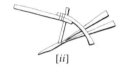

[ii]

Plough (Sk. *hala*). The non-figurative form of many early agricultural deities and subsequently their attribute. In Mesopotamian art it is the symbol of Ningirsu, a god of agriculture whose principal cult centre was Lagash (mod. Telloh) [*ii: Sumerian, 4th mill.* BC]. His plough is first seen on early cylinder seals and recurs in Mesopotamian relief sculpture down to the 7th cent. BC (see also EAGLE; NET; NINURTA). The Greek hero Triptolemus, father of agriculture, may have a plough beside his more regular sheaf of corn. Among Hindu deities the plough is an attribute of SARASVATI, river-goddess originally associated with agriculture. For some Indian deities it also served as a weapon and is an attribute of KARTTIKEYA and Balarama, brother of KRISHNA. The Chinese emperor is depicted with his court conducting a ritual spring ploughing intended to ensure a good harvest. In Christian art ploughing is one of the Labours of the Months (see TWELVE MONTHS). A plough is an attribute of the Silver Age personified (see AGES OF THE WORLD). Trial by ordeal, involving walking on red-hot plough shares, was successfully undergone by St Cunegunda (d. 1033), wife of H.R.E. Henry II, a scene depicted in German and early Florentine painting.

[iii]

Prayer-wheel. A Tibetan aid to devotion: a cylindrical device, held by a handle, containing the mystical prayer, *Om mani padme hum* (see JEWELS). The formula is printed many times over on long strips of paper which are wound round the cylinder [*iii*]. A cover is placed over it and the wheel turned. The written prayer, handled in this way, is regarded as no less effective than the spoken. Prayer-barrels, working on the same principle, stand at the entrance to Lamaist temples.

[*iv*]

Purse. Since antiquity an attribute of HERMES/MERCURY in the role of god of commerce; in Christian art of the apostle Matthew (a tax-collector), St Lawrence (a deacon) and Judas Iscariot. Judas's purse is one of the INSTRUMENTS OF THE PASSION. Three purses identify Bishop Nicholas of Myra. They were his gift to an impoverished nobleman whose three daughters were reduced to prostitution in order to support him. In VANITAS painting a purse symbolizes the transience of worldly wealth. It is an attribute of Vanity personified, of Melancholy, one of the FOUR TEMPERAMENTS, and Avarice, one of the SEVEN DEADLY SINS [*iv: German, 16th cent.*]. An inexhaustible purse is one of the Japanese 'Precious Things', or TAKARA-MONO. See also MONGOOSE.

[*v*]

Quadrant, Sextant. Instruments once used to measure the altitude of the stars, an attribute of Astronomy, one of the SEVEN LIBERAL ARTS [*v: Italian, 17th cent.*].

Quiver. With bow and arrow, an attribute of many gods and goddesses of war, and of the hunter (see BOW) [*vi*]. The quiver of ARTEMIS/DIANA, originally the protector of wild animals, is first seen on a painted Greek vase of the 7th cent. BC. The Mesopotamian ISHTAR, when accoutred as a war-goddess, is widely depicted in neo-Assyrian art (8th–7th cents. BC) with bow, arrow and quiver.

[*vi*]

Ring (Ch. *huan*). A symbol of office and the authority it brings, derived from the signet-ring, which was used in antiquity. To hand over a signet-ring is to delegate authority. Ecclesiastical dignitaries wear different kinds of ring according to their rank; the 'fisherman's ring' worn by the Pope shows St Peter in a boat drawing up a net. The ring also symbolizes union, in particular the bond of marriage, and occurs in various contexts in Christian art: SS. Catherine of Alexandria and Catherine of Siena are symbolically wedded to Christ by the infant Jesus who places a ring on their finger; St Francis of Assisi weds Lady Poverty (see THREE MONASTIC VOWS). Three linked rings represent the TRINITY; three rings, each set with a diamond, formed an *impresa* of Cosimo de' Medici (1389–1464). The so-called rod-and-ring [*vii: Assyrian, 9th cent.* BC] held by various Mesopotamian deities, especially the sun-god SHAMASH, appears to have been a symbol of divine power, or possibly justice. It is also probably a symbol of Shamash in an early non-figurative form. It is thought to represent a measuring rod and line. A somewhat similar motif, but with a very short 'rod', possibly representing a coiled and

[*vii*]

[i]

[ii]

[iii]

[iv]

knotted rope, is the *shen*, the Egyptian hieroglyphic for eternity, and is held in the claws of the FALCON or Horus, the VULTURE of Nekhbet, the *ba,* and by other gods [*i*]. The 'ring-post' in early Sumerian art is thought to symbolize a temple gateway [*ii: later 4th mill.* BC]. A measuring rod is an attribute of Lachesis, one of the THREE FATES, in ancient Greek art. Kalika, one of the sixteen great ARHATS of Buddhism, holds two gold rings, or wears them as ear-rings. Court officials banished by the Chinese emperor were sent one of two rings, a perfect one to denote forgiveness and return or a broken one to remain in exile. *Huan*, ring, is homophonous with the verb 'to return'.

Rope. A symbol of captivity or subjugation, seen on Egyptian reliefs from the beginning of the dynastic period. In Japan, from very early times, a rope of rice-straw (*shimenawa*) was used ritually in Shinto shrines as a symbolic barrier, to mark off a sacred area. It is mentioned in a myth about the sun-goddess AMATERASU who, lured from a cave, was barred from re-entering by a *shimenawa*.[47] It is fastened across the door of a house during the New Year festival to keep evil spirits at bay, and has other ritual uses. It may be decorated with strips of coloured paper and the fruit and leaves of a bitter orange and ferns, symbolizing good fortune [*iii: inro, 19th cent.*]. In Christian art a rope symbolizes the betrayal of Christ. It is an attribute of the apostle Andrew, who was bound to the cross. A martyr dragged by a rope round his neck is St Mark. Round the neck of Charles Borromeo, and others, it denotes the penitent. A hanging man is Judas Iscariot; a hanging woman, Despair personified. The cutting of the Gordian knot by Alexander the Great with a stroke of his sword demonstrated lateral thinking. See also NOOSE.

Rosary (Sk. *mala*; Ch. *nien-chu*; Jap. *nenju*). String of beads of great antiquity, used especially by Buddhists and, since the later Middle Ages, by Christians as a mnemonic when praying. Its origin is unknown and probably predates Buddhism. In art it is an attribute of the Hindu gods BRAHMA, SHIVA in his ascetic role, BRIHASPATI, SARASVATI and GANESHA; of Buddhist deities, the bodhisattva AVALOKITESHVARA in his several Far-Eastern manifestations, PRAJNA-PARAMITA, the Dhyani-Buddha Amitabha (Jap. Amida) and several Chinese Lohans (see ARHAT). The Chinese Buddhist rosary usually has 108 beads, divided into sets like the Christian string. They ensure that the name of Buddha is repeated at least 100 times. Japanese rosaries most commonly have 112. Each bead in the rosary of Kannon (the Japanese identity of Avalokiteshvara) represents an earthly passion which the god in his mercy takes upon himself, thereby liberating the worshipper from his desires. Each sect of Tibetan Lamaism has its own type of rosary [*iv: Tibetan*]. It is carried by all priests and many lay people. In art, especially sculpture, the rosary may be represented with a mere dozen or so beads, or as a decorated ring.

The rosary is used by Catholics while meditating the fifteen mysteries of the Virgin Mary. It has 165 beads divided into fifteen sets, each set having ten small and one large bead. The 'lesser rosary' has 55. Each small bead represents an Ave Maria, each large one a Paternoster and Gloria. The rosary is an attribute of St Dominic who, according to legend, invented it; of Catherine of Siena; of the Compostellan pilgrim and of St Roch, when represented as a pilgrim. It was credited with miraculous powers, particularly in combating Islam and Protestantism. It is a symbol of the Catholic Church in 17th cent. still-life painting of northern Catholic Europe (see also BOOK; VANITAS).

[v]

Rudder. Attribute of the Egyptian goddess ISIS; and of the Roman goddess FORTUNE, one of the deities who guided the destiny of the empire. She was revived in Renaissance allegory, personifying chance, or luck [v: Italian, 16th cent.].

Sack. Aeolus, Greek god of the winds, kept them shut up in a sack.[48] His Shinto counterpart, Fu-jin (or Fu-ten), has the sack slung over his shoulders. He has horns, and his hands and feet may have claws [vi]. The Chinese bodhisattva, Pu-tai Ho-shang, 'The Monk with the Hempen Sack', is worshipped as a manifestation of MAITREYA. In Japan he is known as Hotei and is one of the GODS OF HAPPINESS. He is fat, jolly and reclines on a full sack said, in Japan, to contain the TAKARA-MONO, precious objects symbolizing prosperity. Sacks of RICE are an attribute of Daikoku, another GOD OF HAPPINESS.

[vi]

Sail. The Roman goddess, FORTUNE, has a sail and rudder, possibly some allusion to guiding the imperial ship of state. She retains them in Renaissance allegory, when hazard and uncertainty are implied [vii: Italian, early 16th cent.]. A sail is an attribute of APHRODITE/VENUS who was born of the sea. A black sail may symbolize death, from the Greek myth of the return of Theseus to Athens after slaying the MINOTAUR, in a boat with black sails. A white sail was to have signified the success of his mission, black failure. Theseus forgot this undertaking and his father, seeing the boat approach, threw himself into the sea and was drowned.[49]

[vii]

Saw. Attribute of the Hebrew prophet, Isaiah, one of the FOUR PROPHETS. According to an early N.T. apocryphal book[50] he was martyred by being 'sawn asunder'. The apostle Simon Zelotes, who died in the same way, also has a saw. A saw with pronounced teeth is an attribute of the Mesopotamian sun-god, SHAMASH; the tool appears to have been used ritually to cut branches for cult purposes. As a cutting tool the saw can be destructive like fire and is therefore an attribute of the alchemist who was popularly known as a 'child of fire'; also of Melancholy, one of the FOUR TEMPERAMENTS [viii].

[viii]

Scales. Ancient symbol of judgement, especially of the soul af-

[i]

[ii]

[iii]

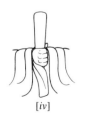

[iv]

ter death. In the Egyptian Hall of Judgement the deceased's heart is weighed against a FEATHER of truth, before OSIRIS, the judge. THOTH, the patron of scribes, stands to one side, ready to record the verdict. It was a popular subject from the beginning of the New Kingdom (*c.* 1567 BC), found almost exclusively in the Book of the Dead (see also CROCODILE). HERMES/MERCURY weighs Greek against Trojan on Attic vase painting. In Christian art, the archangel Michael weighs the souls of the dead before Christ the judge, first seen on French cathedral sculpture from the 12th cent. [*i: German, tomb relief, c. 1237*]. The Hindu Lord of the Dead, YAMA, also judged the dead. He was adopted by Buddhism and presides over the scales in which a person's good deeds, represented as white pebbles, are weighed against black, his sins. In Roman art, Justice personified, one of the CARDINAL VIRTUES, has sword and scales, which she retains to the present day. They are also the attribute of Logic, one of the SEVEN LIBERAL ARTS. Famine, one of the four horsemen of the Apocalypse, has a pair of scales. See also ZODIAC.

Sceptre. Emblem of royal and divine authority. Originally it represented a weapon taken from a defeated enemy and was therefore a token of conquest. The sceptre of Mesopotamian deities was formerly a MACE, its knob representing an animal's head. The sceptre of ISHTAR, goddess of fertility and war, has a dragon's head, sometimes two, facing outwards. Dragon- or eagle-headed sceptres were fixed to Assyrian war-chariots, probably a symbol of their war-god, NINURTA. With a ram's head they are associated with the god of fresh water, EA, in his manifestation as a goat-fish (see FISH).

The *was* sceptre [*ii*] is an attribute of Egyptian deities, too common to be determinative. The head originally represented an animal, perhaps a dog or fox, which magically gave protection. It symbolizes joy and well-being and was placed in the tomb or painted on the coffin to ensure continued prosperity. A sceptre combining *was, djed* (PILLAR) and ANKH is an attribute of PTAH. See also PAPYRUS.

A headed sceptre of a distinctive type is seen in Hindu and, especially, Tantric Buddhist art (Sk. *khatvanga*) [*iii*]. In its earliest form it was a human leg or arm bone topped with a human skull, a weapon of remote, probably Shivaite origin, and once associated with human sacrifice. In Tantric painting two or three small human heads are added to the skull, the whole sometimes being surmounted by a *vajra* (THUNDERBOLT) or TRIDENT. It is an attribute of PADMASAMBHAVA, YAMA, and a class of Tantric goddesses, the Dakinis (see KALI).

The Japanese *shaku* [*iv*] is a type of sceptre which denotes noble rank and is sometimes held by Shinto deities. See also K'UEI HSING.

In the West, the sceptre, often with orb, is an attribute of numerous monarchs, deities and allegorical figures. Its head is often distinctive, thus: eagle (Roman consuls); fleur-de-lys (arch-angel Gabriel, French kings); orb and cross, or dove (English kings); cuckoo (HERA/JUNO, a deceived spouse). St Louis of Tou-louse, who renounced the throne, has a crown and sceptre at his feet. The VIRGIN MARY, when enthroned as Queen of Heaven, may hold orb and sceptre. A sceptre lies at the feet of Melpomene, MUSE of Tragedy. In Renaissance allegory it is an attribute of Europe personified, one of the FOUR PARTS OF THE WORLD, and of PHILOSOPHY. In VANITAS paintings it symbolizes earthly power relinquished at death. See also CROOK; JU-I; STAFF.

[v]

Scroll. Symbol of learning and attribute of the scribe. A scribe with an open scroll of papyrus on his lap sits cross-legged be-fore the throne of THOTH, the Egyptian god of learning. Imhotep, vizier and architect to the pharaoh Zoser (*c.* 2667–2648 BC), also has an open scroll. The Chinese scroll (*chüan*) when used sym-bolically, as in ceramic decoration, is usually rolled. It represents paper or silk, one of the Chinese scholar's FOUR TREASURES. Paint-ing, which includes calligraphy, is one of the FOUR ARTS, usually represented as a pair of scrolls [v]. A scroll is an attribute of Lao-tzu, founder of Taoism. In Buddhist art they symbolize the sa-cred texts, the *Pitakas* and *Sutras*. A scroll is an attribute of AVALOKITESHVARA and certain other bodhisattvas and of the Lohan, Pan-t'o-ka (see ARHAT; EIGHT IMMORTALS). The Japanese god of learning, Jurojin, one of the seven GODS OF HAPPINESS, holds a staff from which two scroll-books hang. In Graeco-Roman art, a scroll is an attribute of the MUSES of history and comedy, Clio and Thalia; of Atropos, one of the THREE FATES; of Rhetoric, one of the SEVEN LIBERAL ARTS; in Christian art of the O.T. prophets and, sometimes, the evangelists. Twelve scrolls, in the scene of Pen-tecost, symbolize the gospels translated into twelve languages. In the Apocalypse cycle, John eats a scroll presented by an an-gel, to digest God's message.[51]

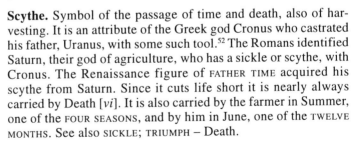

[vi]

Scythe. Symbol of the passage of time and death, also of har-vesting. It is an attribute of the Greek god Cronus who castrated his father, Uranus, with some such tool.[52] The Romans identified Saturn, their god of agriculture, who has a sickle or scythe, with Cronus. The Renaissance figure of FATHER TIME acquired his scythe from Saturn. Since it cuts life short it is nearly always carried by Death [vi]. It is also carried by the farmer in Summer, one of the FOUR SEASONS, and by him in June, one of the TWELVE MONTHS. See also SICKLE; TRIUMPH – Death.

[vii]

Seal. Symbol of authority, or ownership, its impressed image often serving as an amulet. Mesopotamian cylinder seals [vii] appear to have had just such a magical function. For example, they frequently represent animals in combat, probably symbol-izing the conflict of divine powers. An image of this kind would protect the owner from the anger of the gods. Stamp seals used by Chinese Taoist priests were made of peach-wood in the belief

[i]

[ii]

[iii]

[iv]

[v]

that the image would all the better keep off evil spirits. The seven seals of the Apocalypse, according to Christian interpreters, guarded the secrets of divine destruction kept in a scroll book. The seventh seal was used, it is not clear how, to mark the brows of those to be saved from the final calamity.[53]

Set-square, sometimes with a ruler. Attribute of Geometry, one of the SEVEN LIBERAL ARTS; Melancholy, one of the FOUR TEMPERAMENTS; Justice, one of the CARDINAL VIRTUES, who may also have other measuring instruments; the apostle Thomas [i] who was, according to an early tradition, a carpenter and builder.[54]

Shears. Symbol of death, used by Atropos, one of the THREE FATES of Greek mythology, who cuts the thread of life [ii]. An attribute of the Christian St Agatha, whose breasts were shorn. See also HAIR.

Shield. The defensive weapon of many gods and heroes. Some have distinctive bearings: crossed arrows, Neith, the creator-goddess of Sais in the Egyptian delta; Gorgon's head, ATHENA/MINERVA; lion or bull, Fortitude, one of the CARDINAL VIRTUES; human head with snake's body, Deceit personified (see AGES OF THE WORLD – Iron Age); highly polished, reflecting the Gorgon's head, PERSEUS. The shield of Hindu and Tantric Buddhist deities in their ferocious aspect (Sk. *khetaka*) is usually rectangular or circular [iii]. It is carried by SHIVA, KARTTIKEYA, KALKIN, ARJUNA and DEVI (as Durga) among others. In Renaissance art a shield is an attribute of ARTEMIS/DIANA with which she protects her virginity, likewise Chastity personified; also of Rhetoric, one of the SEVEN LIBERAL ARTS. The personifications of History and Victory are seen writing on a shield, recording great events.

Sickle. A crook-shaped sickle [iv: 9th cent. BC], together with a MACE, were the insignia of neo-Assyrian kings and gods (see NINURTA). A sickle is an attribute of the Greek gods of agriculture, DEMETER/CERES and Priapus; also of Summer personified, one of the FOUR SEASONS. The curved sword of the hero Perseus sometimes resembles a sickle. It is an alternative to the SCYTHE with which Cronus castrated Uranus in Greek myth.[55]

Sieve. It sifts the wheat from the chaff, truth from falsehood and the Christian faithful from unbelievers. It is an attribute of Prudence personified, one of the CARDINAL VIRTUES, who discerns these things. It became a symbol of virginity, from the case of the Roman Vestal Virgin, Tuccia, who was accused of adultery and proved her innocence by carrying water in a sieve.[56] A sieve is the attribute of the virgin queen, Elizabeth I, in portraiture [v: Italian, c. 1580], and of Chastity personified, one of the THREE MONASTIC VOWS.

Sistrum. Rattles of various types have been used in the religious rites of many peoples, to induce frenzy or frighten away evil spirits (see also MUSICAL INSTRUMENTS). The sistrum, a kind of

[vi]

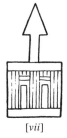

[vii]

[viii]

[ix]

rattle, is seen on a Sumerian cylinder seal of 2500 BC. In Egypt it was sacred to HATHOR, whose rites involved much music-making. Some of the capitals in her temple at Dendera have reliefs depicting sistra. The Egyptian instrument had a handle with the cow-head of Hathor at the top, and a system of jangling disks on cross-bars held in a frame [vi]. The sistrum was deified in the person of Ihy, son of Hathor. It is also the attribute of Bastet, the cat-goddess. It was taken up by devotees of Isis and hence found its way to Rome and beyond. Hathor is not the only deity to be represented on the instrument.

Spade. A triangular spade, the *marru* [vii: neo-Babylonian, 8th cent. BC], was the symbol of Marduk, Mesopotamian god of agriculture and tutelary deity of Babylon. It is seen on cylinder seals of many periods, on boundary stones of the 9th and 8th cents. BC and elsewhere. In Christian art a spade is the attribute of Adam after the Expulsion,[57] Christ 'the Gardener',[58] and St Phocas, also called the 'Gardener'. In Renaissance allegory Spring, one of the FOUR SEASONS, has a spade.

Spear. A common attribute of warriors, hunters and various gods, male and female. It has wider applications. The weapon of Hindu gods is the *shakti* [viii], a Sanskrit word that also came to mean masculine strength and potency, probably because of the weapon's phallic associations. *Shakti*, being a feminine noun, eventually denoted the goddess who is the spouse and active counterpart of male Hindu deities (see DEVI). A Shinto creation myth tells of the Japanese deities Izanagi and Izanami, brother and sister, who created the world from the primeval waters by means of a 'heavenly jewelled spear'.[59] In Egyptian tomb painting a spear, especially that of HORUS, functions as a weapon, destroying evil, usually symbolized by a HIPPOPOTAMUS. A small model of the spear of Horus was placed in the tomb to protect the deceased. In Christian art a martyred saint pierced with spears is the apostle Thomas. The lance of Longinus pierces the side of Christ on the cross. A broken lance sometimes lies at the feet of devotional images of St George. A flaming, golden spear or javelin pierces the heart of St Teresa of Avila, implanting God's love, an image acknowledged to have erotic overtones.

Sphere, Armillary. A spherical skeleton which, by means of a series of metal rings, shows the principal circles of the heavens, including the zodiac belt. Their positions are based on the assumption that the earth is the centre of the universe. It features in Renaissance art as a symbol of the universe, an attribute of learned men and women, and of Astronomy, one of the SEVEN LIBERAL ARTS [ix].

Spindle, Spinning-wheel. An attribute of goddesses who are spinners of fate. Such deities are commonly in groups of three. Of the THREE FATES of Greek myth, Clotho spins the thread of a

[i]

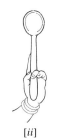

[ii]

[iii]

[iv]

human life. Her spindle is seen in Renaissance painting [*i*]; in classical art she may have a spinning-wheel. The thread which led Theseus safely out of the Cretan LABYRINTH is also a symbol of destiny.

Spoon, or **Ladle** (Sk. *sruk*). Sacred utensil used in Hindu ritual for pouring ghee on the altar fire; the attribute of AGNI and BRAHMA [*ii*]. In Christian art, it is an attribute of Martha who personifies the busy housekeeper.[60]

Staff. Carried by pilgrims, missionaries and other wayfarers for support and, sometimes, protection. The so-called 'alarm staff' (Sk. *khakkhara*; Ch. *hsi chang*; Jap. *shakujo*; Tib. *khar-sil*) with its jangling metal rings is typical of the mendicant Buddhist monk throughout the East [*iii*]. It announces his coming, drowns unwelcome sounds, warns off demons and, according to some, frightens away small creatures that would otherwise be trodden underfoot (for all life is sacred to the Buddhist). It is an attribute of the BODHISATTVAS and AVALOKITESHVARA; of Nagasena, one of the sixteen great ARHATS; of Hachiman, a Shinto/Buddhist deity, once widely venerated in Japan, who is sometimes represented as a monk.

The Christian pilgrim, especially to Compostella, has a plainer staff from which may hang his water-gourd and wallet. It is therefore an attribute of the apostle, James the Greater, whose supposed remains lie in Compostella cathedral. Apostles, such as Philip, in their missionary role may carry a staff. St Ursula, who led eleven thousand virgins on a pilgrimage to Rome, has a red-cross banner flying from hers. The staff of St Christopher, a man of great stature, may be a palm-tree.

A rustic staff is an attribute of the Chinese deity Shou Hsing, god of longevity, one of the three so-called GODS OF HAPPINESS, and of Fuku-roku-jiu and Jurojin, his Japanese counterparts. It has one or two scroll books hanging from it. Sacred staves, kept in Egyptian temples, were surmounted by the head of the resident deity, and were taken into battle by the pharaoh to obtain the god's protection. The staff of HORUS, used to attack SETH as hippopotamus, may be shaped like a harpoon. See also CADUCEUS; CROOK; RING; SCEPTRE; WAND.

Stupa (Sk. 'mound'). Originally a prehistoric burial mound, out of which developed a dome-shaped monumental tomb for Indian princes, subsequently adopted by Buddhism and further developed, embodying a rich symbolism. It held the supposed remains, usually a mere fragment, of Shakyamuni or other BUDDHAS; otherwise it marked a spot made sacred by some episode in Shakyamuni's life. The oldest existing stupa, at Sanchi in central India, was probably founded in the 3rd cent. BC. The later, multi-storey type (usually nine), known as a pagoda (or *dagoba*), is found throughout eastern Asia [*iv: Korean, 12th cent. AD*].

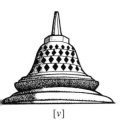

[v]

[vi]

[vii]

[viii]

The central axis of a stupa symbolizes the axis of the universe, like Mt Meru, the sacred MOUNTAIN of Hinduism. In the Japanese wooden pagoda it is an actual pillar forming part of the structure. At the same time the axis is a symbol of the Buddha himself in the state of *Nirvana*. The domed stupa has no pillar, so his statue therefore occupies the central point of the building [*v: Borobudur, Java, later 8th cent. AD*]. The 'cosmic axis' rises through a series of heavenly spheres represented by terraces, storeys or UMBRELLAS [*vi: Gandharan votive stupa, 4th (?) cent. AD*], according to the style of architecture. They also symbolize the progressive stages of meditation that lead ultimately to Enlightenment. The stupa has four monumental doorways facing the four points of the COMPASS. In Mahayana Buddhism each is presided over by one of the four Dhyani-Buddhas (see VAIROCANA). The dome has a square retaining wall or stands on a square base, with the door midway along each side. This is a common type of ground-plan, resembling the MANDALA, and shares its symbolism. An octagonal plan, common in Japanese pagodas, stands for the eight-petalled LOTUS, another cosmic symbol.

Models of the stupa, typically of bronze, were made as votive offerings. A model stupa is an attribute of Abheda, one of the sixteen great ARHATS. A small pagoda, held in the hand, identifies the Japanese warrior, Bishamon, one of the FOUR CELESTIAL KINGS. In Tibetan painting MAITREYA may have a stupa in his diadem. See also DEVI; TREE.

Stylus. Symbol of Nabu, Sumerian god of scribes and writing. It may be set in front of a clay tablet [*vii: Mid-Assyrian, 13th cent. BC*] or be represented as a double stylus standing on an altar. It is occasionally wedge-shaped. Nabu was the son of Marduk and the latter's SPADE is often juxtaposed. Among the Greek MUSES Calliope (epic poetry) and Clio (history) hold a stylus and tablet; the latter otherwise has a scroll. A tablet is an attribute of Atropos, one of the THREE FATES. In Renaissance allegory stylus and tablet are attributes of History, and of Arithmetic, one of the SEVEN LIBERAL ARTS.

Sword. Symbol of power, authority and justice; the attribute of gods, heroes and Christian martyrs too numerous to help identify them. A weapon taken from a beaten enemy became, in the hands of the victor, a symbol of his unconquerable might and authority. Hence, to receive a sword in, say, a coronation rite symbolically confers authority on the monarch. An ogival-shaped sword was one of the insignia of Assyrian kings [*viii*] (see also SICKLE).

Among Hindu deities a sword (Sk. *khadga*) is one of the weapons of SHIVA in his role of 'cosmic hero', KARTTIKEYA, ARJUNA, the war-god, Kala, the god of time, and is among the numerous attributes of Durga (DEVI) and sometimes SURYA. KALKIN, the incarnation of VISHNU as a horse, has a flaming sword. For Buddhists the sword symbolizes wisdom and insight, because it cuts down doubt and ignorance, clearing the way for true knowledge leading to Enlightenment. Thus it is an attribute of several bodhisattvas, in particular MANJUSHRI and PADMASAMBHAVA. In their 'wrathful' Tantric forms it is usually flaming. Mo-li Ch'ing, one of the FOUR CELESTIAL KINGS, wields a sword. When entwined with a snake or dragon it may identify Fudo Myo-O, a Japanese manifestation of VAIROCANA.

For Taoists the sword symbolized victory over the powers of darkness, and is carried on the back of Lu Tung-pin, one of the EIGHT IMMORTALS. He travelled about the Chinese empire using it to destroy dragons and other evils. A magic sword is one of the THREE SACRED RELICS of the Japanese imperial regalia.

The Egyptian dwarf-god, BES, as protector of the household, brandishes a sword.

In Christian art, seven swords pierce the breast of the VIRGIN MARY, symbols of her 'Seven Sorrows'.[61] The image may have originated in an Assyrian goddess who has seven arrows, or swords, radiating from her back, as if from a quiver. A sword is the principal attribute of the Archangel Michael and the apostle Paul (who may have two). Among other Christian martyrs with a sword are: Agnes; Alban; George; James the Greater; Justinia (piercing her breast); Euphemia (likewise, with a lion); Peter Martyr (Dominican friar, embedded in his skull); Thomas Becket (a bishop, likewise); Boniface (a bishop, piercing his book); Adrian (with an anvil); Gervase and Protase (a pair, with whip and sword). Martin of Tours severs his cloak with a sword to share it with a beggar. Lily and sword next to Christ, the judge at the Last Judgement, symbolize the innocent and guilty. A sword emerges from the mouth of Christ, the apocalyptic 'Son of Man'.[62] The sword with which Peter cut off the ear of Malchus[63] is one of the INSTRUMENTS OF THE PASSION.

In medieval and Renaissance art a sword is an attribute of Justice and Temperance, two of the FOUR CARDINAL VIRTUES; Wrath, one of the SEVEN DEADLY SINS; Choler, one of the FOUR TEMPERAMENTS; Rhetoric, one of the SEVEN LIBERAL ARTS; the European SIBYL and Melpomene, the MUSE of Tragedy. The Greek hero PERSEUS has a curved sword. See also AGES OF THE WORLD – Iron Age; BRIDGE; VANITAS.

[i]

Tablet. Two stone tablets of the Law were received by MOSES from God on Mt Sinai.[64] By tradition they are represented on the embroidered curtain that hangs before the 'Ark of the Law' in the synagogue. In Christian art they fall from the hands of the Synagogue personified. A tablet covered with figures is an attribute of Arithmetic, one of the SEVEN LIBERAL ARTS. Victory personified uses a shield for a tablet [*i: Roman, 2nd cent.* AD]. YAMA, Tantric Buddhist Lord of the Dead, records his judgements on a tablet. See also STYLUS.

Tambourine. Like the SISTRUM, once used in ritual dance to

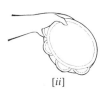

[ii]

[iii]

frighten off evil spirits (see BES), or to induce ecstasy (when held by the Bacchantes, followers of DIONYSUS/BACCHUS). It is an attribute of Erato, MUSE of love poetry, and, in Renaissance allegory, of Hearing, one of the FIVE SENSES, and Vice personified (see VIRTUES AND VICES). The modern instrument is hardly changed from its Roman prototype [*ii: Italian, 15th cent.*].

Temple. Primarily, it was built to serve as the dwelling-place of a god. He or she occupied it in the form of a cult statue placed in the most sacred area. The oldest such buildings are Sumerian and Egyptian. The expression 'house of god' was used widely from Lamaist temple to Christian church. The representation of a temple-like building found in synagogues, Jewish funerary art and on coins, especially in the Graeco-Roman period, is the Torah Shrine [*iii: mid-3rd cent.* AD]. It usually has the form of a portico of three or four columns, sometimes with a pediment. It seems to have been derived from older Near-Eastern models of a temple which housed a god. It is meant to suggest the divine presence and symbolizes the sanctity of the Pentateuch.

A temple also symbolized the universe — heaven, earth and Underworld — in microcosm. The ceiling of the Egyptian temple was painted with STARS and sacred birds to represent the vault of heaven, and plant life sprang as it were from the earth on its carved PILLARS. Likewise, the illusion of a celestial vault was given to the ceiling of the mithraeum with images of sun, moon and planetary deities. The building often had an east–west axis so that the sun-god's first rays fell on his cult image (see MITHRAS). For the temple as the centre of the world axis, see STUPA. Mountain tops, being the abode of many deities, were often the site for a temple, as in the Shinto cult of Sanno. See also ZIGGURAT. The circle and sphere as a symbol of the cosmic mind of God were introduced into Christian architecture influenced by Renaissance humanist thought. Thus, the interior cupola of St Peter's, Rome, by Michelangelo is a perfect hemisphere which, if continued downward to form a sphere, would precisely touch the floor. See also CIRCLE; FOUR PARTS OF THE WORLD – Europe.

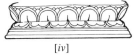

[iv]

Throne. The seat of greater gods and sovereigns and a symbol of their authority, especially in Hindu, Buddhist and Christian art. Sanskrit iconographical treatises [65] describe several distinct types of throne for Hindu deities, two of which are also predominant in Buddhist sculpture and painting: the lotus throne [*iv*], or *padmasana* (which also means 'lotus POSTURE'), and the lion throne, *simhasana*, which has four small lions supporting the corners. LOTUS and LION are both important Buddhist symbols. For a third type, common in eastern Asia, see HOUR-GLASS.

An empty throne had a place in the rituals of many peoples. It evoked the presence of a god, a venerated ancestor or an absent ruler. In Christian art, especially Byzantine, it symbolized God, or the Second Coming or, with a dove and a crucifix (or the book of the gospels), the Trinity. An empty throne was one of the non-figurative images used to represent the Buddha before his human figure had become established. His presence is often indicated by a footstool that shows his footprints.

The devotional image of Christ enthroned is a borrowing from imperial Roman iconography and established itself with the decline of the Western Empire. It presents him as 'Sovereign Lord'. The VIRGIN MARY enthroned is likewise an early image seen first in Byzantine mosaics. Later, in the medieval West, she may be crowned and hold an orb or sceptre as 'Queen of Heaven', a symbol of the Mother Church.

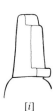

[i]

In Egypt ISIS is represented with a throne as head-dress [i], an allusion to her role as the mother of the pharaoh. A very popular image shows her enthroned suckling her son HORUS, with whom the pharaohs were identified.

Torch. Symbol of life, the fire of love (sacred and profane), the light of truth and the fire of the sun. When turned down and extinguished it denotes sunset, or death. It is an attribute of AGNI, the Vedic fire-god [ii], and of higher ranking priests in the cult of the sun-god MITHRAS, in which purificatory fire rituals were performed. The chariot of the Greek sun-god Helios is preceded by Aurora, the goddess of dawn, holding a torch. It is held by DEMETER/CERES in her search for Persephone. Taweret, the Egyptian HIPPOPOTAMUS goddess, holds a torch to drive off demons. It is one of the weapons of SHIVA, which he inherited from Agni.

[ii]

In Graeco-Roman art Prometheus, who stole fire from heaven, applies a torch, symbolizing life, to the figure of a man when he performs the act of creation. A pair of torches is held by HECATE, goddess of night and the Underworld. A flaming torch held by APHRODITE/VENUS or EROS/CUPID symbolizes the fire of love. A common motif on Roman sarcophagi shows a Cupid, who symbolizes the soul of the deceased, holding a downturned torch denoting death. Occasionally, in his other hand, he holds a crown or garland symbolizing victory over death. These motifs were revived in Renaissance art. In Renaissance allegory the figure of PEACE uses a torch to set fire to a heap of weapons; Temperance, one of the CARDINAL VIRTUES, quenches a torch with a jug of water; Truth sometimes holds one aloft, as does Sight, one of the FIVE SENSES.

A torch is rare in Christian art. It is sometimes one of the INSTRUMENTS OF THE PASSION, from a reference in the fourth gospel to the betrayal of Christ.[66] It is an attribute of certain martyrs burnt at the stake, such as Dorothea. St Dominic may be accompanied by a dog (*Domini canis*) with a torch in its mouth, symbolizing his burning faith. It is an attribute of the Libyan SIBYL. See also FIRE.

Tori-i. The gateway leading to a Shinto shrine, marking symbolically the entrance to sacred precincts. It is regarded by some as a symbol of the 'right direction' of Shinto dogma, the 'Way of

[iii]

[iv]

[v]

[vi]

the Gods'. The *tori-i* at the shrine of the goddess Itsukushima on the island of Miyajima [*iii*] is called the Gateway of Light. There is evidence from Japanese painting that they were introduced at Buddhist temples from about the 16th cent. Whether they evolved from the sculptured gateways (*toranas*) of the early Indian STUPA is uncertain. A possible link is suggested by a 1st cent. AD stupa in the ancient city of Sirkap in North-Western India which has a *torana* carved with birds. *Tori-i* means 'birds' roosting place'.

Tower. The principal attribute of St Barbara whose father locked her in a tower to protect her virginity. It may have three windows, symbolizing the Trinity [*iv: Italian, 15th–16th cent.*]. Barbara is also the Christian patron of armourers and gunsmiths. Her image was once frequent on heavy guns and personal armour, as protector against sudden death. She may have a cannon for attribute. Danaë, a princess of Greek myth, suffered the same indignity but ZEUS/JUPITER, turning himself into a shower of golden rain-drops, entered her chamber and lay with her. The medieval Christian Church saw her as a prefiguration of the VIRGIN MARY who was also impregnated by divine intervention. Hence a tower is one of the attributes in the Annunciation and Immaculate Conception; and in Renaissance allegory of Chastity personified, one of the THREE MONASTIC VOWS.

The twin towers, or pylons, that form the gateway to Egyptian temples (New Kingdom) represent ISIS and her sister Nephthys, guardians of the sanctuary. See also ZIGGURAT.

Trefoil. A combination of three leaves or lobes, a symbol of the Christian Trinity. It is a feature of Gothic church windows [*v: early English, 13th cent.*]. The three-leaved shamrock is said to have been used by St Patrick on an evangelizing mission to the Irish as an example of the Trinity. Hence it became the national emblem and symbol of Ireland. It is occasionally represented in Renaissance painting in scenes of the Holy Family or the VIRGIN MARY in the enclosed garden.

Trident (Sk. *trishula*). A three-pronged weapon first seen on early Mesopotamian cylinder seals where it is the symbol of an unidentified god and probably represents lightning. In the West it became the attribute of marine deities, especially the Graeco-Roman Poseidon/Neptune and of Amphitrite, his wife. It is a symbol of his power to raise storms at sea. Its double-ended form, probably of Assyrian origin, became the THUNDERBOLT. A sacred trident was used in the Israelite rite of sacrifice.[67]

The origin of the Indian trident, or *trishula*, commonly seen in Hindu and Buddhist art [*vi*], is uncertain, as is its relationship, if any, to the western type. Its frequent juxtaposition to the WHEEL of the sun may indicate a former solar symbol. As with the classical trident it evolved a double-ended form which also became a thunderbolt, the *vajra*, symbol of Vajrayana Buddhism

[i]

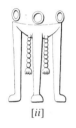

[ii]

[iii]

[iv]

(see BUDDHA). The *trishula* is the most familiar weapon of SHIVA, a connection that has been traced back to the Indus Valley civilization. With a ROSARY, the two together symbolize his destructive and ascetic aspects. Durga (DEVI) slew the buffalo-demon with Shiva's *trishula*. It is the attribute of his spouse and other *shaktis*, especially in their wrathful Tantric forms, also of GANESHA. (See also FLEUR-DE-LIS.)

In Buddhist art the *trishula* may lose its shaft. This type can form the head of Buddha in his oldest non-figurative images. It is placed above the WHEEL, or over the TREE or other column, that forms his body [*i: Sanci, early 1st cent.* BC]. It also stands for the *tri-ratna*, the three symbolic JEWELS of the Buddhist trinity. In Tantric art the *trishula*, with a shaft that transfixes two human heads and a skull, is an attribute of YAMA, Lord of the Underworld, and of PADMASAMBHAVA, the founder of Lamaism, in his wrathful aspect. See also SCEPTRE.

In Christian art, a trident occasionally symbolizes the Trinity, but is also the fork used by Satan and his demons in hell.

Tripod. Originally a form of ancient Greek altar. It became a symbol of achievement in festivals of music and dance from the practice of awarding a tripod as a prize to the *choragus*, or chorus master. It was set up on a monument and dedicated to DIONYSUS. The Choragic Monument of Lysicrates (335 BC) in Athens is well known. A tripod was also associated with prophecy, being the seat upon which the priestess of Apollo at Delphi sat to deliver her oracles [*ii: Greek coin, c. 420* BC]. It is a device on the shield of Ares, Greek god of war, in Attic vase painting.

Trumpet. In some primitive societies it was sounded to ward off evil spirits during rites of circumcision and burial, and at sunset. It was played only by men and had a phallic connotation. Later, the straight bronze trumpet became the instrument of the herald and is associated with the call to arms and proclamations of all kinds [*iii: Roman, 1st cent.* AD]. It is sometimes an attribute of the MUSES Clio, Calliope and Euterpe, though rarely, if ever, in antiquity. In Renaissance art Fame personified has a trumpet, sometimes winged; or two, one short, one long, for good and ill repute. It is also an attribute of Pride, one of the SEVEN DEADLY SINS. In Christian art two angels with trumpets herald the Last Judgement; they also appear to JEROME in a vision. Seven trumpeting angels announce the apocalyptic Day of Wrath.[68] See also BONE (for the Tibetan thigh-bone trumpet); HORN; SHELL; TRIUMPH; VIRTUES AND VICES.

Ts'ung. Chinese JADE object in the form of a hollow cylinder enclosed in a rectangular body. It has been found, sometimes in large numbers, in tombs dating from *c.* 2500 BC. Its purpose and symbolism are unknown, but it may have been intended to protect the corpse [*iv: Chou dynasty*]. From the Sung dynasty the four rectangular surfaces may be decorated with the TRIGRAMS and the YIN AND YANG motif. The corners sometimes bear a stylized face, with prominent eyes, either human or animal (perhaps a dragon). See also CIRCLE.

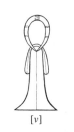

[v]

Tyet. Egyptian amulet of unknown origin, somewhat resembling the knot in the girdle of the gods [v]. From the period of the New Kingdom it was known as the Blood of ISIS and was sacred to the goddess. It was placed in the tomb with the deceased. The *Book of the Dead* calls it a 'knot-amulet of red jasper' through which the power of Isis would protect his body.[69]

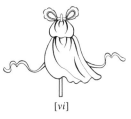

[vi]

Umbrella or **parasol** (Sk. *chatra*; Ch. *t'ien kai*; Jap. *kasa*). Like the CANOPY, an ancient emblem of royalty and high rank throughout the East. Held by VISHNU as a dwarf; by Yashoda, mother of KRISHNA; by Mo-li Hung, one of the Buddhist FOUR CELESTIAL KINGS. It is held over Buddha by Indra, or other attendants. It is one of the Buddhist EIGHT LUCKY EMBLEMS [vi]. The spire of the STUPA may comprise superimposed umbrellas symbolizing the BODHISATTVAS' progressive stages towards *Nirvana*. The Japanese 'umbrella of loving accord' shelters two clandestine lovers.

Urn. The cinerary urn, a receptacle for human ashes, symbolizes death and mourning. It is widely represented in western funerary art with this meaning. A flame issuing from it denotes the renewal of life, or resurrection. In Renaissance art it is the attribute of Artemisia, widow of Mausolus (died 353 BC), ruler of Greek Asia Minor, whose tomb, the Mausoleum, was at Halicarnassus; and of Agrippina, widow of the Roman general Germanicus (died AD 19), who brought his ashes back to Rome.[70] Both women are personifications of conjugal fidelity.

An overturned urn from which water flows is the attribute of river-gods. The god reclines on it; he is bearded and usually crowned with reeds. He is encountered only rarely in Graeco-Roman sculpture, but is widely represented in Renaissance and later art (sometimes with an OAR). He personifies many rivers of classical myth; also the Nile (Finding of Moses[71]) and the Jordan (Baptism of Christ[72]). River-god and urn also stand for Water, one of the FOUR ELEMENTS. See also VASE.

In ancient Rome, an urn symbolized fate since it was used as a receptacle for voting tablets [vii].

[vii]

Vase (Portmanteau word including bottle, flask, jug, pitcher, pot and similar vessels, but see also BUCKET, CHALICE, Canopic JAR, URN). In the most ancient traditions a round vessel symbolized the womb and should be understood in this sense in the very oldest Mesopotamian images of a goddess holding a flowing vase (late 4th to early 3rd mill. BC). It symbolized simply the female principle of fertility and only later came to denote the sacred 'water of life' (see RIVER). In Egypt a pot likewise symbolized creation and birth and was associated with the coming of the

[i]

[ii]

new day. Egyptian goddesses guard the water of life in pots. The pharaoh's offerings to the gods of milk, water or wine were made in round pots. The symbolism of the womb is also present in the Canopic JAR and funerary URN.

A vase or pitcher held by a Hindu or Buddhist deity contains either the divine liquor of immortality or water. The liquor, *amrita* (cognate with *ambrosia*), was obtained, according to a famous myth, by churning the ocean.[73] The *amrita* vessel has various shapes [*i: Tibetan, 19th cent.*]. It is an attribute of the bodhisattva AVALOKITESHVARA and his Chinese and Japanese manifestations, Kuan-yin and Kannon; of the bodhisattva/Buddha MAITREYA and the Tibetan Lamaist saint PADMASAMBHAVA. The ordinary Indian water-pot (Sk. *kamandalu*), commonly seen in stone-carving and bronzes, has various simple shapes. It is an attribute of BRAHMA, SHIVA, DEVI as Durga, VISHNU as a dwarf, and ascetics generally.

A vase, or jar, with a lid [*ii*] is one of the EIGHT LUCKY EMBLEMS of Buddhism and would hold relics or ashes. A similar vase, to store hidden treasures, was added by Lamaists to the Buddhists' SEVEN TREASURES. A pair of ritual goblets, each decorated with a long-tailed animal, is one of the TWELVE ORNAMENTS on Chinese imperial robes.

In early Christian art of the Roman catacombs a vase denotes the receptacle for the deceased's soul. Later, it is an attribute of Mary Magdalene, holding oil of myrrh,[74] and of the women at Christ's tomb.[75] A vase of scented unguent, probably derived from the Magdalene's, is an attribute of Smell, one of the FIVE SENSES in Renaissance allegory. A water-flask may identify St Omobuono and pilgrims generally. A collection of earthenware pots is the attribute of the Spanish martyrs SS. Justa and Rufina.

The wine-vessel of the Greek Dionysus and the Satyrs is usually a *kantharos* (see WINE), sometimes an *amphora*. Hebe, the cup-bearer of the Olympian gods, may hold one or, in Renaissance painting, a pitcher. Temperance personified, one of the four CARDINAL VIRTUES, pours water from one pitcher to another, to dilute wine, while Grammar, one of the SEVEN LIBERAL ARTS, waters plants. An overturned vessel symbolizes VANITAS (emptiness) in still-life paintings. A flaming vase is held by CHARITY and APHRODITE/VENUS as a symbol of Sacred Love (see FIRE).

Vina. Ancient stringed instrument of India, mentioned in the *Vedas*. It is the attribute of the Hindu god Narada, a legendary sage and storyteller, who was said to have invented it. It is also among the instruments of the heavenly musicians, the *Gandharvas*, whose leader was Narada. It is played by Sarasvati, a Hindu RIVER-goddess, spouse and *shakti* of BRAHMA. She is also goddess of speech and learning and the popular tutelary deity of Indian musicians. The vina has a gourd near each end of the finger-board for resonance, but is often represented in a very stylized manner [*iii: Tibetan, 17th cent.*]. The instrument of

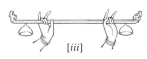

[iii]

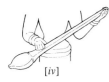

[iv]

[v]

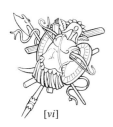

[vi]

Narada is sometimes a long lute [*iv: S. Indian bronze, early 19th cent.*].

Wallet. Part of the gear of the pilgrim and one of his attributes in western Christian art. It hangs from his shoulder or staff. It may carry the badge of his destination: scallop shell for Compostella [*v: French, c. 1500*], crossed keys for Rome, cross for the Holy Land. A wallet is the attribute of the Capuchin monk, Felix of Cantalice, near Rome (*c.* 1513–87). It held the alms he collected for his convent. The Greek god PERSEUS sometimes carries a wallet (containing Medusa's head).[76]

Weapons. The attribute of many gods and heroes, male and female, often symbolizing their power to drive away evil and ignorance. But the symbolism of individual weapons is sometimes contradictory: thus, the arrows of the Vedic god Rudra and Greek APOLLO deliver disease and death while those of EROS/CUPID may kindle the fires of love. Weapons alone are seldom enough to identify their owner. Among the twelve Olympians, the greater Greek gods, Ares/Mars, god of war, wears armour and holds a variety of weapons. Among Hindu gods, the DISK, or discus, Indian CLUB and conch-SHELL (used as a war-trumpet) are typical of Vishnu. Shiva's most characteristic weapons are a TRIDENT, battle-AXE, skull-topped CLUB and a flaming TORCH. Tantric Buddhist deities, especially Tibetan with their strong Shivaist roots, have many weapons in their multiple hands, when represented in their wrathful aspects. They are used to destroy evil and protect devotees. Besides those mentioned above, the following are commonly seen: ARROW; BOW; DAGGER; DRUM; GOAD; KNIFE; MACE; NOOSE; SPEAR; SWORD; THUNDERBOLT.

A trophy in the original sense (Gk. to turn, or put to flight) is a symbol of military victory in imperial Roman art. It was a memorial set up on the field of battle to mark the spot where a defeated enemy turned, and consisted of a wooden post hung with his weapons. In Renaissance allegory it is an attribute of VICTORY personified [*vi: Italian, 16th cent.*]. The figure of PEACE sets fire to a heap of weapons or breaks them under her chariot wheels. The weapons of Europe, one of the FOUR PARTS OF THE WORLD, denote her skill in the arts of the war. They are an attribute of the Iron Age personified, one of the AGES OF THE WORLD; of Fortitude, one of the CARDINAL VIRTUES. In allegories of War, overcome by Love, Cupid stands in triumph on a heap of weapons; amoretti play with Mars' weapons and armour while he dallies with Venus. In VANITAS paintings they are a reminder that arms afford no protection against death. See also LANCE; QUIVER; SHIELD.

Wheel. In ancient Greece, Celtic Europe and in the East a symbol of the sun, which evolved from the earlier solar disk (see SUN). Its spokes were the sun's rays and its rotation suggested the sun's course across the sky. The Greek myth of Ixion, whose punishment was to be tied to an ever-turning fiery wheel, was an echo of primitive human sacrifice to a sun-god.[77] The wheels that 'sparkled like topaz' in the vision of Ezekiel, one of the FOUR PROPHETS, may well have been inspired by a Babylonian solar image.[78] In India the wheel (Sk. *cakra* or *chakra*) was primarily a symbol of the turning year, dependent on the sun. The spokes, according to their number, denoted the season, months or days. It was set in motion by VISHNU.[79] When the wheel was adopted as a Buddhist symbol, the Buddha took over Vishnu's role, taking the title Cakravartin, 'He who turns the Wheel', that is, he who rules the universe.[80] Before he was represented in human form the wheel symbolized the person of the Buddha himself, and was sometimes surmounted by a *trishula* (see TRIDENT). It later became the symbol of Buddhist teaching itself, the 'Wheel of Doctrine', or 'of the Law' (*Dharma-cakra*). In this sense, it is an attribute of VAIROCANA and AVALOKITESHVARA. Wheel and LOTUS are closely associated, both being solar symbols. The latter was given fresh layers of meaning by Buddhists. The flower sometimes forms the hub of the wheel, or its petals the spokes. In this

[i]

form it is also an attribute of Vishnu, which he may retain in his various incarnations [i]. The wheel is one of the symbols of the Buddha's FOOT. It is also sometimes seen on the open palm of his raised HAND. It is one of the EIGHT LUCKY EMBLEMS of Chinese Buddhism (see also SEVEN TREASURES).

A different aspect of Buddhist doctrine is represented by the 'Wheel of Life', the *Bhava-cakra*. It symbolizes the unending cycle of rebirth which mankind suffers and from which Enlightenment offers the only escape. It is seen mainly in Tibetan painting and takes the form of a wheel, usually with six spokes. It is clutched by a demon, a symbol of mankind, clinging desperately to life. At the hub are a cock, snake and pig, symbols of lust, anger and ignorance. The six sectors depict the regions of the gods, demi-gods, mankind, animals, tortured spirits and hell. Human misery is the theme of mankind's sector. Round the rim, we see twelve succeeding stages of human life from birth to death, each complete revolution of the wheel leading inexorably to rebirth. Birth is symbolized by a potter fashioning a man on his wheel, like the Egyptian creator-god, Khnum (see RAM). Death is represented as a corpse carried off to cremation or burial.

In Christian art a broken wheel is the principal attribute of Catherine of Alexandria; a wheel with lighted candles set round the rim identifies Bishop Donatian of Rheims. In Renaissance allegory Dame FORTUNE turns the wheel of fate, on which mankind rises and falls. See also MUDRA; PRAYER-WHEEL; SWASTIKA.

Whip. Symbol of authority, punishment, penance. In Christian art, it is one of the INSTRUMENTS OF THE PASSION. It is an attribute of the penitent Mary Magdalene; the Spanish martyr Vincent of Saragossa and the Agrippine SIBYL. Two figures with whip and

[ii]

[iii]

sword are the Milanese martyrs Gervase and Protase. A whip with three knots, symbolizing the Trinity, belongs to Ambrose, one of the FOUR LATIN FATHERS. In early Greek art, EROS/CUPID chastises the gods with a whip. It is an attribute of the goddess HECATE. In Renaissance allegory Grammar, one of the SEVEN LIBERAL ARTS, chastises her pupils with a whip [ii]. Envy, one of the SEVEN DEADLY SINS, holds a whip.

Window. The image of a woman's face at a window is widely represented in Near-Eastern art, especially on ivory plaques [iii: neo-Assyrian, 8th cent. BC]. It is believed to represent the goddess Astarte (see ISHTAR), or her priestess or votary, beckoning from a temple window, and to symbolize the ritual prostitution that was part of the goddess's cult. The image has been found at several sites in Mesopotamia. Herodotus describes how the women of Babylon were obliged, once in their lives, to visit the temple 'and there consort with a stranger', by way of honouring the goddess.[81]

In Christian art, three windows in a TOWER symbolize the Trinity.

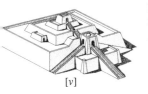

[iv]

Yoke. As a Christian symbol, it belongs to Obedience personified, one of the THREE MONASTIC VOWS. We see it placed on a monk's shoulders by his abbot. In Renaissance allegory it may also symbolize a husband's marital condition [iv: Italian, 17th cent.].[82] Yoga, the Hindu/Buddhist system of spiritual exercises, is connected etymologically with yoke and denotes spiritual discipline. The yoke does not feature in Indian iconography.

[v]

Ziggurat. A staged, pyramidal tower, the typical form of sacred architecture in many cities of Mesopotamia. One of the earliest known was built at Ur about 2200 BC [v: reconstruction]. The best known was at Babylon (7th–6th cents. BC), the biblical Tower of Babel, which was some 300ft high and had seven stages.[83] A ziggurat symbolized the sacred MOUNTAIN that linked heaven and earth. At the top was the shrine of the local deity, where a sacred marriage was performed annually (see ISHTAR). The tower is represented on neo-Babylonian seals [vi: Babylonian, late 2nd mill. BC] sometimes surmounted by a god's symbol, most often the crescent of the moon-god, SIN. See also NINURTA; SHAMASH.

[vi]

Zither (Ch. ch'in). Symbol of Music, one of the FOUR ARTS of the Chinese scholar [vii], sometimes wrongly called a lute. The long zither, of which there are several types, is the oldest stringed instrument of China and existed in Chou times. When played by a philosopher or sage it was said to reveal to him the ultimate truths of life.

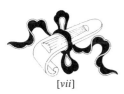

[vii]

4. Earth and Sky

[i]

Aureole. Radiance that surrounds the whole body, or most of it, unlike the HALO, which is round the head only. An aura, seen as flames emanating from the body, was once believed to denote divinity, like the flame flickering on the brow of Ascanius, son of the Trojan prince Aeneas, when his father bore him from Troy.[1] The Pentecostal fire would appear to be a similar phenomenon.[2] The same belief was held by Hindus; in Indian art from the 2nd–4th cents. sacred figures, especially in groups, are framed in an arch of flames (Sk. *prabhatorana*) that springs from the tops of two pillars. The ring of flames surrounding dancing SHIVA has been interpreted in various ways. As a symbol of the light of truth, the energy of divine wisdom emanating from the god, it corresponds to the flaming aureoles that surround the Tantric forms of certain Buddhas and bodhisattvas in India, Indonesia, China and Japan [*i: Japanese, 13th cent.*]. A pointed aureole represents the leaf of the pipal, or bodhi tree of Buddhism (see VAIROCANA: Acala). In Christian art devotional images of the Virgin Mary and Christ at the Transfiguration are often depicted within an aureole (see MANDORLA).

[ii]

Bubbles. Symbol of the brevity and transience of life in VANITAS paintings, and in allegories of time and death. Its source is a Latin proverb, *Est homo bulla*, man is but a bubble, which was revived in the Renaissance. Bubbles are usually blown by infants or putti [*ii: French, 17th cent.*].

[iii]

Carbuncle, 'a glowing coal'. Semi-precious type of garnet which glows dark red in certain lights. It was once believed to emit light spontaneously. Carbuncles adorned the chariots of APOLLO[3] and Aurora. It is a Christian symbol of the blood of Christ and martyred saints. Five carbuncles on the arms and in the middle of a medieval crucifix symbolize Christ's wounds [*iii*].

Cloud (Ch. *yün*; Jap. *kumo*). The oldest cloud symbol is Chinese, described in the *Po-ku-t'u* as a 'cloud-and-thunder pattern'.[4] It is a type of MEANDER which evolved from primitive pictographs and is first seen in Han dynasty art. It symbolizes plenty, which is a heavenly gift brought by the rain. One of the many roles of the Chinese DRAGON was bringer of spring rain, represented as the 'dragon-among-clouds' (Ch. *yün lung*). A glimpse of this heavenly creature, quickly obscured by cloud, symbolized not merely the promise of abundance but the momentary vision of the Tao itself (see EIGHT IMMORTALS). The theme was popularized in Sung painting and reached Japan where the setting is often the sacred Mt Fujiyama. Clouds with rain, or a dragon, also represent the YIN AND YANG and may denote sexual union.

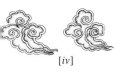

Clouds form the throne or vehicle of numerous Chinese and Japanese deities and immortalized heroes. Formalized cloud patterns occur as decorative motifs on Han dynasty utensils, coffins and elsewhere. They were firmly established on ceramic ware from the T'ang dynasty, generally symbolizing happiness or good luck. *Yün* (cloud) is a near homonym for 'luck' [*iv*]. (They often resemble the more stylized renderings of the FUNGUS of immortality.) In the West, Yahveh veiled himself from Moses' sight in a cloud on Mt Sinai.[5] (See also PILLAR.) A hand emerging from a cloud belongs to God the Father, who was not represented in person before *c.* 13th cent. A cloud receives Christ at his Ascension; he will be borne on a cloud at his Second Coming.

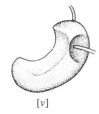

Comma. The *magatama* [*v*] is a comma- or claw-shaped stone of great antiquity found in Japan. Some have also been discovered in Korea. The best examples are made of jade. They were usually strung to form a necklace, and were offered ritually to certain Shinto deities. The jewels offered to AMATERASU to tempt her from her cave were *magatamas*.[6] Together with the sacred mirror and sword they are one of the THREE SACRED RELICS of the Japanese imperial regalia.

Coral. Once worn as an amulet by Mediterranean peoples, especially by children, as a protection against sickness and the 'evil eye'. A necklace of red coral beads appears in pictures of the Virgin and Child. In Graeco-Roman myth it was formed from seaweed petrified by the Gorgon's head, when severed by Perseus [*vi*]. In China coral stands for longevity and is sometimes included among the EIGHT TREASURES. Coral is one of the Japanese group, the TAKARA-MONO, where it symbolizes the power to ward off evil. A coral necklace is an attribute of Africa, one of the FOUR PARTS OF THE WORLD.

Crescent. Symbol of lunar deities, male and female, in many civilizations; also of the Mother-Goddess, when it may be represented as a cow's horns. Chief among Egyptian lunar deities were KHONSU, a mummy with crescent and disk on his head, and THOTH, represented as an ape and similarly crowned. For OSIRIS the moon's phases symbolized his life, death and resurrection. ISIS was identified in Ptolemaic times with the Greek moon-goddess Selene.

The crescent is the symbol of the Sumerian moon-god Nanna (see SIN) [*vii*], who crossed the heavens in a crescent-shaped barque. It is first seen on cylinder seals from Ur. ISHTAR, his daughter, may also have a crescent. The crescent was acquired by SHIVA and is worn in his hair, one of several symbols of his power to create and destroy.

In the West pre-Hellenic Greeks worshipped the moon as a cow from the resemblance between crescent and horns. Thus Io, a moon-goddess, was represented with small horns (see COW). In

classical Greece Artemis and Selene had a crescent for attribute, also Hecate who was associated with them as a lunar
goddess. The woman of the Apocalypse, 'robed with the sun, beneath her feet the moon',[7] whom the Middle Ages saw as the
VIRGIN MARY, stands on the moon, though it is seldom a crescent before the 17th cent. As an Islamic symbol it was introduced by the Seljuk Turks in the 13th cent., perhaps borrowed
from the crescent that had been an emblem of the city of By-
zantium since antiquity. For Chinese and Japanese references,
see MOON.

[i]

Dew. On Greek vase painting Eos (Aurora), the winged goddess
of dawn, sprinkles dew from an amphora. The episode of the dew
on Gideon's fleece[8] was taken to prefigure the impregnation of
the Virgin by the Holy Ghost and is associated with the scene of
the Annunciation. In still-life painting, especially 17th cent.
Dutch, a dew-drop on a leaf [i] or petal symbolizes the evanes-
cence of human life.

Fire or **Flame.** Fire is the manifestation of a god in many religions. The Hindu AGNI, originally Indo-European and prominent
in the *Rig-Veda*, was present in the fire on the sacrificial altar.
The cult of the altar fire, also of Indo-European origin, existed
in ancient Iran and became personified in a god of fire, Atar, son
of the supreme deity of light, Ahura Mazda. The fire emanating
from SHIVA, whose origins were pre-Aryan and can be traced to
the Indus Valley civilization, was initially regarded as a destructive force but subsequently signified his divine energy which
activates the universe. The ring of flames round dancing Shiva
is comparable to the fiery AUREOLE that encircles certain Buddhist
deities. In earliest Buddhist art Shakyamuni himself is represented
as a flaming pillar, symbolizing the radiance shed by his wisdom.
In his later, human form, flames may spring from his shoulders
while water pours from his feet, an illustration of one of his
legendary miracles.[9] In Tantric art the sword of MANJUSHRI is
aflame.

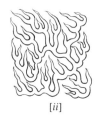

[ii]

In China, fire (*huo*) is masculine (*yang*) and generally has a
positive symbolism: wrath, danger, speed, lust, etc. It denotes
zeal, as one of the TWELVE ORNAMENTS embroidered on imperial
and official robes [ii: *Chinese silk, 17th cent.*]. The Chinese god
of fire is Chu Jung. Like Shiva he has a third eye in the middle
of his forehead. In Egypt, fire was purifying: Taweret, the HIPPO-
POTAMUS goddess, holds a torch to exorcize demons; it was used
for this purpose in Egyptian funerary rites from the Hellenistic
period. It was both protective and destructive: the royal URAEUS
spat flames which protected the pharaoh and destroyed his enemies. Coffin Texts describe various fiery aspects of the next
world, such as a river of fire for sinners, not unlike medieval
Christian images of hell.[10]

The god of the Hebrews manifested himself in a burning
bush[11] (see also THORN), as a pillar of fire[12] and as a fiery pres-

[iii]

ence on Mt Sinai.[13] The 'pentecostal fire' that descended on the brows of the apostles[14] was a manifestation of the Holy Ghost. Fire is purificatory in the Christian doctrine of purgatory and is retributive in hell. A flame, especially a flaming heart, symbolizes religious ardour and is the attribute of St Anthony of Padua, St Augustine and CHARITY personified [iii]. Ordeals by fire, to test faith or innocence, were undergone by the infant Moses,[15] the three in the fiery furnace,[16] St Francis before the Sultan of Egypt, and other figures from history. In Renaissance allegory the flames of passion surround Lust, one of the SEVEN DEADLY SINS. See also FOUR ELEMENTS; FOUR TEMPERAMENTS — Choleric.

[iv]

Globe. Held by a deity or monarch it represents the earth or universe and symbolizes his sovereignty over it. In Christian art, surmounted by a cross, it is held by Christ and God the Father. In this form it is also one of the insignia of English kings (since Edward the Confessor) and of Holy Roman Emperors. A globe is the attribute of gods and allegorical figures, denoting their universality, especially Truth, Fame, Abundance, Justice (one of the CARDINAL VIRTUES), Geometry (one of the SEVEN LIBERAL ARTS), EROS/CUPID, and Lachesis (one of the THREE FATES). Under FORTUNE's feet it indicates instability, i.e. her waywardness [iv: after Mantegna]. Under the feet of PHILOSOPHY it denotes her superior status. In VANITAS still-life paintings a terrestrial globe stands beside the earthly possessions that death will take away. A celestial globe (which should show the constellations) belongs to Urania, MUSE of Astronomy, and to Astronomy personified, one of the SEVEN LIBERAL ARTS. It was borne on the shoulders of the Titan Atlas, as a punishment, a burden temporarily assumed by HERCULES.[17] The sphere, in general, symbolizes the heavens, concentric spheres, usually nine, representing the universe in medieval and Renaissance art. See also SPHERE, ARMILLARY.

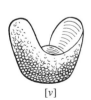

[v]

Gold. The colour of the sun and sun-gods. In Egypt RE and HATHOR are described as golden. Being impervious to change it symbolized survival after death; hence the pharaoh's and nomarch's death masks were made of gold. Masks of lesser folk were painted yellow. Gold is a symbol of Buddhist illumination or Enlightenment, and of the Buddha's own nature. Gilding is therefore used for effigies of Buddhas, in particular of MAITREYA. In paintings, gold pigment is used typically for the aureoles of gods. In Chinese painting a gold or silver ingot shaped like a boat or shoe [v] expresses the hope of future wealth, especially at the new year or at a wedding. Such ingots were first produced in the Yüan dynasty, and were given as presents bearing appropriate good luck inscriptions. Three ingots denote 'May you succeed in the three state examinations.' As a Christian symbol gold is the pure light of heaven. Alternatively it denotes idolatry, as in the case of the golden calf.[18]

[i]

Halo, or **Nimbus.** In the oldest images of sun-gods the halo takes the form either of a plain disk or of beams of light radiating from their heads (see SUN). At first the solar disk framed the whole body, subsequently the head only. This development probably began with Ahura Mazda in Persia , or SURYA in India. (In Egypt the disk of RE, HATHOR and Sakhmet appears above the head as part of a crown.) The radiant type of nimbus is typical of AMATERASU, MITHRAS, APOLLO and Helios/Sol [*i: Roman, 2nd cent.* AD], and hence of certain deified Roman emperors. The oldest extant images of Hindu deities with a nimbus belong to the 2nd–4th cents. AD. It is either a plain circle or a lotus in full flower. Hindu iconographic texts[19] call for a nimbus (Sk. *shirash-chakra*) for all deities, but that is by no means regularly observed. In Buddhist art the Wheel of the Law, one of several symbols used to represent Shakyamuni in his earliest, non-figurative phase, was originally a solar disk. A plain nimbus and aureole round his human figure are first seen on coins and sculpture from N.W. India (W. Pakistan) about 2nd–3rd cents. AD, probably a Greek stylistic influence. Nimbus and aureole in various forms remained a feature of Buddhas, some BODHISATTVAS (e.g. AVALOKITESHVARA; Kshitigarbha) and ARHATS wherever Buddhist art penetrated.

The nimbus appears in Christian art about the 5th cent. when the western Roman Empire was collapsing and the Church, adopting many imperial formulae, elevated Christ into a symbolic sovereign, all-powerful ruler. The Mithraic cult may also have been an influence: as Christianity gradually supplanted worship of the sun-god, churches were built over Mithraic temples (e.g. Santa Prisca and San Clemente in Rome) where haloed images of Mithras and Sol may still be seen. The nimbus was at first confined to the three persons of the TRINITY and angels. A cruciform nimbus usually belongs to Christ alone [*ii: Venetian, 13th cent.*]; a triangular shape (the Trinity) to God the Father. A square denotes living persons and a hexagon virtues personified. The nimbus is seldom seen in post-Renaissance Christian art. See also DISK, AUREOLE.

[ii]

Hill. An early Egyptian creation myth from Heliopolis describes a hill, or mound, emerging from the primeval waters.[20] It was identified with Atum, the Heliopolitan sun-god and creator. The city itself came to be regarded as the 'primeval mound', the centre of the universe. Atum was originally worshipped in the form of an obelisk, called *benben*; later, in human form, he is depicted enthroned upon the mound. A similar cult at Memphis was devoted to a local fertility god, Tatenen, the deity responsible for providing the silt left when the Nile inundation receded annually. He later became identified with PTAH. In Heliopolitan funerary rites the pharaoh's statue was placed on a heap of sand in the tomb, symbolizing his ascent to meet the god. The Coffin Texts (Middle Kingdom, *c.* 2050–1786 BC) introduce a new

[iii]

concept of the after-life. The deceased spends it in the Field of Reeds carrying out agricultural work to ensure his material well-being (later delegated to a *ushabti*). The field has fourteen hills, or mounds, on which gods and spirits dwell who protect the deceased. The second is the hill of Re-Harakhte (see RE), the sun-god, who rises from it each day [iii].[21] In New Kingdom funerary art Osiris, as ruler of the Underworld, is enthroned on the mound to judge the dead. See also MOUNTAIN, the abode of other deities.

Jade (Ch. *yü*). The most highly prized of Chinese gem-stones. A Han scholar wrote: 'Jade is the fairest of stones. It is endowed with five virtues. Charity is typified by its lustre, bright yet warm; rectitude by its translucency, revealing the colour and markings within; wisdom by the purity and penetrating quality of its note when the stone is struck; courage, in that it may be broken, but cannot be bent; equity, in that it has sharp angles, which yet injure none.'[22] The earlier Chou period had seen the production of a variety of jade objects to which magical powers were attributed. They served as amulets and had ritual functions. Others symbolized the four quarters of the universe. Jade objects were used to protect the body after death, especially the *pi* [iv] and TS'UNG. A CICADA of jade was placed in the mouth of the deceased. An entire suit made of pieces of jade has been discovered on the body in a Han dynasty tomb. See also MUSICAL STONE; TIGER.

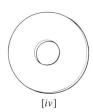

[iv]

Mandorla. The almond-shaped AUREOLE, also called a *vesica piscis* (fish-bladder) that, since early Christian art, sometimes frames Christ at the Ascension.[23] Originally it represented the cloud in which he ascended and gradually assumed the characteristics of an aureole. It also surrounds Christ at his Transfiguration; the VIRGIN MARY at her Assumption and elsewhere [v], and Mary Magdalene at her Assumption.

[v]

Moon. The Mother-Goddess and related female deities were always associated with the moon, since the moon's phases coincided with women's menstrual cycle that the moon was once believed to control. All Greek goddesses were once lunar deities and some, such as Selene and DIANA/ARTEMIS, retain the moon as an attribute, especially in the form of the CRESCENT. Hecate, goddess of the Underworld and patron of witches, has three bodies, or three faces, one for each of the moon's phases. Some earlier primitive societies regarded the moon as male, impregnating women and causing the growth and productiveness of crops.

This aspect of moon-worship was also present in the cult of Soma in India and in Iran (where it is called Haoma). Soma was a greatly revered plant from which a concoction was made and was drunk ritually for the sake of its hallucinatory properties. It was ambrosial, an offering to the gods, promising immortality

[i]

to all who drank it. It became deified and was later personified by the moon, where it was believed to grow.

In China the moon (*yueh*) is the subject of many folk-tales. It is *yin* (feminine and negative), unlike the sun, which is *yang* (masculine and positive). The most important of the various Festivals of the Moon is still celebrated by women and children at full moon at the autumn equinox, when little images of a HARE were given sacrificial offerings. The hare inhabits the moon, like the three-legged toad, or FROG. The Chinese moon-goddess, Ch'ang-O [i] was transformed into the moon-toad (Ch. *ch'an ch'u*) as a punishment for stealing the elixir of immortality. 'Moon-blossom', which occasionally falls to earth, makes pregnant any woman who swallows it. The moon with its hare is one of the TWELVE ORNAMENTS on Chinese imperial robes. In Japan the old Shinto deities of sun and moon (*tsuki*) were female and male respectively, the opposite of Chinese. They were born from the left and right eye of the god of creation, Izanagi.[24] Since the emperor was descended from the sun-god, the moon came to symbolize the empress. Much Chinese lunar folk-lore made its way to Japan, including the festival of the Japanese moon-god, Susano-O, which was celebrated at the same season of the year. In the Far East, as in Mediterranean civilizations, the phases of the moon symbolized regeneration, that is, the fertility of crops and, later, resurrection in the after-life. For Buddhists the circle of the full moon symbolizes perfect truth, the full knowledge of *dharma*, the Law. See CRESCENT for references to Egypt, Sumer, India, Greece, Virgin Mary. See also HORUS; KHONSU.

Mountain. Throughout the ancient world there were many sacred mountains that were the abode of gods and which provided a link between heaven and earth. According to some cosmologies the sacred mountain was also the centre and axis of the whole universe (see also OMPHALOS). Twin peaks were sometimes the dwelling-places of the sun and moon. In Egypt the moon-god THOTH dwelt in a temple on the mountain range west of Thebes. In the Egyptian netherworld was a mountain topped by a throne to which the pharaoh ascended by a ladder after death. The cities of Mesopotamia constructed their own sacred mountain, the ZIGGURAT, with a temple at the summit. The principal Mesopotamian Mother-Goddess was called Lady of the Mountain (Ninhursag) since mountains were the ultimate source of water and hence fertility.

India has many sacred mountains. Mt Kailasa in the Himalayas is the home of SHIVA and a centre of pilgrimage (see also DEVI). Buddhism taught that the earth was flat and circular with a mountain (Mt Meru) at the centre which formed the throne of the Buddha (see also HOUR-GLASS). The STUPA and pagoda were symbolic representations of Mt Meru with the cosmic axis running through the centre of the building (see further VAIROCANA).

The home of the bodhisattva AVALOKITESHVARA was the mythical Mt Potala. The hill on which the palace of the Dalai Lama stands at Lhasa was given the same name when he occupied it in the 16th cent., since he is regarded as the reincarnation of the bodhisattva.

Mountain deities are numerous in Japan. Originally Shinto and gradually incorporated into Buddhism, they are often associated with the fertility of the land and are the object of pilgrimages and annual festivals. Fujiyama is the most revered. Its tutelary deity was the goddess Sengen, to whom a temple was built on the summit in AD 806. She is widely represented in Japanese art carrying a branch of wisteria and wearing a large hat. Her cult was replaced by a trio of Buddhist deities who are represented on three peaks towards which a file of pilgrims makes its way. Among others are Sanno of Mt Hiei; the fierce Shingon deity, Zao Gongen, of Mt Kimpu; and the numerous deities of the Kumano region with its sacred waterfall, near which Mt Potala, sacred to AVALOKITESHVARA, was believed to be situated.

[ii]

A mountain is one of the TWELVE ORNAMENTS on Chinese imperial robes. In Taoist myth it represents the Isles of the Blest, the abode of the Immortals where the sacred FUNGUS grows, or the Hills of Longevity (see EIGHT IMMORTALS). It is a popular scenic subject in ceramics and lacquer painting where three, occasionally five or seven, peaks, very stylized, rise out of the waves of the Eastern Sea [*ii: Ming, late 15th cent.*]. Mountains were a retreat for Chinese hermits, like the Theban desert for early Christians. Here they hoped to discover the gateway to the Immortals' paradise through some crevice in the rocks. The Taoist mountain is also sculptured depicting the Immortals together with Taoist symbols. It was an object of contemplation for scholars. (See also CENSER.)

In the Old Testament Jehovah spoke to Moses from the top of Mt Sinai (or Horeb). Medieval world maps, which were generally circular, placed Jerusalem in the middle so that Calvary, traditionally described as a hill, was at the very centre of the Christian universe. (See also HILL.)

[iii]

Omphalos. The belief that one's own country, or, more specifically, a sacred hill or mountain within it, was the centre of the earth or even the axis of the cosmos was held by the Egyptians, Babylonians, Assyrians and others. (See MOUNTAIN.) For the ancient Greeks the place was marked by the omphalos, or navel, the stone monument in the temple of Apollo at Delphi [*iii: pre-Hellenic*]. According to Strabo[25] the spot was determined by Zeus who let fly two eagles (some say crows) from the east and west ends of the earth. Delphi was the place where they met.

[iv]

Rainbow (Gk. *Iris*). The throne of sky-gods and a link between heaven and earth. Christ at the Last Judgement may sit on a rainbow which, if three-coloured, denotes the Trinity [*iv: Italian,*

[i]

15th cent.]. The Hebrew Yahveh set a rainbow in the clouds as a token of his covenant with Noah.[26] Iris, the messenger of the Greek gods, is represented on Attic vases with wings and holding a CADUCEUS (as the female counterpart of Hermes), but she is without a rainbow until the Renaissance. In China a rainbow symbolized the union of YIN AND YANG and is therefore an emblem of marriage.

River. A sacred source of fertility, nourishing life. River deities are therefore often female. Mesopotamian deities hold vases from which streams flow, often dividing into four. Examples from the royal palace at Mari on the Euphrates [*i: 20th–19th cent.* BC] show flowing vases held by attendants of the Mother-Goddess, ISHTAR; they are also seen on her temple (of Inanna) at Uruk (15th cent. BC). There are late Assyrian examples that could well be the inspiration for the biblical four rivers of Paradise (which medieval Christians interpreted as symbols of the four gospels).[27] The idea that certain rivers confer immortality was widespread. It occurs in a Sumerian myth of Inanna's descent into the Underworld,[28] in the Greek myth of Achilles dipped in the Styx,[29] and in the practice of bathing in the Ganges. It is also present in rites of baptism, Christian and pagan.

Three principal rivers of India, Ganges, Jumna and Sarasvati, are identified with life-giving Mother-Goddesses, who are widely represented in Hindu art. They are often found as guardians at Temple gateways, accompanied by wild ducks and other water birds, and may be mounted on a marine monster or turtle, or a lotus. The Ganges, whose deity is Ganga, is the most sacred of Indian rivers. It descends from the heavenly dwelling-place of SHIVA in the Himalayas, according to a myth which is strikingly represented in a famous rock-carving at Mamallapuram, near Madras.[30]

Two male gods are associated with the Nile: the ram-headed KHNUM, who regulates the annual inundation, and Hapy, fully human with pendent breasts, who personifies the inundation itself. Greek river-gods were also male and are typically crowned with reeds, reclining on an overturned urn from which water flows.

The Greek Underworld had four rivers: Acheron, Styx (the principal river), Phlegethon (a river of fire) and Cocytus.[31] A fiery river also confronted the deceased in the Egyptian Underworld,[32] as did the flaming river of hell in Byzantine representations of the Last Judgement. (See also FOUNTAIN.)

Rock. For many early peoples certain rocks and stones, in their original, natural state, were the abode of a god and therefore holy. The Mother-Goddess of Asia Minor, Cybele, was worshipped in the form of a meteoric stone, which in 204 BC was brought to Rome where a temple was built for it on the Palatine. The stone at Bethel (= 'house of God') in Canaan, which the Hebrew patriarch, Jacob, used as a pillow, was a similar case.

[ii]

[iii]

[iv]

(See LADDER.) Anointing it, as Jacob did, was common practice. A rock is a symbol of Christ, the Church, steadfast faith and a metaphor for the apostle Peter. Water struck from the rock by Moses[33] is the spiritual refreshment the Church provides.

Rocks are a popular motif in Chinese paintings and ceramic decoration. They are typically given outlandish shapes, often having birds perched on them and sometimes sprouting plants. They symbolize the stability, permanence and calm of the Taoist paradise. Cracks and holes in the rock are said to afford glimpses of constellations in that far-off region [ii: Ming, 16th cent.]. For the Chinese, rocks also stand for long life and firm friendship among the old. Sacred stones once existed in various parts of China and were invoked to produce rain and, by women, in the hope of conceiving male children. See also MOUNTAIN; OMPHALOS; PILLAR; STONE.

Shadow. It was once widely believed that a person's shadow was an intrinsic, vital part of his being, able to influence for good or ill those on whom it fell. Christian art depicts an episode from the ministry of the apostle Peter when the sick were carried into the street in the hope that his shadow would fall on them.[34] In Egyptian tomb painting of the New Kingdom the deceased's shadow is seen leaving his body, sometimes accompanied by the *ba*, his soul [iii]. (See also BIRD.) The shade of the flabellum, or fan, gave divine protection to the pharaoh. In China a so-called 'shadow wall', sometimes painted with a large red sun, was erected before the entrance to official buildings to keep harmful influences away.

Sibitti, the 'Seven'. A group of seven unnamed Mesopotamian gods. They are first represented on early Babylonian cylinder seals (1st half of 2nd mill. BC) and later on boundary stones and stelae. They take the form of seven disks or hemispheres, arranged in two rows or as a rosette [iv: Mitannian, 15th–mid-14th cent. BC]. They became identified with the Pleiades and then were arranged like the constellation. They were derived from a set of seven pebbles, originally used for casting lots, later for divination, and hence they became deified. Thus they are depicted above scenes of battle, sickness, or other situations where fate hangs in the balance. In neo-Assyrian reliefs they are seen among other non-figurative images of deities guarding the king. They are also associated with the goddess ISHTAR, as a planetary deity, when they may be represented as rosettes (see ROSE).

Star. The belief that stars and planets are gods and goddesses was common in many religions. They were deities who had the power to influence people and events on earth below, a concept that was expanded into an elaborate pseudo-science in ancient Babylonia. Stellar motifs are a feature of much ancient art, serving as symbols and attributes of the gods. The Mesopotamian Mother-Goddess, ISHTAR, who was identified with the planet

[i]

Venus, was represented as an eight-pointed star, probably derived from a cuneiform sign that denoted divinity [i]. It often forms a triad with lunar crescent and solar disk. Ishtar's horned cap may bear an eight-pointed star (see also SIBITTI). The star that led the Persian magi to Bethlehem[35] is taken to be the planet Venus. It is also a symbol of CHRIST, the 'bright star of dawn'.[36]

[ii]

The Pyramid Texts indicate a very early Egyptian cult of the stars. They mention Sothis, goddess of the annual Nile flood, who gave birth to the morning star[37] – she was later identified with the dog-star, Sirius, and wears a five-pointed star on top of her crown. Seshat, goddess of writing, has a head-dress of a seven-pointed star, or possibly a rosette (the symbolism is obscure), and holds the serrated leaf of a PALM. Specially venerated were the circumpolar stars, the 'imperishable ones' because they never set. Stars existed in the Underworld and so were known as 'followers of OSIRIS', its ruler. Thus, ceilings of royal tombs are decorated with stars, always five-pointed [ii]. Tomb paintings may also depict the goddess Nut who personified the vault of the heavens, or firmament. She is typically represented with her body arched over the earth (see ARCH) and may be sprinkled with stars.

[iii]

For the Chinese, too, the stars and constellations were deities who influenced earthly affairs. Three stars form one of the TWELVE ORNAMENTS on the emperor's robes and decorate the robes of the GODS OF HAPPINESS who are called Star Gods. The Pole Star symbolized a virtuous emperor. The Great Bear, or 'Northern Dipper', because of its resemblance to a rice-scoop, was a measure of material prosperity. It was also the abode of K'UEI HSING, god of examinations. It is represented as seven small circles linked by lines [iii], like the three on the imperial robes. The stars Aquila and Vega symbolize two separated lovers, he a herdsman, she a weaver, in a Chinese legend very popular with artists in China and Japan.[38] Once a year, in July when the stars were in conjunction, a flock of MAGPIES formed a bridge – the Milky Way – that allowed the girl to cross and meet her man, a symbol of faithful yet thwarted love.

The Graeco-Roman family of astral deities (Venus, Mars, Mercury, Castor and Pollux, etc.) had its roots in ancient Babylonia. In spite of opposition by early Christian writers the idea of a link between gods and stars crept into Christian thought and art. Christ, as we saw, had a stellar epithet, as did the VIRGIN MARY who was 'Star of the Sea' (Stella Maris). She wears one on her cloak and is crowned with a circlet of stars as Virgin of the Immaculate Conception. A star is an attribute of SS. Dominic (on his brow) and Thomas Aquinas (on his habit). In Renaissance allegory a crown of stars is worn by Urania, MUSE of Astronomy. Together with flowers and fish stars adorn the robe of PHILOSOPHY. See also COMPASS; ZODIAC.

Stone. For its principal symbolism see ROCKS; OMPHALOS; JADE;

[iv]

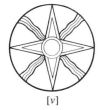

[v]

MUSICAL STONE; COMMA; JEWELS; CRANE. Among Christian saints Bavo has a falcon on his wrist and carries a heavy stone, symbol of his former sins; Jerome, one of the FOUR LATIN FATHERS, as a penitent hermit beats his bare breast with a stone; Stephen, stoned to death, has, in devotional images, one or more stones resting on the crown of his head [iv: Italian, late 15th–early 16th cent.]. Poverty personified holds a heavy stone (see THREE MONASTIC VOWS).

Sun. Once worshipped worldwide as a supreme, all-seeing god of light, source of fertility and life; also, because of its setting and rising, a symbol of death and resurrection. The god was generally male and had links with the MOON who was female (see YIN AND YANG), though in Japan the sexes are reversed. Vestiges of sun-worship have survived in a variety of symbols, such as the equilateral CROSS, SWASTIKA, TRISKELE, ROSETTE and WHEEL, which travelled from one country to another.

The Mesopotamian sun-god, SHAMASH, first took the form of a four-pointed star with four flames or rays [v: Sippar, 9th cent. BC]. It is also the form of the storm-god ADAD. Erected on a post it stood at the entrance of the temple. It was also used as an amulet. The sun-symbol in Egypt was usually a plain disk. The oldest Egyptian solar god, whose cult dates from the Early Dynastic period, was RE, worshipped principally at Heliopolis (the 'sun-city'). His disk is encircled by a URAEUS. Re had links with HORUS who may wear the same symbol. The Egyptians, like some other peoples, divided the sun's passage across the sky into three phases, sunrise, noon and sunset, which they represented by a SCARAB, the disk of Re, and RAM-headed gods such as AMUN and Khnum. The sun-god Aten, whose cult reached its peak in the 18th Dynasty, is depicted curiously as a disk shedding its long rays towards the earth, each ray terminating in a hand, one or two of which hold an ANKH. The sun's disk may crown other deities, mostly linked in some way to Re: the sacred BULLS, Apis and Mnevis; the ram-god of Middle Egypt, Heryshaf; the cow-goddess HATHOR, and MONTU, the war-god of Thebes.

The cult of the sun among the northern Indo-European peoples is seen in the *Rig-Veda*, which describes five solar gods, all having human form, some of whom drive their CHARIOTS across the heavens.[39] They are MITHRAS, the golden Savitri, Pushan who guards the well-being of flocks and herds, VISHNU and SURYA. Vishnu crossed the universe in three strides,[40] symbolizing the three phases of the sun's journey across the sky. Surya, the 'all-seeing', eventually became the dominant solar deity of Hinduism and had numerous temples in India. He may have a solar disk or hold a lotus bloom in each hand that resembles the solar ROSETTE. In late bronzes he wears a halo. For other sun-gods in human form, see HALO. For the solar aspect of the Buddha Shakyamuni, see WHEEL.

There are traces of former sun-worship among the Chinese, perhaps due to the influence of Zoroastrianism which reached the Far East during the T'ang dynasty. But primarily the sun embodies the male principle, *yang*, and was a symbol of the emperor and his powers. It is one of the TWELVE ORNAMENTS on the imperial robes where the solar disk encloses a three-legged raven or cock (see also TRISKELE). A solar eclipse was a sign that the emperor was being overshadowed by the empress, who was symbolized by the moon (*yin*). In Japan, too, the sun was closely associated with the imperial family who claimed to be descended from the Shinto sun-goddess, AMATERASU. The sun on the Japanese national flag, *Hi no maru* ('Flag of the Sun'), was derived from the Chinese flag.

The tendency of the early Christian Church to absorb and transmute pagan cults brought sun, moon and stars into art. Sun and moon accompanied images of Persian and Greek solar gods, and thence were introduced on Roman coins depicting the emperor. From there they were transferred to images of Christ enthroned, which deliberately imitated imperial formulae. Christ was then known as the Sun of Righteousness.[41] Sun and moon are also introduced into the scene of Christ's baptism and crucifixion. The VIRGIN MARY, when represented as the Immaculate Conception, is from the mid-17th cent. 'robed with the sun, beneath her feet the moon, and on her head a crown of twelve stars'. This is a description of the Woman of the Apocalypse,[42] who was assumed in the Middle Ages to symbolize the Virgin. In Renaissance allegory the sun is an attribute of Truth. See also SNAKE.

[i]

Thunderbolt. The representation of a lightning-flash, believed by ancient peoples to be the destructive weapon of a sky-god. In Mesopotamia it is first seen on Akkadian cylinder seals in the form of a two- or three-pronged fork [*i: Assyro-Kassite, late 12th cent.* BC]. In the neo-Assyrian period (9th–8th cent. BC) the fork with three prongs became double-ended, making a kind of double TRIDENT (see NINURTA). In this form it was the symbol of the storm-god ADAD and Near-Eastern deities related to him: Hadad in Syria, Phoenicia and Canaan, and the Hittite Teshub. It reached Greece from Asia Minor where it became the classical thunderbolt of ZEUS/JUPITER, sometimes held in the claws of his EAGLE. It spread across Roman Gaul, appearing on pagan monuments in the early Christian era. The thunderbolt was revived in the Renaissance with various embellishments [*ii: Italian, 17th cent.*] as an attribute of Jupiter and also of Fire personified, one of the FOUR ELEMENTS.

[ii]

In the East the thunderbolt (Sk. *vajra*; Jap. *kongo*) was originally the weapon of INDRA, chief god of the Vedic pantheon and bringer of rain. With it he slew Vritra, the demon of drought and darkness. It was among the numerous Hindu symbols taken over by Buddhists who gave it wide, metaphysical dimensions.

[*iii*]

Thus the weapon that gave the rain-god his invincibility became a symbol of the adamantine, diamond-hard core of Buddhist philosophy (Ch. *chin-kang-shih* = diamond, adamantine), the state of *Nirvana* which cannot be undone or dissolved. It also came to represent a magical power which the believer, through prayer and contemplation, could compel the gods to grant him. This was the doctrine of a Buddhist sect called the 'Vehicle of the Thunderbolt', or Vajrayana. (See further, BUDDHA; DEVI.) The typical image was a double-ended trident [*iii*], sometimes two together forming a cross. It pervades all Vajrayana imagery and is also used as an implement in the sect's rituals. Thunderbolt and BELL together complemented each other as symbols of PHALLUS and womb respectively. A bell with a *vajra*-shaped handle is also used in their ritual. The *vajra* is an attribute of many sacred figures of the Mahayana sect of Buddhism, e.g. the Dhyani-Buddhas, Akshobhya and Amoghasiddhi (see VAIROCANA); the BODHISATTVA Vajrapani, an attendant of the Buddha; PRAJNA-PARAMITA; the Lamaist saint PADMASAMBHAVA and other lesser Tibetan deities; Zao-Gongen, the fierce tutelary god of the Shinto Buddhist cult of the same name; and the Gate Guardians of Buddhist temples (see FOUR CELESTIAL KINGS). It may form a border (repeated eight, sixteen, or thirty-two times) on the MANDALA where its purpose is to exclude harmful influences. See also MEANDER.

Water. The primeval element from which all was created, therefore an archaic symbol of the womb and of fertility; also purification and rebirth. Among the many creation myths of India, the Near East and Egypt those that postulate the existence of a cosmic ocean before the world came into being have a prominent place. The *Rig-Veda* says 'In the beginning everything was like the sea and without light.'[43] In later texts BRAHMA, the creator, raises the earth from the waters at the beginning of each cosmic age, or *kalpa*,[44] a role subsequently taken over by VISHNU. The latter is first depicted in Gupta sculpture reclining asleep on the waters. His couch is the thousand-headed snake, Ananta. From his navel grows a LOTUS, on which Brahma sits.[45] In Hindu households a jar of water, symbolizing the divine presence, is kept for daily ritual. Water and lotus were a Buddhist symbol, taken over from the orthodox Hinduism [*iv: Japanese bronze, 8th cent. AD*].[46]

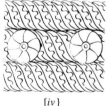

[*iv*]

The vault of heaven, or firmament, that separates the upper from the lower waters is a feature of Hindu and other cosmologies. The ancient Babylonian poem of creation, *Enuma Elish*, dating from the early 2nd mill. BC, tells how 'all lands were sea' until the creator, Marduk or Bel, created the firmament.[47] It was followed by the complete creative process which took seven days, culminating with man. This would appear to be the source of the Hebrew account in Genesis.[48] In Christian art the days of creation form the first part of a cycle of scenes, common in medieval churches, that makes a statement, in microcosm, of the Christian universe.

Water is the primeval matter in several Egyptian creation myths. In the beginning a mound arose from the water bearing the creator-god of Heliopolis, Atum.[49] The mound was the centre of earth and the city was built upon it. Alternatively a lotus bud floated on the surface and opened to reveal HORUS in the role of sun-god whose rays spread over the earth, like the much later Hindu creation myth. Water, as the source of fertility for dwellers in the Nile valley, symbolized the female creative process, yet at the same time the deity who personified it was Nun, a male. He was present in the sacred lakes within Egyptian temples where priests performed purificatory rites of ablution. Similar baths, or water tanks, are part of Hindu temples, and one has been excavated at the ancient Indus Valley city of Mohenjo-Daro (3rd–2nd mill. BC). The neo-Assyrian temple of the god of fresh water at Assur had a similar tank (see EA). Symbolic purification by washing was a necessary preliminary to ensure that subsequent rituals would be effective. Its meaning was extended in the rite of baptism, practised by many peoples. For Christians it is not only a cleansing of sin but also a symbolic rebirth within the Church. The crossing of the Red Sea by the Israelites[50] and the story of the Flood[51] were seen as prefigurations of Christian baptism.

For Egyptians water had other magical properties, symbolically life-giving. A libation of water during funeral rites ensured the reanimation of the deceased in the after-life. It was also prophylactic. An inscription promising protection against scorpions and snakes was sometimes carved at the foot of a statue. It was drenched with water which, when drunk, made a magical medicine.

The oldest Greek creation myth associates the primordial water with a Mother-Goddess. 'In the beginning Eurynome, the goddess of all things, rose naked from Chaos, but found nothing substantial to rest her feet upon and therefore divided the sea from the sky'[52] (the firmament again). The myth is probably an echo of the matriarchal religion of the prehistoric inhabitants of Greece, the Pelasgians (whose name means 'water'). A later myth makes Eurynome the daughter of Oceanus. He personified the waters that girded the earth, out of which all living things were born.[53] In classical times the ruler of the sea was Poseidon/Neptune who ordered his subjects with a TRIDENT. The goddess APHRODITE/VENUS was born of the sea and worshipped as creatrix in many seaports and islands of the eastern Mediterranean.

Water is one of the FOUR ELEMENTS (five in China). Aquatic grass, or water-weed, is one of the TWELVE ORNAMENTS on Chinese imperial robes [i: Chinese silk, 17th cent.]. To water plants to make them grow symbolizes the nourishment of the intellect (see SEVEN LIBERAL ARTS – Grammar).

[i]

In ancient art water is represented by a variety of curvilinear motifs. The Minoans of Crete made much use of the SPIRAL, often together with fish and other marine creatures. See also FISH; FOUNTAIN; RIVER; STAR (the Egyptian firmament); VASE; WAND.

Wind. Some ancient peoples regarded the wind as a god. He controlled the fate of seafarers in particular. The Greek Aeolus and Japanese Fujin kept the winds in a SACK. The Egyptian god of air, Shu, had power over the 'four winds of heaven'.[54] He was also known as the 'pleasant north wind', not so welcome to some Europeans. The Greeks recognized eight winds, all represented on the Horologe of Andronicus, or Tower of the Winds, in Athens (1st cent. BC). Those facing the cardinal points are Boreas (north), warmly clad and blowing a conch shell; Apeliotes (east) with flowers and fruit; Notos (south), pouring a shower of rain from an urn; Zephyrus (west) throwing flowers in the air from his lap. In Roman funerary art the winds may be personified as Tritons blowing conch shells to speed the soul on its way to the Isles of the Blessed. More often they are represented as a bust, or merely a head, with pursed lips, occasionally with a sort of horn issuing from the mouth [*ii: Gallo-Roman, 1st cent.* AD]. Wings may sprout from their temples to suggest speed. Bodiless heads with puffed cheeks, sometimes with horn or conch, recur in medieval and Renaissance art, especially in marine subjects. (See also MITHRAS.)

[*ii*]

5. *Human Body and Dress*

Aegis. Goat-skin cloak or apron usually bearing a Gorgon's head and sometimes fringed with serpents. A symbol of protection, worn by the goddess ATHENA/MINERVA in classical Greek sculpture [*iii: Pergamum, 2nd cent.* BC]. According to Herodotus[1] the Greeks copied it from the everyday dress of Libyan women. A semi-circular aegis, a collar-like necklace, is the attribute of Bastet, Egyptian CAT goddess.

[*iii*]

Angel (Gk. *angelos*, messenger). Winged messengers communicating between god and man are common to many religions. The winged deities and *genii* of Egypt were probably the prototypes of Mesopotamian winged human and animal figures, transmitted through military conquest and trade. They in turn probably inspired the winged gods of Greece and Rome, and Hebrew and Christian angels. Descriptions by O.T. prophets, such as Ezekiel's winged creatures,[2] which became Christian cherubim and seraphim [*iv*], must have been based on actual monuments, probably Babylonian. Roman funerary reliefs also had some influence on the appearance of angels in early Christian art. The nine choirs, the heavenly host surrounding the

[*iv*]

throne of God, were formulated in the *Celestial Hierarchy* by pseudo-Dionysius (*c.* AD 500). Only the two lowest categories, archangels and angels, mediate directly with man. They announce God's will, protect the righteous and punish wrong-doers, featuring in these roles in many O.T. and N.T. scenes. The nine choirs all together represent heaven in Byzantine and western art and are often depicted as musicians.

The *Rig-Veda*[3] refers to a class of youthful demigods, the *angirases* (probably cognate with *angelos*), one of whom was AGNI. Their function was mediatory, bringing the god's gifts to mankind. Hindu myth has another class of celestial beings, the *apsarases*, nymphs who inhabit the Paradise of INDRA. They are represented as young, sensuous females and are dancers and musicians. Like most of the Indian pantheon they have no wings (see also NYMPH). Originally water spirits and tree spirits, they have no mediatory function. They were adopted, perhaps surprisingly, by Mahayana Buddhism as the attendants of Buddhas and bodhisattvas. The *apsaras* in China (*t'ien-jen*) and Japan (*tennin*) has wings and may hold a lotus flower.

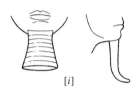

[*i*]

Beard. A man's hair was traditionally the source of his strength and virility. The sage is usually bearded and of venerable appearance, especially in the East: thus Shou Hsing, one of the THREE GODS OF HAPPINESS, several of the EIGHT IMMORTALS and BRAHMA. Egyptian gods generally have a long beard, curled at the end, in contrast to pharaohs who have a short tuft cut square at the end [*i*].

[*ii*]

Belt. The meditation band (Sk. *yoga-patta*) is a belt of cloth worn by Indian sages to support the body in the course of meditation [*ii: S. India, 17th cent.*]; also sometimes by VISHNU in his incarnation as a man-lion (Narasimha). See also GIRDLE.

Blindfold. Symbol of moral and spiritual ignorance. In Christian art a blindfold woman personifies the Synagogue [*iii: Reims, 13th cent.*]; in Renaissance allegory, Avarice, one of the SEVEN DEADLY SINS, and Ignorance. EROS/CUPID is sometimes blindfold. Also blindfold are FORTUNE and Nemesis (for their randomness) and, for her impartiality, Justice, one of the CARDINAL VIRTUES. A blindfold is one of the INSTRUMENTS OF THE PASSION.

[*iii*]

Blood. Among primitive peoples the blood of a sacrificed animal or human, mixed with seed or spread on the ground, magically fertilized it. Hence ears of corn sprout from the blood of the bull sacrificed by MITHRAS. Similarly in Greek myth, ANEMONES sprout from the blood of the dying Adonis. Kali, the destructive aspect of the Hindu Mother-Goddess DEVI, slays a demon whose drops of blood give birth to thousands more.[4] In such ways it symbolizes new life arising from death. Tantric images show Kali beheaded, with life-giving blood streaming from her, the goddess' cosmic energy [*iv: Kangra, c. 1800*]. Known as Lha Mo in Tibet, she is depicted in *tankas* riding over a sea of blood and drinking it from a skull-cup. The blood from Christ's sacrifice of his own life symbolizes the doctrine of the Redemption: angels catch it in a chalice as it spurts from his body. Red flowers are the symbols of the blood of Christian martyrs. For the 'Blood of Isis', see TYET.

[iv]

[v]

Bones. A club-like weapon (Sk. *khatvanga*), made of a human thigh-bone with a skull attached to one end, was an early attribute of SHIVA and could be a vestige of human sacrifice practised by primitive, pre-Aryan Indian tribes. A somewhat similar weapon is held by Tantric deities of demonic aspect in Tibet, where traces of cannibalism are more marked. Thigh-bone trumpets are used by Lamaist priests in funerary processions to ward off evil spirits and in other rites [v: *Tibetan, 19th cent.*]. The Tibetan shaman wears an apron made of carved human bones when performing his rites. See also SKULL.

[vi]

Bowels. Once thought to be the seat of the emotions, hence 'bowels of compassion.' The inspection of entrails for the purpose of divination was once widespread. In them was sometimes seen the face of a Mesopotamian monster Humbaba [vi: *neo-Babylonian, c. 7th–6th cents.* BC] who was killed by Gilgamesh. Humbaba was the prototype of the Greek Gorgon. Disembowelling, a former method of execution, was suffered by the Christian saint, Erasmus of Formiae (died *c.* 303), whose intestines were wound round a capstan. The latter is therefore his attribute. Envy, one of the SEVEN DEADLY SINS, gnaws her own entrails. See also COMBAT; KNOT.

Breast. Symbol of the fertilizing power of Mother-Goddesses. Small clay effigies, often with pronounced breasts, dating from neolithic times, have been found in large numbers in different parts of Europe and Asia. The ancient association of Mother-Goddess and snake (both symbolic of the Earth) is seen in the Egyptian Renenutet, sometimes with a cobra's head, who suckles an infant. Figurines of a similar snake-headed goddess holding a child to her breast have been found in Mesopotamia at Ur (first half of 4th mill. BC). Hapy, the male god of the Nile inundation, has pendulous breasts and a sagging belly, symbolizing his powers of fertility. The former is also characteristic of Taweret, the HIPPOPOTAMUS goddess. ISIS suckling HORUS symbolizes her role as protector of the pharaoh.

[vii]

The Indian Mother-Goddess Lakshmi (see DEVI) supports one breast with a hand [vii]. Hariti, the so-called Buddhist Madonna, formerly a demoness reprieved by the Buddha, suckles one or more infants at her ample breasts in the manner of the figure of CHARITY in western art. The many breasts of the well-known ARTEMIS/DIANA of Ephesus (an untypical cult image, 1st cent. AD) represent, according to some, not breasts but dates, also symbols of fertility. In Christian art the VIRGIN MARY suckling the infant Christ, the *Virgo Lactans*, appeared first about the 6th cent.

In Baroque painting she presses milk from her breast which wets the lips of the kneeling St Bernard of Clairvaux, an ardent Mariolater. The MILK of Hera/Juno made Hercules immortal. Milk from the breasts of the MUSES is the source of artistic inspiration and, in Renaissance allegory, is seen falling on a book or musical instrument. The tradition that Amazon women of Asia Minor removed their right breast to facilitate drawing a bow is not observed in classical art.

[i]

Chasuble. Church vestment, derived from the ancient Roman *paenula*, or travelling cloak, worn by the priest celebrating Mass. The embroidered Y represents Christ hanging from the cross. There is usually a cross on the back [*i*]. In art, it is worn by SS. Ignatius of Loyola, Martin of Tours, Philip Neri, Thomas Becket. The Virgin robes St Ildefonso in a chasuble.

[ii]

Cloak. In western art a symbol of protection, given especially by persons of high rank to inferiors. The 'Virgin of Mercy', or Misericordia, stands and holds out her cloak to protect her supplicants kneeling beneath [*ii: Italian, 15th cent.*]. St Martin, on horseback, divides his cloak with his sword to share it with a beggar. A cloak is also a disguise, to dissimulate evil, and may be worn by Satan. See also DRESS; HERMES/MERCURY.

Cope. A richly embroidered semicircular cloak which evolved, like the CHASUBLE, from the Roman *paenula*, donned for specific liturgical occasions. In art it is one of the identifying vestments of a bishop. The bands, usually embroidered with gold thread, illustrate cycles of scenes from the gospels, or lives of the Virgin or saints. The garment itself symbolizes innocence and purity [*iii*].

[iii]

Crown (see also HAT). The crown is a symbol of sovereignty, power, victory, the attainment of honours. The Christian martyr's crown signifies victory over death. Christ's crown of THORNS symbolizes his Passion. The VIRGIN MARY, when crowned, is Queen of Heaven. Christ crowns St Catherine of Siena, making her his symbolic bride. Among other saints, Louis of Toulouse, a monk, has a crown at his feet symbolizing his renunciation of the French throne in favour of the Church; Bridget of Sweden and Onuphrius, who abandoned a life of ease, are similarly represented. Crown and armour lie at the feet of a monk, William, duke of Aquitaine, who gave up his title and the profession of soldier. A crown is often among the objects in a VANITAS still-life. As an omen of his future victory, the child MOSES tramples on the pharaoh's crown.[5] In Christian allegory a crown falls from the head of the BLINDFOLD Synagogue, in contrast to the Church, who is crowned and holds a chalice; HOPE reaches up to grasp her crown. A musician wearing a crown is DAVID, king of Israel. TIARA and MITRE are also Christian symbols. In secular allegory Europe, one of the FOUR PARTS OF THE WORLD, wears a crown; Asia has a crown of flowers; the crown of PHILOSOPHY may

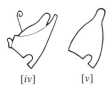

[iv]   [v]

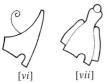

[vi]   [vii]

[viii]

[ix]

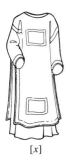

[x]

have three heads. See also LAUREL; MUSES.

The varied headgear of Egyptian deities and kings was, like the HAIR of Shiva and others, a magical source of power and strength. The pharaoh wears a double crown, the *pschent* [iv], which is a combination of the white crown of Upper Egypt [v] and the red crown of Lower Egypt [vi]. They symbolized the powers of the tutelary goddesses of the two regions, Nekhbet (see VULTURE) and Wadjet (URAEUS), who were the king's guardians. The *pschent* is also worn by Atum, sun-god of Heliopolis, known as father of the king, and by HORUS who personified the king. From the beginning of the Old Kingdom the king also wore two upright ostrich plumes (FEATHER). The Atef crown [vii], worn principally by OSIRIS, combined the white crown, double plumes and a small solar disk. Royal crowns were a popular image on amulets. For the headgear of other Egyptian deities see ARROW; BASKET; CRESCENT; GAZELLE; GOOSE; HORN; LOTUS; PALM; SCORPION; SPIRAL; STAR; SUN; THRONE. The Phrygian Mother-Goddess, Cybele, wears a turreted crown [viii] (see ROCK).

A crown or similar headgear, symbolizing a sovereign deity, is worn by Assyrian gods (HORN); by SHIVA and his *shakti* and several Buddhist divinities (TIARA; HAIR). A crown is held in the hand of Rahula, one of the sixteen Protectors of the Law of Far-Eastern Buddhism (ARHAT). The Shinto sun-goddess AMATERASU wears a pagoda-like crown. The ancient Chinese imperial crown [ix] was strung with a row of gems that hung front and back. By inclining his head the emperor caused a curtain of jewels to be lowered before his eyes, obscuring any ill-omened or other unwanted sight. It is also worn by YAMA, Hindu Lord of the Dead, in his Chinese manifestation.

Dalmatic. The traditional vestment of the deacon [x], cut in the form of a cross. It is said to symbolize joy, justice and salvation. The following deacons are depicted wearing it: SS. Lawrence, Leonard (with fleurs-de-lis on it), Stephen, Vincent of Saragossa.

Demon. A harmful spirit and a symbol of evil, though in the East its influence is more often benign. Unlike the hybrid MONSTER, which is mainly animal, the demon usually has human form with certain animal appendages. Christian art represented the demon in the likeness of the Greek god Pan, with his horns, tail and sometimes cloven hoof, though omitting his erect phallus. Worship of Pan, together with other fertility gods like Dionysus (see BULL), survived into the Christian era and became the epitome of evil for the early Church. Pan, and the somewhat similar Satyrs, the attendants of Dionysus, therefore made a fitting image for Satan and his retinue. Wings and clawed feet, for which the art of the ancient world could supply many models, are also typical of Christian demons. Wings, in particular, were a reminder to the faithful of Satan's 'fallen angels'. As a symbol of all that is evil according to Christian teaching the demon has an important place in art. As the messenger of Satan he bears sinners away to hell, the counterpart of God's angels who carry the righteous to heaven. Demons contend with angels for the possession of a dying man's soul; they bear away the soul of the impenitent thief at Christ's crucifixion; at the Last Judgement they, or Satan, try to tip the scales of St Michael. Demons were the cause of disease and insanity for which the cure was exorcism. In art the rite is performed by a saint, several of whom were well known for their powers to heal, often with the aid of an ASPERGILLUM. Small black demons can be seen fleeing from the mouth of the exorcized person. Demons symbolize the temptation to sin – usually withstood – and, as such, are an attribute of SS. Antony the Great, Catherine of Siena and Norbert, among others. A demon blows out the candle of a nun, Geneviève; lies at the feet of Geminianus; and whispers in the ear of Judas. As the agents of Satan they have numerous other roles in Christian art.

[i]

The terrifying aspect of demons does not necessarily bode ill. Its purpose may be to protect, to ward off the forces of evil. In this role they act as guardians of Egyptian royal tombs, especially in the 20th Dynasty, where they are depicted on the entrance walls. Their dual character appears again in Mesopotamia, where both good and evil demons existed who carried out the will of the gods. They were rarely represented, though several images survive of a late Assyrian/Babylonian demon, Pazuzu. He has four wings, a scaly body, clawed hands and feet and a fierce expression, remarkably like Satan's fallen angels [*i: Bronze, 1st half of 1st mill.* BC]. He personified the south-west wind that brought disease. Yet he was the enemy of an evil spirit, Lamashtu, who caused miscarriages and the death of new-born babies. Pregnant women therefore wore protective amulets depicting the head of Pazuzu.

The idea of a band of demons headed by a demon-king, or lord of evil, at war with a corresponding company of the righteous is common to several cultures. In ancient Persian religion it took the form of a symbolic struggle between the powers of light and truth against darkness and falsehood. They were personified by the god Ahura-Mazda (see WINGED DISK) and his retinue of 'arch-angels', and Ahriman, prince of demons, who had a large, very varied horde of followers.[6] Hindu myths tell of many symbolic contests, often between those who maintain the ordered universe and the forces of chaos. There are two main classes of demons: the *asuras*, aerial spirits, led by the demon-king Bali, and constantly at war with the gods; and the more feared, earth-bound *rakshasas*, who prey on men and women at night.[7] The leader of the latter, Ravana, was slain by VISHNU in his seventh incarnation as Rama. Ravana has human form and carries weapons, and sometimes has ten heads and twenty arms. In his fourth incarnation as a man-lion he slew the demon Hiranyakashipu.[8]

The art of the Vajrayana sect of Buddhism (see BUDDHA), that
is, the 'Vehicle of the Thunderbolt', has a class of figures, male
and female, of fearful, demonic appearance. Their ferocity, however, disguises their true nature, which serves a benevolent purpose. Some are guardians of temples (FOUR CELESTIAL KINGS),
whose looks and weapons will drive away evil spirits; some are
directing their wrath at ignorance and illusion, the evils which
impede the way to Enlightenment. These deities, who were taken
over by Buddhism from Shivaite myth and imagery, accompanied
the spread of Tantrism to Tibet, China and Japan [*ii: Japanese
bronze, 12th cent.*], where their numbers greatly multiplied from
the mid-1st mill. AD. They are characterized by a third EYE and,
especially in Tibet, more than one head and many arms. They hold
an assortment of WEAPONS: thunderbolt, flaming sword, noose,
bow and arrow, dagger and elephant goad, among others, with
which they conquer evil. They have flaming aureoles. In Tibetan
painting and sculpture they are typically joined to their *shakti*
in the YAB-YUM position; their heads are crowned and bodies
garlanded with human skulls; as well as their weapons they may
hold a skull-cup filled with human blood; they may have fangs
(TOOTH). In Tantric doctrine certain beings have a dual nature,
calm (Sk. *shanta)* or wrathful (Sk. *krodha),* a vestige of their
Shivaite origin, where the god is both creator and destroyer.
Thus in Tantric art Buddhas and bodhisattvas may be represented in either form. Among the more widely depicted in their
fierce aspect are Acala (Jap. Fudo Myo-O), a manifestation of
the Adi-Buddha VAIROCANA, the bodhisattvas AVALOKITESHVARA
and MANJUSHRI and, especially in Tibet, the legendary founder
of Lamaism, PADMASAMBHAVA. (See further BODHISATTVA; BUD-
DHA; DEVI.) The Chinese god of literature, K'UEI HSING, is demon-
like.

[*ii*]

Dress. Royal robes, like the crown, are a symbol of sovereignty.
The decorations on the ritual robes of the Chinese emperors symbolized the various qualities essential to a good ruler. They came
to be regarded as a compendium of Confucian ethical doctrine
and a symbolic image of the universe (see TWELVE ORNAMENTS).
The emperor himself was a symbol: the Son of Heaven. It was
said of his robes that 'the straightness of the seam at the back
and the rectangles of the embroidered collar remind the wearer
that his administration should be impeccable and his justice in-
corruptible' [*iii*]. The imperial DRAGON, which was represented
on his robes, throne and household articles, held all the cosmic
significance historically attributed to it by the Chinese. The
Twelve Ornaments, of great antiquity, belonged to the emper-
or alone, at least from 1759, while the 'dragon robes' were also
worn by courtiers and officials. The ceremonial robe worn to
commemorate the emperor's ancestors included the Buddhist
EIGHT LUCKY EMBLEMS and the emblems of the Taoist EIGHT IM-
MORTALS.

[*iii*]

The Buddha in the Mahayana art of Indo-China appears, untypically, in royal robes from about the 15th cent., probably an influence of the cult of the god-king in the Khmer Empire. This image spread to Burma, Nepal and Tibet. Among the different ranks of Buddhist figures the ARHAT is distinguished by his plain monk's garb. (See also JEWELS.)

In the solar cult of MITHRAS, the mystagogue, or initiated priest, wore a robe bearing the signs of the ZODIAC. This marked him as a person who had, symbolically, passed through the sun's ecliptic. In Renaissance allegory the robe of PHILOSOPHY is adorned with flowers, fish and stars.

Several Christian church vestments have a symbolic meaning: COPE; DALMATIC; MITRE; PALLIUM; STOLE. Headwear, like robes, may be symbolic: CROWN; HAT; HELMET; TIARA; TURBAN; VEIL. See also AEGIS; BELT; CLOAK; GIRDLE; SANDALS; SASH; SHROUD.

[i]

Dwarf. The fifth incarnation of VISHNU was as the dwarf Vamana. SHIVA dances on a black dwarf that attempted to kill him. The grotesque image of BES, the Egyptian dwarf-god [i: 26th Dynasty] warded off evil, in particular protecting women in childbirth.

[ii]

Ear. In Egyptian funerary art, especially on stelae, an ear meant that one's prayers had been heard and was a sign of the god's goodwill. Elongated ears are typical of BUDDHAS, BODHISATTVAS and ARHATS. They were a mark of royalty in the East, perhaps from an Indian custom of wearing heavy ear-pendants [ii: Nepal, 10th cent.]. (See also BRAHMA; KRISHNA; VISHNU.) The Tibetan ascetic, Mila-ras-pa (1038–1122), a prolific and popular religious poet, is always depicted with his right hand cupped to his ear. In the West, Pan and the Satyrs have pointed ears; the court jester wears asses' ears. In Christian art a severed ear is one of the INSTRUMENTS OF THE PASSION.[9]

[iii]

Eye. Symbol of gods as all-seeing, all-knowing. Early Mesopotamian cult statues (3rd mill. BC) typically show deities with large, staring eyes, compellingly powerful. The eye was also a potent protective talisman: Marduk held one between his lips in his victorious battle against Tiamat. In Egypt the eye is seen everywhere, functioning mainly as a protective talisman. The URAEUS snake worn by the pharaoh to ward off evil was regarded as an eye. A pair of eyes, painted on early coffins, enabled the deceased to see his way in the after-life; from the New Kingdom an eye on a coffin or mummy was apotropaic. The commonest form in Egyptian art is a human eye with the addition of certain markings of the falcon. This is the 'eye of HORUS' [iii] and is his right, or solar, eye; his left, or lunar, eye is the 'wedjat' or 'udjat' eye ('made whole, restored'), both having been cut out by Seth (see OSIRIS).

In Hindu myth SHIVA has a third eye which emits destructive

fire. It is usually vertical in the centre of his forehead. His spouse Pidari, which is also an aspect of Kali (DEVI), the destroyer, may also display it. It entered Tantric Buddhist art and is a regular feature of BUDDHAS, BODHISATTVAS and lesser deities in their ferocious aspect (see DEMON; FLAME; URNA); AVALOKITESHVARA, the 'thousand-eyed', is depicted in Tibetan mandalas with eyes in his/her multiple hands and many heads, and also has a third eye.

In Greek myth the Cyclops were a race of one-eyed giants (though occasionally depicted with two); Polyphemus was the best known. Argus had one hundred eyes which, on his death, Hera placed in the peacock's tail.[10] In Christian art an eye symbolizes God the Father; it may be framed in a triangle, the TRINITY. Two eyes on a dish or on a stalk are the attribute of St Lucy.

[iv]

Eyebrow. Very long eyebrows sometimes reaching to the ground are the attribute of several Chinese Lohans; eg. Chia-li-chia (Sk. Kalika) [iv] and A-shih-to (Sk. Ajita) (see ARHAT).

[v]

Finger. HORUS, when depicted as a wholly anthropomorphic child, holds a finger to his lips, enjoining silence [v: Thebes, 23rd Dynasty]. It alludes to his being hidden in the papyrus of the Delta and brought up in secret, like MOSES. See GESTURE for symbolism of fingers and hands.

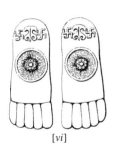

[vi]

Foot, Footprint. Head and feet are respectively highest and lowest in the scale of metaphysical values that Indians attribute to various parts of the body. The feet of a god, being the part nearest to man, are an object of worship. The feet and footprints of Vishnu are worshipped as the consequence of a well-known myth which tells how he created the universe by taking three great steps.[11] (Sk. *pada* means step, foot and footprint.) (See also BRAHMA.) Images on the soles of his feet typically show them decorated with his numerous attributes and other sacred signs. Veneration of the feet of the BUDDHA followed upon this. The representation of his footprints, with or without symbols, was one of the non-figurative ways of indicating his presence in the earliest phase of Buddhist art. The oldest images of the soles of his feet show the Wheel of the Law [vi: Indian, c. 100 BC]. Later they bear more symbols though the number varies. They are sometimes known as the Seven Appearances, or EIGHT LUCKY EMBLEMS. They are found in Buddhist temples in India, China and Japan. It is one of the many kinds of good-luck charm devised by the Japanese.

In the West bare feet symbolize humility or poverty. Christ and the apostles, Franciscan friars, the Virgin of Humility and Poverty personified are all depicted thus. In Gothic art Christ's Ascension is shown as two feet about to disappear into a cloud. Washing a pilgrim's feet is the first symbolic act of hospitality performed in monasteries along the pilgrimage roads, in memory of the Last Supper.[12]

Gesture. (For Hindu/Buddhist hand gestures see MUDRA.) Hand

and arm gestures in Christian art were greatly developed in the Middle Ages and many of them also appear in secular works. In the Latin Church the priest's sign for giving absolution or blessing is a raised right hand with thumb and two fingers extended, to symbolize the Trinity [i]. In the Greek Church the forefinger is extended, the third half curled, the fourth held down by the thumb, and the fifth half curled. They are meant to form the Greek letters ICXC, the abbreviation of 'Jesus Christ', but are seldom correctly depicted [ii]. In eastern Church art, this sign is made by Christ, apostles and archangels. Signs made in everyday life are often self-explanatory. Among others the following (with examples) are commonly represented in the West. Raised hand, or hands, open, palm outwards: acceptance (Virgin of the Annunciation) [iii]; right hand alone raised: protection (Christ, apostles, prophets); right hand placed on left breast: obedience (Adam at his creation); left index finger raised and pointed towards or touching right palm: argument, discussion (Job and his friends) [iv]; hand resting on cheek or chin: grief (mourners at the Crucifixion) [v]; forearms crossed, fists clenched: betrayal, deceit (heretics); crossed hands hanging down, palm inwards: rejection, refusal (Pilate dismissing Christ) [vi]; hand on thigh: firmness of purpose (king giving orders); one hand grasping the other: intense grief (mourners at a saint's tomb) [vii]; baring one's breast with both hands: wrath (Wrath personified) [viii]. In Renaissance double-portraits a man resting his hand on a woman's breast symbolizes betrothal.

The Chinese custom of grasping one's own hands, often hidden by the sleeves, was a salutation, corresponding to the western custom of shaking hands, and indicated that they would not be used aggressively. This gesture was accompanied by seven other clearly defined degrees of self-abasement culminating in repeatedly kneeling and striking one's head on the ground. The gods were entitled to different degrees according to their importance. The emperor received the seventh. In China there are several systems of using the fingers to denote numbers. The Chinese also use a large number of well-understood gestures in everyday social intercourse but they are seldom depicted in art. Covered hands are, in East and West, a sign of respect towards a monarch. The motif was introduced into Byzantine Christian art when Christ assumed the role of divine sovereign.

The position of the hands in prayer takes several forms. Clasped hands are typical of Mesopotamian worshippers from the late 4th to early 3rd mill. BC onwards. They are seen almost invariably on votive statuettes. On Etruscan and Roman monuments the praying figure stands with arms and hands outstretched horizontally, palms forward, the *orans* figure. To the Romans it signified devotion to the gods of filial piety and love of one's fellow-men (Pietas, Humanitas). It was adopted by early Christians and can be seen widely in catacomb painting. Christians also clasped their hands and, especially in the eastern

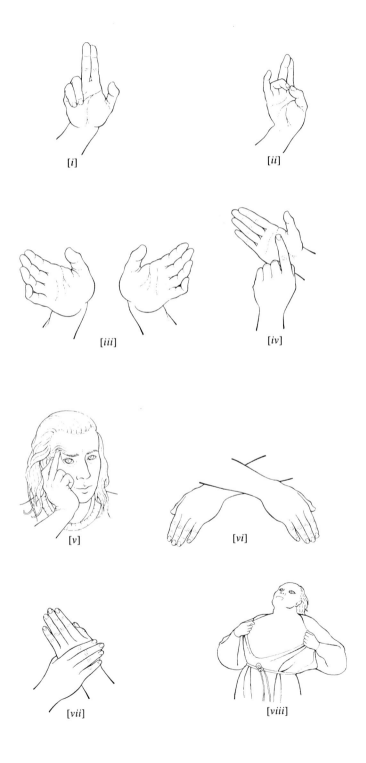

[i]

[ii]

[iii]

[iv]

[v]

[vi]

[vii]

[viii]

Church, prostrated themselves before sacred images. (Prostration before sovereigns, human and divine, was a widespread custom in East and West.) The familiar Christian attitude of prayer – hands joined with palms and fingers flat – is also commonly seen in Hindu and Buddhist art (see MUDRA).

Egyptians knelt before the deity like Christians, Chinese and others, and touched the ground with nose and forehead. In prayer, the arms were raised with open palms facing the god's image, symbolizing submission. In funerary art from the Old Kingdom onwards the deceased has his hand on his knee, palm upwards, reaching out for food, on a table, to sustain him in the after-life. See also FINGER; HAND.

[i]

Girdle. Symbol of power, as in the case of the 'shemset' girdle [i] worn by Egyptian gods and kings of the Archaic period. The girdle of APHRODITE/VENUS bestowed sexual attraction, i.e. power, on the wearer. It is also worn by HERA/JUNO. In antiquity, worn by a wife, it denoted marital fidelity. The girdle of the VIRGIN MARY denotes chastity or purity and is also an attribute of doubting Thomas, to whom she threw it as evidence of her Assumption, which he had doubted. The THREE MONASTIC VOWS of poverty, chastity and obedience are symbolized by the three knots in the Franciscan's girdle.

Hair. Regarded by many peoples as the repository of physical strength and inner power. Thus, the pharaoh holds a vanquished foe by the hair to symbolize his subjection, and Samson was fatally weakened when his locks were shorn.[13] The 'ambrosial locks' of ZEUS/JUPITER were a symbol of his divine power. SHIVA, as the divine embodiment of the ascetic yogi, wears a high pile of densely matted hair resembling a crown which, for much the same reason as Samson's, was untouched by scissors (Sk. *jata-mukuta*) [ii: S. India, 19th cent.]. It is the magical source of the power and energy that inspires Shiva, the ascetic. It is usually decorated with a CRESCENT, also sometimes a SKULL, a figurine of the river-goddess, Ganga, and the flowers of the THORN-APPLE. It is also worn by Rudra, Shiva's antecedent in the *Vedas*, and by BRAHMA and his wife, Sarasvati. A somewhat similar hair-style with a knob on top (Sk. *kirita-mukuta*) is worn by VISHNU, while that of goddesses is usually more conical, with two or three knobs (Sk. *karanda-mukuta*). See also ARJUNA.

[ii]

Buddhism followed a different tradition. On leaving his father's palace Shakyamuni, as a token of repudiating his princely rank, cut off his hair with a sword, leaving only the close-cropped curls that we see in his images. He threw the top-knot (Sk. *ushnisha*) into the heavens where it was caught by Indra in a jewelled casket (though the Buddha is always shown wearing it).[14] Buddhist ascetics, monks and priests shave their heads to indicate renunciation of the flesh and submission to the divine will. (The tonsure is a modification of the same custom.) Priests of the Jain sect in India go to the extreme length of removing hair from all parts of the body. In art, Chinese Lohans, Japanese Rakans (see ARHAT) and other disciples of Buddha have the head shaved, though a fine stubble is often visible in Japanese painting.

To cut off a lock of one's hair is a token gesture of mourning, as ISIS did when mourning the death of Osiris. The long plaited tress, worn in Egyptian art by royal children, the so-called 'sidelock of youth' [*iii: Karnak, 18th Dynasty*], perhaps symbolizes eternal youth. It is also seen on the child HORUS and KHONSU. In Christian art long flowing hair denotes a penitent woman, as with Mary Magdalene. It also denotes virginity or, at least, the unmarried state, as with some virgin saints, and in Renaissance portraits commemorates a betrothal or wedding. The Renaissance courtesan more usually has her hair tied up and braided, as does the 'earthly' Venus (see APHRODITE/VENUS).

[*iii*]

Hand. Early Mesopotamian amulets in the shape of an open hand or a clenched fist protected the wearer against the evil eye (4th–3rd mill. BC). Models of clenched fists were embedded in the walls of neo-Assyrian royal palaces to ward off evil (Nimrud, Nineveh, Assur: 9th cent. BC). On early cylinder seals an open hand, upright between two deities, denoted divine or regal power, known as the 'Hand of Justice'. The hands of the Egyptian creator-gods PTAH and Khnum, at their potter's wheel, symbolize their creative powers. A Heliopolitan myth tells that the sun-god Atum performed the act of creation by masturbation, his semen producing further deities. His hand therefore became a female entity, the two being depicted in funerary art as a divine pair. The rays of the sun-god Aten terminate in hands, some holding the ANKH, which denote his creative powers. Egyptian funerary art depicts a pair of bodiless outstretched arms bent vertical at the elbows, hands with palms forward [*iv*]. This is the *ka*, a symbol of the beneficent divine power that is transmitted from the gods to man. Each person has his own *ka* which, when placed on his effigy in the tomb, will ensure his immortality. It is very frequent also in royal cartouches from the 4th Dynasty.

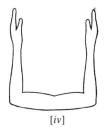

[*iv*]

Hindu deities tended to accumulate many attributes, often through the process of syncretism. The problem of representation was solved by providing the deity with multiple arms and hands to hold them, a fairly rare convention before the 9th or 10th cent. DEVI, given the weapons of other gods to help her fight the BUFFALO-demon, has eight or ten, sometimes twelve. In Tibetan paintings of Tantric Buddhist deities their many limbs, regardless of attributes, become an aspect of the god's divine power: fierce tutelary deities may have forty arms or more. The Mother-Goddess, Devi, in her fierce Tantric aspect, as Kali, wears a garland of human hands. The right hand of the Buddha making the mudra-gesture of teaching or protection may show the Wheel of the Law on the palm [*v*].

[*v*]

[i]

[ii]

[iii]

[iv]

[v]

On Roman stelae a man and woman clasping each other's right hand, the *dextrarum junctio* of the Roman marriage ceremony, symbolizes their reunion in the after-life. In Christian art a hand in the act of striking is one of the INSTRUMENTS OF THE PASSION. Emerging from a cloud it represents the supreme power of God the Father, especially before the 12th–13th cents. when the First Person was not represented in human form. Subsequently it represents him in the TRINITY. A hand giving coins alludes to Judas's payment; holding straws, to the drawing of lots for Christ's tunic. The washing of hands symbolizes innocence, from Pilate's action;[15] hence Innocence personified washes her hands. A severed hand is the attribute of the Tiburtine SIBYL.

The hand's infinitely expressive power to convey religious and social symbols, as represented in art, especially Christian and Chinese, is dealt with under GESTURE; for Buddhist gesture see MUDRA.

Hat. The head-covering of the shepherd or traveller in ancient Greece was the *petasus*, round and broad-brimmed against the sun. With wings, it is the headgear of HERMES/MERCURY. The European pilgrim's hat was similarly broad-brimmed, sometimes turned up at the back and sides [*i: English, 14th cent.*]. With a scallop SHELL, it identifies the apostle James the Greater, St Roch, or Christ on the journey to, or sharing supper at, Emmaus.[16] A cardinal's hat is an attribute of Jerome, one of the FOUR LATIN FATHERS. The 'Phrygian cap', or 'bonnet', is a conical cap with the top falling forward. It was originally the headgear of the magi, the priests of Mazdaism in Achaemenid and Sassanian Persia [*ii: Dura-Europos, c. AD 240*], and hence of MITHRAS whose cult they promoted. It is used in western art to identify Trojans and other peoples of western Asia. Priests of the several Lamaist sects of Tibet wore distinctive headgear. The founder of Lamaism, PADMASAMBHAVA, is distinguished by his mitre-like cap [*iii*]. The reformer and founder of the 'Yellow Hat' sect, still dominant today, Tson-k'a-pa (died 1417), can be identified by his cap, a type still worn by the Grand Lama [*iv*]. The ceremonial head-covering which identifies the pharaoh in Egyptian art is the *nemes* [*v*]. See also CROWN.

Head. (See also BEARD; EAR; EYE; HAIR; JAR; NOSE.) Among sacred figures multiple heads are more characteristic of the East, severed heads of the West. Four-headed deities have been found in early Babylonian bronzes. In Hindu art BRAHMA usually has four, which face the four quarters of his creation, the universe. SHIVA sometimes has three heads (or three faces), like his predecessor, the 'Lord of the Beasts', in the Indus Valley civilization. A famous sculpture at Elephanta (8th cent.) shows a Shiva Trinity. The head in the middle, impassive and other-worldly, represents the deity in his transcendent, absolute aspect. At the sides, in profile, are the heads of Shiva and his *shakti*, repre-

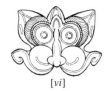

[vi]

[vii]

[viii]

senting the male–female principle that creates the world of appearances. The Gorgon's head, set on the pediment of a Greek temple to ward off evil, has its Hindu counterpart in the *kirtimukha* ('Face of Glory'). It represents Shiva in his wrathful aspect[17] and is seen at the top of the aureole-like arch framing various deities and over the door of Shivaite sanctuaries [*vi: S. Indian, 19th cent.*]. The six heads of KARTTIKEYA, in some texts the son of Shiva, refer to the myth of his multiple conception by the Seven Sisters, in the constellation of the Pleiades (one of whom declined to be impregnated).[18] Shiva's consort, Kali (DEVI), prominent in Tantric art, and embodying his destructive powers, wears a garland of her victims' heads, as do some other Tibetan gods in their 'wrathful' aspect (see PADMASAMBHAVA). The demon-king Ravana often has ten heads, a boon conferred on him by BRAHMA; when they were severed in battle, they grew again like the heads of the Greek Hydra. (It was Ravana who abducted Sita to Sri Lanka (see APE).) Multiple heads are a feature of the Tantric forms of many Hindu and Buddhist figures, especially the so-called fierce, tutelary deities whose heads are usually crowned with human skulls. Of Buddhas themselves, the Adi-Buddha VAIROCANA may have four heads (or faces). Among BODHISATTVAS Lokeshvara has four, MANJUSHRI has nine and AVALOKITESHVARA, in certain forms, eleven. Among other Buddhist figures the monk is distinguished by his shaven head (see ARHAT).

The head of Shakyamuni has several distinguishing features. In the earliest images (2nd cent. AD) it is entirely shaven. The established type, which was widespread by the late 4th to early 5th cents. under the Gupta Empire, shows him with short curly hair topped by the *ushnisha*, elongated EARS and, where an appropriate surface exists, a plain halo. The *urna*, a small protuberance between the eyebrows (from which wisdom emanates to illuminate the universe) is absent in the Gupta period [*vii: Gandharan, 1st cent. AD*].

The Greek goddess, HECATE, sometimes has three heads. JANUS, the Roman god of doorways and of beginnings of all kinds (e.g. January), has two faces, both bearded. Originally only one was bearded; they then symbolized sun and moon respectively (see also TWELVE MONTHS – January). A severed head on a platter belongs to JOHN THE BAPTIST,[19] an image once believed to have the power to cure sickness. A blindfold head on a platter belongs to PAUL, executed according to tradition, in the reign of Nero. See also HERMES/MERCURY. Execution by beheading was a common fate of early Christian martyrs. Cephalophores, such as Denis and the English bishop Cuthbert, hold their own head. A hatchet embedded in the skull of a Dominican friar identifies St Peter Martyr (1205–52), who died at the hands of Catharists whom he had oppressed [*viii*]. In late medieval and Renaissance art Prudence personified has three heads, symbolizing her essential nature: memory, intelligence and foresight, or past, present and future. A severed head, pierced by an arrow, is an attribute of America, one of the FOUR PARTS OF THE WORLD. A flaming head: see FOUR ELEMENTS – Fire.

Heart. In ancient Egypt a symbol of life and the seat of the emotions and intellect. In the Hall of Judgement the deceased's heart was placed in the scales and weighed against the ostrich feather of Maat, goddess of truth and justice. For the Chinese the heart (*hsin*) was also the seat of the intelligence and emotions and is one of the Buddha's Eight Precious Organs (see EIGHT TREASURES). In the West the heart symbolizes, above all, ardour, either religious and spiritual or profane and sexual. A flaming heart is the attribute of Augustine (see FOUR LATIN FATHERS), Antony of Padua and, from the Renaissance, of CHARITY personified and APHRODITE/VENUS [*i*]. Pierced by an arrow it is the attribute of EROS/CUPID. St Teresa of Avila experienced a vision, often depicted, of an angel piercing her heart with a flaming arrow. A heart with a crown of thorns is the emblem of the Jesuits and their founder, Ignatius of Loyola. The 'sacred heart' (i.e. Christ's) has been an object of devotion since the Middle Ages and much more widely from the 17th cent., when it is represented pierced by the nails of the cross and encircled with the crown of thorns. In Renaissance allegory an old hag gnawing her heart is Envy, one of the SEVEN DEADLY SINS.

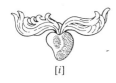

[*i*]

Helmet. An attribute of ATHENA/MINERVA at all periods, often with a panache; also of FAITH, as a protection against heresy, and Fortitude, one of the CARDINAL VIRTUES, in her conquering aspect. A helmet with a wolf's head, see AGES OF THE WORLD – Golden Age. The Greek hero PERSEUS wears a winged helmet of invisibility, one of the weapons he used to overcome the Gorgon, Medusa [*ii*]. Chinese children playing with a helmet symbolize, through a play on words, an argument as to who won the highest grade in an examination. The 'children' stand for sons, whose advancement to high office was a father's primary ambition.

[*ii*]

Infant, Child. The Hindu lotus-goddess, Padmapani or AVALOKITESHVARA, among his/her many subsequent transformations, became in Chinese Buddhism a goddess of mercy, Kuan-yin, who holds a young child in her arms. She is known as Kannon in Japan. The Hindu fertility-goddess, Hariti, a demon who devoured children, was similarly converted by Mahayana Buddhism into a protector of the young. She is first seen in Gandharan art (2nd–6th cents. AD), a motherly figure surrounded by children. She is known in China as Kuei-tze Mu-chin and in Japan as Kishimojin.

[*iii*]

   Children have a symbolic role in much Chinese art, influenced by Confucianism and Taoism [*iii*]. In that once strongly patriarchal society, they represent sons and, when associated with various objects, they symbolize, by a play on words, parental hopes, especially for success in public examinations leading to high office (see HELMET). Hence Lu Hsing, Taoist god of wealth and salaries, one of the GODS OF HAPPINESS, usually holds a child or has one at his feet. Children with pomegranates and peaches are expressing the wish 'May you have sons, long life and fortune.' A child holding a JU-I sceptre signifies 'May you have male offspring.'

In Egypt the child Horus holds a FINGER to his mouth and wears his HAIR in the 'side-lock of youth'. This image, popular in the Graeco-Roman era, was placed in a house to protect it from evil spirits. The image of ISIS suckling Horus similarly had the power to protect children from harm. It may have been a formative influence on the oldest image of the Virgin nursing Christ, the *Virgo Lactans*, in Coptic painting.

[iv]

The death of Christ is implicit in his image as an infant. It is often stressed by an APPLE, POMEGRANATE, or GOLDFINCH, etc, in his hand, which allude to Christian doctrines of Redemption and Resurrection, and his coming crucifixion. The child Christ is an attribute of SS. Antony of Padua, Augustine (see FOUR LATIN FATHERS) and Vincent de Paul and is carried on the shoulders of Christopher who wades across a river. Children are venerated as symbols of innocence in the cult of Holy Innocents, which commemorates the massacre by Herod the Great.[20] From the Renaissance the figure of CHARITY suckles one or two infants (see also FOUR ELEMENTS – Earth). A winged female holding a white and black infant is Nyx, the Greek goddess of night, with her children Sleep and Death, a theme represented in post-Renaissance painting. See also PUTTO.

[v]

Leg. St Roch, who protected Christian pilgrims from the plague, is shown lifting his cloak to reveal a plague-spot on his thigh [*iv: French, 15th cent.*]. Commonly seen in French and Italian pilgrimage churches from the early 15th cent.

Liver. One of the forms of divination practised by ancient peoples, in order to discern the will of the gods, was the study of the liver of a sacrificed animal, or haruspication. The Etruscans were well known for this skill [*v: Etruscan, c. 400 BC*]. The liver is one of the Eight Precious Organs of the Buddha (see EIGHT TREASURES) and, for the Chinese (*kan*), is the seat of courage and symbolizes filial piety.

[vi]

Man. The belief that the human body represented the universe in miniature, being composed of the same elements, was widespread in the ancient world and was revived in the medieval West. The existence of a physical causality between the two – between macrocosm and microcosm – was central to astrology. It is the subject of countless diagrams in astrological works, which show how each limb or organ of the body is governed by its own planet or sign of the zodiac. Christians taught that the perfect human body belonged to Christ [*vi: Italian, 1554*] and that this should be reflected in the proportions of the cruciform church. Leonardo, in a well-known drawing, illustrating Vitruvius, demonstrated that the perfect body could be inscribed within a circle and also a square.[21] A man is one of the four so-called APOCALYPTIC BEASTS.

[i]

Maniple. Christian church vestment, worn by the celebrant of the Mass, consisting of a long band of material hung over the left arm and usually embroidered with three crosses. It represents the rope by which Christ was led to Calvary, and is a symbol of good works, vigilance and penitence [i].

[ii]

Mask. Of prehistoric origin, still used in the rituals of primitive peoples and believed to transmit magically the character of the image to the wearer. (See p. x) It was used in the religious drama of the ancient Greeks at the festivals of DIONYSUS and would have been derived from older cults. In the Far East the convention of masked actors survives today in the Japanese Noh play, and is a popular motif in *netsuke*. In Tibet masked dances are still part of religious drama, where the masks represent gods and demons in conflict. Greek actors wore masks appropriate to their parts, more grotesque in comedy. They are therefore the attribute of the MUSES of comedy and tragedy, Thalia and Melpomene [ii: *Roman sarcophagus, 3rd cent.* AD]. The tragic mask is sometimes worn by Cupid on Roman sarcophagi. In Renaissance Venice the mask was popularized in the *ballo mascherato*, inviting freedom from social restraints. Hence, in art, it is a symbol of Venus, deceit, vice in general and Night personified (see VIRTUES AND VICES).

[iii]

Milk. The milk of goddesses bestowed divinity and immortality. Thus the image of the Egyptian ISIS suckling HORUS is a symbol of the pharaoh receiving divine nourishment. It has points in common with the VIRGIN MARY suckling Christ. In Greek myth[22] the infant HERCULES, son of a mortal woman, was ensured immortality by being put to the breast of HERA/JUNO. (Some of her milk splashed across the heavens, creating the Milky Way [iii: *after Tintoretto, 1560s*].) Somewhat similar effects were claimed for the act of libation, often performed with milk. The liquid was poured on to an altar as a sacrifice to a deity, the remainder being ritually consumed by the priest. Indian Brahmins mixed milk with the juice of the *soma* plant, producing an hallucinogenic drink which was offered to the gods to secure their continuing immortality. The *haoma* of the Iranians was related to it. A Hindu creation myth[23] tells how the gods and demons churned the primeval waters, transmuting them into milk, then sacramental butter (*ghee*) and ultimately *soma* and a poisonous antithesis. The ensuing battle between gods and demons for possession of the elixir symbolizes the opposing forces of universal creation and destruction. *Soma* is sometimes called honey in Hindu texts. A mixture of milk and honey was a form of sacrament offered to DIONYSUS, and was used in Jewish and subsequently Christian ritual for several centuries. In Roman catacomb painting a shepherd with a milk-pail symbolizes the Christian sacrament.

[iv]

Mitre. The liturgical hat of the Jewish high-priest on special occasions and of bishops and some abbots in the eastern and western Churches. As a Christian vestment it was established in Rome in the 10th cent., and was formerly worn by cardinals [iv]. It is divided crosswise forming a double, pointed crown, said to symbolize the Old and New Testaments, also the two rays of light that shone from Moses' brow on receiving the Ten Commandments.[24] SS. Bernard and Bernardino, both said to have thrice refused a bishopric, are depicted with three mitres lying at their feet.

Mouth. Egyptian funeral rites included the ceremony of 'Opening the Mouth'. It was performed on the mummy and statue of the deceased by touching his face with various sacred utensils in order to reanimate the senses so that he could answer for himself in the Hall of Judgement. The officiating priest wore a jackal-mask of Anubis. The rite is known to date from the Old Kingdom but it is not depicted in detail until the 18th Dynasty. Funerary paintings show PTAH, the god of craftsmen, performing the rite with an adze. In medieval Christian art, and later, the entrance to hell is represented as the gaping mouth of a great beast, probably intended as the biblical Leviathan[25] [v: French, 12th cent.]. See also FINGER.

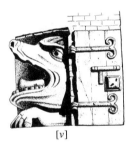

[v]

Mudra (Ch. *shou yin*; Jap. *shu-in*). A series of symbolic, stylized positions of the hands widely seen in images of Hindu and Buddhist divinities. Indian dance-drama, in which meaningful hand gestures always played an important part, originally served a religious purpose. From there they found their way into Hindu rituals and thence into Buddhism where they were given fresh meanings in accordance with Buddhist doctrine. *Mudra*, a Sanskrit word, once meant a seal or its impression, so, when applied to a gesture performed by a priest, it was a guarantee of the efficacy of a rite, rather like the Christian sign for absolution. The *mudra* is first seen in Indian art in images of Shakyamuni, the historical BUDDHA, about the 2nd cent. AD. By the 7th cent., mainly due to the influence of Tantrism, a wide range of gestures had been established, each with its own precise meaning, and holding latent magical powers. In this form they spread east with Buddhism to Tibet, China, Indonesia and Japan. The following are the most commonly represented (see p. 133):

1. *Abhaya-mudra*. When made by a god the raised right hand grants protection to his devotees and dispels fear. A similar gesture is seen in images of the Persian Ahura-Mazda, of later Roman emperors and in early Christian art, of Christ, apostles and prophets. Among Hindu deities the gesture is made by BRAHMA,

SHIVA, VISHNU, KRISHNA, KARTTIKEYA and others. The first images of Shakyamuni show him in this pose. With seated figures the left hand may rest in the lap, as shown.

2. *Varada-mudra*. A gesture of the left hand, often combined with no. 1, as shown. It denotes a deity's charity, power to grant a wish or fulfil a vow. Typical of AVALOKITESHVARA in most of his/her eastern manifestations and of the chief Hindu deities cited in no. 1 above.

3. *Dhyana-mudra*. Both hands lying in the lap of a seated figure denote intense concentration during meditation. Traditionally it is the pose of Shakyamuni when he received Enlightenment under the bodhi tree. There are several variations of which two are shown. In the second, the circle formed by the fingers and thumbs symbolize the Wheel of the Law in its divine and human aspects. Both are typical of the Buddha Amitabha in China, Indonesia and Japan.

4. *Dharmacakra-mudra*, the 'turning of the Wheel of the Law', a symbol of Buddhist doctrine and a gesture of teaching (see WHEEL). It has several variations but the thumb and forefinger of the right hand are usually joined to represent the Wheel. It is seen throughout Buddhist Asia and is reserved solely for Buddhas, including the future Buddha, MAITREYA, and PRAJNA-PARAMITA, the 'Mother of all Buddhas'.

5. *Vitarka-mudra*, denoting exposition or argument, is another gesture of teaching. It is usually made by the right hand, sometimes the left, or both. It is similar to no. 4, is found in the same contexts and, more widely, among bodhisattvas. It is the gesture of the ARHAT Vajriputra. The thumb may touch the second or third finger when, in the latter case, it resembles the sign for absolution, made in the Greek Church.

6. *Vajra-mudra* symbolizes the supreme wisdom of Adi-Buddha, VAIROCANA, and is almost exclusively associated with him, especially in his Japanese manifestation as Dai Nichi. The five fingers of the right hand symbolize the five elements of the material world grasping the Adi-Buddha's flame of knowledge (see FOUR ELEMENTS). Alternatively for Tantric adepts, the gesture symbolizes mystical sexual union (see YAB-YUM).

7. *Bhumisparsha-mudra*, 'touching the earth', another gesture that was, according to various legends, made by Shakyamuni at the moment of his Enlightenment. The most popular account tells of his temptation by Mara, the Buddhist Satan and enemy of Enlightenment, while he sat under the bodhi tree. Shakyamuni touched the ground to invoke the Earth spirit who answered in a voice of thunder confirming the righteousness of his Buddhahood.[26] It is found throughout the Far East and is the most common type of *mudra* in Thailand from the 14th cent.

8. *Anjali-mudra*. A symbol of supplication or adoration widely used by Hindus, Christians and others as a gesture of prayer. Among Hindu deities it is typical of the images of HANUMAN and GARUDA; also of the Tamil philosopher and teacher,

1.

2.

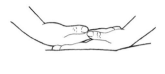

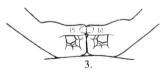

3.

4.

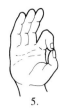

5.

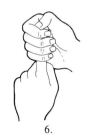

6.

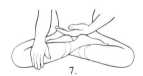

7.

8.

Ramanuja (died *c.* AD 1137). When the tips of the fingers are interlocked they symbolize the union of the spiritual and material aspects of the cosmos. The gesture is associated with bodhisattvas and lesser figures when they are attendant on a Buddha.

The Dhyani-Buddhas, when facing the four quarters, over which they reign (see COMPASS; VAIROCANA), are distinguished by their *mudras*: east, Akshobhya, no. 7; south, Ratnasambhava, no. 2; west, Amitabha, no. 3; north, Amoghasiddhi, no. 1. See also GESTURE; HAND.

[*i*]

Mummy. In Egypt embalming the body in order to preserve it in the after-life is known to have been practised from the 4th Dynasty. In art, the gods PTAH, OSIRIS and KHONSU are depicted partially wrapped like a mummy. Figurines, called Ushabtis, modelled and painted as if mummified, were placed in the tomb of the pharaoh to act as his servants. Sacred animals were also mummified, sometimes in large numbers, for example, the CAT of Bastet [*i: Bubastis, Late Period*], the BULL of Apis, and the IBIS and baboon of Thoth (see APE).

[*ii*]

Nose. To press the nose with a short, blunt rod [*ii: stele, neo-Babylonian, 8th cent.* BC] was a ritual gesture made by Mesopotamian royalty, and appears to symbolize humility before a god. (Lesser mortals prostrated themselves.)

Nudity. Attitudes to nudity have changed over the ages especially in relation to worship. Sumerian priests and their attendants celebrating the New Year festival approached the deity's image naked as a sign of abasement [*iii: Uruk, later 4th mill.* BC]. Nudity and fasting, to mortify the flesh, were practised by more extreme Indian ascetics, for example Vardhamana, the founder of Jainism, who spent his later life completely naked. Nudity was at first the rule in Jainist monasteries until disagreements arose which ended in schism.

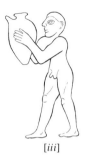

[*iii*]

A goddess of love, like Qadesh in Egypt and the Graeco-Roman APHRODITE/VENUS, was generally represented nude, though Aphrodite is usually robed in early vase painting. The classical Greek sculptor's aim of creating, in the service of religion, an ideally perfect human body was copied, generally for secular reasons, by the Romans. The nude in classical art was condemned by the Christian Church as the work of Satan.[27] The medieval Church recognized certain categories of nudity in art. It symbolized Innocence (Adam and Eve before the Fall), Poverty (Job), Penitence (Mary Magdalene) and Truth personified.[28] Renaissance humanists made the female nude a symbol of 'sacred' love in contrast to her 'profane' sister who was richly adorned and bejewelled (see APHRODITE/VENUS).

Nymphs. Ancient Greek demigods, the young and beautiful daughters of Zeus. They were of various classes, each inhabiting her own realm: spring, river, sea, mountain, tree, etc. Similar spirits appear in Indian folklore, particularly in association with trees, like the Greek Dryads. The *apsarases* in the *Vedas* were water-nymphs, who later became celestial musicians. They were the attendants of Kama, the Vedic equivalent of Eros, and the mistresses of gods and mortals. They were, surprisingly, adopted by Buddhism and are widely depicted among the retinue of the Buddha, or hovering above the gateways of STUPA and pagoda [*iv: Cambodian, early 12th cent.*].

[*iv*]

Pallium. Archbishop's vestment, a Y-shaped band of white wool with a front and back pendant bearing six purple crosses [*v: German, 10th cent.*]. It comes from the Pope and was formerly his gift to specially honoured prelates. Its shape symbolizes the crucifixion.

[*v*]

Phallus. A symbol of male sexual potency and the generative forces in nature. The phallus was the object of many ancient fertility cults. Worship of the PILLAR seems to have had a phallic origin and vestiges live on in European folk traditions such as the maypole dance. The Egyptian fertility god MIN is typically ithyphallic (having an erect penis) and AMUN, GEB and OSIRIS are, in some contexts, represented in the same way. Artefacts from the Indus Valley (3000–2000 BC) show an ithyphallic god who is thought to have been the prototype of SHIVA. Of his many-faceted cult, the image of Shiva as a phallus (Sk. *lingam*) appears to have entered Hinduism about the 2nd or 1st cent. BC. He is typically shown standing inside it in a kind of niche. Or he may be replaced by his *shakti* (see DEVI). In Tantric Hinduism the *lingam* may be combined with the YONI (vulva) [*vi: Himachal Pradesh, 19th cent.*], symbolizing the creative energy of god and goddess in sexual union. The *vajra* (THUNDERBOLT) is the principal cult object of the Vajrayana sect of Buddhism; together with the temple BELL, they symbolize *lingam* and *yoni* respectively. Phallic worship entered Greece, probably from Thrace, in the rites of DIONYSUS and his followers, Pan, Silenus and the Satyrs. They are commonly ithyphallic in Greek vase painting. Priapus, the rustic god of fields, orchards and flocks, came from Asia Minor. His typical monument was the *herm*, a pillar serving as a boundary stone. It was crowned by the god's bust with an erect phallus lower down. Similar stones were dedicated to HERMES/MERCURY. See also ARCH; TRUMPET; UNICORN.

[*vi*]

Posture. One of the disciplines of the yoga adept is to sit with legs and feet in certain fixed positions, which are felt to neutralize the senses and therefore aid meditation. They must be of great antiquity for there is evidence that some such postures were known to the Indus Valley people (3rd–2nd mill. BC). They are generally known by their Sanskrit name, *asana*, which has been defined as a 'mystic position of the lower limbs'. The word also means pedestal. Hindu and Buddhist deities, when represented

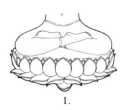

1.

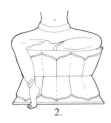

2.

3.

4.

5.

6.

seated in this manner, acquire a sacred aura that sets them apart from the everyday world. The following *asanas* are the most often represented:

1. *Padmasana*, the 'lotus posture', also called *dhyanasana* ('profound meditation') and *vajrasana* ('adamantine'). It is the well-known pose of the Buddha. Since *padmasana* also means 'lotus pedestal' he is usually represented enthroned on lotus petals, which carry the full force of the flower's Buddhist symbolism (see LOTUS). The posture is first seen in Indian sculpture in the late 2nd cent. AD and in due course spread throughout Buddhist Asia. The pose is not confined to Buddhas but is also used for bodhisattvas, especially MANJUSHRI, and other sacred figures, like PRAJNA-PARAMITA. The *virasana*, or 'half lotus', is a modified form in which the right foot is invisible, being pressed into the opposite thigh.

2. *Lalitasana*, 'posture of relaxation'. Either foot hangs, usually the right. It contrasts with the strictly formal, meditative pose of the Buddha (no. 1) and is typical of certain bodhisattvas, in particular AVALOKITESHVARA, more often in his/her Chinese manifestation as Kuan-yin (T'ang and Sung dynasties) and as Kannon in Japan (from the 8th cent.). This informal pose is appropriate to bodhisattvas, complementing their normal princely garb. It is also often used for the chief Hindu deities, when seated, such as BRAHMA, INDRA, VISHNU and SHIVA.

3 and 4. *Rajalilasana*, 'royal ease'. Some variation occurs in the position of the right arm. It is used for bodhisattvas, especially MANJUSHRI and AVALOKITESHVARA in their Far-Eastern identities.

5. 'Posture of Maitreya', also called 'European posture'. The legs are sometimes crossed below the knees. It is almost exclusively used for MAITREYA. The posture is said to symbolize his readiness, as Buddha-to-be, to step down and appear before the world.

6. 'Pensive posture', associated particularly with Manjushri and Avalokiteshvara in China, from the beginnings of Chinese Buddhist art, and in Japan; sometimes also Maitreya. The position of the hands and fingers may vary.

See also YAB-YUM.

Putto. The winged infants, ubiquitous in high Renaissance and Baroque painting and sculpture, were descended from Greek *erotes*, messengers of the gods and guardian spirits of earthly mortals. They themselves were derived from Eros (see EROS/CUPID). Such spirits, or daemons, were also known to the Egyptians, Persians and Babylonians. They are seen bearing garlands in Indian Buddhist sculpture of the Gandhara period (1st–2nd cent. AD), which was subject to Graeco-Roman influences. The *genii*, or guardian spirits of Roman religion, who conducted the soul to heaven, feature prominently in Roman funerary sculpture and were taken over to represent angels in early Christian sepulchral art. They are absent from medieval art, reappearing in their angelic role in the Renaissance [*i*]. In profane art they are the attendants of APHRODITE/VENUS, Cupid and the MUSE, Erato.

[*i*]

Sandals. Shod feet are often a distinguishing mark of royalty and the gods, usually represented as sandals in Mesopotamian and Egyptian art [*ii: neo-Assyrian, 8th cent.* BC]. The pharaoh's captured enemies were represented on the soles of his sandals, so that he continued to tread them underfoot. The deceased before OSIRIS in the Hall of Judgement wear white sandals as a sign of purity and innocence. Sandals were removed in the presence of a deity or on sacred ground; thus God ordered Moses to remove his before the burning bush.[29] (They may be represented as boots in northern art.) The custom remains among Moslems who go unshod into the mosque. Winged sandals are an attribute of the Greek gods HERMES/MERCURY and PERSEUS. Sandals are an attribute of the Greek goddess of VICTORY.

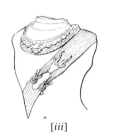

[*ii*]

Sash. The sacred, or 'Brahmanic' sash, or cord (Sk. *yajnopavita*), was originally a deer-skin. It was usually worn over the left shoulder, diagonally across the chest to the right hip and up the back. The deer's head hung over the chest. As a cord, or sash, it is worn by high-caste Hindus, and symbolizes the *sutratman*, a spiritual thread to which all individuals are attached, like pearls.[30] It is represented in Hindu sculpture from the Gupta period [*iii: 4th–6th cents.* AD] in modified form, sometimes knotted at the front. It is the attribute of several Hindu deities, in particular AGNI, BRAHMA, VISHNU, SHIVA and his followers, and BODHISATTVAS. Shiva's sash may take the form of a snake.

[*iii*]

Shroud. In Christian art the attribute of Joseph of Arimathaea who, after the crucifixion, placed Christ's body in his own tomb.[31] The raising of Lazarus, who is shrouded and who would have been entombed upright [*iv: mosaic, Ravenna, 6th cent.* AD], was said to prefigure Christ's Resurrection.

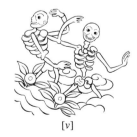

[*iv*]

Skeleton. Death personified as a skeleton is a familiar figure in western art from the early Renaissance onwards, inspired by Petrarch's TRIUMPHS. At Death's triumph his chariot is drawn by black oxen. A young woman, sometimes with her lover, is often his victim, a reminder that her beauty, which inspires love, is at his mercy. He confronts the soldier. On horseback he cuts down his prey with a SCYTHE. He may hold an HOUR-GLASS. He features in funerary sculpture from the 17th cent. The 'Danse Macabre', a late medieval theme, depicts a row of figures of descending social rank from Pope to peasant, a skeleton between each, to signify that Death is no respecter of persons.

In Tibetan Lamaist paintings a pair of skeletons (*citipati*) [*v: Tibetan, c. 1800*] are attendants of YAMA, Lord of the Underworld. They link arms and dance on corpses. They may carry sceptres topped with skulls, or a skull-cup and a vase.

[*v*]

Skull. (Sk. *kapala*). The human skull features in the iconography of certain Hindu and Tibetan Buddhist deities, either as personal ornament (singly, or strung on a necklace or girdle) or as the head of a club or sceptre, or, in half, as a drinking bowl filled with blood. These are vestiges of primitive religions that involved human sacrifice and ritual cannibalism, though their symbolism was subsequently much modified. SHIVA has a human skull in his head-dress and may wear a skull-necklace, symbols of death and a reminder of his role as destroyer. His spouse, Parvati, in the same role (see DEVI) may also have a necklace of skulls. The bowl of blood belongs particularly to Tibetan Tantric gods, male and female, in their fierce aspect. It is a non-determinative attribute, but is specially associated with PADMASAMBHAVA. Numerous deities in their wrathful aspect, such as YAMA, god of death, also have a crown and/or garland of skulls [*i: Tibetan, 17th cent.*].

[*i*]

A skull-bowl containing fermented liquor is still used in Lamaist rites.

In the West the skull symbolizes death in Christian art from the Middle Ages onwards. From the 16th cent. a winged skull may be seen on funerary monuments. A skull is an object of contemplation and the attribute of several saints, in particular Francis of Assisi, Romuald, Jerome, one of the FOUR LATIN FATHERS, and Mary Magdalene. In VANITAS still-life painting it symbolizes the fleeting nature of life on earth but, crowned with evergreen ivy, offers hope of immortality. An old man with a skull symbolizes the last of the AGES OF MAN. It is an attribute of Melancholy, one of the FOUR TEMPERAMENTS. In portraiture it denotes the sitter's Christian piety. A skull at the foot of the cross belongs to Adam, whose original sin was redeemed by Christ's death. His blood may drip on it. See also BLOOD; BOWL; SCEPTRE; SKELETON.

Soul. The Egyptian idea of the soul was a combination of ANKH, *ka* (see HAND) and *ba* (BIRD). The *ba* was a human-headed bird and corresponded to the Greek conception of the soul personified by Psyche,[32] who is represented in the same way on early Greek vases. Later she became a winged human figure. In Byzantine Christian art the soul was an infant, often winged, a type that became general in the West [*ii: Italian, 13th cent.*]. It usually emerges from the deceased's mouth. See also BUTTERFLY.

[*ii*]

Spittle. A god's spittle can create life and also has the power to heal. That of the Babylonian god, Marduk, was called the 'spittle of life'. The Egyptian sun-god, Atum, created the first goddess, Tefnut, by the act of spitting.[33] Another early text tells how the earth was created from the spittle of Khepri, the scarab deity.[34] The stolen EYE of Horus was restored in place by the spittle of THOTH. The healing power of spittle was also demonstrated by Christ when he restored the sight of a man blind from birth[35] [*iii: after Duccio, early 14th cent.*]. To spit may denote contempt and is also a means of warding off the evil eye. A human head in

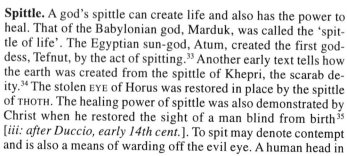

[*iii*]

the act of spitting is one of the INSTRUMENTS OF THE PASSION.

Stigmata. Marks similar to the wounds on Christ's body, usually five, which have appeared on the hands, feet and side of certain exceptionally devout Christians [*iv*]. In art they identify SS. Francis of Assisi and Catherine of Siena.

Stole. Christian liturgical vestment, long and narrow, worn round the neck. As worn by a deacon it goes over the left shoulder and is fastened under the right arm. On others the ends fall straight down [*v*]. It signifies the priest's dignity and power of office, his Christian duties and hope of immortality.

[*iv*]

[*v*]

Swaddling bands. A symbol of the Mesopotamian fertility-goddess, Ninhursag, also known as Nintu, 'the lady who gave birth' [*vi: early Babylonian, 1st half, 2nd mill. BC*]. It is first seen on reliefs of the Larsa period (early 2nd mill. BC), later on cylinder seals and boundary stones. It is depicted as if hanging from a peg on a temple wall, where it would be used in some rite connected with childbirth. In ancient Athens, swaddling bands were made out of clothes worn by the parents for their initiation ceremony at Eleusis. Their magical property was enhanced with the addition of various amulets which both protected and identified the new-born child.

[*vi*]

Tiara. Ornamental head-dress characteristic of Hindu and Buddhist deities and their *shaktis*, especially when in sexual union (see YAB-YUM). A tiara usually distinguishes bodhisattva from Buddha [*vii: Tibetan bronze, 18th cent.*]. However, the Buddha sometimes wears a tiara in Mahayana art of Thailand and Cambodia (from the 16th cent.). It is found more widely on Buddha in the art of the Vajrayana sect in eastern Asia. It is worn by Dhyani-Buddhas, by MAITREYA and by the Buddhist 'goddess of wisdom', PRAJNA-PARAMITA. The Pope's tiara is first mentioned in the 8th cent. Its present form with three superimposed crowns dates from 1315. They symbolize the Trinity. See also Gregory (one of the FOUR LATIN FATHERS); CROWN; SEVEN DEADLY SINS – Pride.

[*vii*]

Tongue. For the Egyptians the tongue was the visible manifestation of the spoken word by means of which the creator-god PTAH brought the universe into being (see WORD). It was, with his heart, the organ of creation, and a symbol of his power and authority. Atum-RE had similar powers. THOTH, patron of scribes, was called the 'tongue of Re'. To stick out the tongue would ward off harmful spirits, as in images of the Egyptian god, BES, who protects women in childbirth; the Graeco-Roman Gorgon [*viii: Attic, 6th cent. BC*], whose head was carved on temple pediments; and various guardian monsters, Tantric deities such as Kali (DEVI), YAMA, and others, in their wrathful aspect.

[*viii*]

Tooth. Protruding carnivorous teeth are a common feature of Shivaite and Buddhist deities, such as Kali (DEVI), YAMA, and others in their wrathful aspect (see DEMON) [*i: Mandi, c.* AD *1800*]. See also PINCERS.

[*i*]

Turban. Head-dress of several Near-Eastern peoples, especially Mohammedans. Introduced into the West by returning crusaders, it was often used by artists to characterize Old Testament figures, the Saracen, the SIBYLS and Orientals in general [*ii: after Rembrandt, 1642*]. In medieval Spanish manuscript painting the Moors are distinguished by their turbans.

[*ii*]

Urna. A tuft of hair, one of the distinguishing marks of the BUDDHA, though not always shown. It is situated in the centre of the forehead just above the eyebrows. It is described in Buddhist texts[36] as a white lock, curling to the right, the auspicious direction. It is generally represented as a small, round excrescence and on carved images may be of crystal or precious stone. (For illustration, see HEAD.) The urna emits the light of wisdom and symbolizes the state of Enlightenment. It is seen on Dhyani-BUDDHAS and BODHISATTVAS. In Tantric art it is replaced by the Shivaite third eye [*iii*]. See also EYE.

[*iii*]

Veil. A curtain or screen veils the inner sanctuary of temple or church in many cults, past and present. The officiant at a Roman sacrifice drew his toga over his head to veil himself from any distraction that would nullify its effect [*iv: Ara Pacis, c. 13* BC]. A nun's or bride's veil symbolizes chastity and submission; thus Rebecca, a virgin, covered her face on meeting Isaac.[37] The VIRGIN MARY, when enthroned, is veiled; as is HERA/JUNO in classical art. In medieval art Chastity personified, one of the THREE MONASTIC VOWS, is veiled. In Renaissance allegory a veil drawn aside reveals the figure of Truth. See also VERNICLE.

[*iv*]

Vernicle. The cloth (*sudarium* or vernicle) used to wipe the sweat from Christ's face as he bore the cross to Calvary. As a result, the image of his features was miraculously imprinted on it [*v*]. The woman who brought the cloth was named Veronica (*vera icon*, true image). She was canonized and, with SS. Peter and Paul, is a patron saint of Rome. The episode is not mentioned in the gospels and seems to have been an invention of medieval religious drama. It does not appear in art before the 15th cent. Veronica is depicted wiping Christ's face or kneeling and holding out the vernicle. It appears on badges worn by pilgrims returning from Rome.

[*v*]

Wrestlers. Wrestling is often a symbolic act. For the Greeks, especially later Stoics, contests of this kind had a parallel in the struggle between human passions that degrade and the contemplative life that leads to wisdom. Graeco-Roman tombs may represent wrestlers, usually children, engaged in this ethical contest. Early Mesopotamian votive plaques (turn of 4th–3rd mill. BC) show scenes of wrestling which are thought to have been part of some ritual occasion, possibly a sacred banquet. Japanese *sumo*

[*vi*]

wrestling also once had a ritual aspect, having been performed at religious festivals in Shinto shrines [*vi: wood-carving, 13th cent.* AD], a priest acting as referee. The ritualistic features of present-day *sumo* reflect its religious origins.

The mysterious wrestling match between the Israelite patriarch, Jacob, and an initially unidentified opponent at the ford of Jabbok[38] has many interpretations, Rabbinic, Christian and folkloric. In early Christian art, Jacob's adversary was God, later an angel. As an allegory of good versus evil, it may be a demon. It also symbolized the conflict of Church and Synagogue. Unidentified human wrestlers are often seen among the relief sculptures of Romanesque churches, but their meaning and artistic lineage are uncertain.

[*vii*]

Yab-Yum. Tibetan term (lit. 'father-mother') for the posture of ritual sexual intercourse (Sk. *maithuna*) between Hindu and Buddhist Tantric deities in their 'fierce' aspect, very common in Tibetan art [*vii*] though unknown in Japanese. The female, or *shakti*, represents the active, creative energy of the male. For Buddhists it is said to symbolize a fusion of the dual aspect of the Buddhist universe, the eternal (god) and temporal (goddess). It has been compared to the 'sacred marriage' of Babylonian religion and the Dionysiac and Priapic rites of ancient Greece and Rome. (See also DEVI.)

[*viii*]

Yoni. The concept of a Mother-Goddess, the universal creatrix, is of great antiquity and first took shape among very early, prehistoric communities. One common type of ritual object associated with the cult, found in all ages, is a representation of the vulva (Sk. *yoni*), the female external genital organ. It symbolizes the goddess's womb, the ultimate source of all creation. The image survives in Indian Tantric art as an attribute of the spouse of Shiva or as a devotional image [*viii: S. India, 19th cent.*]. It may be combined with the *lingam* of Shiva in the form of an oblong shallow basin with a *lingam* in the centre, a common object in Shivaite temples (see PHALLUS). Votive images and cave paintings of the Mother-Goddess displaying her vulva are found in western Europe, especially France, and appear to date from 2000 to 1400 BC. The Egyptian hieroglyphic sign for 'woman' is a vulva. See also TRIANGLE.

6. Plants

[i]

Acanthus. The distinguishing feature of the Corinthian capital; given more varied treatment in Byzantine capitals [*i: Constantinople, 6th cent., with Justinian's monogram*]. The scroll forms – a continuous curving stem with branching spirals – is found on ceilings of Italian churches (Rome and Ravenna, 5th–13th cents.), where it symbolizes heaven. The Tree of Jesse is often based on the acanthus.

Almond. Symbol of spring, from its early blossoming. A Christian symbol of divine favour, from the flowering of Aaron's rod.[1] The rod of Joseph, husband of the Virgin, also flowered as a mark of divine favour, whence the almond became a symbol of the Virgin's purity. For the Chinese it symbolizes feminine beauty and fortitude in grief [*ii*]. See also MANDORLA.

[ii]

Anemone. Scarlet and purple varieties are common in the Near East [*iii*]. It is an ancient symbol of death and sorrow from the Greek myth of the dying Adonis from whose spilled blood anemones sprouted.[2] They sprouted likewise from the blood of Christ on Calvary, according to a medieval tradition, and hence appear in paintings of the Crucifixion and of the Virgin of Sorrows.

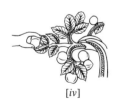

[iii]

Apple. In Christian art, the fruit of the Tree of Knowledge, plucked by Eve [*iv: French, 12th cent.*], hence a symbol of the Fall; held by the infant Christ it alludes to the doctrine of Redemption (see VIRGIN MARY). In Greek myth the apple of discord was thrown into the banquet of the gods and later awarded by Paris to APHRODITE/VENUS whose attribute it is; also of her attendants the THREE GRACES. The golden apples of the Hesperides symbolize immortality, and are an attribute of HERCULES. In China wild apple blossom denotes female beauty.

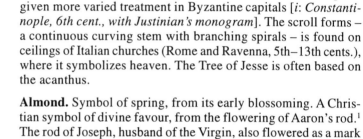

[iv]

Bamboo (Ch. *chu*; Jap. *sho*). Bamboo painting first flourished as a genre in Northern Sung art, though its origin is much earlier [*v*]. Pliant yet strong it symbolized reliability, courage in adversity, good breeding and similar virtues; also longevity, being evergreen. With the PINE and PLUM blossom it forms a very common group on Chinese ceramics and Japanese lacquer known as the THREE FRIENDS, standing for good fortune and longevity. See also HSI WANG MU.

Bread. The symbol of Christ's body. Bread and wine denote the Eucharist. They are seen together in VANITAS still-life paintings, especially north European. Bread, symbolizing spiritual refreshment, was brought to desert hermits by a bird, usually a raven.

[v]

[vi]

[vii]

[viii]

[ix]

[x]

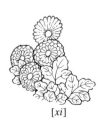

[xi]

A dog brought a loaf to St Roch in prison [*vi: French, 15th cent.*]. Bread and wine were used in Mithraic mysteries. In Egypt bread was offered to the gods, in particular to funerary deities. It was found in the tomb of Tutankhamun. It is usually represented as small, round or oval loaves. See also BASKET.

Cane. Stalk of sugar cane [*vii*], an attribute of SARASVATI, Indian goddess of vegetation.

Carnation. Emblem of the VIRGIN MARY, often a substitute for the ROSE. Red carnations symbolize the blood of Christian martyrs; white, virginal purity. In Renaissance portraiture when held in the sitter's hand, it denotes a betrothal. It is an attribute of Smell personified, one of the FIVE SENSES. In China it is associated with marriage and may feature with the lily and butterfly in ceramic and textile decoration [*viii: Sung textile*].

Cedar. Symbol of Christ, according to the Old Testament typology;[3] also an attribute of the Virgin of the Immaculate Conception (see VIRGIN MARY) [*ix*]. Evergreen trees such as cedar, pine and cypress symbolized the hope of life beyond the grave for many Mediterranean and Asian peoples. In ancient Mesopotamia the cones of the cedar and pine were used ritually to promote fertility or as a protection against harmful influences, especially disease (see PINE CONE).

Cherry. *Prunus Japonica* (Jap. *sakura*) is a Japanese national emblem. In China and Japan its flowers are a symbol of Spring and of feminine beauty [*x*]. In Christian art cherries are the 'Fruit of Paradise' enjoyed by the blessed and are sometimes held by the infant Christ (see VIRGIN MARY).

Chrysanthemum (Ch. *chu hua*; Jap. *kiku*). Commonly seen on Chinese ceramics as an emblem of Autumn (see FOUR SEASONS) – *chu* being a near-homophone of 'nine' and 'long time' – it is associated with the ninth month and with long life (sometimes with a PINE TREE). It may symbolize geniality, and a life of ease, especially after retirement [*xi*]. The sixteen-petalled chrysanthemum is a Japanese national emblem and the badge (MON) of the imperial family. The sun on the national flag, adopted in 1859, is styled to resemble a chrysanthemum. The Chinese legend of the 'Chrysanthemum Boy' is known in Japan, where he is called Kikujido.[4] See also GRASSHOPPER.

Citron. Jewish cult object, the *ethrog*, represented in wall painting and mosaic in Graeco-Roman synagogues; also on coins, lamps, tombstones and other artefacts [*i*]. It is one of the FOUR SPECIES and is carried at the Feast of Tabernacles, originally a harvest festival. The lemon was a Christian symbol of fidelity in love and associated with the VIRGIN MARY.

Columbine. The 'dove-like' aquilegia, its flowers somewhat resembling doves in flight [*ii*]; hence it is a Christian symbol of the Holy Ghost and may therefore accompany the VIRGIN MARY. Seven blooms symbolize the 'seven gifts of the holy spirit' (see DOVE).

Convolvulus. In Christian art it denotes humility, like the violet [*iii*]. In China it is a common symbol of love and marriage, perhaps entwining the pine-tree of longevity.

Corn. Ears or sheaves of corn are the universal attributes of the many corn deities of Europe and, especially, the Near East. Their rites, of which vestiges remain today, are among mankind's oldest. The annual death and rebirth of vegetation was reflected in their common myth: DEMETER/CERES and Persephone (Greece) [*iv*]; Astarte, or APHRODITE, and Adonis (Syria); Cybele and Attis (Phrygia); ISIS and OSIRIS (Egypt); Tammuz and ISHTAR, or Inanna (Sumer). Ears of corn, belonging to Tammuz, are depicted on cylinder seals from Uruk (Warka), *c*. 2500 BC. The cultivation of corn, symbolizing its life-preserving powers, is frequently depicted in Egyptian tomb painting, to ensure the deceased's survival (see also OSIRIS). In European painting corn is the attribute of Summer, one of the FOUR SEASONS, of Abundance, Concord and the Silver Age personified (see AGES OF THE WORLD). In Christian art corn and vine together symbolize the eucharistic elements and may be held by the infant Christ (see VIRGIN MARY). See also MITHRAS; TWELVE MONTHS – July.

Cornucopia, the 'horn of plenty', is a large horn, from which the fruits of the earth flow [*v: French, early 17th cent.*]. It is the attribute of gods, goddesses and benign personifications too numerous to be useful for identification. Noteworthy are the Graeco-Roman corn-goddess, DEMETER/CERES, PEACE, the Cimmerian SIBYL and, from the Renaissance onwards, CHARITY, Concord and FORTUNE. (See also AGES OF THE WORLD; FOUR ELEMENTS; FOUR PARTS OF THE WORLD.) In Greek myth the infant Zeus was suckled by the goat Amalthea, in return for which he changed one of her horns into a cornucopia, overflowing with everything she desired.[5] See also HORN.

Creeper. The ultimate in Jain asceticism was motionlessness. The standing figure of their saint, Gommateshvara, is therefore

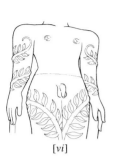

[vi]

[vii]

[viii]

[ix]

[x]

[xi]

[xii]

[xiii]

represented with tendrils climbing his legs and arms [*vi: Mysore, 10th cent.* AD]. (See also IVY.)

Cyclamen. Dedicated to the VIRGIN MARY, the red spot at the centre of the flower denoting her sorrows [*vii*]. Alternatively, a symbol of voluptuousness from the use of its root in the concoction of love potions in antiquity.[6]

Cypress. Like other evergreens, a symbol of immortality, that is, life beyond the tomb, hence found beside graves in ancient Greece and Italy, the Near East, India and China, as well as Christian Europe. It was also claimed for its funerary connections that it preserved the body from decay, that once cut down it died and that its dark foliage symbolized death [*viii*]. On Mithraic monuments seven cypresses denote the seven planetary spheres through which the soul passes on its journey to heaven.

Daisy. Symbol of the innocence of the Infant Christ, especially in scenes of the Adoration in Italian painting from the later 15th cent., where it may replace the Virgin's LILY [*ix*].

Dandelion. Christian symbol of grief, seen mainly in paintings of the crucifixion by the early Flemish and German schools [*x*].[7]

Date. Clusters of dates were a symbol of fertility in Egypt and Mesopotamia [*xi: Nimrud, 8th cent.* BC]. Some of the earliest representations of the SACRED TREE appear to depict a date palm. (See also PALM.)

Fig. For the bodhi-tree or *ficus religiosa*, the Buddha's Tree of Enlightenment, see TREE. Its leaf is an emblem of the BUDDHA and is sacred to Buddhists and Brahmins. Its characteristic shape, sharply pointed, is reflected in the shape of the AUREOLE of Buddhist deities. The child KRISHNA lying on a fig leaf [*xii: S. India, 19th cent.*] is said to symbolize the god brooding over the destruction of the universe at the end of the *kalpa*, or cosmic age.

Fleur-de-lis. The origin of the well-known emblem of French kings and the city of Florence is uncertain [*xiii: French, late 15th* *cent.*] It is possibly a stylized rendering of an IRIS or three lilies, or may have been derived from the head of a weapon such as Shiva's *trishula* (see TRIDENT). If a flower, it would once have been a symbol of life. In Christian art it may replace the LILY as the principal flower of the VIRGIN MARY. In the scene of the Annunciation[8] it forms the tip of Gabriel's sceptre. Adopted as the emblem of the French monarchy in 1147 it became the attribute of later French saints of royal blood, Louis IX and Louis of Toulouse. Charlemagne (died 814) and Zenobius, bishop of Florence, may have a fleur-de-lis.

Flowers. Flower deities are generally female, being descended from more ancient fertility goddesses. Thus Flora, the old Italian goddess of flowers – who also watched over the vine, olive and other crops – made a barren heifer fecund by touching it with a flower.[9] Flower-goddesses hold garlands or baskets of flowers, or strew their blooms about. The Taoist goddess of flowers, Hua Hsien, may have attendants holding flower baskets. She is not the same as Lan Ts'ai-ho (Jap. Ransaikwa), one of the EIGHT IMMORTALS of Taoism, who holds a basket and wears only one shoe [*i*]. Lu Hsing, one of the GODS OF HAPPINESS, also holds a basket of flowers, as sometimes does HSI WANG MU, Queen Mother of the West. Sengen, the Shinto goddess of Mt Fuji who causes trees to blossom, carries a flowering branch. Garlands and flowers are an attribute of the Hindu SARASVATI and of YAMA, the Hindu god of the Underworld, who wears them in his hair; of Eos/Aurora, the Graeco-Roman goddess of dawn; and of personifications of Spring, one of the FOUR SEASONS, HOPE, Logic, one of the SEVEN LIBERAL ARTS, Smell, one of the FIVE SENSES, and Asia, one of the FOUR PARTS OF THE WORLD. In Renaissance allegory flowers, fish and stars decorated the robe of PHILOSOPHY. Flowers are among the still-life objects in VANITAS paintings.

[*i*]

Many individual species (qq.v.) have their own symbolism. Christian painting and Chinese ceramic decoration are both, in their different ways, very rich in this respect. In Chinese art each of the FOUR SEASONS and the TWELVE MONTHS is distinguished by its own flower. Another Chinese group, the THREE FRIENDS, is also popular in Japan, especially in lacquer work.

Garden. Egyptian symbol of life after death often depicted in tomb paintings of the 18th and 19th Dynasties with palms and sycamore trees. The idea of a heavenly garden as the abode of the dead and of the gods occurs also in Sumerian and Babylonian myth. Dilmun, the Sumerian Paradise, was probably the origin of the Garden of Eden. The Buddhist heaven, the Pure Land of the West (Sk. *sukhavati*; Ch. *Ch'ing T'u*), was a Chinese doctrine of the 4th cent. AD later adopted by the Japanese. Its magnificent gardens surrounded a palace where the Buddha Amitabha dwelt (see BUDDHA). A somewhat similar Taoist Paradise was ruled by HSI WANG MU, Queen Mother of the West, who guarded

[*ii*]

the peaches of immortality in her gardens. In the garden of the Greek Hesperides, which also lay in the west, grew a tree of golden apples guarded by the dragon Ladon. The garden of Flora, the Roman goddess of FLOWERS, was the gift of the West Wind, Zephyrus. She and her garden were popular with Post-Renaissance painters. In Christian art an enclosed garden symbolizes virginity and is particularly associated with the VIRGIN MARY of the Immaculate Conception[10] and the Annunciation [*ii: Flemish, early 15th cent.*].

Gourd. The hollow dried fruit of the calabash, once used by travellers as a water-bottle; an attribute of James the Greater, patron of Christian pilgrims. The 'double gourd' (Ch. *hu-lu*) [*iii*], sometimes with smoke rising from it, symbolizes the union of YIN AND YANG, heaven and earth, and good augury. It is an attribute of Li T'ieh-kuai, one of the Taoist EIGHT IMMORTALS; of Shou Hsing, one of the GODS OF HAPPINESS; and sometimes of HSI WANG MU, Queen Mother of the West. Gourds strung on a pole are the military standard of Hideyoshi (1537–98), a famous Japanese soldier and statesman. The gourd tree that sheltered Jonah[11] was made a symbol of Christ's Resurrection.

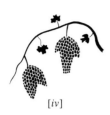

Grapes. Bunches of grapes belong to DIONYSUS/BACCHUS, the Greek god of wine [*iv: Attic, 5th cent.* BC]. In Christian art they symbolize the Eucharistic wine, hence the blood of Christ. The infant Christ, in the arms of the VIRGIN MARY, may hold grapes. Two Israelites bearing a very large bunch of grapes between them on a pole became a prefiguration of Christ on the cross.[12] Grapes are an attribute of Vincent of Saragossa, patron of Spanish winegrowers, and of Autumn personified, one of the FOUR SEASONS. In the cycle of the LABOURS OF THE MONTHS they are harvested in September. See also VINE.

Hemlock. Umbelliferous plant, a symbol of death; the draught taken by Socrates on his death-bed, a popular theme in French neoclassical painting [*v*]. An attribute of Treason and Death personified.

Holly. Sacred to Saturn, Roman god of agriculture. It featured in his festival, the Saturnalia, which was celebrated in mid-December and was the prototype of Christmas. Its leaves later symbolized Christ's crown of thorns, its berries his blood. The tree may be introduced into paintings of Jerome, one of the FOUR LATIN FATHERS, when meditating on the Passion of Christ, and of JOHN THE BAPTIST who foretold it [*vi*].

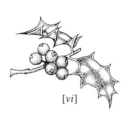

Honeycomb. Renaissance paintings depict Cupid, the god of love, stung by a bee, having stolen a honeycomb, which he is still holding [*vii*]. It illustrates the notion that 'love is bitter-sweet' and comes from Theocritus.[13] A honeycomb is an attribute of JOHN THE BAPTIST.[14] See also AGES OF THE WORLD – Golden Age; BEE, BEEHIVE.

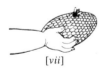

[i]

[ii]

[iii]

[iv]

[v]

Hyacinth. The subject of one of a number of related Greek myths probably derived from ancient fertility rites. In Greek myth the flower sprang from the spilt blood of the youth Hyacinthus who died when accidentally struck by a discus thrown by his lover Apollo.[15] Ovid says the flower 'took on the shape of a lily, but was purple in colour'. Artists interpret it freely according to the species most familiar to them [i]. It is seen in the garden of Flora in Renaissance painting. It is also a Christian symbol of Prudence, fairly rare in art, apparently derived from the myth.

Hyssop. Christian symbol of penitence and humility. As a purgative[16] it became a symbol of innocence regained, hence of baptism [ii].

Iris. The flower of the VIRGIN MARY, an alternative to the LILY. It appears first in early Flemish painting, where it may accompany, or replace, the lily. It is rare in German art, and common in Spanish [iii]. As the emblem of the Greek god Iris, it is unknown before the Renaissance. See also FLEUR-DE-LIS.

Ivy. Sacred to DIONYSUS/BACCHUS in antiquity, and consumed by his followers, the Bacchantes, in their frenzies. Dionysus wears a garland of ivy, or it entwines his THYRSUS. As an evergreen it is a symbol of immortality. It is also a symbol of death because 'it is a mischievous plant for it destroys and starves any tree by withdrawing the moisture'.[17] Ivy crowning a skull denotes immortality in VANITAS paintings. Antinous, a favourite of the Roman Emperor Hadrian, who committed suicide and is immortalized in Roman sculpture [iv: Roman, 2nd cent. AD], may be crowned with ivy. See also CREEPER.

Laurel. Once believed to be a protection against disease, the bay laurel was sacred to APOLLO, one of whose roles was that of healer and patron of medicine. It featured in Greek and Roman festivals in honour of the god; victors in his Pythian games at Delphi, which included contests of poetry and music, were awarded a laurel crown. It was bestowed by the Greek goddess Nike (Victory). In early Greek art EROS/CUPID bestows a laurel wreath on loving couples. It was worn by Roman emperors when celebrating a triumph [v: Ara Pacis, c. 13 BC]. The practice of awarding a laurel crown for poetry was revived at Padua in 1315, and it remains a symbol of literary and artistic achievement. In Renaissance paintings laurels grow on Mount Parnassus, home of the MUSES, whose leader was Apollo. It is an attribute of Apollo, the MUSES Calliope and Clio, the Greek poets Orpheus, Homer and Arion (who rides a dolphin); in allegory, of Fame (with trumpet) and naked Truth. See also AGES OF THE WORLD – Iron Age; VIRTUES AND VICES. In Greek myth the nymph Daphne on being pursued by Apollo was changed into a laurel tree.

Leaf. In Chinese ceramic decoration a leaf of artemisia is one of the EIGHT TREASURES [*vi*] and is a symbol of joy. See also FIG; HOLLY; IVY; VINE and other florae.

[*vi*]

Lettuce. The long-leaved variety (*Latuca sativa*) was sacred to MIN, the Egyptian god of fertility [*vii*]. It was offered ritually in the belief that it was an aphrodisiac that would maintain his sexual energy. The earliest image, seen on tombs, dates from 4500 BC, but as an attribute of Min, from the 6th Dynasty.

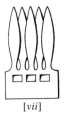

[*vii*]

Lily. The white lily is a widely accepted symbol of purity in the West. In ancient Greece it was believed to have sprung from the milk of HERA/JUNO. As a Christian symbol it also denotes virginity and is pre-eminently the flower of the VIRGIN MARY [*viii*]. It therefore features in the Annunciation, either held by the archangel Gabriel or standing in a vase. A lily and sword in the scene of the Last Judgement symbolize the innocent and guilty. A lily is an attribute of virgin saints, in particular Catherine of Siena, Clare, Euphemia, Scholastica; also of Antony of Padua, Dominic, Francis of Assisi, Francis Xavier, Joseph the husband of Mary, Philip Neri, Thomas Aquinas, and the Erythraean SIBYL. It is an attribute of Smell, one of the FIVE SENSES. See also FLEUR-DE-LIS.

[*viii*]

Lotus (Sk. *padma*; Ch. *lien-hua*; Jap. *renge*). The name of various species of water-lily, revered in ancient Egypt and in many parts of Asia. Its sacred character was derived initially from its watery habitat, WATER being an archaic symbol of the primeval ocean out of which the universe was created. The lotus, floating on the surface, was its womb. In both Egyptian and Indian myth and art the petals open to reveal a creator-god. Its opening at sunrise and closing at sunset linked it also to the sun, itself a divine source of life. The Egyptian sun-god and creator, RE, is depicted as a child reclining on a lotus (or his head emerges from it) at the beginning of his daily journey across the sky. The lotus was personified by Nefertum, a deity associated with Re and worshipped principally at Memphis. He wears a lotus crown, usually topped with two feathers. HATHOR, a sky-goddess in one of her aspects, was also connected with Re and sometimes holds a lotus. Capitals of columns in Egyptian TEMPLES may be carved to represent a lotus, either in bud [*ix*] or open and bell-shaped. A lotus is the emblem of Upper Egypt.

[*ix*]

In the 8th cent. BC the lotus image was transmitted to Phoenicia and thence to Assyria and Persia, where it is sometimes substituted for the SACRED TREE. Phoenician goddesses hold a lotus flower as a symbol of their creative power. It often features in Sassanian Persian ornament (3rd–7th cents. AD).

In India, too, the lotus was linked to a sun-god. The Vedic deity, SURYA, who personifies the sun, typically holds a lotus in each hand. It was also associated with the worship of Indian Mother-Goddesses from very early times, as a symbol of the cosmic womb. The oldest example is from the Indus Valley (3rd mill.

[i]

[ii]

BC) (see DEVI). Following the Aryan conquest (2000–1500 BC) the Indian pantheon became predominantly male. It was headed by BRAHMA, the creator-god of the *Vedas*. A later myth, adumbrated in the *Rig-Veda*,[18] tells how the universe came into being through a golden lotus floating on the cosmic waters, from which Brahma was born. When his cult yielded place to VISHNU he was then depicted sitting on a lotus that grows from Vishnu's navel (from 5th to 6th cents. AD).[19] (See also KRISHNA.)

The cult of the Mother-Goddess in India never wholly died out. She emerged again as the Hindu goddess Padmapani, 'She who holds the lotus' [i] (see AVALOKITESHVARA). She is present in some degree in all female deities (see DEVI). The *shaktis*, spouses of the gods, representing the procreative energy that drives the universe, nearly always have a lotus among their numerous attributes, which symbolizes this universal life force. Lakshmi, wife of VISHNU, and Parvati, wife of SHIVA, are directly descended from the Indus Valley goddess and feature in several myths linking them to the lotus. The symbol was bequeathed to their offspring, Skanda, the son of Shiva and Parvati, who holds a lotus in each hand (see KARTTIKEYA). Lakshmi may be enthroned on a lotus, or stands on it, flanked by elephants that spray her with water, a symbol of her fertilizing power. The principal lotus goddess of Buddhism was PRAJNA-PARAMITA, consort of the Adi-Buddha, who holds a lotus with a book lying on it [ii] (see also MANJUSHRI). Goddesses of the RIVERS of India are sometimes mounted on a lotus (see SARASVATI).

In Buddhist teaching the lotus goes far into the realm of metaphysics. It is a symbol of the pure essence of human nature which is undefiled by *samsara*, the endless cycle of rebirth, or by the ignorance that the physical world generates; in other words, the lotus is Enlightenment itself. It shares this symbolism with the WHEEL of the Law and the two together therefore often form a composite image. The Buddhist heaven, the Pure Land of the West, a concept introduced by the Mahayana sect, is symbolized by the lotus and is an attribute of its presiding deity, Amitabha (see VAIROCANA). Thus it is represented at the centre of decorated ceilings in Buddhist temples, especially in central Asia. The plan of the eight-sided pagoda is also related to the lotus (see BUDDHA; STUPA).

Statues of the Buddha seated on a lotus throne mark him as ruler of the created universe and as the personification of the doctrine of Enlightenment. They appear first in the art of Gandhara and Mathura (3rd or 4th cents. AD). Even earlier he is seated in the 'lotus position' (see POSTURE). Later, nearly all Buddhas and bodhisattvas either sit or stand on the lotus; when seated it may form their footstool. These enthroned deities appear in the art of Nepal, Tibet, China and Japan, the throne signifying the sitter's divine origin. Mahayana Buddhism in China and Japan developed, in the 4th and 5th cents. AD, the idea of the 'Pure Land of the West', a celestial Paradise at whose head was a Redeemer, the Dhyani-Buddha Amitabha (Jap. Amida). He and his attendant deities are usually enthroned on the lotus (see also THRONE). The lotus features regularly in the Tantric art of Tibet. The *Shri-Yantra*, one of the Tantrists' objects of contemplation may be encircled by the lotus motif (see TRIANGLE). The motif often features in the Tibetan MANDALA.

A lotus is among the EIGHT LUCKY EMBLEMS on the sole of the Buddha's foot. It is the attribute of Ho Hsien-ku, one of the Taoist EIGHT IMMORTALS; and of several Japanese sennins and other holy men. It is a Chinese emblem of Summer, one of the FOUR SEASONS.

[*iii*]

Magnolia (Ch. *mu-lan*). In ancient China the magnolia was the exclusive property of the emperor who might bestow a plant as a token of royal favour [*iii*]. The flower symbolizes gentleness and feminine beauty. Mu-lan (magnolia) was a famous Chinese heroine (between AD 220 and 588) who, disguised as a man, took her ailing father's place on the battlefield.

[*iv*]

Marigold. The golden flower of the VIRGIN MARY though rare as her attribute in art [*iv*]. Like the sunflower, it turns its face towards the sun. A Greek myth tells how a Nereid, Clytie, having been spurned in love by the sun-god, APOLLO, was turned into a 'sunflower' (more probably a marigold) and so continued to gaze upon him ever after.[20] In China it is sometimes called the 'flower of eternal life' and symbolizes longevity.

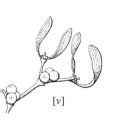

[*v*]

Mistletoe. In European folklore a symbol of life, a healing plant and a protective talisman [*v*]. As an evergreen it is parasitic on the oak (among other trees). It ensured, so long as it was not cut, the continued existence of the tree-spirit in winter. In Teutonic myth the god Baldur, apparently identified with his oak-tree spirit, died on being struck by a twig of mistletoe. It was sacred to the Druids who cut it ritually when performing a bull-sacrifice. The Trojan hero Aeneas, on descending to the Underworld, carried a branch of the 'golden bough', or mistletoe, to protect his life. Mistletoe at Christmas derives, like HOLLY, from the Roman festival of the Saturnalia.

[*vi*]

Mon. Badge worn by Japanese imperial and noble families and their military retainers to distinguish one from another, especially when warring among themselves. It first came into general use in the 12th cent., being derived from much older battle standards. They eventually numbered over 500. The majority of the motifs are floral but there are many abstract patterns and miscellaneous objects. The principal badge of the emperor, called the *Jo-mon*, comprised the leaves and blossoms of the Japanese flowering tree, the Paulownia (Jap. *kiri*) [*vi*]. A somewhat similar device, the *Kae-mon*, was used by other members of the imperial family. A third imperial badge, the *Kiku-mon*, was a CHRYSANTHEMUM with sixteen petals and another sixteen just visible behind them [*vii*].

[*vii*]

[i]

[ii]

[iii]

[iv]

Myrtle. Aromatic evergreen, a symbol of love and sacred to APHRODITE/VENUS and her attendants, the THREE GRACES [i]. A crown of myrtle was awarded to Roman victors, a lesser honour than the laurel. The myrtle is one of the FOUR SPECIES of the Jewish religion. In Christian art it symbolizes the martyrs and confessors, following a vision of the prophet Zechariah.[21] It is occasionally an attribute of the VIRGIN MARY.

Narcissus. For the ancient Greeks a symbol of youthful death, from the myth of the beautiful youth of that name who pined away gazing at his reflection in a pool. At his death he was changed into the flower.[22] It was believed that a person's soul resided in his reflection (see MIRROR) which, in the case of Narcissus, was stolen by the water nymphs. In China, as in Greece, the narcissus (*shui-hsien-hua*) means water-immortal or nymph. Since it blooms at the Chinese New Year it will bring good fortune for the next twelve months [ii: *Ch'ing ceramic*]. Narcissus, stones and bamboo, depicted together, denote by a play on words, 'The immortals wish you a long life.'

Oak. Sacred tree, the abode of the gods of thunder and rain, worshipped by many early communities throughout Europe. Probably the oldest cult centre was that of ZEUS/JUPITER at Dodona in Epirus, where the rustling leaves of the sacred tree were regarded as his voice, uttering oracles [*iii: Roman relief from the Forum, early 2nd cent.* AD]. At Plataea in Boeotia a sacred marriage was performed between Zeus and HERA/JUNO in the role of oak-goddess, when they were crowned with oak-leaves. An oak-leaf crown was awarded to a Roman citizen if he saved the life of a fellow Roman in battle. The oak and its parasite MISTLETOE were at the centre of Druidic rites. The tree was sacred to Silvanus, Roman god of forests, and to Donar, or Thor, the Teutonic god of Thunder. A bishop wearing canonicals, his foot resting on a fallen oak, is St Boniface (*c.* 675–754), an English missionary to northern Europe. His pose symbolizes his conversion of Druids to Christianity.

Oil. Anointing with oil was part of the Hebrew ritual of consecrating high priests and kings, as in the case of Aaron anointed by Moses[23] and David by Samuel,[24] with oil poured from a horn [*iv: English miniature, 12th cent.*]. David was regarded by the Christian Church as a prefiguration of Christ (= the anointed), hence his place in Christian art.

Olive. Symbol of peace, sacred to ATHENA/MINERVA though, in her earliest, pre-Hellenic manifestations, she was a war-goddess. An olive crown was awarded to victors in the Panathenaea, the games held in her honour at Athens. It is worn by ZEUS/JUPITER as patron of the original Olympic games. Early Christians took over the olive as a religious symbol: in the Roman catacombs one sees a sprig of olive carried by a dove with the inscription '*In pace*', that is to say, may the soul of the deceased depart in peace.

In later Christian art the olive is an attribute of the VIRGIN MARY, sometimes as a substitute for the lily; of St Agnes and, in Renaissance allegory, of Peace and Concord personified [*v*] (see also AGES OF THE WORLD – Golden Age). In China the scented olive, with white or yellow flowers, is a symbol of Autumn, one of the FOUR SEASONS.

[*v*]

Orange. In the West white orange blossom is a symbol of purity and virginity and is therefore often carried by a bride. The tree may be depicted beside the VIRGIN MARY, or its fruit in the hand of the infant Christ. It may sometimes replace the apple tree in scenes of Paradise, as a symbol of the Fall. Oranges are a popular gift at Chinese and Japanese New Year festivals. For the Chinese the gift expresses the wish for good fortune in the coming year or, if to a married daughter, that she may speedily bear children. In Chinese, *chü* (orange) is a near homophone for 'to pray for happiness' [*vi*].

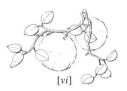

[*vi*]

Palm, Palmette. The date palm was an important source of food in ancient Mesopotamia and one of several trees that featured in fertility rites in the region. The sacred marriage between the Mother-Goddess and the corn-god Tammuz was described as a coupling between the 'holy palm tree' and the 'holy corn plant'.[25] The SACRED TREE, a fertility symbol, is typically crowned with some form of palmette motif [*vii: neo-Assyrian, 7th cent.* BC], especially on Assyrian monuments from the 10th cent. BC, though known much earlier.

[*vii*]

In Egypt the palm symbolized the fertility of crops generally and, with the PAPYRUS, formed the heraldic signs of Upper and Lower Egypt. The date palm was sacred to the sun-god RE and was regarded as his abode. The notched palm-rib [*viii*] is the characteristic attribute of Heh, the god of eternity who was invoked to grant eternal life. In the New Kingdom it is also seen as the attribute of Seshat, goddess of writing and of royal record-keeping.

[*viii*]

A palm branch, called *lulab*, is one of the FOUR SPECIES carried by Jewish priests at the Feast of Tabernacles, formerly a harvest festival. In the Graeco-Roman era the four are sometimes represented by the palm alone. The palm, a symbol of military victory in the Roman army, was taken over by early Christians to symbolize their victory over death. It appears first in the funerary art of the Roman catacombs and is subsequently used in many contexts. It became the attribute of most Christian martyrs. It features at the death of the VIRGIN MARY, the death of John the Evangelist and at Christ's last entry into Jerusalem. (See also THREE MONASTIC VOWS.) It is an attribute of the Virgin of the Immaculate Conception. A loin-cloth of palm leaves is the dress of some desert hermits, especially St Paul the Hermit. A palm-branch is the attribute of the personifications of VICTORY, Fame and Asia, one of the FOUR PARTS OF THE WORLD. Eros and Anteros contend for a palm branch. (See EROS/CUPID.)

[i]

Papyrus, the 'growth of the river' (i.e. the Nile). Its reeds were treated in such a way as to provide a smooth surface for writing. It was the 'heraldic' plant of Lower Egypt (cf. PALM), where it once thrived, and symbolized the creation of the world, which had risen from the primeval waters [i]. It forms the sceptre of Wadjet, the ancient tutelary goddess of the Delta region. The capitals of temple columns in the New Kingdom are carved to represent the flower-like umbel, either closed or open (at night or in daytime), to symbolize the path of the sun-god. (See HATHOR; PILLAR; SA.)

[ii]

Peach (Ch. *t'ao*). The tree and its fruit are popular motifs in Chinese art, especially ceramics. Peaches are a symbol of the coming of spring, eternal renewal and hence long life. With a JU-I sceptre the message is 'Long life just as you would wish'; with a BAT, 'Long life and happiness'. Peaches bring happiness to newlyweds for the written character *t'ao* denotes both peach and marriage. Peach blossom would be inappropriate for them, for being short-lived it conveys the idea of early death. Fallen blossom symbolizes a prostitute. A peach is an attribute of Shou Hsing, one of the GODS OF HAPPINESS, and of his Japanese counterpart, Fuku-roku-jiu, and Jurojin. A common motif in ceramic decoration shows a peach tree with a twisted trunk that forms the character SHOU, meaning longevity [*ii: Ch'ing Dynasty*]. The Queen Mother of the West, HSI WANG MU, of Taoist legend, guards the peaches of immortality that grow in her palace gardens. The wood of a peach tree repels evil spirits and so is chosen for the figures guarding doorways, and by Taoist priests for the carved seals they use to stamp amulets. In Christian art a peach, when substituted for the more usual apple in the hand of the infant Christ, is a symbol of salvation. A peach with one leaf denotes the heart and tongue speaking with one mind and is therefore a symbol of Truth.

[iii]

Peony (Ch. *mu-tan*; Jap. *botan-kwa*). Popular motif on Chinese ceramics, especially early 15th cent., typically in scroll form [*iii*]. Though it is *yang* it expresses love, feminine beauty and similar sentiments. The tree peony is a symbol of Spring, one of the FOUR SEASONS and is depicted with the other three seasonal flowers. Peony and peach together denote 'long life, riches and good repute'. For the Japanese it is an emblem of imperial power and wealth, besides sharing some of the Chinese symbolism.

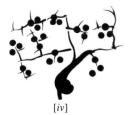

[iv]

Persimmon (Ch. *shih*). Brightly coloured fruit, somewhat like an apple, also called Chinese fig, or date plum. Seen mainly in ceramic decoration, where it symbolizes joy [*iv*]. Persimmon, lily and sacred fungus together denote 'May everything come about as you would wish.'

Pine cone. An object resembling a pine cone is depicted in the rites surrounding the SACRED TREE. It is held in the hand of a priest or winged *genius* and pointed at the tree as if to touch it. Various explanations have been offered for the meaning of the rite. The object itself is thought to have been the inflorescent bud of the date palm or a cone of the pine, fir or cedar, the scene as a whole perhaps representing an actual or symbolic fertilization of the tree. The motif appears in Mesopotamian art following the arrival of Indo-European settlers around the 18th cent. BC and is prominent in late Assyrian monumental reliefs [*v: 8th cent.* BC]. The wand of Dionysus is tipped with a pine cone (see THYRSUS). The pine cone is commonly seen in Roman funerary art as a symbol of Immortality, the tree itself being evergreen.

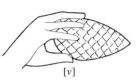
[*v*]

Pine tree (Ch. *sung shu*; Jap. *matsu*). Chinese symbol of Longevity, friendship and constancy especially in time of adversity; with bamboo and prunus, one of the THREE FRIENDS. It is common in ceramic decoration from the 15th cent. [*vi*]. The pine tree may personify Shou Hsing, one of the GODS OF HAPPINESS. The Japanese spirits of the pine tree are Jo and Uba, an aged couple, he with a rake, she with a broom. They are often accompanied by a TORTOISE and CRANE, symbols of Longevity. They are the subject of a 15th cent. No play and are popular in painting and carved *netsuke*. (See also PINE CONE.)

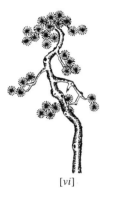
[*vi*]

Plantain (Ch. *pa-chiao*). The stiff leaves of this species of banana are a popular motif in Chinese blue and white ceramics from the 14th cent. onwards, especially round the necks of vases and flasks [*vii*]. They symbolize the self-taught person from a legend of a student too poor to buy paper who used dried plantain leaves instead.

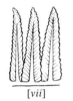
[*vii*]

Plum (Ch. *li*; *mei hua*). The wild plum (of the genus *prunus*), which blossoms early before the leaves appear, is a Chinese emblem of Winter, one of the FOUR SEASONS [*viii*]. With the bamboo and pine it is one of the THREE FRIENDS of winter. Plum blossom is a symbol of the integrity of the Confucian scholar and of steadfastness generally, the tree being a very sturdy growth. It is a popular source of inspiration for poets and artists. With peach blossom, or a QUAIL, it expresses the wish for joy. Plum blossom is the attribute of the Shinto patron of poetry and the arts, Kitano Tenjin (845–903). He was deified and became the object of a cult; many of his sanctuaries are well known for their plum trees.

[*viii*]

Pomegranate. Its many seeds made it a widespread symbol of fertility and abundance among the peoples of the Mediterranean, Near East, India and beyond. It is an attribute of the Greek goddesses DEMETER/CERES, Persephone and HERA/JUNO and was believed by some to be an aphrodisiac, or to induce pregnancy. Hence it was associated with fertility-goddesses. Persephone was given a pomegranate seed to eat before departing from Hades' kingdom. This ensured her periodical return below and the future cycle of death and rebirth of nature.[26] The pomegran-

[i]

ate as a Christian symbol of resurrection and immortality was derived from this myth. It is seen in the hand of the infant Christ (see VIRGIN MARY). It is also a Christian symbol of chastity (see UNICORN).

It is one of the fruits of the SACRED TREE. It is an attribute of Hariti, a demoness of Buddhist legend[27] who devoured children until, in some versions, the Buddha cured her by giving her a pomegranate to eat. She is represented in Buddhist art in the Far East holding a child and is widely invoked by infertile Japanese women under the name of Kishimojin. In China the pomegranate symbolizes fertility and is widely represented in ceramic painting [i]. A painting of the fruit cut open to reveal its seeds makes a popular wedding present, expressing the wish 'May you have as many children as there are seeds!'

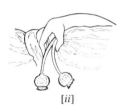

[ii]

Poppy. Well known in antiquity for its sleep-inducing properties. In Graeco-Roman funerary art it symbolizes the sleep of death. It is an attribute of Hypnos, Greek god of sleep and features in Graeco-Roman funerary art [*ii: late Roman sarcophagus*]. He may hold a horn from which opium drips. Some early images of DEMETER/CERES show her holding poppies, an allusion to the death of nature in winter. Among pre-Hellenic peoples it was a symbol of fecundity, and was taken medicinally to induce pregnancy. In Renaissance allegory a crown of poppies is worn by Nyx, the goddess of night, and Morpheus, god of dreams. More rarely it is an attribute of APHRODITE/VENUS.

[iii]

Quince. Sacred to APHRODITE/VENUS and a symbol of fertility. Plutarch advised Greek brides to eat a quince in preparation for their wedding night.[28] In Renaissance wedding portraiture the woman may hold a quince [*iii*]. In the hand of the infant Christ it has the same meaning as the APPLE.

Reeds. Bundles of reeds, bound up in a distinctive way [*iv: Early Sumerian, 3rd quarter, 4th mill.* BC], represent the Sumerian Mother-Goddess, Inanna (ISHTAR), and perhaps also ANU. They appear to have been placed round the shrines of the goddess (3500–3250 BC). They are still seen after the Early Dynastic Period. Reeds of the Nile sometimes sprout from the body of GEB, the Egyptian earth-god. Pan-pipes, the instrument of Greek shepherds, were perhaps once made of reed canes. A myth tells how the god Pan pursued a nymph, Syrinx, who escaped from him at a river's edge by being transformed into reeds. Pan cut them and made from them the first set of pipes.[29] The Buddhist monk, Bhodidharma, crossed the Yangtze river on a reed (see ARHAT).

[iv]

Rice. 'Staff of life' in the East, sharing some of the symbolism of corn. Daikoku, one of the Japanese GODS OF HAPPINESS, sits or stands on bales of rice. The Shinto god of rice, Inari, carries sheaves of rice over his shoulder (see also FOX). Rice is one of the offerings in Lamaist temple ritual. The 'grain' symbol on

[v]

Chinese imperial robes [v], one of the TWELVE ORNAMENTS, was once thought to be rice, but is probably millet.

Rose, Rosette. The two should be distinguished. The rose is a common symbolic flower in western classical and Christian art (though of little significance in the East), while rosette denotes a shape, not necessarily based on a rose. The red rose was sacred to APHRODITE/VENUS, her attendants, the THREE GRACES, and Flora, the Italian goddess of flowers, for all of whom it symbolized love and beauty. It was an early Christian symbol, found in the Roman catacombs, where possibly it denotes Paradise. It became closely associated with the VIRGIN MARY, who was sometimes designated 'rose without thorns', that is, without sin. A red rose symbolizes the Christian martyr's blood, a white one virginity. Roses are an attribute of several female saints, among them Dorothea, Elizabeth of Hungary, Rosalia of Palermo, Rose of Lima.

[vi]

The rosette, like the wheel which it sometimes resembles, was primarily a solar symbol, and thus may be seen on the WINGED DISK and the FOOT of Buddha. It personifies several Near-Eastern sun-gods. It was a popular decorative motif in Mesopotamian art in later times, sometimes possibly as a symbol of ISHTAR [vi]. As a decoration for jewellery and on tombs and buildings its purpose may have been apotropaic. It is found with the crescent in the funerary art of Roman Gaul, symbolizing sun and moon respectively. See also SIBITTI.

[vii]

Rosemary. From its lasting scent, a symbol of remembrance. As an evergreen, denoting immortality, it used to have a place in funeral rites [vii].

Sa. An Egyptian hieroglyph said to represent a herdsman's shelter made of papyrus that has been rolled up and tied. It was a magical symbol of protection, and is the attribute of BES and Taweret, the HIPPOPOTAMUS goddess [viii: Middle Kingdom].

[viii]

Sacred Tree. The belief that a spirit dwelt in certain trees and plants that were beneficial to man goes back into prehistory. The image of a tree flanked by a pair of animals, demigods or human figures appears in Mesopotamian art about the 18th cent. BC. It is likely it was then regarded as a manifestation of the Mother-Goddess, ISHTAR, and not just an impersonal spirit of fertility. The image subsequently spread throughout the Near East and far beyond, its meaning continually modified to suit the cultures in which it took root. Early Mesopotamian examples depict a cypress, vine or pomegranate, most often the date-palm, or sometimes a combination of more than one [ix]. (See DATE; PALM.) It is widely represented on Assyrian monuments from the 10th cent. BC, becoming gradually more stylized and elaborate. There are two main types: the tree flanked by animals confronting each other; or flanked by human (or partly human) figures apparently performing a fertility rite (see PINE CONE). The

[ix]

tree with human figures reached the Far East, undergoing many adaptions on the way. The tree flanked by animals likewise spread eastwards to Persia and hence to India where it was introduced into Buddhist art. It was also among the decorative motifs that Byzantine artists borrowed from Sassanid Persia. Thence it entered medieval Christian art of the West, as part of a large repertoire of fantastic creatures and other motifs of Near-Eastern origin (see also TREE).

[i]

Sycamore. Several kinds of tree were venerated by the ancient Egyptians, each being the abode of one or more deities. The so-called 'Egyptian sycamore' (*Ficus sycamorus*) is related to the fig and bears fruit.[30] It was sacred to RE. A pair stood at the eastern gate of heaven from which he emerged each morning.[31] It was also one of the forms in which the sky-goddess, Nut, manifested herself. Her head and shoulders emerge among its branches. Sycamore leaves as amulets would bring prosperity. The tree commonly represented in the *Book of the Dead* would be the sycamore [i].

[ii]

Thistle. Christian symbol of sorrow and sin, from God's curse upon Adam,[32] when it is coupled with the THORN. Hence it sometimes grows at the foot of the cross in crucifixions by northern European painters [ii].

[iii]

Thorn. According to Thomas Aquinas thorn branches are for Christians a symbol of minor sins; briars and brambles, major ones.[33] The bush, burning yet unconsumed, out of which God spoke to Moses,[34] though commonly called a thorn, was a bramble (Vulg. *rubus*). It was likened to the VIRGIN MARY, whose virginity remained intact while yet wrapped in the flames of divine love.[35] She is sometimes represented by German painters in a flaming bush. As the 'lily among thorns'[36] she sits in a rose-garden whose roses have exaggeratedly large thorns. The Crown of Thorns[37] placed on Christ's head to mock him travestied the Roman victor's crown. It is one of the INSTRUMENTS OF PASSION. It is an attribute of Louis IX, king of France, who brought the supposed relic back from Constantinople; of Catherine of Siena who received it from Christ in a vision (having refused the alternative offer of a golden crown); and of the Delphic SIBYL. It is also a heraldic device [iii].

[iv]

Thorn-apple, or **Datura.** Narcotic plant, which is smoked and also fermented to make an intoxicant [iv]. Its flowers sometimes decorate the head-dress of SHIVA, as an attribute.

Thyrsus. A staff entwined with ivy and vine shoots and topped with a PINE CONE, denoting fertility [v: *Herculaneum, bas-relief*]. It is hence a phallic symbol. It is an attribute of DIONYSUS/BACCHUS and his followers, the Bacchantes.

[v]

Tree. Worshipped by many ancient peoples as the abode of a god or, indeed, as the god himself; also a symbol of the universe, and a source of fertility, knowledge and eternal life. There were many tree cults in the Nile valley: tree spirits, usually female, were especially identified with Nut, the sky-goddess, and HATHOR. They are depicted in the *Book of the Dead* half emerging from the branches and pouring water over the deceased to nourish his soul.[38] The latter is sometimes represented as a BIRD, his *ba*. The tree is generally a type of SYCAMORE. According to one tradition certain gods were created within a tree from which they emerged, as it were like a butterfly from a chrysalis. Thus RE was born from a sycamore and Wepwawet, a jackal-headed god of Upper Egypt, from a tamarisk.

[*vi*]

One of the most potent images of a tree representing a super-natural being is the bodhi tree (bo-tree, pipal, *ficus religiosa*), the tree of Enlightenment under which the Buddha Shakyamuni sat when he attained his transcendental state [*vi: Sanci, early 1st cent. BC*]. It is the image most frequently used to represent his actual presence in early Buddhist art before he is shown in human form. It is seen first in relief sculpture (*c*. 150 BC) with an empty THRONE beneath it. In later, narrative scenes of his life he sits enthroned under the bodhi tree, an image found throughout the Buddhist world. Veneration of the pipal was older than Buddhism and was not the only ancient Indian tree cult to penetrate Buddhist art. A flowering tree, the ashoka (*Saraca indica*), is depicted in re-liefs decorating the outer gateways and railings of the oldest stupas. A female tree spirit, a Yakshi or dryad, stands embracing the trunk and apparently kicking it. It is a vestige of an ancient ritual intended to make the tree bear fruit. In a Buddhist context, however, the Yakshi symbolizes *maya*, the everyday world of sensory illusion that surrounds the central sanctuary. See also NYMPH.

The sacred grove was a typical feature of early tree-worship among the ancient Greeks. Offerings were made to one specially chosen tree within the grove. Best known was the OAK of Do-dona, sacred to Zeus, which was also consulted as an oracle, the rustling of its leaves being the voice of the god. At a later stage of Greek religion an image of a tree became the symbol of a god. Finally, when deities assumed human form, it evolved into an attribute, like the LAUREL of Apollo, the OLIVE of Athene and the MYRTLE of Aphrodite. The image of a tree flanked by devo-tees, human or animal, was a Mesopotamian fertility symbol that migrated westwards with several changes of meaning (see SACRED TREE).

It was once believed that the earth was flat and circular. It was covered by a kind of inverted bowl, the firmament, which re-quired some central support such as a MOUNTAIN, PILLAR, or tree to hold it up. This world axis, the 'cosmic tree', was known to the Babylonians and to European peoples. It occurs in Hindu myth[39] and was borrowed by Buddhism to become part of the symbolism of the STUPA. The sacred ash tree of Scandinavian myth, the Yggdrasil, also supported the universe. Its branches symbolized heaven, its trunk the earth and its roots hell. An eagle perches on its top branch while a dragon gnaws a root.

The Tree of Life in the Garden of Eden whose fruit bestowed immortality[40] is thought to be related to the Hindu cosmic tree of the *Rig-Veda*.[41] From it was distilled *soma*, or *amrita*, the drink of Hindu gods, comparable to the Persian *haoma* and Greek nectar, all of which granted eternal life, perfect knowledge, happiness and other desires. The origin of the biblical Tree of Knowledge is less certain but may be derived from the image of the Assyrian sacred tree flanked by two human figures or from the tree in the garden of the Hesperides that was guarded by a snake.[42] As a Christian symbol tree and cross are connected through a medieval legend that the wood from the Tree of Knowledge was used for the cross, Christ thereby redeeming the Original Sin. The genealogy of Christ is represented in medieval art by a tree springing from the loins of Jesse, father of David.[43] Other ancestors occupy the trunk and branches; the VIRGIN MARY or Christ is at the top. It is an attribute of the Virgin of the Immaculate Conception. A Christian hermit praying in a hollow tree is Bavo. A bishop, one foot resting on a fallen oak, is Boniface, whose mission took him among the Druids. A flowering tree is an attribute of the bishop Zenobius. See also CYPRESS; OAK; PALM; PINE; SYCAMORE; etc.

Vine. Shares much of the Christian and Dionysian symbolism of GRAPES. Its leaves form a crown for DIONYSUS/BACCHUS and his followers. They entwine the THYRSUS of his devotees, the Bacchantes. The vine scroll is a feature of temples of Bacchus, a motif that travelled to Asia with his cult, where its symbolism was lost [*i: Gandhara, 2nd–3rd cent.* AD]. In Christian art and architecture it is a continually recurring motif. For early Christians it symbolized CHRIST. Together with ears of corn it symbolizes the eucharistic elements. It was sacred to OSIRIS, in his role of agricultural deity, for he was believed to have introduced it into Egypt. In Renaissance allegory it is the attribute of Autumn personified, one of the FOUR SEASONS, and features in the TWELVE MONTHS. It is worn as a crown by Gluttony, one of the SEVEN DEADLY SINS.

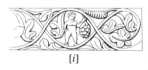

[*i*]

Violet. Christian symbol of humility and modesty, associated with the infant Christ and VIRGIN MARY particularly in paintings of the Adoration of the Virgin and Child, from the early Renaissance [*ii*]. White violets are an attribute of St Fina (d. 1253); they sprouted around her death-bed.

[*ii*]

Wand. In the hand of the thaumaturge its touch works miracles. With it, MOSES struck water from a rock.[44] In catacomb paintings the same scene symbolizes God's power [*iii*]: later, it stood for the spiritual refreshment provided by the Church. The Roman catacombs also depict Christ, as a man or as a lamb, touching baskets of bread with a wand to make them multiply and feed

[*iii*]

the five thousand.[45] He uses a wand to bring Lazarus to life.[46] A flowering wand is the attribute of the Israelites' high priest, Aaron,[47] and, by derivation, of Joseph, husband of the VIRGIN MARY. A wand is the attribute of the Greek sorceress, Circe. In Attic vase painting she uses it to stir a magic potion[48] which turned Odysseus' companions into pigs. The CADUCEUS of Hermes could 'cast a spell upon our eyes or wake us from the soundest sleep'.[49] In Renaissance painting Hypnos, Greek god of sleep, holds a wand whose touch brings sleep and oblivion. See also STAFF.

[iv]

Willow (Ch. *liu shu*; Jap. *yanagi*). Among the many species of willow the *salix babylonica*, or weeping willow, has captured the imagination of poets and artists, especially in the East. It is a native of China in spite of its name. It was a popular motif with Sung dynasty painters [*iv: early 13th cent.*] and with the Japanese. It was the harbinger of spring but above all symbolized female grace and beauty. Its branches swaying in the wind reflected a Japanese wife's submission to her husband's will. For Buddhists it was a symbol of meekness, and is an attribute of the bodhisattva Kuan-yin (see AVALOKITESHVARA). Willow-pattern chinaware, designed by the English potter, Minton, in 1780, illustrates a Chinese folk-tale.

In the West the willow is mainly a symbol of mourning, from its biblical connection: the Jews, during the Babylonian exile, wept for Zion and hung their harps on willow-trees.[50] It features in funerary art and is especially popular on English tombstones of the later 19th cent. See also FOUR SPECIES.

[v]

Wine/Wine-press. The wine drunk ritually by worshippers of the Greek DIONYSUS/BACCHUS symbolized his blood and promised them eternal life. In vase painting the god is crowned with vines or ivy and holds a wine-vessel, typically a *kantharos* [*v: Attic vase painting*]. Wine had a long history of sacramental use by the Jews and probably for this reason became established as the preferred eucharistic element among early Christians. Wine and bread symbolize the blood and body of CHRIST (see also VANITAS). Wine spilling from a broken glass is an attribute of Benedict. The Mystic Wine-Press, an allegory seen mostly in French stained glass, especially 16th cent., is a double image depicting Christ treading grapes and being crushed in a press. His cross forms the wine-press, while his blood is caught in a chalice. The themes are an interpretation in Christian terms of two Old Testament passages.[51]

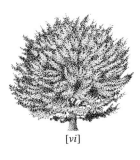

[vi]

Yew. Symbol of grief and mourning and therefore a feature of English churchyards [*vi*]. It was grown in Celtic sacred groves where it was said to signify immortality. This alternative symbolism was inherited by the Christian Church when it took over such places for its own worship. It is rare in Christian art.

Collectives

Adad. Mesopotamian storm-god of Akkad, known as Hadad in Syria, Phoenicia and Canaan. He is the same as Ishkur, the storm-god of Sumer. His cult dates from the Early Dynastic Period, if not earlier. His power was both beneficial and destructive, bringing lightning and floods but also fertilizing rain. Like many sky- and storm-gods he holds a lightning-fork (see THUNDERBOLT). On Akkadian cylinder seals he stands on a hybrid, dragon-like creature; in the neo-Assyrian period, on a BULL, which is the god's zoomorphic form and also a symbol of his power. He may wear a horned cap (see HORN), which is sometimes surmounted by the Mesopotamian type of solar disk (see SUN). In neo-Assyrian reliefs he may be represented by the sun symbol alone. The Hittite storm-god Teshub, who was Adad under another name, may have, besides the lightning-fork and bull, an AXE or MACE.

Ages of Man. Theme known in antiquity and revived at the end of the Middle Ages. The number varies from three to twelve, usually three: childhood, youth and old age; occasionally seven, when they may be linked to the planetary deities. Always implicit is the idea of the transitory nature of youth and beauty and the inevitability of death (cf. VANITAS). Children at play and loving couples represent the first two; the third is an old man with a SKULL, or counting COINS. A fourth sometimes follows the lovers, a soldier in ARMOUR or a man holding COMPASSES, that is, learning his craft. The four ages are sometimes linked to the FOUR SEASONS; twelve to the TWELVE MONTHS. In Titian's allegory of Prudence youth, maturity and old age symbolize past, present and future.

Ages of the World. Hindu, Persian and Greek myths all tell how the world evolved through a sequence of ages. They marked the stages in the decline of the human condition from primal innocence to misfortune and woe. Certain similarities suggest a common origin, probably Aryan. In both Hindu and Greek the ages (Hindu, *yuga*) are called Golden, Silver, Bronze and Iron.[1] The Hindu ages are most often numbered four to one (*krita*, *treta*, *dvapara*, *kali*), after the four-sided dice used by Indian gamblers. Only in Persia is mankind finally delivered, by a righteous god (but see KALKIN). The Greek myth, the only one to produce a significant iconography, is first told by Hesiod (who introduces a Heroic age after Bronze).[2] It was adapted by Ovid,[3] whose version was the principal source used by artists. The subject seems to be unknown in antiquity but became popular from the end of the Middle Ages. From the early 17th cent. the older narrative scenes were replaced by allegorical figures with appropriate attributes, derived from a newly published mythographical dictionary.[4] Three ages were the usual number:

Golden Age: Pastoral landscape; men, women and animals mingle peacefully. Cupid steals a HONEYCOMB. Shells used for cups and platters. *17th cent.* – CORNUCOPIA or OLIVE branch, BEEHIVE.

Silver Age: Ploughing and sowing, humble dwellings being built. The figure of Justice, one of the FOUR CARDINAL VIRTUES, with sword and scales, surveys the scene. *17th cent.* – PLOUGH, sheaf of CORN, a primitive hut.

Iron Age: Soldiers looting, violating women and children, and slaying a LAUREL-crowned female (personifying learning and the arts). *17th cent.* – SWORD,

SHIELD bearing an image of Deceit (human head with body of a snake). HELMET with a wolf's head on it. See DEVI; KALKIN.

Agni. Hindu god of fire who is present in the flames of the sacrificial altar and is also worshipped at the domestic hearth. He was one of the principal deities of the Aryan-(Indo-European) speaking peoples of the northern steppes who invaded India in the first half of the 2nd mill. BC bringing their culture with them. Their religious literature is contained in four books, the oldest, the *Rig-Veda*, was written about 1500 BC and was probably based on older, oral traditions. Its language is Sanskrit, the oldest member of the Indo-European family (which includes Greek and Latin – cf. Agni: Lat. *ignis*, fire). The *Rig-Veda* consists of hymns in praise of the Aryan gods. They are mostly male and gradually over-took the cults of the Mother-Goddess and other indigenous Indian deities. It tells how Agni is born every day from two fire-sticks who are his parents.[5] He has a buttery face and hair, the altar flames having been fed with ritual offer-ings of *ghee*.[6] He is the messenger between men and gods: the flames drive off demons and at the same time bear the sacrificial offering to heaven. Another early tradition identified him with the goat, as a sacrificial animal, which in later myth became his mount, or 'vehicle'. Agni, in human form, holds a ladle or SPOON of a type used in ritual to pour *ghee* on the altar fire. He also holds a TORCH or flaming vase (see FIRE). He may have an AXE, to cut wood for the fire, and a FAN, which serves as bellows. He may wear a Brahmanic SASH. See also ANGEL; KARTTIKEYA.

Amaterasu Omikami. Sun-goddess and the principal deity of Shintoism, 'the national religion of Japan'. Shinto, 'The Way of the Gods', like many other ancient cults, originally had to do with man's relationship to the world of na-ture. Natural objects were felt to possess a numinous, divine quality or power, known as a *kami*, which became a focus of worship. So trees, rivers, mountains, plants, etc dominated the earliest Shinto art (see also ROCK). A *kami* later came to denote an anthropomorphic god, ancestor, or indeed any historical figure who was felt to be divine. Its presence was also felt in their devotional images in painting and sculpture. A fitting site for a deity's shrine was one that was itself imbued with this mystical quality. The principal shrine of Amaterasu is at Ise on the Pacific coast of Honshu.

A Shinto text of the 8th cent. AD claimed that the Japanese imperial family were direct descendants of the sun-goddess and were therefore themselves di-vine. It gives a mythical account of the origin of the imperial regalia, the THREE SACRED RELICS.[7] These precious objects were offered to Amaterasu to entice her out of a cave where she had hidden to escape her wily brother, the earth-god Susano-O. They were subsequently handed down to succeeding generations of emperors. While the goddess was in hiding, the world was plunged into dark-ness, which suggests that the myth reflects ancient rites connected with winter and the changing seasons.

Following the establishment of Buddhism in Japan in the 6th cent. AD a proc-ess of syncretism slowly took place in which Buddhist deities were incarnated as *kami*. By the 11th cent. all the major Shinto gods had their Buddhist counter-parts. Amaterasu was identified with the Adi-Buddha, VAIROCANA.

The goddess is represented with a HALO of the sun's rays, like MITHRAS, APOLLO and other solar deities. She may have ARROWS, which are symbols of the rays. She holds a SWORD, or a MIRROR (two of the sacred relics). She may wear a pa-

goda-shaped reliquary, a *sharito*, as a CROWN. The COCK that heralds the rising
sun is sacred to her. (The birds are kept in the grounds of her temple at Ise.) Her
messenger is a three-legged CROW. See also ROPE.

Amun. Very early Egyptian creator-god of Hermopolis Magna (al-Ashmunayn),
first mentioned in the Pyramid Texts. His cult moved to Thebes after the 11th
Dynasty and, from the New Kingdom onwards, he became supreme state god.
He formed a trinity with Mut and KHONSU. He became identified with the sun-
god, RE of Heliopolis, and was then known as Amun-Re. His name means the
Hidden One, probably an indication that his worshippers had no visual impression of him. He is represented in human form and wears a modius-crown topped
with two long FEATHERS. He is often enthroned, when he may hold a CROOK and
flail, insignia of the pharaoh whom Amun protected. His erect PHALLUS refers
to his procreative powers (see BULL; MIN). The RAM, a typical image of sexual
energy, was especially sacred to him and was probably one form in which he
was originally worshipped; also the GOOSE, possibly a link with the Heliopolitan myth of creation out of the primeval waters (see WATER). As creator-god he
was worshipped as a SNAKE at Hermopolis and Thebes. As Amun-Re he may
have a solar disk (see SUN) and a LION.

Anu (Sum. An). Mesopotamian sky-god. The supreme deity and father of the
Sumerian pantheon. His realm was heaven and he was creator of the universe.
His oldest temple, which surmounted a ZIGGURAT at the Sumerian capital, Uruk
(mod. Warka), probably dates from the beginning of the dynastic period (*c.* 3000
BC). His rites were noted for their splendour. In later times his cult was superseded by that of ENLIL. His iconography is meagre and uncertain. He appears to
have been represented by the symbol of the horned cap (see HORN), which he
shares with Enlil and other gods. The so-called reed-post (see REEDS) and the
STAG have also been attributed to him.

Aphrodite/Venus. Graeco-Roman goddess of love, beauty and fertility, probably originally from Cyprus and, in pre-Hellenic times, related to ISHTAR. The
Greeks identified her with the Egyptian HATHOR. In Greek myth she took numerous lovers. Her principal attributes are a scallop SHELL and DOLPHINS (she
was born from the sea), DOVES or SWANS (to draw her chariot), a flaming HEART,
TORCH and magic GIRDLE (to kindle love). The red ROSE (stained with her blood)
is sacred to her; also, though less often depicted in art, the SWALLOW, SPARROW,
APPLE, POPPY. Her attendants are her son EROS/CUPID and the THREE GRACES.
Renaissance art depicts an 'earthly' Venus, richly dressed with JEWELS and
braided HAIR who is contrasted with her heavenly sister who is nude and holds
a flaming VASE, symbolising the fire of divine love (see NUDITY). She personifies Spring, one of the FOUR SEASONS, and appears among TWELVE MONTHS in
February and May.

Apocalyptic Beasts, or Tetramorph. Symbols of the four evangelists, derived
from Ezekiel[8] and, following him, the book of Revelation[9]: Matthew, MAN; Mark,
LION; Luke, OX; John, EAGLE. There were numerous medieval interpretations.
Most commonly they stood for Christ's birth, death, resurrection and ascension.
They usually surround the figure of Christ, especially above the portals of
Romanesque and Gothic churches. In Renaissance allegory they draw the chariot
of Eternity (see TRIUMPH).

Apollo. Greek god who had many roles. Originally pre-Hellenic, he came to personify the classical Greek spirit that emphasized reason, intellect and *sophrosyne*, that is, temperance, or 'nothing to excess', in contrast to man's passionate nature exemplified by Dionysus. In Greek myth he is the son of ZEUS/ JUPITER and Leto, and the twin brother of ARTEMIS/DIANA. He is widely represented in art of all periods, beginning with Greece in the 7th cent. BC. As leader and inspirer of the MUSES he wears a LAUREL crown and plays a stringed instrument appropriate to the period. On Greek vase painting it is a *kithara*, a forerunner of the LYRE; in the Renaissance it is a viol or similar instrument. His BOW and ARROW, used to destroy enemies and protect his votaries, also made him patron of archers. In the classical period he is seen struggling for possession of a TRIPOD belonging to his sanctuary at Delphi, which HERCULES tried to steal. His attribute of a SNAKE was derived from an ancient ophidian cult at Delphi and also recalls the myth of his slaying a python. His WOLF may reflect an early identity with a wolf-god or at least suggests a former role as guardian against its depredations. His CROOK denotes a one-time god of shepherds whose principal enemy was the wolf. The Romans identified Apollo with their SUN-god, a role revived in Renaissance painting. He drives the sun-god's CHARIOT, drawn by four white horses, and has a radiant HALO. His arrows also symbolize the sun's rays. Minor attributes include a SWAN (a symbol of beauty) and GLOBE (his universal sovereignty). In the Renaissance he may be accompanied by a three-headed monster (wolf, lion, dog), borrowed from the Graeco-Egyptian deity Sarapis (see HEAD).

Apostle (Gk. messenger, ambassador). The twelve chief disciples of Christ, especially as missionaries after his death. In early Christian art they are represented as twelve SHEEP, more rarely as twelve DOVES. When first represented as men each has a sheep for attribute. From the 6th cent., when seen as a group, they are distinguished as follows; Peter, KEYS or FISH; Paul, SWORD, sometimes two; Andrew, saltire CROSS; James the Greater, pilgrim's STAFF; John, CHALICE with snake, or EAGLE; Thomas, SET-SQUARE; James the Less, fuller's CLUB; Philip, CROSS, cross-staff; Bartholomew, flayer's KNIFE; Matthew, PURSE; Simon (an alternative to Paul), SAW; Thaddeus (Jude) and Matthias, LANCE. Mark and Luke (see APOCALYPTIC BEASTS) may replace Simon and Matthias. The apostles are very widely represented as a series in church sculpture and painting, both as devotional figures and in narrative scenes.

Arhat (Sk. 'Worthy One'; Ch. *Lohan*; Jap. *Rakan*). In early Buddhism one who had reached the state of enlightenment, usually a monk, and would enter Nirvana upon his death. Unlike the BODHISATTVA his influence on early affairs then ceased for he was no longer subject to the cosmic cycle of rebirth. Nevertheless, arhats were worshipped as representatives of the Buddhist ideal, especially by the Hinayana ('Lesser Vehicle') sect (see BUDDHA). The cult of the arhat was prominent in eastern Asia. It flourished in China from about the 8th cent. AD, in Tibet from the 11th and in Japan between the 12th and 15th.

Arhats were traditionally regarded as historical figures, like Ananda and Kashyapa, the two disciples closest to Gautama Shakyamuni. They are depicted as his attendants and, like arhats in general, wear the simple robes of a monk. Another, greatly venerated, is the Indian monk Bodhidharma (Ch. *Ta-mo*; Jap. *Daruma*). He was the reputed founder of the Ch'an (Zen) sect in China about AD 500 and is widely represented in China and Japan. Besides his devotional images, episodes from his legendary life make popular subjects. He makes a miraculous crossing of the Yangtze on a REED, or walks with one shoe, carrying the other.

As their numbers multiplied, arhats were organised into groups. At the same time their relationship to historical figures, where it existed, grew ever more tenuous. Unlike the bodhisattva, however, arhats generally remained earthbound and usually had a specific dwelling place, especially on a mountain-top. Members of a group were given attributes to tell them apart, though there are many inconsistencies, especially between Chinese and Tibetan figures. Ananda and Kashyapa became heads of a group promoted by the Mahayana ('Great Vehicle') school in the Far East, called the Ten Great Disciples. A group of sixteen, the Protectors of the Law (i.e. the Buddhist faith), was nominated in a 7th cent. text.[10] They are widely represented in painting and sculpture in Buddhist monasteries in China, Japan and Tibet though as a group they are not found in India. They are usually robed as monks, with shaven HEAD, long EAR-lobes (a sign of their wisdom) and a HALO. Some wrathful Tantric forms are found in Tibetan art. In Tibetan *tanka* paintings they attend Buddhas and some bodhisattvas. Only the first eight in the following list have clearly determinative attributes:

Abheda (holds a model STUPA); Ajita (meditates with hands clasping knee, long EYEBROWS in Chinese examples); Angaja (CENSER), Bakula (MONGOOSE vomiting jewels); Kalika (two gold RINGS, long eyebrows); Kanatavatsa (NOOSE); Nagasena (alarm-STAFF); Rahula (holds a CROWN). Badhra (BOOK); Cudapanthaka (meditates); Gopaka (book); Kanakabharadvaja (meditates); Panthaka (book); Pindolabharadvaja (book and begging BOWL); Vajriputra (FAN or FLY-WHISK, right hand in teaching gesture: *vitarka*-MUDRA); Vanavasi (fan or fly-whisk, sometimes long eyebrows).

Arjuna. A prince, one of five brothers, the main protagonist in the Indian epic poem, the *Mahabharata* (*c.* 200 BC–AD 300). It tells of their struggle to win the kingdom of the Kurus against a rival family who were their cousins. The martial exploits are interspersed with much religious and philosophical discourse. Arjuna is a paragon of knighthood and a symbol of valour. He exemplifies the *Kshatriyas*, the warrior class, who are second only to the priesthood in the Indian caste system. In art his royal status is shown by his HAIR, done as a *jatamakuta* crown, or similar; he wears JEWELLERY and may be shod in PATTENS. His weapons are usually a BOW, or sometimes SWORD and SHIELD. KRISHNA is his charioteer. Arjuna may be represented with his brother, Bhima, who is similarly attired and generally holds a CLUB.

Artemis/Diana. Graeco-Roman goddess, originally worshipped in pre-Hellenic times in Greece, Crete and Asia Minor as a Mother-Goddess concerned with the fertility of crops, animals and women. In classical myth she was the daughter of ZEUS/JUPITER and Leto, and twin sister of APOLLO. Her role then changed and she became the familiar virgin huntress who reappears in Renaissance and later art. The BOW, ARROW and QUIVER of the huntress are seen on Attic vases of the 6th cent. BC. She may also have a SPEAR or javelin and be accompanied by hunting DOGS. A STAG, or doe, beside her, usually regarded as her quarry, may be derived from her role as protectress of wild life. This is suggested by some vase paintings. As goddess of chastity she may hold a SHIELD to protect her virginity. In this role her CHARIOT is drawn by stags. Her crescent

MOON comes from the Italian moon-goddess, Diana, whom the Romans identified with Artemis, though she had earlier associations with a moon cult in Attica.

Assur, or **Ashur**. One of the greater Mesopotamian gods; tutelary deity of Assyria and its capital, Assur (mod. Ash Sharqat). He came to the fore with the rise of Assyrian power in Upper Mesopotamia in the mid-14th cent. BC. His rites and iconography owed much to other, older gods, especially to his Babylonian counterpart, the state-god, Marduk. In his temple at Assur was a sacred DAGGER, symbol of invincible power, on which oaths were sworn. It was probably handed down from more ancient cults. In neo-Assyrian reliefs and wall-paintings (from c. 883 BC) he is represented in his principal role as god of war and protector of the state. He hovers above the king's army, framed in a WINGED DISK, his BOW drawn against the enemy. In another context a hand emerging from a cloud and holding a bow probably denotes Assur. He usually wears a horned cap (see HORN), which he may have acquired from ANU. His mount, common to several gods, is a four-legged hybrid with a snake's head, body and tail, lion's forepaws and bird's talons at the rear (see also MONSTER). Like Marduk and other old Mesopotamian gods Assur also personified the fertility of beasts and crops. The typical image of the deity in this role shows plants sprouting from his body while goats feed upon them (cf. OSIRIS, as god of vegetation).

Athena/Minerva. The foremost goddess of classical Greece. She was the patroness of Athens, with her temple, the Parthenon, on the Acropolis; a warlike protectress who was born fully armed and is sometimes accompanied by Nike, goddess of VICTORY. She was the guardian of various skilled crafts and the personification of wisdom. In Greek myth she was the daughter of ZEUS/JUPITER. He swallowed her mother while she was still pregnant and Athena sprang from his head already clad in armour. Attic painting and reliefs depict her emerging, wearing plumed HELMET and holding SPEAR and SHIELD. She wears a goat-skin cloak or AEGIS. In pre-Hellenic times she was worshipped in Crete and Mycenae under other names, in association with snake and tree cults, from which she may have acquired her SNAKE and OLIVE. Her warlike attributes may be from the same source. In Greece Athena became identified with the OWL, the sacred bird of Athens. Later, through its association with her, it became a symbol of wisdom. BOOKS, which have the same meaning, are a late acquisition. As a symbol of Virtue she is a popular figure in Renaissance allegory (see VIRTUES AND VICES).

Avalokiteshvara ('The Lord who Looks Down'; Ch. *Kuan-yin*; Jap. *Kannon*). The most revered of all bodhisattvas in the Mahayana ('Great Vehicle') school of Buddhism; the personification of infinite mercy and compassion. His origin lies in the ancient, pre-Aryan Mother-Goddess of India, Padmapani ('Lotus Bearer'), who was adopted by Buddhism as a male god, also known as Avalokiteshvara. In his primary role he holds a LOTUS or is framed by one on each side. His right hand makes the gesture of charity (MUDRA: *Varada-m*). He wears the princely adornments typical of the bodhisattva, including the Brahmanic SASH. As the 'son' or emanation, of the Dhyani-Buddha, Amitabha, he wears a small effigy of the latter in his hair (his determinative attribute). The oldest example of this feature is from Mathura (1st or early 2nd cent.), where he also holds an *amrita* VASE. His POSTURE when seated is usually 'royal ease', when he is deemed to be in his abode at the top of the sacred MOUNTAIN, Potala. In Indo-China and Indonesia he is known as Lokeshvara ('Lord of the World'), retaining the Amitabha motif and sometimes having four heads facing the compass points. In these regions he makes up a trio with the bodhisattva Vajrapani and the Buddha Shakyamuni. See also BODHISATTVA; BUDDHA.

In China he is known as Kuan-yin, 'He who heeds sounds', i.e. prayers, and holds a LOTUS, or sprig of WILLOW or JU-I blade. Here and in Japan he is depicted as the messenger of Amitabha, leading the souls of the dead towards the Dhyani-Buddha's heavenly kingdom, the 'Pure Land of the West'. (See also BUDDHA.) Devotional paintings of Amitabha (known as Amida in China and Japan) show him attended by Kuan-yin and sometimes the FOUR CELESTIAL KINGS. Towards the end of the Sung period (13th cent.) images of Kuan-yin assume somewhat feminine traits which may denote a change of sex (not accepted by all scholars). He/she may then hold an infant, an image that has been compared to the Christian Madonna and Child, though more likely to reflect the fact that, though still a male deity, he was invoked by women desiring children.

In Tibet and Japan (where he is known as Kannon) the bodhisattva's cult and imagery were deeply tinged with Tantric Buddhism which spread from north-eastern India to Nepal and Tibet (see PADMASAMBHAVA). It was introduced independently into Japan in the 8th cent. by a Japanese Buddhist priest, Kobo Daishi, who had studied Shivaism and other Hindu cults in India. In his many Tantric manifestations he may have multiple arms and heads, and benign and wrathful aspects. He has a flaming AUREOLE, wish-granting JEWEL, WHEEL of the Law, ROSARY and *amrita* VASE. A popular image in his wrathful aspect gives him three heads surmounted by a HORSE's head. This is Bato-Kannon, redeemer of the animal kingdom, and is derived from a Hindu horse-god, Hayagriva. He then has a FLY-WHISK and Shivaite attributes such as the third EYE, a garland or crown of SKULLS and various weapons: SWORD, NOOSE and GOAD. Also found in Japan and Tibet is an eleven-headed figure, perhaps representing the concentrated energies of eleven bodhisattvas, and a symbol of an all-seeing deity who searches out good and evil. The heads are typically arranged in tiers and surmounted by the Amitabha motif. This form may also have a 'thousand' eyes (simply a very large number), which are depicted on extra hands, stretched out as though to succour the oppressed. Avalokiteshvara also has a wrathful YAB-YUM form (not found in Japan). He then holds an alarm-STAFF, skull BOWL and flaying KNIFE. The Tibetan Dalai Lama has been regarded since the 17th cent. as the incarnation of Avalokiteshvara. To symbolize this concept the bodhisattva has a BOOK, rosary, lotus and, sometimes, SCROLL and conch-SHELL. The lamasery at Lhasa then became known as Potala, after the sacred mountain.

Bes. A popular Egyptian household god, protector of women in childbirth, also associated with music and dancing. He is widely represented from the New Kingdom onwards, especially on domestic artefacts. From the Late Period he is depicted on the walls and columns of the *mammisi*, a temple chamber where rites were performed celebrating divine and royal births. His image has also been found in the Near East, mainly disseminated by the Phoenicians. Bes is a DWARF of fierce aspect. Like many tutelary deities of Asia, his threatening appearance, brandishing a SWORD or knife, is intended to ward off evil, and disguises a benevolent temperament (see DEMON). Originally he wore a LION's skin, which is usually reduced to ears and tail. He is bearded and, like Tantric guardian deities, his TONGUE sometimes sticks out. He may have a crown of feathers. In the 18th Dynasty he can have WINGS. His principal attribute is the SA, which he shares with the HIPPOPOTAMUS goddess, Taweret, who is also a guardian of childbirth. As a patron of music and the dance he may have a HARP or TAMBOURINE, the latter also possibly to frighten evil spirits.

Bodhisattva (Sk. 'He whose essence is Enlightenment'; Ch. *P'u-sa*; Jap. *Bosatsu*). The highest goal of the Buddhist is to achieve the state of Enlightenment, or Nirvana, following the example and teaching of Gautama Shakyamuni. In early Buddhism those who reached this end were regarded as Buddhist saints and were known as 'Worthy Ones', or ARHATS. Once they had entered the state of Buddhahood, however, their ability to influence the rest of mankind ceased. In order that this beneficent influence might continue, the Mahayana ('Great Vehicle') school of Buddhism developed the idea of the bodhisattva. Like the arhat, he had attained Enlightenment and the immediate right to enter Nirvana, but chose instead to remain in the world (through further incarnations) to succour his fellows (see also BUDDHA). Bodhisattvas comprise real and legendary figures from the past – monks, teachers and pilgrims – but the greatest number are abstract, metaphysical beings, the embodiment of compassion and charity. They rank next to the Buddha in the sacred hierarchy. They are anthropomorphic and make up a formidably large galaxy of figures in Buddhist art.

Images of bodhisattvas accompanied the spread of Mahayana Buddhism. They are found in South-East Asia, Indonesia and, in particular, China, Japan and Tibet. There was a tendency to merge with local gods, especially with Japanese Shinto deities and the ancient cult figures of Tibet. In Tibetan art the bodhisattva's image is considerably affected by Shivaite Tantrism in having both benign and wrathful forms and in his sexual embrace with a goddess, or Tara. (On Tantrism see DEVI; SHIVA; PADMASAMBHAVA).

Some of the oldest images date from the 3rd cent. AD and come from Gandhara in N.W. India (now Pakistan). In contrast to the serene immobility of the Buddha (a sign that he has entered Nirvana), the bodhisattva, whether seated or standing, has a relaxed pose to signify his continuing relationship with mankind (see POSTURE). Unlike the Buddha figure he is richly attired (necklace, armlets, anklets, etc.) with an elaborate head-dress or diadem – perhaps in allusion to Shakyamuni's earlier princely status. Bodhisattvas' attributes are not often determinative; they share such things as SWORD, *amrita* VASE, SCROLL and LOTUS. Some have the Buddha's URNA on the forehead and a HALO or AUREOLE.

Foremost among bodhisattvas are AVALOKITESHVARA and his/her various manifestations of goodness and mercy; MANJUSHRI and PRAJNA-PARAMITA, the essence of supreme wisdom; PADMASAMBHAVA, the founder of Tibetan Lamaism; MAITREYA, the Buddha-to-be. The following are also widely worshipped:

Samantabhadra (Ch. *P'u-hsien*; Jap. *Fugen*). A so-called Dhyani-Bodhisattva, the 'son', that is, a spiritual emanation created by the meditation of a Dhyani-Buddha, in this case VAIROCANA. His mount is an ELEPHANT, which may have six tusks. He and Manjushri are the attendants of Shakyamuni. His name signifies

universal benevolence. In China he is old and unkempt and may hold a JU-I
sword. He is patron of the contemplative Japanese sect, the Nichiren.

Vajrapani ('Thunderbolt Bearer', Jap. *Kongo*). Another Dhyani-Bodhisattva,
'son' of Akshobya. He holds a THUNDERBOLT to chastise the impious. His early
images from Gandhara, whose art has Hellenistic features, recall ZEUS. He is
coupled with Lokeshvara (see next) as an attendant of the Buddha, especially
in Indonesia. See also GARUDA.

Lokeshvara, 'Lord of the World', a manifestation of Avalokiteshvara. The
rulers of the Khmer empire in the 13th cent. were regarded as his incarnation
and his carved image is common in Indo-China, especially Cambodia. It may
have four HEADS, facing the four compass points, a symbol of the emperor's universal dominion.

Kshitigarbha (Ch. *Ti-tsang*; Jap. *Jizo*). The 'Womb of the Earth', a merciful
judge of the souls of the dead in hell. His image is found in Central Asia, China
and in Japan where he became very popular from the 11th cent. He is dressed
as a monk and may have an alarm-STAFF, but is distinguished from other religious by an *urna*, halo, and *cintamani* JEWEL. In Japan he forms the main devotional figure in many painted MANDALAS. His image is rare in India.

Brahma. Hindu creator-god. In the oldest sacred literature, the *Rig-Veda*, the
word *brahman*, or *brahma*, signified not a recognisable deity but an abstract,
metaphysical concept. It was a wholly impersonal creative power that was
present in the spoken WORD, i.e. the various sacred formulae uttered by the priest
(cf. the Egyptian PTAH). Later, *brahman* came to denote the priest himself. The
meaning was again extended in the *Upanishads* (c. 700 BC). *Brahman* there
became a process of creation, continually active and pervading the universe,
and was the source from which the gods themselves originally arose. The individual's perception of his own inner self, or soul, called *atman*, is in fact identical with *brahman*. He is hindered from recognizing this because of the material
distractions of daily life but, by mental and physical disciplines, by contemplation, the disability can be overcome and a state of Enlightenment achieved. It
is the annihilation of self within the universal *brahman* that brings release from
the otherwise endless cycle of birth and death (see AGES OF THE WORLD). The
cosmic creative process eventually evolved into an anthropomorphic god,
Brahma.

He was the driving force in several creation myths. He created the primeval WATERS and was born from a golden EGG, fertilized by his own seed, that
floated on them.[11] He took the form of a BOAR and lifted up the earth above the
waters.[12] He was born from a LOTUS that grew from the navel of VISHNU.[13] During the Gupta dynasty (4th–6th cents. AD) there evolved a trinity of gods,
Brahma, VISHNU and SHIVA. They symbolized the universal forces of creation,
protection and destruction, and are seen as a group, especially in Vishnavite
temples. From this period the cult of Vishnu grew as that of Brahma declined,
so that the latter came to be depicted in a subservient role: he is among the deities
attendant on Vishnu. He is seen washing Vishnu's FOOT when Vishnu takes the
'three steps' that brought the universe into existence. He is the charioteer of
Shiva.

In carved devotional images Brahma is represented with four HEADS, one
of them sometimes bearded, and they should face the four quarters. They are
said to symbolize the four *Vedas*, the four castes of Hindu society and the four

yugas. The *yuga* is one of the four subdivisions of the great Hindu cycle of creation and destruction called the 'day of Brahma' (see AGES OF THE WORLD). His commonest attributes are a BOOK, made of palm-leaves in older sculptures, which represents the *Vedas*, and a ROSARY. With four arms he may also have a water-pot (see VASE) to wash Vishnu's foot, or have his hands in the *abhaya* and *varada* poses (see MUDRA). His HAIR is dressed in the *jata-makuta* style. He wears EAR-ornaments and sometimes the Brahmanic SASH. His mount is a GOOSE. In later art he wears a TIGER-skin loin-cloth. Brahma's consort was Sarasvati, goddess of speech and learning (see VINA), who shares some of his attributes: rosary, book, *jata-makuta*, water-pot and goose. She may also hold, or stand on, a LOTUS, indicating her origin as a pre-Aryan Mother-Goddess. Brahma was adopted by Buddhism and, with INDRA, is depicted as the attendant of Shakyamuni and of the Redeemer-Buddha, Amitabha, especially in China and Japan. See also TWELVE HEAVENLY KINGS.

Buddha, Buddhism. The founder of Buddhism, Siddhartha Gautama, was born about 563 BC in north-east India. He was the son of the chief of the Shakya (Scythian) tribe and so became known as the Sage of the Shakyas, or Shakya-muni. The colourful metaphysical doctrines that were developed by later schools and which produced the great wealth of symbolic art and architecture owed little, if anything, to the founder who appears to have taught a fairly uncomplicated ethical system.

The essence of Buddhism is an eight-fold code of conduct involving self-denial and meditation that leads the devotee towards the ultimate wisdom of Enlightenment (Nirvana), that is, the state of Buddhahood. It may take him many lifetimes to achieve it. Until he does so he will be reborn time and again in the endlessly recurring cycle of cosmic ages (see AGES OF THE WORLD). On finally entering Nirvana the chain of transmigrations will be broken. It is said that Shakyamuni himself lived through countless previous existences in preparation for his latest, final incarnation. One who has yet to achieve Buddha-hood is known as a BODHISATTVA.

The later developments had three main branches, each with its own iconographical features. They were the 'Lesser Vehicle' (Hinayana), the 'Great Vehicle' (Mahayana), both of which emerged around the first two centuries AD, and the 'Vehicle of the Thunderbolt' (Vajrayana), which appeared in the 8th century. Hinayana or, more correctly, Theravada, the 'Doctrine of the Elders', adhered closest to what was regarded as the founder's original teaching. It also recognized that Shakyamuni was not unique but had been preceded by other Buddhas (usually seven) and one, MAITREYA, was still to come. The sect's greatest following was in southern India and Sri-Lanka and spread to Burma, Siam and other parts of S.E. Asia. As to images of the Buddha, it always preferred the oldest type, which portrayed him in the form of symbols (see below). Unlike Mahayana it had no great pantheon of sacred figures, except for certain highly revered monks, especially Japanese. The series of narrative scenes from the legendary life of Shakyamuni was also allowed.

Mahayana doctrine had a strong metaphysical slant. Like Hinayana, it recognized the existence of other Buddhas in other ages. Shakyamuni was now conceived as an eternal, divine saviour and became identified with a mythical universal ruler, adumbrated in the *Vedas* and subsequently known as Cakravartin, 'He who turns the WHEEL' (see also SEVEN TREASURES). Mahayana enlarged the concept of the bodhisattva, the striver towards Buddhahood. He was now one who had reached his goal but chose to postpone entry into Nirvana, to remain on earth and help other mortals along the same path. These bodhisattvas form a large gallery of devotional figures throughout the Buddhist world. They merge with and take on the characteristics of many local deities. In Tibet they are coupled with the female 'energies', or *shaktis* of Tantrism (see DEVI).

The Vajrayana sect derives its name from its principal symbol, the *vajra* or THUNDERBOLT, which for them has a mystical power that they can call on by performing magical rituals. Its doctrines were established in Bengal and Bihar and soon spread to Nepal and Tibet. Its imagery pervades the art of Tibetan Lamaism, and eventually reached Indonesia through the export of portable bronze statues. The *shaktis*, known to this sect as Taras, or 'Saviouresses', together with the associated sexual rituals, are central to its worship and imagery. A separate offshoot, which ignored *shaktism*, invoked the god, whether Buddha or bodhisattva, through the contemplation of various magical symbols in the form of the written or spoken word, even a single written letter, abstract signs and ritual gestures. This approach to worship was practised especially in Japan and China (see A; JEWELS; MANDALA; MUDRA; TRIANGLE; WORD).

On the oldest Buddhist monuments Shakyamuni is represented by symbols. Carved stone pillars, erected by the Emperor Ashoka in the 3rd cent. BC, feature the Wheel of the Law and sometimes the LOTUS. Early STUPAS were similarly regarded as his personification, like certain motifs that decorate them: the TREE of Enlightenment, a PILLAR of fire, the empty THRONE and his FOOT-PRINTS, which may bear a set of symbols. The Buddha in human form is first seen in the 1st to 2nd cents. AD, a development probably influenced by the rise of the Mahayana sect and its veneration of sacred figures. His image, serene, unadorned and seated in the mystic state of Nirvana, the position of his hands in the *dhyana-mudra* denoting the utmost concentration, is familiar to Buddhists throughout China, Japan and Indonesia. He may adopt other *mudras*, in which case the WHEEL is visible on the palm of his right hand. The Buddha's head has characteristic features which were established by the end of the 4th cent. – *ushnisha* and *urna* (see HEAD), short, curly HAIR, long EARS and sometimes a HALO.

The Buddha's image evolved in response to developments in Mahayana thought, especially in eastern Asia. The historical Shakyamuni, already an eternal divine saviour, became one essential part, or hypostasis, of a trinity, the 'Three Bodies of the Buddha'. The Body of Essence was immanent, pervading the universe. It corresponded to *brahman* of orthodox Hinduism (see BRAHMA) and was the source of the other two: the Body of Bliss, a kind of heavenly father, called Amitabha, who dwelt in an upper, ethereal realm; and the Created Body, incarnate on earth as Shakyamuni. The cult of Amitabha had a large following in the Far East from the 4th cent. AD. He was a Redeemer, presiding over a heavenly kingdom, the 'Pure Land of the West', an alternative haven for the multitude who would never reach Nirvana. He is widely represented as an enthroned Buddha in, or before, his PALACE, surrounded by a host of bodhisattvas (see also AVALOKITESHVARA). In a further development Amitabha became one of a group of five metaphysical beings, the 'Buddhas of Meditation', sometimes called Dhyani-Buddhas. The leading figure, the supreme Absolute (Adi) Buddha, was VAIROCANA, who is represented in stupas and pagodas on the axis of the universe, while the other four, distinguished by their mudras, face the four quarters. See further, COMPASS; VAIROCANA.

Calendar. The Chinese calendar is a veritable bestiary of symbolic animals. Each year is assigned to a different animal, twelve in all, in an endlessly recurring cycle known as the Twelve Earthly Branches. The cycle begins with the RAT (whose next appearance will be 1996), followed by OX, TIGER, HARE, DRAGON, SNAKE, HORSE, GOAT, APE, COCK, DOG, BOAR. A further cycle of ten written signs, called celestial stems, when set beside the twelve, produces a great cycle of sixty years. This notation can be used to express a person's birth, marriage and other significant events, and his fate determined accordingly. A similar system is known in Japan and is used by Lamaist priests in Tibet. The group of twelve is certainly as old as the 1st cent. AD and was probably copied from a zodiac of Turkish origin, though tradition claims it was invented in the 3rd mill. BC.

The magical power of a mirror to reveal the future made it a natural object on which to represent the signs. An often quoted example from the T'ang dynasty (AD 618–906) is a compendium of such astrological lore.[14] The symbols are arranged in concentric circles round the central boss. First are the animals symbolizing the four quadrants of the heavens: DRAGON (east), PHOENIX (south), TIGER (west), TORTOISE (north). They are also linked to the FOUR SEASONS and FOUR ELEMENTS (five in China). The next circle consists of the EIGHT TRIGRAMS and next to them the Twelve Earthly Branches. The outer circle contains twenty-eight animals that correspond to the constellations of ancient Chinese astronomy, seven belonging to each quadrant. In the western zodiac the twelve signs corresponding to the Earthly Branches begin with *Aries* = Rat, the rest following in their normal order (see further ZODIAC; TWELVE MONTHS).

In Japan the Tendai sect of Shinto-Buddhism worships thirty deities (the *Sanju Banshin*) who are guardians of one of the most sacred Buddhist texts, the *Lotus Sutra*, one deity being assigned to each day of the month. They are depicted as courtiers, soldiers, monks and include several females. Among them is Kasuga Myojin, the tutelary deity of the Kasuga cult seated on a DEER. The group's origin may date from the 9th cent. AD, though their collective image, often painted on silk, is not seen before the 15th cent.

Cardinal Virtues. The ideal city, according to Plato, should be governed by 'the wise, brave, temperate and just'. As a group they are unknown in Graeco-Roman art, though the figure of Justice with her SCALES is found on Roman reliefs and coins. Christian theologians, in particular Ambrose, Augustine and Thomas Aquinas, placed them next to the three supreme THEOLOGICAL VIRTUES, recommending them as benefits to be derived from the Eucharist. As a group of seven female figures, the Theological and Cardinal Virtues are widely represented in later medieval and early Renaissance painting and relief sculpture, sometimes paired with appropriate Vices and with the SEVEN LIBERAL ARTS. Their principal attributes are:

Justice. Scales, SWORD, FASCES, SET-SQUARE, COMPASSES, BLINDFOLD, LION, GLOBE. See also AGES OF THE WORLD – Silver Age.

Prudence (Wisdom). SNAKE, MIRROR, BOOK, COMPASSES, SIEVE, STAG. For Prudence with two faces, see HEAD.

Fortitude. CLUB and LION's skin (of Hercules), PILLAR (of Samson), HELMET, WEAPONS.

Temperance. Typically she dilutes wine with water, in the act of pouring liquid from one jug to another. She also has, later, a BRIDLE, sheathed SWORD, TORCH, CLOCK. See also APOLLO.

Charity (Gk. *agape*; Lat. *caritas*). Its primary meaning is not almsgiving but the Christian concept of love, which is directed both towards God and one's neighbour. The latter was originally depicted in Gothic art as a woman performing the Six Works of Mercy.[15] This was later shortened to only one: clothing the naked. Charity as an allegorical figure embraces both concepts. From the 13th cent. she has a flame (see FIRE), a symbol of love's ardour, or a CANDLE, the light of faith. From the 14th cent. she holds up a flaming HEART or VASE, offering it to God. From this time love of one's neighbour is symbolized by a CORNUCOPIA or a bowl of FRUIT. Opposed to Charity in medieval art is Avarice, who has a PURSE or puts riches in a chest. Giotto, and others after him, replaced Avarice by Envy who gnaws a heart. From the earlier 14th cent. a new type appeared, first seen in Italian art: a woman suckling INFANTS and, later, others clustering round her. The PELICAN became her attribute from the 16th cent.

Christ. From a very early date the person of Jesus was represented by symbols, perhaps partly because Christians under persecution felt safer using a sign language understood only among themselves. The symbols are found in the Roman catacombs, on sarcophagi and on lamps and seals. Not all come from the Bible. The FISH, an alternative eucharistic element for the first Christians, was probably taken over from an older Jewish ritual meal. Orpheus, the legendary Greek poet, is made to represent Christ in catacomb painting. The reason is not clear but may reflect a wish to attract to the Christian faith devotees of the mystery cult of Orphism, which then had many followers in the Roman Empire. Christ as the Good Shepherd, another early symbol, is mentioned in the gospels.[16] The image itself, of a shepherd carrying a sheep round his shoulders, had Graeco-Roman antecedents (see HERMES/MERCURY). The paschal LAMB, originally a Jewish sacrificial offering, was used to symbolise Christ who made the redemptive sacrifice for Christians. Among other early symbols are the VINE, from Christ's own words;[17] PELICAN; STAR;[18] and the CROSS itself. To regard the BREAD and WINE of the Eucharist as symbols is incorrect according to those for whom they constitute the 'Real Presence' of Christ's body and blood, though they are widely used symbolically in art, for example in VANITAS paintings. See also TRIUMPH – Eternity.

Combat. The scene of a fight between individual combatants is common to the art of many peoples and can often be interpreted symbolically. It frequently takes place between man and animal. In the East it can assume cosmic dimensions, symbolizing the unending struggle for supremacy between the forces of light and darkness, or order and chaos, that pervade the universe. In the West the influence of the Christian ethic makes it more often into a contest for the soul of man, between the opposing virtues and vices that make up human nature.

Mesopotamian art is rich in symbolic images of combat, where we typically see a pair of animals contending with each other or tackled by an unarmed, naked human hero. Scenes of this kind are common on cylinder seals and ivories from the early Sumerian period onwards. They are believed to represent the gods in their early zoomorphic forms as the divine forces that controlled mankind, contending for supremacy. The popular theme of a lion-headed eagle attacking a bull perhaps represents the Mother-Goddess ISHTAR (who was also a war-goddess) setting about some rival deity. Gilgamesh, the hero of Mesopotamian epic myth and the forerunner of many dragon-slayers like St George, overcomes the monster Humbaba[19] and the Bull of Heaven.[20] In the Babylonian epic of creation, *Enuma Elish*, the god of Babylon defeats the sea-monster Tiamat, a symbolic victory of order over the primeval, watery chaos.[21] Comparable struggles engage the gods of Indian mythology, like INDRA and VISHNU, and the goddess DEVI in her warlike roles. In Egypt the forces of darkness and chaos are symbolized by the underworld snake-goddess Apophis, who is never permanently quelled. For other aspects of symbolic combat, see DRAGON; EAGLE; HERCULES; TORTOISE; VIRTUES AND VICES; WRESTLERS.

David. King of Israel, musician, supposed author of the psalms and an O.T. prefiguration of Christ. He wears a royal CROWN and plays a stringed instrument, usually a HARP or, in medieval Books of Psalms, often a psaltery. A LION alludes to his feat of killing one with his bare hands,[22] said to symbolize Christ overcoming Satan. His HORN refers to his anointing by the prophet Samuel and symbolized his sanctity as a future king. See OIL.[23]

Demeter/Ceres. Graeco-Roman goddess of agriculture, especially corn. She was descended from much older earth-goddesses who were worshipped to ensure the fertility of crops. Rituals were performed in the autumn at the sowing of the seed corn, which had been harvested and stored some four months earlier. From this arose the myth of Persephone, her daughter, who annually passed a third of the year in the Underworld,[24] (not, it seems, the winter months, as the myth relates, but the period between harvest and sowing). Demeter's attributes are ears or a sheaf of CORN, a CORNUCOPIA, SICKLE, and TORCH with which she searched for her daughter. Herbal medicine, once used to assist women's various reproductive functions, included the POPPY and POMEGRANATE, which were her attributes in early Greek art. The PIG, being very prolific, was sacrificed to her and was another early attribute. The SNAKE, because of its ancient connection with fertility goddesses, was another. It was revived in Italian Renaissance painting in the form of dragons that draw her CHARIOT. In Renaissance allegory she personifies Summer, one of the FOUR SEASONS. See also TWELVE MONTHS – August and September.

Devi. The general term for the great goddess of Hindu myth and art, descendant of the Mother-Goddess worshipped by the Indus Valley peoples (3rd mill. BC) and probably much earlier still. The ancient cult must have survived locally alongside the mainly male Vedic gods brought by the Aryans from Central Asia in the first half of the 2nd mill. BC. From about the 5th cent. AD she began to assume an increasingly dominant role under various names, first as the wife of the Vedic gods, then as a powerful, independent being. God and goddess together were seen as a symbol of the continual process of creation. The male was the passive, absolute element; the female was the active, creative energy, or *shakti*, derived from him. (See also SPEAR.) The male–female relationship was very significant in the tradition of Tantrism. This was originally part of the cult of SHIVA, its texts (the *Tantras*) taking the form of a dialogue between Shiva and his *shakti*, Parvati. The sex act has a central place in the myth, ritual and imagery of the sect. Its devotees, when in the act of ritual intercourse, see themselves identified with the god and goddess. The concept of the *shakti* began to influence Buddhist thought with the rise of Vajrayana (Thunderbolt sect) about the end of the 6th cent. AD and eventually became a feature of Tibetan Lamaist art (see YAB-YUM).

Devi (strictly Maha-Devi, the Great Goddess) is the omnipresent female deity of Hinduism, but she appears in many guises and has many names according to her various roles. As the wife of VISHNU she is called Lakshmi ('Fortune') or Shri-Lakshmi. Her link with the ancient Mother-Goddess is the LOTUS. She may stand on the flower or hold it in her hand; she is flanked by ELEPHANTS that spray her with fertilizing waters. This image is seen on a seal from the Indus Valley and reappears in a 7th cent. AD relief at Mamallapuram, and elsewhere. Lakshmi accompanies Vishnu and also KRISHNA, as Vishnu's *avatar*. As a lotus-goddess she entered Buddhism at an early date and can be seen among other deities from one of the oldest Buddhist STUPAS (Bharhut, 2nd–1st cent. BC).

Parvati ('Daughter of the Mountain'), the wife, or *shakti*, of Shiva, is virtuous and chaste. She sits beside him in his palace on the sacred MOUNTAIN, Kailasa. Below them, imprisoned in the mountain and struggling vainly to escape, is the demon Ravana. The god and goddess here symbolize their creative power, or *brahman* (see BRAHMA), which the demon is powerless to destroy.

Many Hindu deities have a dual aspect: in the throes of violent emotion they display a ferocious, destructive side in which they sometimes assume animal forms. These contrasting aspects are called *shanta* (gentle and calm) and *krodha* (wrathful). Parvati in her wrathful aspect is known as Durga ('difficult of access') or Kali, the Black Goddess. In this role her most famous exploit was to slay the BUFFALO demon, Mahisha.[25] The other gods ceded their weapons to her – the symbols of their power – which she takes in her many hands. She is mounted on a LION, the symbol of her ferocious identity. The demon, in spite of protean cunning, is finally pierced with a TRIDENT and beheaded. See also DISK; GOAD; NOOSE.

The Great Goddess as destroyer is also prominent in Tantric myth and art where she is also known as Kali. She has carnivorous fangs (TOOTH), protruding TONGUE and a garland made of the severed HANDS of her victims, whose entrails she devours. But she is not a symbol of evil and is widely revered. Her name, Kali, means Time, in other words, that which creates and ultimately devours all things. The present Iron Age, the last in the cosmic cycle of four, is called the Kali-yuga, the Age of Kali, which will end in universal destruction by fire and flood (see AGES OF THE WORLD; KALKIN). On a personal level, as a bringer of death, Kali's devotees resort to cemeteries to worship her. (On Tantrism see further PADMASAMBHAVA. See also BODHISATTVA; BUDDHA; PRAJNA-PARAMITA; SARASVATI.)

Dionysus/Bacchus. Graeco-Roman god of fertility, probably originally from Thrace and closely associated with the cultivation of the vine. He was worshipped principally in the form of a BULL, sometimes as a GOAT. His wild, orgiastic rites involved eating the beasts' raw flesh and were the occasion of much drunken revelry (see WINE). His cult spread through Asia and became highly popular in Rome. In classical myth he is the son of ZEUS/JUPITER and the mortal Semele.

In the act of copulation she was consumed by Zeus's lightning but the infant was saved and sewn into Zeus's thigh until due to be born.[26] Dionysus is widely represented in classical art, and themes from the myths were popular in the Renaissance and later. He holds a sprig or branch of VINE, or IVY, either of which may make a crown. He holds a wine vessel (usually a *kantharos* in Greek vase painting) and a sacred wand, the THYRSUS. These attributes also belong to his male and female followers, the Satyrs and Bacchantes. The latter may, besides, play CYMBALS and TAMBOURINE, or hold SNAKES, since handling snakes seems to have been a part of Dionysiac rites. A DOLPHIN recalls his punishment of sailors, by whom he was kidnapped, by turning them into dolphins.[27] Dionysus is associated with TIGERS and LEOPARDS, probably through the spread of his cult to the East. He and his followers may wear their skins. In Renaissance and later art they, or sometimes goats, draw his triumphal CHARIOT. In Renaissance allegory he personifies Autumn, one of the FOUR SEASONS. See also TWELVE MONTHS – October.

Ea (Sum. Enki). Mesopotamian god of fresh water. According to a Sumerian myth the god, there called Enki, dwelt in the ocean of fresh water *abzu* that surrounds the earth and on which the earth floats.[28] The *abzu* fed rivers and springs, bringing fertility to the land, and was also the source of all wisdom and knowledge. The god's principal temple was in the Akkadian city of Eridu (where he would have been known as Ea). Cylinder seals of the first half of 2nd mill. BC show the god, usually enthroned, with streams of WATER flowing from his arms and shoulders, interspersed with fishes. In sculpture and wall-painting of all periods of Mesopotamian art, he holds a vase from which streams and fishes flow, an image also associated with other deities as a symbol of fertility in general. Ea wears a horned cap (see HORN) and may have a TURTLE or RAM-headed sceptre for attributes. Another Sumerian text, with Enki in the role of creator, has striking parallels with the account of creation in Genesis.[29] See also RIVER; VISHNU (*avatar* of a fish).

Eight Immortals (Ch. *Pa Hsien*). A group of figures seen widely in Chinese art. They are Taoist in origin and typify Taoism, whose supposed founder was the legendary sage, Lao-tzu, in the 6th cent. BC. Taoism was a religion in the true metaphysical sense, unlike the rival doctrines of Confucius, which were essentially a moral code of public service (see TWELVE ORNAMENTS). It taught that there is a way (*tao*), a natural order of the universe and its motive forces, with which the individual must be in harmony. It required a passive, receptive frame of mind, best found in the solitude of the mountains. To its devotees it brought long life and the promise of immortality. During the Han dynasty (206 BC–AD 220) Taoism became a popular mass movement. This was mainly due to shaman-priests and other charlatans who offered various magical prescriptions which guaranteed immortality. It was believed by Taoists that a divine plant, a kind of FUNGUS, grew on legendary islands in the Eastern Sea, the 'Isles of the Blest', perhaps Japan. The inhabitants, having eaten it, became immortal (see CENSER). Out of these beginnings developed the Chinese reverence for longevity, which is expressed in their art by many symbolic motifs, for example, BAMBOO; BAT; CORAL; CRANE; HARE; JU-I; PEACH; PINE; PLUM; STORK; TORTOISE.

A Taoist pantheon of gods and goddesses began to take shape in the Han dynasty. Among them was a God of Longevity, Shou Hsing, one of the THREE

GODS OF HAPPINESS. The Eight Immortals, who also symbolize longevity, date from the same period, though the members of the group were not finalized until the 13th or 14th cent. Like other Taoist deities, some are based on supposed historical persons, three of them quite well authenticated. They are distinguished by their attributes, which also feature, without their owners, on ceramics, silks and other forms of decorative art. The canon of Eight are:

Chung-li Ch'uan. Leader of the Eight, a bearded sage with a FAN.

Ho Hsien-ku. Young girl, holding a LOTUS.

Chang Kuo. Bearded and holding a bamboo DRUM. He may be mounted back to front on a white mule or ASS.

Lu Tung-pin. Patron of barbers. Bearded, with FLY-WHISK and SWORD, the latter usually slung across his back.

Han Hsiang-tzu. Youthful patron of musicians, playing a flute (see PIPE).

Ts'ao Kuo-chiu. Patron of actors, elderly and bearded, holding CASTANETS.

Li T'ieh-kuai. A beggar with an iron CRUTCH and GOURD.

Lan Ts'ai-ho. Patron of florists, a woman holding a basket of FLOWERS, and wearing only one shoe.

Lao-tzu himself is often represented holding a JU-I sceptre and a BOOK or SCROLL. He is mounted on a black BUFFALO which, according to legend, is carrying him to the West in search of Buddhist doctrines, alternatively to the Taoist paradise, the Hills of Longevity (*Shou Shan*). See further, MOUNTAIN.

Eight Lucky Emblems (Ch. *Pa chi hsiang*). Buddhist symbols of good augury, originally supposed to have figured on the Buddha's FOOT. They are most commonly seen on Chinese ceramics, but are also used as motifs in Buddhist architecture and on Lamaist prayer-flags. The group usually consists of the WHEEL of the Law, conch SHELL, UMBRELLA, CANOPY, LOTUS, VASE or jar, with lid, pair of FISH and mystic KNOT. See also HUNDRED ANTIQUES.

Eight Treasures (Ch. *Pa pao*). A group of symbolic objects often represented on Chinese ceramics, textiles and carpets. Its composition varies with time and place. The objects are thought to have once symbolized valuable offerings but later came to denote, as a group, a wish for material prosperity. They are usually entwined with red ribbon, which indicates their use as charms. They have a very simple, stylized treatment. The commonest group consists of: BOOK; LEAF; pair of HORNS; LOZENGE; COIN; MIRROR; Pearl (see JEWELS); stone chime (see MUSICAL STONE).

Enlil. Mesopotamian god who became the supreme deity of Sumer; god of air and the winds, 'king of heaven and earth', 'king of all the lands', generally beneficent to mankind. He was the father of NINURTA. His principal temple at Nippur in the north of Sumer was called Ekur, the 'Mountain House',[30] perhaps an indication of his origin in the mountains of western Iran. At the end of the Old Babylonian period (*c.* 1600 BC) he became, with ANU and EA, one of a great Mesopotamian trinity. In neo-Assyrian reliefs the trio are symbolized by three horned caps (see HORN). See also SIN.

Eros/Cupid. Graeco-Roman god of love, first mentioned by Hesiod as one of the oldest deities, the son of Chaos, who stands for the primeval power out of which the universe was created. He 'unnerves the limbs and overcomes the mind and wise counsels'.[31] Later myths made him the son of APHRODITE/VENUS by various fathers. He is represented in Greek vase painting and reliefs from the 5th cent. BC as a youth or child, often with his mother. He has WINGS and hovers above nuptial couples, sometimes about to crown them with a LAUREL wreath; or he pursues gods and goddesses with a WHIP. As Cupid he is widely represented in Renaissance and later painting and sculpture, often simply as a symbolic presence in scenes of love-making. From this period his attributes are BOW, ARROW and QUIVER; a golden arrow inspires love, a leaden one kills it. A burning TORCH symbolizes the fires of passion while, when turned down and extinguished, they are extinct. A GLOBE denotes Cupid's universal power. When BLINDFOLD he symbolizes love's blindness and moral darkness. An arrow piercing a HEART alludes to the motto *Omnia vincit Amor*, 'Love conquers all'. It is also implied when he stands triumphantly on a heap of WEAPONS. Surrounded by BOOKS or musical instruments, he is victorious over intellectual pursuits. His triumphal CHARIOT is drawn by four white horses or by goats. Greek myth gave Eros a brother, Anteros, who symbolized love reciprocated. Renaissance humanists made them symbols of earthly and heavenly love, like the same twin aspects of the Renaissance Venus. They contend for a PALM branch, or embrace in reconciliation. Eros may be distinguished from his brother by a blindfold. See also TRIUMPH.

Faith. One of the three THEOLOGICAL VIRTUES. In medieval art she has a CROSS, CHALICE and sometimes a FONT. Her opposing vice, sometimes forming a pendant, is Idolatry, a man worshipping an APE. In Counter-Reformation art, Faith holds a book with a cross lying on it and her foot rests on a CUBE. She may hold a CANDLE, the light of faith, and wear a HELMET to ward off heresy.

Father Time. The Greeks personified Time, or Chronos, as an old man. He became identified with Cronus (having a similar name), a Titan who, in Greek myth, castrated his father with a sickle.[32] The Romans identified their god of agriculture, Saturn, with Cronus and kept the sickle, or made it a SCYTHE. Saturn thus also came to personify Time, and had the means wherewith to reap, like Death. As an old man he is given a CRUTCH. The *ouroboros*, or SNAKE with its tail in its mouth, a symbol of eternity, became his attribute in late antiquity. The Renaissance figure we call Father Time is based on Saturn. At this period also he acquired WINGS and HOUR-GLASS. He then had several symbolic roles. He records the deeds of heroes in a book, uncovers naked Truth, reveals Innocence (with her lamb), destroys youth and beauty and, finally, accompanies the figure of Death. See also VIRTUES AND VICES; TRIUMPH – Time.

Five Elements, see FOUR ELEMENTS.

Five Poisons. Chinese medicine was traditionally based on various groups of five. Thus a tincture concocted from five supposedly venomous creatures was prescribed for various ills, on a homeopathic principle. They were CENTIPEDE, SCORPION, SNAKE, gecko LIZARD and toad (see FROG). Their collective image was made into a charm to ward off sickness and evil spirits. They also symbolize different social evils. The Chinese god and mythical queller of demons, Chung K'uei, is depicted as a fierce warrior chasing the five creatures with a sword. The image is hung up on the 5th day of the 5th month to scare them away. Chung K'uei is especially popular in Japan, where he is called Shoki. He is depicted in comical pursuit of small imps.

Five Senses. They are first mentioned as allegories in a 12th cent. mythographical manual, which claims that the five daughters of the Greek sun-god, Helios, in reality stand for the Five Senses.[33] The Renaissance humanist movement inspired the production of numerous similar works, much used by artists from the 16th to 18th cents. The five, represented as female figures, are given a variety of appropriate attributes:

Hearing. Musical instruments such as LUTE, TAMBOURINE or portative ORGAN; from the 17th cent. often a bowed instrument; the sharp-eared STAG.

Sight. She gazes admiringly into a MIRROR or, occasionally, holds a flaming TORCH; sharp-eyed EAGLE and LYNX.

Taste. BASKET or dish of fruit; APE with fruit in mouth.

Smell. Bunch of FLOWERS, especially LILIES or CARNATIONS; VASE of scent; DOG.

Touch. HEDGEHOG and ERMINE together (harsh and soft sensations); SPIDER, SNAIL, TORTOISE (all sensitive to touch); Leda's SWAN; FALCON.

Dutch *genre* paintings may allude to the senses, as in tavern scenes depicting drinking (Taste), smoking (Smell) a fiddler and singers (Hearing), man embracing woman (Touch). Touch is sometimes depicted as a physician letting blood.

Fortune. She first emerges as a goddess in Hellenistic Greece when the power and influence of the great gods of Olympus were in decline. She personified the element of chance that was now perceived to govern the destinies of mankind. The Greeks called her 'That which happens', or Tyche, and usually represented her wearing a mural CROWN and holding a CORNUCOPIA. The Romans identified her with an old Italian fertility goddess, Fortuna. They gave her a RUDDER and prow of a BOAT because she was feared by seafarers; sometimes a GLOBE or WHEEL (both inconstant because they turn). She may have WINGS. Fortune enjoyed a strong revival in Renaissance allegory. Marine attributes now include a SAIL, SHELL and DOLPHIN. She may be BLINDFOLD, or have DICE, to indicate her random behaviour; more rarely, a BRIDLE, from an ancient confusion with Nemesis. Fortune's wheel was a popular allegorical theme in the Renaissance. The wheel has a handle, which is turned by Dame Fortune, while figures, rising and falling, cling desperately to the rim. The topmost wears a crown, he at the bottom falls off.

Four Arts. To be a musician, writer and bibliophile, painter and chess-player were the necessary accomplishments of every Chinese scholar besides his formal qualifications, providing him with spiritual refreshment. A scholar was one who had passed all the state examinations and was therefore intimately acquainted with the work of Confucius. For Confucius, music in particular was an essential ingredient of Chinese culture because it promoted social harmony, combining earthly and spiritual values, YIN AND YANG respectively. The four arts are symbolized by a LUTE (or ZITHER), BOOKS (with brush-pens), two SCROLLS (painting and calligraphy) and a CHESSBOARD. They are often represented together on ceramics. A group of young women, known as the 'Ten Learned Women', may be depicted practising the four arts. See also CARP (state examinations); K'UEI HSING (god of literature); FOUR TREASURES (the scholar's tools of trade).

Four Celestial Kings, or Four Guardians of the World (Sk. *Lokapala*), are found in Buddhist temples, each one facing one of the four cardinal points (see also

COMPASS). They probably originated in one of the various categories of guardian spirits that abound in Indian folk-religion, namely the *yakshas*, genii of the earth who protect its treasures. They are first seen on the exterior of stupas at Bharhut (1st cent. BC), and are later very widely represented in eastern Asia, typically in armour and trampling on DEMONS. In Chinese painting and sculpture they are royally robed, sometimes crowned, often with wrathful expressions. According to one tradition they represent four legendary brothers who were military leaders. They are distinguished by their attributes:

East. Mo-li Ch'ing, brandishing a fiery SWORD that destroys all evil-doers.

South. Mo-li Hung, holding an UMBRELLA that brings darkness and chaos when opened.

West. Mo-li Hai, playing a LUTE whose sound causes the enemy's settlements to catch fire.

North. Mo-li Shou, holding a MONGOOSE, which devours evil-doers. A separate tradition identified the Guardian of the North with a legendary Japanese warrior, Bishamon, who is also worshipped as one of the seven GODS OF HAPPINESS. In Japan he enjoyed a separate cult as protector of the monastery of the Sanno sect of Buddhism on Mt Hiei near Kyoto. His attribute is a small pagoda, held in the hand.

The four kings are distinct from the two Gate Guardians (Sk. *Dvarapala*) who stand one on each side of the entrance to many Buddhist temples. They may also stand at the edge of paintings of the Buddhist hierarchy. They are usually represented as fierce, half-naked warriors and may hold a *vajra* (THUNDERBOLT).

Four Elements. Beliefs about the elements were closely bound up with the practice of alchemy. The ancient pseudo-science was supposed to have originated in Egypt and was known in the East and West long before the Christian era. The four elements made contrasting pairs, earth and air, fire and water. The Chinese recognized five: water, fire, metal, wood, earth which, in various ways, were also related to one another. In Chinese art they are symbolized by pig, hen, dog, sheep and ox respectively, or five TIGERS. They are also related to the seasons, winter, summer, autumn, spring, and their symbolic animals (see COMPASS). (See also MUDRA – 6) In the West the four elements are first represented in Italian Renaissance painting as female allegorical figures or, especially in the 16th cent., as classical deities:

Earth. Her attributes are derived from the old fertility goddesses: CORNUCOPIA, SNAKE (Demeter/Ceres), SCORPION (Tellus Mater), turreted CROWN (Cybele). She may suckle one or two children (Ops). *Genre* scenes in 17th and 18th cent. painting depict various horticultural activities.

Air. CHAMELEON. The goddess Hera/Juno with her PEACOCK and other BIRDS. Or she hangs in the air with an ANVIL tied to each foot.[34] *Genre*: Children with windmills or blowing bubbles.

Fire. SALAMANDER, THUNDERBOLT, HEAD aflame, or PHOENIX for a head-dress. The blacksmith of the gods, Hephaestus/Vulcan.

Water. A river-god with flowing URN. Poseidon/Neptune with his train, accompanied by DOLPHINS and HIPPOCAMPI. *Genre*: anglers beside a river or in a boat.

See also FOUR TEMPERAMENTS; PHILOSOPHY.

Four Latin Fathers, or Four Doctors of the (western) Church. The title was first used in the Middle Ages for four celebrated Christian theologians, Jerome (*c.* 342–420), Ambrose, bishop of Milan (*c.* 339–97), Augustine, bishop of Hippo Regius (354–430) and Pope Gregory I ('the Great') (*c.* 540–604). The first three, who lived in an age torn by doctrinal controversies, were paramount in establishing orthodoxy. As a group they may be depicted on their own or attending Christ in Majesty, the Virgin enthroned or Virgin and Child. They usually hold books. Their distinguishing attributes include:

Jerome. Dress: cardinal's HAT; LION (from the legend that he befriended one after drawing a thorn from its paw), MODEL of a church. Jerome, when depicted by himself as a desert hermit, has a STONE to beat his breast; SKULL and HOURGLASS.

Ambrose. Dress: bishop's canonicals; WHIP, with three knots symbolizing the Trinity, to castigate Arian heretics; BEEHIVE, his mellifluous eloquence.

Augustine. Dress: bishop's canonicals or monk's habit; flaming HEART, his religious ardour; ARROWS piercing his breast, remorse for a misspent youth. When alone, by the sea-shore, he has an INFANT at his feet, an allusion to his work *De Trinitate, On the Trinity,* in which the child symbolizes the infant Christ.[35]

Gregory. Dress: papal TIARA and pontifical CROSS; a DOVE at his ear, inspiring his words.

Their counterparts in the eastern Church are the Four Greek Fathers, John Chrysostom, Basil the Great, Athanasius and Gregory Nazianzen, sometimes joined by a fifth, Cyril of Alexandria. They wear bishop's vestments and have no attributes, being distinguished by their inscriptions.

Four Parts of the World. As allegorical female figures they appear in the sculpture of Christian churches, especially Jesuit, from the late 16th cent., where they symbolize the world-wide extension of Catholic doctrine. Their attributes were established in Ripa's mythographical manual.[36]

Europe. CROWN and SCEPTRE, as queen of the world; holds a TEMPLE; WEAPONS and HORSE denote supremacy in war; CORNUCOPIA of fruit.

Asia. CROWN of flowers; JEWELS adorn her robe; she holds a CENSER containing oriental perfumes, a spray of flowers or fruit, or a PALM. A CAMEL sits beside her.

Africa. Black complexion; crowned with the head of an ELEPHANT; CORAL necklace; holds a SCORPION and CORNUCOPIA of ears of corn. A LION and SNAKE are nearby.

America. American-Indian head-dress of FEATHERS holds BOW and ARROW; severed HEAD (suggesting cannibalism), pierced by an arrow, lies at her feet. A caiman is nearby.

Four Prophets. Of the authors of O.T. prophetic books, Isaiah, Jeremiah, Ezekiel and Daniel frequently form a group in Christian art, when they are known as the Four Greater Prophets. They first appear, beside other sacred figures such as O.T. prefigurative types of Christ and the SIBYLS, in 13th cent. cathedrals and churches, often at the west door. They may hold a scroll bearing an inscription from their writings, or a book. Their distinguishing attributes are:

Isaiah. SAW, the instrument of his death; TONGS holding a glowing coal.[37]

Jeremiah. CROSS, as a prophet of Christ's Passion.

Ezekiel. WHEEL, or double wheel, an allusion to his vision.[38]

Daniel. LION, or its skin.[39]

Four Seasons. The Greek goddesses who controlled the order of nature and the changing seasons were the Horae. They were originally worshipped as spirits of fecundity and in the oldest myths are only three in number.[40] At first they are indistinguishable from one another, but in later Graeco-Roman painting and sculpture, when they are four, they acquire appropriate attributes, which in general they retain until the 18th cent.

Spring. Spray of FLOWERS. In Renaissance and later painting her hair may be garlanded with flowers and she holds a SPADE or HOE. From this period she may be personified by a classical deity, Flora or APHRODITE/VENUS.

Summer. SICKLE or SCYTHE, ears or sheaf of CORN. Ren.: also fruit. Deity: DEMETER/CERES.

Autumn. GRAPES, VINE leaves. Deity: DIONYSUS/BACCHUS.

Winter. Thickly clad. Ren.: old man, wrapped in cloak, sometimes by fireside. Deity: Boreas (North wind), or Hephaistos/Vulcan, blacksmith of the gods.

The seasons had links with ancient astronomy: *Horae*, in Greek, also means the four quadrants of the heavens. In China the seasons formed part of a comprehensive scheme of cosmology that took in the quadrants, terrestrial directions, the four supernatural creatures (see COMPASS) and the elements (see FOUR ELEMENTS). In the decoration of Chinese ceramics, textiles, etc, the seasons are symbolized by the PEONY, LOTUS, CHRYSANTHEMUM or OLIVE, and PLUM. See also CALENDAR; FOUR TEMPERAMENTS; TWELVE MONTHS.

Four Species (Heb. *arbaah minim*). Four plants used ritually during the Jewish Feast of Tabernacles. They are traditionally a PALM branch (*lulab*), an *ethrog* (CITRON), three sprigs of MYRTLE and two WILLOW twigs. Old Rabbinical commentaries suggested various allegorical meanings such as parts of the body or four types of Jew. They are now thought to have been symbols of the earth's fruitfulness that accompanied prayers for rain.

Four Temperaments. The Middle Ages, following a tradition that goes back to ancient Babylonian astrology, believed that man was a microcosm of the universe and that his body was therefore governed by various planetary influences. They worked through his internal organs that produced four kinds of bodily fluids, or humours, which determined his temperament. There were terrestrial influences too. The humours were of the same essence as the FOUR ELEMENTS and were also associated with the FOUR SEASONS, four times of day, four rivers of Hades and other groups comprising the same magic number. They were also linked to four animals that were said to share their character. Thus:

Sanguine (blood), air, spring, morning, Acheron, APE.

Choleric (bile), fire, summer, midday, Phlegethon, LION.

Melancholic (black bile), earth, autumn, dusk, Styx, PIG.

Phlegmatic (phlegm), water, winter, night, Cocytus, LAMB.

As a group of allegorical figures they appear in 15th cent. Books of Hours, thereafter mainly as single figures accompanied by their animals. Choler, sometimes a soldier, may be unsheathing his SWORD and be surrounded by flames. Melancholy, a temperament that Renaissance humanists associated with the contemplative, intellectual and artistic type of person, was the only one widely represented. In astrological terms she was one of the 'children' of Saturn and so wears a gloomy, saturnine expression, while she broods over a BOOK. She may have WINGS, and a DOG (associated with Saturn) instead of a pig. A SKULL indicates the vanity of her efforts. A PURSE or cash-box symbolizes typical Saturnian parsimony. Saturn presided over Geometry, one of the SEVEN LIBERAL ARTS, so Melancholy borrows her COMPASSES, SET-SQUARE, ruler, etc. Among the children of Saturn were carpenters, so she may have some of his tools, such as a SAW.

Four Treasures. The four 'priceless jewels' of the Chinese scholar's study are PAPER, BRUSH, INK and INKSTONE. They reflect the deep veneration for literary skills, inherited from Confucius, of which calligraphy later became an intrinsic part. See also the FOUR ARTS of the scholar.

Ganesha (or Ganapati). Popular elephant-headed Hindu god. His origin is likely to have been Indian, not Aryan. His cult and imagery were insignificant before the 7th cent. AD. He symbolizes wisdom, charity and is the patron of literature. He was said to be the amanuensis of the author of the Indian epic, the *Mahabharata* (*c.* 100 BC–AD 300). He is called 'Remover of Obstacles' and is invoked at the start of difficult undertakings. There are various myths about his birth, the majority making him the 'son' of Parvati and SHIVA.[41] His iconography is very varied. He is pot-bellied and has a broken tusk. The latter must surely have been inspired by an actual image – its first reference is in a *Purana* of *c.* 4th–10th cent. AD.[42] His mount is a bandicoot, the large Indian RAT; occasionally a LION. He usually has four arms, but sometimes as many as twelve. His commonest attributes are weapons, especially the elephant GOAD and NOOSE. He may also have a battle-AXE, BOW and arrow, TRIDENT, conch-SHELL and DISK. Ganesha appears occasionally in Tibetan art as a god of wealth, when he dances on a jewel-spitting MONGOOSE and holds a BOWL of jewels and various weapons, in particular battle-axe and trident; also a ROSARY.

Garuda. Sacred bird of Hindu myth, the mount of VISHNU, usually taken to be an EAGLE, sometimes a wild goose. The image of a god standing or sitting on an animal or bird, his so-called 'vehicle' (Sk. *vahana*), is a convention that appears to have originated in Mesopotamia and is an aspect of several Indian deities (see, e.g. BULL; GOAT; LION; PEACOCK; RAT). It is probably to be understood not as a symbol but as a representation of the god himself – a survival of the deity in his more ancient, wholly zoomorphic form. Certainly, the eagle was once widely identified with sun-gods and Garuda is referred to as the 'golden sun-bird', while Vishnu personified the sun in the myth of his three strides across the heavens.[43] The myth of the conflict between bird and snake (see EAGLE) occurs in the East and West. In the sacred literature of India it takes place between Garuda and the evil, poisonous serpent Kaliya.[44] It is a symbolic encounter between heaven and earth, or between birth and creation – from the bird's cosmic egg – against death (see further KRISHNA). Garuda may be represented wholly as a bird, though later he is usually in human form with WINGS and sometimes a beaked nose. His hands may be in the *anjali* position (see MUDRA), especially when he accompanies Vishnu. Garuda was adopted by Buddhism and features particularly in Tibetan painting and sculpture as the vehicle of the Dhyani-BUDDHA Amoghasiddhi and as one of the manifestations of the BODHISATTVA, Vajrapani. As the latter he has human form with wings and talons and stands on a snake or demon. See also ELEPHANT.

Geb. Egyptian god who personified the earth and its fruitfulness. A creation myth from Heliopolis made him the father of OSIRIS, ISIS, SETH, Nephthys and

THOTH, by his sister/spouse, the sky-goddess Nut (see COW). He is described in early texts[45] but is not widely represented before the New Kingdom. He has human form and reclines under the heavenly ARCH of Nut, sometimes with erect PHALLUS. As an earth-god REEDS and other plants may sprout from him and he may be coloured green (see DEVI). The hieroglyph of his name is a GOOSE, which he sometimes wears on his head. Some myths identify him with the goose from whose egg the sun-god RE was born. Otherwise his head-dress is the red CROWN of Lower Egypt.

Gods of Happiness (Ch. *Fu lu shou san hsien*). A triad of Chinese stellar gods represented as a group in painting and carving. In Japan they merge with others to form a group of seven (Jap. *Shichi-fuku-jin*).

Shou Hsing. God of longevity. A bearded sage easily distinguished by his high, domed head. He holds a PEACH, a long, knotted STAFF from which one or two scrolls may hang, and sometimes a GOURD (containing cinnabar, used to make the elixir of immortality). He may be accompanied by a DEER or CRANE.

Lu Hsing. God of riches (and salaries), holds a basket of FLOWERS and may be accompanied by one or two children.

Fu Hsing. God of happiness, holds a JU-I sceptre.

The robes of all three are sometimes decorated with STARS. Artists are not always reliable in allocating their attributes, those of Fu and Lu sometimes being reversed. The group may be represented simply as symbols: BAT (Happiness), DEER or stag (Riches), PINE (Longevity).

The origins of the Japanese seven are Indian and Chinese as well as Japanese. As a group they date only from the early 17th cent., though individually some are much older. Typically they are seen aboard the legendary Treasure Ship (see BOAT).

Fuku-roku-jiu, meaning Happiness, Prosperity, Long Life. He shares the staff, peach and crane of his Chinese counterpart, Shou Hsing.

Hotei. Known as the 'calico-bag monk', he is shaven headed, has a large SACK and, like Lu Hsing, is generally accompanied by children.

Daikoku is, like Lu Hsing, a God of riches. He stands on bales of RICE and holds a miner's HAMMER and SACK containing the precious stones he has mined. His messenger is a white RAT.

Jurojin. God of scholarship and literature, originally Chinese and reflecting the Chinese love of learning. His attributes, too, are borrowed from Shou Hsing: domed head, staff with scrolls attached, peach, and riding a deer.

Ebisu, 'the smiling one'. God of food, once worshipped in every home; patron of fishermen who holds a large FISH under his arm.

Bishamon has mixed affiliations, Hindu, Buddhist and Japanese. In his Buddhist aspect he is identified with the Guardian of the North (see FOUR CELESTIAL KINGS) and holds a pagoda (STUPA). In the Treasure Ship he wears armour, like a war-god.

Benten. The only female in the group, worshipped in Japan principally as a goddess of love. Like the Hindu SARASVATI, from whom she may be descended, she is also a goddess of speech, letters and music, and holds a Chinese LUTE. Other occasional attributes are the so-called 'pearl', or light-giving jewel, one of the SEVEN TREASURES, and a KEY. Her early myths suggest she was originally a river-goddess, which explains the presence of a SNAKE in some shrine images. She also has a Tantric form with eight arms holding typical Tantric WEAPONS:

sword, axe, disk, trident, sceptre, noose, bow and arrow. In household shrines she is represented with fifteen sons, each of whom symbolizes one of the various tasks of daily life.

Hathor. Egyptian COW-goddess, worshipped from the beginning of the dynastic period, possibly earlier. Her cult was widespread, having its main centre at Dendera. She is represented in human form with a crown of cow's horns and, between them, a solar disk (see SUN) sometimes with the URAEUS. The disk indicates a link with the sun-god RE, whose lotus she sometimes holds. Alternatively she is wholly bovine. From an early period Hathor was regarded as the divine mother of the pharaoh whom, as a cow, she suckles. The PAPYRUS was sacred to her and may decorate the cow's body. She was also goddess of love, music and dancing and was identified with Aphrodite (A./VENUS) in Ptolemaic times. In this role she has a SISTRUM and MENAT, instruments used by priestesses during her rites. Hathor's cult spread abroad in the wake of trade. Her images have been found at the Phoenician city of Byblos, at Mari on the Euphrates, and elsewhere in the Near East and North Africa. See also ISIS.

Hecate. Greek goddess of pre-Hellenic origins, perhaps Anatolian, associated with the MOON and witchcraft. As a moon-goddess her worshippers were female. They left offerings before her statue which stood at crossroads where three ways met. It has three HEADS, or three bodies, which faced three ways. They were also said to symbolize the moon's phases. As a goddess of night and darkness she inhabited the Underworld and was known as Queen of the Dead. She holds two TORCHES to light her way. She used them to help DEMETER/CERES search for Persephone.[46] Some votive images give her six arms. She then holds pairs of torches, WHIPS, and DAGGERS. On her head is a tall wicker BASKET or a CRESCENT. She may be flanked by a pair of SNAKES. Black DOGS were among the animals sacrificed to her: one is her attribute. In Renaissance and later painting Hecate may be concealed in an underworld cavern while the search for Persephone goes on over her head.

Hera/Juno. Originally a Mother-Goddess, probably Minoan, the chief pre-Hellenic deity of Argos and later the pre-eminent goddess of the Greek pantheon, wife and sister of ZEUS/JUPITER. She was goddess of matrimony and looked after women's reproductive functions, for which she has a POMEGRANATE, once used in herbal medicine. Early Greek art shows her enthroned, sometimes holding a SCEPTRE and wearing a VEIL. The PEACOCK and CROWN were sacred to her. Her sceptre may be surmounted by a CUCKOO, an allusion to the many loves of Zeus. In Renaissance and later art she wears a magic GIRDLE and rides on a CHARIOT drawn by peacocks. As one of the FOUR ELEMENTS Hera symbolizes Air. See also MILK.

Hercules (Gk. Herakles). Greek hero, possibly once an historical figure, later worshipped as a saviour and benefactor of humanity. He personifies strength and courage. In classical myth he was the son of ZEUS/JUPITER and a mortal woman, Alcmene. His many exploits are widely represented in Greek, Roman and later art, and are the main source of his attributes. They are principally two: his weapons and lion's SKIN. In earlier Greek vase painting the weapons are usually BOW, ARROW and QUIVER. In later art he has a massive, knotted CLUB. The skin was taken from the Nemean lion that he strangled to death. There are minor attributes. As an infant he strangles two SNAKES, one in each hand.

A golden APPLE in his hand came from the garden of the Hesperides. A DISTAFF refers to his transvestite phase while the lover of Omphale, queen of Lydia. See also APOLLO; GLOBE; LION; MILK; VIRTUES AND VICES (Hercules at the Crossroads); TWELVE MONTHS – July.

Hermes/Mercury. Graeco-Roman deity with many functions. In parts of Arcadia and Attica he was, at an early date, worshipped as a fertility god in the form of an erect PHALLUS set up at the roadside. Later it took the form of a pillar, known as a Herm, which was crowned with a head, usually of Hermes, and with a phallus halfway down. In classical myth he was the son of ZEUS/JUPITER. He was messenger, or herald, of the gods, escorted the souls of the dead to the Underworld and was the guardian of wayfarers. In this role in early Greek art he wears a broad-brimmed HAT, travelling CLOAK and SANDALS or boots that may have WINGS. He is bearded and carries the messenger's staff, a CADUCEUS. Later he becomes a beardless youth, sometimes naked, a form he retains in the Renaissance. He was god of commerce, and then has a PURSE. As a protector of shepherds he has a RAM. He sometimes carries it around his shoulders, the prototype image of the Christian Good Shepherd (see CHRIST). As inventor of the LYRE, he may have a TORTOISE. A severed HEAD under his foot belongs to Argus, a hundred-eyed giant, whom he slew.[47]

Hope. One of the three THEOLOGICAL VIRTUES. In Gothic art she reaches heavenwards for a CROWN, her hands joined in prayer. An ANCHOR is half hidden under her robes. In the Renaissance and later she has a ship for headgear, indicating that to reach safe harbour was once a matter for hope (see BOAT). She has a CROW because it calls 'Cras-cras' (Lat. tomorrow, tomorrow). A basket of FLOWERS alludes to the hope of fruit to come.

Horus. Egyptian sky-god taking the form of a FALCON. From pre-dynastic times the king was identified with the god and the bird was therefore a symbol of his divinity. Images of Horus show him wholly bird-like at all periods, though from about the Middle Kingdom a falcon's head on a human body is more usual. As a child he is a normal human being. The falcon-headed Horus, as the personification of the king, wears the double CROWN of Upper and Lower Egypt. As a sky-god his eyes were the SUN and MOON and his WINGS were the sky itself. In this role he had links with RE, the ancient solar deity of Heliopolis, and, like Re, he then wears the disk of the sun and royal URAEUS (see also EYE; WINGED DISK). Early myths make Horus the son of Isis and enemy of SETH, who is either his brother or uncle (see OSIRIS). Their rivalry is an echo of struggles for the throne in a period when Lower and Upper Egypt were separate kingdoms and Horus and Seth were their respective tutelary deities. Horus's victory is symbolized by his killing an ANTELOPE, HIPPOPOTAMUS or other animal that was sacred to Seth. Images of the two gods together symbolize the union of the two kingdoms. Horus as a child is suckled by Isis, symbolizing her role as the king's protector; he touches his lips in a symbolic gesture (see FINGER); and may wear the 'sidelock of youth' (see HAIR). For the Four Sons of Horus, see JAR, CANOPIC.

Hsi Wang Mu ('Queen Mother of the West'; Jap. *Seiobo*). Immortal queen of Taoist legend. She lived in a palace on the K'un-lun mountains in Central Asia. In the palace gardens grew a PEACH tree that bore fruit once every three thousand years. It was jealously guarded by the queen and her attendant spirits, for anyone who ate of it became immortal. She is represented in paintings, ceramic decoration, small bronzes and *netsuke*, usually as a beautiful young woman in royal robes. She is attended by two handmaidens, one who holds a basket or dish of peaches, the other a FAN. She is mounted on a PEACOCK, the traditional vehicle of Chinese immortals or, more often, a CRANE. Blue-winged birds that fly about her are her messengers. She may sometimes have a GOURD, BAMBOO or basket of FLOWERS. There are reasons to think that her name, Wang Mu, may have been linked to some historical person or place. There are also parallels with the Greek myth of the garden of the Hesperides.

Hundred Antiques. The delight of the Chinese artist in depicting symbolic motifs is most apparent in the so-called Hundred Antiques that often decorate ceramics, especially larger vases. A hundred means merely a large number. The objects are mainly Taoist and Buddhist and are arranged quite informally. They usually include the EIGHT LUCKY EMBLEMS, EIGHT TREASURES, FOUR TREASURES, FOUR ARTS, the attributes of the EIGHT IMMORTALS and symbolic animals and flowers that have no classification. The message seems to be that material well-being, however achieved, is a continual source of joy.

Indra. Hindu sky-god of Aryan origin, primarily a thunder-god, having affinities with Zeus (z./JUPITER) and Thor; the pre-eminent deity of the *Rig-Veda*. Indra was also a war-god who slew the SNAKE-demon, Vritra, thereby bringing rain that the demon had been mischievously withholding.[48] There may be a distant echo here of the Mesopotamian myth of Marduk slaying Tiamat (see COMBAT). As a warrior Indra's companions were the Maruts, storm-gods and sons of Rudra (see SHIVA); they sped, fully armed, across the heavens in golden, HORSE-drawn chariots. Indra's attendants in the court of heaven were water-nymphs, the *apsarases* (see ANGEL). He is represented holding a THUNDERBOLT, BOW and arrow, and, when he has four hands, an elephant GOAD and lance. His mount is the ELEPHANT, Airavata, who also serves as his throne (Elura, *c.* 200 BC). Indra and BRAHMA were taken into the Buddhist hierarchy as attendants of Shakyamuni. They are seen in the Buddhist art of Gandhara, and in the Far East, where they are temple guardians. In China Indra is known as Ti-Shih, or Yintolo. See also VISHNU.

Instruments of the Passion. A group of objects, most of them mentioned in the closing chapters of the gospels, which symbolize Christ's trial and crucifixion. There is no definitive list and the number varies. The objects are sometimes represented with no narrative context and little formal arrangement. This type of devotional image was once believed to have magical properties. They may appear in the background of subjects such as the Man of Sorrows and the Mass of Gregory the Great. They are sometimes carried by angels. The oldest examples are 13th cent. and usually consist of: PILLAR, to which Christ was bound; crown of THORNS; CROSS; NAILS, SPONGE; LANCE. From the 15th cent. the number grows: thirty COINS; PURSE, sometimes hanging round Judas's neck; LAMP or TORCH of Malchus and his EAR, cut off by St Peter with his SWORD or KNIFE in the scene of the Betrayal; BLINDFOLD; HAND striking; head spitting (SPITTLE); COCK that crowed; FETTERS; WHIP; Pilate's jug and BOWL of water; VERNICLE; DICE, cast by soldiers; LADDER and PINCERS used at the Deposition.

Ishtar. Akkadian name for a deity descended from a prehistoric Mother-Goddess. Her most important rite involved sexual intercourse as a magical means of promoting fertility in all its aspects. She was known as Inanna in Sumer and was the counterpart of Astarte in Syria and Canaan. The consort of Ishtar was Tammuz (Sum. Dumuzi), a shepherd. The symbolic rite of 'sacred marriage' was performed at the New Year festival between the king and a priestess of Ishtar, who symbolized Tammuz and the goddess. Its purpose was to ensure a good harvest in the coming year (see also ZIGGURAT; WINDOW). A Sumerian myth tells of the death of Dumuzi/Tammuz, his descent into the Underworld and rescue by the goddess.[49] It symbolized the annual cycle of decay and regeneration of vegetation and is analogous to the Greek myth of Aphrodite (A./VENUS) and Adonis; ISIS and OSIRIS in Egypt; and Cybele and Attis in Asia Minor. Ishtar, like other goddesses of love and fertility, was also a goddess of war and was invoked by kings on going into battle. On neo-Assyrian cylinder seals she is armed with BOW, arrow, QUIVER and other weapons, and stands on, or is accompanied by, a LION. In the person of Astarte her cult reached Egypt in the 18th Dynasty, a time when the Egyptian empire extended as far as northern Syria. She rides on a horse-drawn CHARIOT, brandishing weapons, or she may be on horseback. She wears bull's HORNS, possibly a symbol of her strength and invincibility. From the Early Dynastic period in Mesopotamia Ishtar was identified with the planet Venus. In this role she has an eight-pointed STAR on her head and may be surrounded by other heavenly bodies such as the CRESCENT moon (according to one tradition she was the daughter of the moon-god SIN), the SIBITTI and, sometimes, the sun-disk of SHAMASH. The rosette (see ROSE) is also thought to denote Ishtar, perhaps being an alternative to the star. She may wear a horned cap (see HORN). See also COW; NUDITY; SCEPTRE; SIN.

Isis. Egyptian Mother-Goddess, wife of OSIRIS and mother of HORUS. (For the relationships of the gods and associated myths, see OSIRIS.) Since the pharaoh was regarded as the living embodiment of Horus, Isis had a special role as his symbolic mother and guardian. This is illustrated by her crown, which is in the form of a rudimentary THRONE and by the popular and very widespread image of her suckling the child Horus, who is seated on her lap. (The latter seems to have influenced the image of the Virgin and Child in Coptic art, if not more widely.) According to myth, Isis and her sister Nephthys took the form of kites in their search for the body of Osiris; they are sometimes depicted on coffins and sarcophagi in human form with open WINGS, protecting the deceased. In the New Kingdom Isis became associated with the cow-goddess HATHOR, acquiring her horns and solar disk, and her SISTRUM and MENAT. From this period she also has the TYET symbol. From the Ptolemaic period she became the protectress of mariners and may have a RUDDER for attribute. See also CRESCENT.

Janus. Old Italian god of doors and gates, invoked at all kinds of openings and beginnings. The first month is named after him. His HEAD has two faces that look in opposite directions – indoors and outdoors, or to past and future. On Roman coins from the 2nd cent. AD he may have as many as four. He holds a KEY in his right hand. In Renaissance allegories of Time he has a SNAKE, the ouroboros, a symbol of eternity.

John the Baptist. Called the forerunner or messenger of Christ, whom he baptized in the Jordan. He is very widely represented in Christian art, especially through his patronage of baptisteries and cities like Florence. As an ascetic desert-dweller he is clothed in a shaggy hide and may hold a HONEYCOMB, which comprised half his diet.[50] He holds a LAMB, the symbol of Christ and a reference to his words, 'Behold the lamb of God!'.[51] He may also hold a simple CROSS made of reeds, especially when represented as a child with the Holy Family. See also HEAD.

Kalkin. In Hindu myth, a horse, the form to be taken by VISHNU in his tenth and last incarnation, still to come. He will arrive at the end of the present 'Iron Age', or *Kali-yuga* of myth, which will bring universal destruction, and the overthrow of alien tyrants and false teachings. (See AGES OF THE WORLD.) Vishnu will come in 'power and glory', riding a white horse and brandishing a flaming sword, to prepare the way for a new 'golden age', or *Krita-yuga*.[52] It is a late myth. Its messianic tone has invited comparisons with western apocalyptic literature of the same era, like the Christian Book of Revelation. Kalkin is usually represented, not as a rider on horseback, but as a human figure with a horse's head. He usually has four arms and holds various weapons, a conch-SHELL (his war-trumpet, to herald the last day), DISK, SWORD, and SHIELD or ARROW. He has a fierce expression.

Karttikeya. In Hindu myth, the 'commander of the army of the gods'. He is also known as Skanda and, in southern India where his cult is still alive, as Subrahmanya. His origins appear to be non-Aryan and related to the indigenous peoples of the south, in particular the Tamils. There are various accounts of his birth. As Skanda he is the son of SHIVA and Parvati and may be represented with them, holding a LOTUS bud in each hand. In the *Mahabharata* he is the son of AGNI who seduces six astral deities, miraculously transformed into one for the occasion. They were the stars of the Pleiades (more usually observed as seven than six). Karttikeya was therefore born with six HEADS and twelve arms, which is the way he is usually represented. With six mothers his suckling was managed conveniently.[53] His image is found in many temples in southern India. His mount is a PEACOCK. As a war-god he has numerous weapons, most commonly BOW and arrow, SWORD, SHIELD, NOOSE and DISK; also conch-SHELL and DRUM. His war standard is topped by a COCK. Right and left hands may be in the *abhaya* and *varada* poses respectively (see MUDRA).

Khonsu. Egyptian moon-god, exceptional among lunar deities in being male. His principal cult centre was Thebes. His name means 'traveller', a reference to the moon's course across the sky. Khonsu is represented as a MUMMY. His hands are free and hold the royal insignia, the CROOK and flail, presumably derived from his father, AMUN. He is crowned with an upturned CRESCENT which holds a circular lunar disk. His sacred animal was the baboon (see APE; THOTH). At Thebes he is represented as one of a trinity of gods, beside Amun and his mother, Mut (see VULTURE). In this context, as a divine child he has the 'side-lock of youth' (see HAIR). An alternative iconography depicts Khonsu with the head of a FALCON, but distinguished from HORUS by the crescent and disk.

Krishna. The varied character of Krishna's iconography is the result of bringing together many Hindu legends of diverse origin. He was epic hero of the *Mahabharata* and also a pastoral deity and divine lover. In later recensions of the poem he becomes one of the incarnations of VISHNU. Being thus transformed from a mortal into a god he acquires Vishnavite traits. Some episodes in his story have marked parallels with western religious myth and epic. He is seen in Hindu art of all periods from the 3rd cent. AD. He is typically adorned with necklace, armlet, bracelet, etc in the manner of Vishnu and other greater gods (see JEWELS). He has heavy EAR-pendants and wears the jewelled, conical HAIR-style, the *kirita-makuta*, of Vishnu, or has his hair tied in a top-knot. His commonest weapons are also Vishnu's: the conch-SHELL and DISK. He usually has two arms, but with four or eight he may also hold a NOOSE, battle-AXE and LOTUS. An empty hand is often in the *varada* or *abhaya* pose (see MUDRA).

Krishna is widely represented dancing on a cobra, with one foot on its raised hood and one hand holding its tail. It illustrates the symbolic conflict between heavenly and earthly powers which, in Hindu myth, takes place between GARUDA and the serpent Kaliya. It was terminated by Krishna who exiled Kaliya to the distant ocean.[54] In this image Krishna's other hand is in the *abhaya* pose or holds a BALL of butter. The ball refers to a childhood incident when he stole milk, curds and suchlike from his mother.[55] It is also the subject of a separate image which shows him as a child on all fours holding a butter-ball. The figure of Krishna dancing, very common in southern India, symbolizes his joy at having obtained it.

As a pastóral god, Krishna is a flute-player (see PIPE), a very popular image. Like Orpheus, he enchanted the whole of nature – birds, beasts and humans – with his music. In this role he sometimes has up to eight arms, two for the flute, the rest for the attributes mentioned above. His listeners are cows, who turn their heads attentively, and numerous maidens, who are cow-herds. the latter are erotically attracted to the god, a symbol, it was claimed, of his love for the human race, which was strongly reciprocated.[56]

In the *Mahabharata* Krishna is the charioteer of the hero ARJUNA. He is seen holding the reins while mounting a chariot. He was also Arjuna's teacher. Interpolated in the epic is Krishna's discourse, forming a separate poem, the famous *Bhagavad Gita*, a compendium of orthodox Hindu doctrine. Krishna, as an incarnation of Vishnu, also has links with the cosmos. His mother, on looking into his mouth, saw there the whole universe at a glance.[57] Another text[58] likens the parts of his body to the different elements that make up earth and sky – the trees and rivers, stars and planets – which recalls the teaching of Babylonian astrologers that man was the universe in miniature, its microcosm. The Hindu cycle of creation, the cosmic 'day of BRAHMA' is alluded to in an image found on late ivories and bronzes of southern India. It represents Krishna reclining on a leaf of the Indian fig-tree (Sk. *vata*) and symbolizes the god contemplating the annihilation of the universe at the end of the cycle (see FIG).

K'uei Hsing (Jap. *Bunshosei*). Chinese god of literature, one of the Taoist pantheon, also venerated by Confucians as the patron of those taking the state examinations (see also EIGHT IMMORTALS; TWELVE ORNAMENTS). His origin appears to be astral for *k'uei* (dragon or spirit) which is the name of part of the constellation of the Great Bear. As a stellar god he is represented as an ugly, horned DEMON. As god of literature he holds a BRUSH-pen and a BOOK inscribed 'Heaven determines literary success'. He may hold a cup instead of a book. He stands on a large FISH or TURTLE. He may be accompanied by another god of literature, Wen Ch'ang, with whom he has sometimes been identified. The second god is an august figure, seated, wearing mandarin robes and sometimes holding a SCEPTRE.

Maitreya (Ch. *Mi-lo-fo*; Jap. *Miroku*). A very widely revered Buddhist deity; a Messiah-like figure who will appear on earth at some future date as another BUDDHA, the successor to Shakyamuni. At present he is therefore still a BODHISATTVA. He is first mentioned in a Buddhist text traditionally assigned to the 1st cent. BC.[59] His image appears first in Gandharan art (2nd–5th cents. AD) and subsequently spread, with his cult, throughout eastern Asia. There are accounts of colossal figures of Maitreya that once existed in India, Tibet and China. He is portrayed in stone and bronze and in painting. He is usually seated, with both legs hanging, as if about to descend from his throne, a posture very characteristic of him. Alternatively he assumes the so-called 'pensive' position (see POSTURE, 5, 6). His hand signs vary but most commonly show one of the 'teaching' gestures, the *dharmacakra* or *vitarka* (see MUDRA). He has a HALO, elongated EARS and, a personal feature, a small STUPA in his hair or diadem. In paintings, in the role of teacher, he is typically surrounded by bodhisattvas and other disciples. In Tibetan painting especially, he sits on a lotus THRONE in the *padmasana* or lotus posture and holds the *amrita* vessel (see VASE).

Manjushri (Ch. *Wen-shu*; Jap. *Monju*). Bodhisattva of transcendental wisdom worshipped throughout Buddhist Asia, especially in the Far East. He and Samantabhadra (moral perfection) are the attendants of Shakyamuni (see BODHISATTVA; BUDDHA). They are easily distinguished by their mounts, LION and ELEPHANT respectively, symbols of the power to overcome all spiritual obstacles. As a single figure Manjushri sits on a lotus THRONE in the full lotus POSTURE, wearing the princely ornaments and garments of the bodhisattva. In Chinese art he is often mounted on his lion. He holds a SWORD in his right hand, typically raised diagonally just above his head. He uses it to dissipate the darkness of ignorance and error. Like PRAJNA-PARAMITA he has a LOTUS with a BOOK resting on top of it (having the same symbolism).

In Tibetan art Manjushri has several Tantric forms with multiple heads and arms. With four arms he also holds a BOW and arrow which, with the sword, are the most traditional weapons of the bodhisattva in his benign, contemplative form. In his wrathful aspect he is most commonly depicted, in *tanka* paintings, as the conqueror of YAMA, king of death. He is then known as Yamantaka. In this role he has a ferocious BULL's head and seven others of fierce aspect, all surmounted by Manjushri's head in its benign form. He is in sexual union with his *shakti* (see YAB-YUM). He tramples various demons underfoot, among them Yama. He has many symbolic attributes, mainly of Shivaite origin, that are typical of the wrathful aspect of Tantric figures. He is framed by a flaming AUREOLE, carries a TIGER skin and wears a garland of SKULLS or human heads. He has thirty-four arms and therefore holds many weapons, besides the above-mentioned, that belong to this class of image. See further, WEAPONS.

Min. A very old Egyptian god of human procreativity and, later, of the fertility of crops. He was first represented in pre-dynastic times in the form of a fetish, thought to depict either a thunderbolt, or the dart-shaped, so-called 'thunderbolt' fossil, or even the act of copulation. There are texts which indicate that Min had taken human form by the beginning of the dynastic era. He stands rigidly upright, crowned, like AMUN, with a modius surmounted by two tall FEATHERS. His most striking feature is his long, horizontally erect PHALLUS, again like some images of Amun. His raised right hand supports a FLAIL. As a god of vegetation, Min's most personal attribute is a bed of LETTUCES, which were among the offerings made to him at his festivals. His principal cult centre, dating from the Old Kingdom, was at Koptos (Qift), near Luxor, where caravans setting out for the eastern desert and the Red Sea invoked him for a safe journey.

Mithras. Sun-god of Aryan origin first heard of in the oldest sacred literature of India, the *Rig-Veda*, where he is the attendant of the sovereign Lord of Heaven, Varuna. The sun itself is called the 'eye of Mitra and Varuna'. He appears among the Persian pantheon as the ally of the god of light, Ahura-Mazda, in his struggle against Ahriman, god of darkness. The cult of Mithras spread widely in the empire of Alexander the Great and reached Rome in the 1st cent. BC. It was made the official religion of the Roman Empire by Commodus (180–192). It had a particular appeal for the army who were instrumental in spreading it through the provinces. Mithraic temples have been found in Germany, Gaul and England as far north as Northumbria. In the Roman era Mithras is represented as a sun-god with radiant HALO. He rises into the heavens on a horse-drawn CHARIOT. His inscriptions call him Unconquerable Sun-god, *Deus Sol invictus*, which appears to identify him with the Roman solar deity, Sol, though the two are sometimes represented side by side. He may also be accompanied by two figures who personify sunrise and sunset, Cautes (with a COCK) and Cautopates (with a downturned, extinguished TORCH). The trio symbolizes the sun in its three aspects.

The focus of Mithraic ritual was the sacrifice of a BULL, a symbolic re-enacting of the god's most famous exploit as bull-slayer. The shedding of the animal's blood was a beneficial, creative act of cosmic dimensions, which secured material and spiritual well-being for devotees. An image of the mythical act, usually in relief sculpture, was placed on the rear wall of every Mithraeum. The god, with one knee in the animal's back, forces it down. One hand grasps a horn or nostril to raise its head, the other plunges a dagger into its heart. Ears of CORN sprout from the fallen BLOOD. A SCORPION, agent of the evil Ahriman, bites the bull's genitals. A DOG, the companion of Mithras, or a SNAKE, may lick the blood to absorb its life-giving qualities. The god wears a flowing cloak and the so-called Phrygian cap (see HAT). The scene may include solar elements such as Cautes and Cautopates, and the signs of the ZODIAC, which form an arch overhead.

Mithras is sometimes represented as a naked standing figure, his body entwined by a snake. In relief sculpture and painting he is framed by an oval-shaped zodiac, with the four WINDS in the corners. The image recalls antique renderings of Kronos-Saturn (see FATHER TIME) and symbolizes the passage of time as it is measured by the sun. The coils of the snake represent the course of the sun through the zodiac.

Animal sacrifice was followed by a sacred meal in which parts of the beast were consumed. In the case of the Mithraic meal symbolic elements were usually substituted which sometimes consisted of bread and wine. This led the Christian apologist Tertullian to describe it as a 'devilish imitation of the Eucharist'. Images of the meal suffered from iconoclasts of the early Church. Roman Mithraism was superseded by Christianity in the 4th cent.

Moses. Leader and lawgiver of the Jewish people who, according to the Pentateuch, brought them out of Egyptian slavery and gave them their religious and social institutions. He may have lived in the 13th cent. BC. Christians regard him as a biblical prefiguration of Christ. In earlier Christian art he is young, usually beardless and holds a WAND with which he magically strikes water from a rock.[60] Later, as lawgiver, he is typically of venerable appearance, with a forked BEARD and holds the TABLETS of the Law. Rays of light shine from his temples. From the 12th cent. they are represented as short, straight HORNS. This was a misreading of *cornutam* in the Latin Vulgate, meaning both 'shining' and 'horned'.[61]

Muses. Greek deities of arts and sciences, the daughters of ZEUS/JUPITER and Mnemosyne, goddess of memory. Originally three in number, they were established as nine from the early classical period. Their attributes, generally appropriate to their calling, mostly date from the Roman era, but are liable to change at different times:

Clio (history): STYLUS and SCROLL or TABLET, BOOK, LAUREL crown, TRUMPET, occasionally SWAN.

Euterpe (music, lyric poetry): PIPE, usually a flute, TRUMPET or other instrument.

Thalia (comedy, pastoral poetry): comic MASK, SCROLL, musical instrument such as a viol.

Melpomene (tragedy): tragic MASK, HORN, SWORD or DAGGER, CROWN in her hand, SCEPTRE at her feet.

Terpsichore (dancing and song): LYRE or other stringed instrument such as HARP or viol.

Erato (lyric and love poetry): TAMBOURINE, LYRE, viol, SWAN, PUTTO.

Urania (astronomy): GLOBE, COMPASSES, crowned with a circlet of STARS.

Calliope (epic poetry): TRUMPET, STYLUS, BOOKS, LAUREL crown in her hand.

Polyhymnia (or *Polymnia*) (heroic hymns): portative ORGAN, LUTE or other instrument, wears a solemn expression.

Musical Instruments. The earliest musical instruments were used by primitive peoples worldwide to provide a rhythmic accompaniment to dance. The function of the dance was magical. It imitated the actions of the hunter and warrior in order to bring success to future enterprises, or to celebrate a past success. The first instruments were purely rhythmic – various kinds of rattles and drums. They had the power to bring good luck or ward off evil, and miniature examples were worn as amulets. The sound of the gourd rattle, in particular, had powerful magic and was the most favoured instrument of the shaman in his ecstatic rituals. Drums had powers connected with human fertility. Drum and drumstick symbolize womb and phallus in the rites of many peoples. Pipe instruments also had a phallic connotation from very early times which has survived in myth and folklore, for example in the Greek myth of Apollo and Marsyas (see LYRE). The trumpet had a varied symbolism. As a martial instrument it was originally intended to scare the enemy and was also used to drive off evil spirits, especially in funeral rites. The conch-shell trumpet was also used for this purpose, but having once been a living, marine creature it was believed to derive magical power from the tides and hence the moon. It was therefore an attribute of moon-deities and associated with female procreative functions. See also BAGPIPE; BONES; CASTANETS; CYMBALS; DRUM; GONG; HARP; LUTE; MUSICAL STONE; PIPE; SISTRUM; TAMBOURINE; TRUMPET; VINA; ZITHER.

Ninurta. Very old Sumerian god whose role combined war and agriculture;

called 'trustworthy farmer of ENLIL', who was his father. His wife was Gula (see DOG). His principal temple was at the Sumerian city of Nippur. His identity tended to merge with a god of similar functions, Ningirsu, whose PLOUGH may perhaps symbolize either deity. As a war-god he was promoted by the Assyrian kings, with a temple at Nimrud. The ZIGGURAT at Nimrud may also have been dedicated to him. Ninurta the war-god may hold a MACE, BOW or arrow, and have an eagle-headed SCEPTRE. (See also NET.) A well-known relief from his temple at Nimrud shows a winged deity, probably Ninurta, apparently in pursuit of a dragon. He wears a horned cap (see HORN) and holds a triple-pronged THUNDER-BOLT in each hand, and carries a SICKLE-sword.

Osiris. Besides the myths about the creation of the world, which are the source of many symbols in Egyptian art, there are those that tell of the genealogy of the gods, their rivalries and battles. They are distant echoes of real struggles for power between tribal leaders in pre-dynastic times, and generated their own symbolic imagery. Osiris was an early god of fertility and also ruler of the Underworld. Pyramid Texts of the 5th Dynasty, which reflect the priestly doctrines of Heliopolis, record that he was descended from the ruling deity of that city, the sun-god and creator, Atum. He was a former king of Egypt who brought the knowledge of agriculture and wine-making to its people. He was the oldest child of the earth- and sky-gods, GEB and Nut, and the brother of ISIS, SETH, Nephthys and THOTH. Isis was both his sister and wife and their son was HORUS. There are varying accounts of different dates[62] that tell how Osiris was murdered by his brother, the usurper, Seth, who threw his body into the Nile, later dismembered it and scattered the remains throughout the Nile Valley. (This may be an aetiological myth seeking to explain the many cult centres that claimed to possess a relic of the god.) The grieving Isis collected her husband's remains and, having reassembled them, was successfully inseminated by him and conceived Horus. She is depicted in the form of a kite hovering over the mummified, yet ithyphallic, Osiris. Together with Horus who, like Hamlet, sought revenge for his uncle's murder of his father, they succeeded in bringing Seth before a tribunal of the gods. Osiris was thereafter king of the Underworld.

From pre-dynastic times the king of Egypt was, during his lifetime, regarded as a god and was identified with Horus. In the light of the later Heliopolitan myth he became, upon his death, identified with Osiris and ruled the Underworld as an immortal. The successor to the throne, a new Horus, was thus, aptly, a divine son of a divine father. Osiris is first represented in the 5th Dynasty. His body is encased in a mummy's wrappings, his hands free, holding the royal insignia, the CROOK and flail. He usually wears the Atef CROWN. In the *Book of the Dead* he presides, enthroned, in the Hall of Judgement (see SCALES). As a god of vegetation Osiris, in funerary art, was symbolized by CORN. The grains, trodden underfoot by goats or pigs, denoted Seth's victory; corn sprouting from the supine body of Osiris symbolized his resurrection. See also ISHTAR; PILLAR (the *Djed*); CRESCENT.

Padmasambhava. 8th cent. Indian Buddhist teacher, an adept in magical rites. His name, meaning 'Lotus Born', refers to the myth of his birth 'at the age of eight' in a lotus flower. He visited Tibet to promote the growth of Buddhism which had been introduced into the country in the previous century. Its form was Tantric, that is, derived from the cult of SHIVA. Its main features were (*a*) the worship of female deities, singly or in sexual union (YAB-YUM) with a male counterpart, either a BUDDHA or BODHISATTVA (see DEVI); (*b*) the view that the gods had two opposite aspects, benign and wrathful (see DEMON); (*c*) the practice of yoga, also related to Shivaism. Padmasambhava enlarged the Buddhist pantheon by introducing certain gods and rituals from the primitive nature-religion of Tibet, called Pön. Eventually they numbered many hundreds, comprising Tibetan versions of Indian Buddhist deities, local gods, demi gods and nature-spirits, and deified animals and birds, many of whom had twin aspects. The magician-priests of the Pön, the shamans, may well have contributed to the image of the wrathful type of Tantric god through their ecstatic devil-dances.

Tibetan art is religious, highly figurative and deals entirely in magical symbols. It consists of paintings and metal sculpture, chiefly bronze. Paintings are of two kinds, the MANDALA and the *tanka*. The latter is a portable icon with a central figure of a Buddha or bodhisattva. He, or she, is seated, usually in the lotus-POSTURE on a lotus THRONE. The god is surrounded by many smaller figures usually arranged in rows. They may be attendants, disciples, protectors or other established groups; or alternative manifestations of the main figure. The wrathful form, in which the yab-yum may feature, is less rigidly structured. The *tanka*, like iconic images of other religions, is regarded as the magical dwelling-place of the deity. By intense meditation upon it, the god's powers are transferred from his image to the devotee.

Padmasambhava is taken to be the founder of Tibetan Lamaism and is worshipped as a bodhisattva, especially by the Red Cap sect which he inaugurated. He has benign and wrathful forms. He is distinguished by his mitre-like headgear of the unreformed Red Hat sect (see illus. HAT, *iii*). It should be mentioned that his other attributes are common to many deities in Tibetan art. He holds a double-ended *vajra*, or THUNDERBOLT, skull-BOWL and has a *khatvanga*, or TRIDENT-headed staff, resting against his shoulder. He is enthroned in his palace in the 'Pure Land of the West', the heavenly kingdom of Amitabha (see BUDDHA), where his miraculous lotus-birth took place. Chief among his many attendants are two female disciples of royal birth who flank him on either side, and who were said to have accompanied him on his missions. His wrathful aspect, as destroyer of evil, takes various forms. Additional weapons, in this role, include a flaming SWORD (*khadga*) or DAGGER (*phurbu*), DRUM (*damaru*) and SCORPION. Other accoutrements, typical of the wrathful type, include a crown of SKULLS, garland of severed HEADS or skulls, TIGER skin. He tramples on a prostrate body. The earliest *tankas* of Padmasambhava date from about the 14th cent. and are rare before the 16th cent.

Peace. The worship of Peace as a divinity may go back to the founding of early city-states. Eirene, the Greek goddess of peace, is first described in an early myth[63] as one of the Horae (see FOUR SEASONS). She was represented, in a sculpture formerly on the Acropolis (*c.* 380 BC), holding the infant Plutus, god of the earth's abundance. The wealth that flows from peace is also symbolized in Greek art by a CORNUCOPIA. She may also have a TORCH and a *rhyton*. In Rome she was Pax. In AD 13 an altar, the *Ara Pacis Augustae*, was dedicated to her in honour of the success of the Emperor Augustus in making peace in the empire. One of its reliefs is an allegory depicting the many benefits peace brings. In Renaissance and later art she retains her cornucopia and uses her torch to set fire to a pile of WEAPONS. She may have WINGS, an OLIVE branch or crown and the DOVE of the Ark, which is associated with the olive.[64]

Perseus. Mythical Greek hero, the son of Danaë, a princess of Argos, and ZEUS/ JUPITER, who appeared to her in a shower of golden rain. In ancient Greek art he wears SANDALS and HELMET, both having WINGS. He carries a SWORD, sometimes curved like a sickle, SHIELD and WALLET. Two of his exploits are widely depicted in antiquity and again in Renaissance and later art. He beheaded the Gorgon, Medusa, whose terrible appearance turned to stone all who looked on her. Her head, which has SNAKES for hair, is the attribute of Perseus. After this, his mount is the winged HORSE, Pegasus, which sprang from Medusa's blood as she died.[65] Perseus flew on Pegasus to the rescue of an Ethiopian princess, Andromeda, who was chained to a rock to be sacrificed to a sea-monster.[66] The theme is illustrated on Greek vases, coins, gems and frescoes, first on an early 6th cent. relief. Medusa's head, engraved on medieval gem-stones, gave magical protection against thunderstorms.

Peter. First of the twelve APOSTLES. The many narrative scenes from his life in Christian art testify to his important place in the history of the early Church. The belief that, with Paul, he founded the apostolic succession and was martyred in Rome in the reign of Nero (probably AD 64) is supported by very early tradition. When depicted beside Paul they symbolize respectively the Jewish and gentile elements in the early Church. His principal attributes are a triple CROSS-staff, as bishop of Rome; an inverted cross, from the tradition that he was crucified head downwards; KEYS and, more rarely, a SHIP, both symbols of the Church; the FISH of Christ; a BOOK, the gospels or perhaps his epistles; a COCK, which crowed after he had thrice denied knowing Christ.[67]

Philosophy. The allegorical figure of Philosophy occurs mainly in medieval and Renaissance art. The source of the image is a description by the late Roman poet and philosopher, Boethius (c. 480–524) in *Consolations of Philosophy*, which he wrote while in prison. He tells how Philosophy came to console him in his cell (while he awaited death).[68] She was a woman of mature years, at one moment of normal height, the next so tall she reached the heavens. Her clothes were neglected and torn. She held a SCEPTRE in her right hand and several BOOKS in the other. Medieval and Renaissance artists added more attributes. Her robe was in three parts, decorated with FLOWERS at the bottom, FISH in the middle and STARS at the top. They correspond to three of the FOUR ELEMENTS, earth, water and air and symbolize three branches of philosophy, moral, natural and contemplative. She may wear a CROWN, sometimes with three heads on it, symbolizing the same. Her books sometimes have titles: two books are *Moralis* and *Naturalis*; one book, *Causarum cognitio*, 'the knowledge of things through their highest causes'. Known as the mother of the SEVEN LIBERAL ARTS, she sometimes accompanies them, her foot resting on a GLOBE, denoting her superior rank.

Prajna-Paramita (Sk. The 'Perfection of Wisdom'). A body of philosophical texts that underlie the doctrines of the Mahayana ('Great Vehicle') school of Buddhism (see BUDDHA). Wisdom was the highest virtue. In this context it meant the intuitive perception of the essential unity of matter and spirit. It transcended the old dualism between the world of illusion (with its unending cosmic cycles) and Enlightenment, and was perceived as a kind of void. One of the most important texts was the *Diamond Sutra*, which was translated into Japanese and Chinese. With the growth of Tantric Buddhism and the introduction of *shaktis*, or goddesses, as the consorts of Buddhas and bodhisattvas (see DEVI), Prajna-Paramita assumed human form as the *shakti* of the supreme Adi-Buddha, VAIROCANA, and was known as 'Mother of all Buddhas'. This purely symbolic figure, comparable to the Christian Sophia, appeared in India, southern and eastern Asia, Japan and Tibet. Her most famous image (Leiden) shows her seated in the full lotus POSTURE on a lotus THRONE, her hands in a teaching gesture (see MUDRA). Beside her rises a LOTUS flower on which rests a BOOK (the *Prajna-Paramita Sutras*) (see also MANJUSHRI). She is richly adorned in the style of bodhisattvas and has an URNA. In her Tantric form she can have four or six arms and a Shivaite third EYE instead of the *urna*. While still making the teaching gesture, with four arms she holds the book and a THUNDERBOLT and, with six, a ROSARY and BOWL.

Ptah. Egyptian creator-god of Memphis. His cult dates from the beginning of the dynastic era, if not earlier. He has human form and wears a close-fitting cap. His body is wrapped as a MUMMY, with his hands left free. He holds a sceptre that terminates in a *djed* PILLAR topped either by the ANKH symbol or *was*, or both (see SCEPTRE). He was the head of a trinity comprising his wife, Sakhmet (see LION), and son, Nefertum (see LOTUS). As a creator Ptah brought the world into being simply by the power of his command, through the spoken word. This concept, formulated by the priests of Memphis, was unique among Egyptian creation myths. It was a remarkable foreshadowing of later Hebrew belief and one that was ultimately adapted to Christian doctrine. It was somewhat analogous to the Hindu concept of *brahman* (see BRAHMA; WORD). An alternative, probably older tradition made Ptah the god of craftsmen; like Khnum, he fashioned mankind, especially the pharaohs, on a potter's WHEEL. As patron of artisans of all kinds, Herodotus identified him with Hephaestus, the Greek blacksmith of the gods. See also HILL; MOUTH.

Re. Major Egyptian sun-god, having his principal sanctuary at Heliopolis; a creator whose sovereignty extended over the earth and the Underworld as well as the sky. The growth of his cult led to the merging of his identity with other gods having similar functions.From the 5th Dynasty the pharaoh called himself 'son of Re'. This was not his only title to divinity since the king was also identified with HORUS. Re usually has a human body and head of a FALCON and is crowned with the SUN's disk and URAEUS. This was the result of merging with Horus who is represented in the same way. One of the roles of Horus was god of the rising sun, when he was known as Harakhti. The composite deity was therefore called Re-Harakhti. He may hold the royal insignia, the CROOK and flail. At night the sun-god descended to the Underworld and returned to the east in his solar BOAT enveloped by the protective coils of the SNAKE-god, Mehen. As ruler of the Underworld Re has a RAM's head, the type with lateral horns. Re, the creator, was born from a LOTUS, the womb of the universe that floated on the primeval ocean. He is depicted as a child resting on the flower, or his (human) head is emerging from it. See also AMUN; GEB; OBELISK; PALM; PHOENIX; SHAMASH.

Sarasvati. One of a group of three Indian river-goddesses, identified with a river – now a mere stream – of the same name in Gujarat. The others are Ganga (the

Ganges) and Yamuna (or Jumna). As a group they share certain functions and attributes (see RIVER). Sarasvati, like other female Indian deities, was probably descended from the Mother-Goddesses of pre-Aryan times. In Hindu myth she is the wife of BRAHMA. Sarasvati was also the guardian deity of speech, letters, music and the arts generally. Her distinguishing attribute is a musical instrument, the VINA, or sometimes an Indian lute. She may have two or four arms. Her other attributes include a BOOK, ROSARY, LOTUS bud, PLOUGH and various weapons. When playing the vina she sometimes sits on a lotus throne.

Seth. Egyptian god with good and evil aspects. He was renowned for his strength. He was originally worshipped as the tutelary deity of Upper Egypt and was regarded as the brother of HORUS who ruled the Lower Kingdom. An alternative Heliopolitan myth, which eventually prevailed, made him the uncle and enemy of Horus (see OSIRIS). The Greeks identified him with Typhon, a monster of Tartarus. Seth is represented with animal's head and human body, otherwise wholly animal. The creature has been variously identified and appears to be hybrid. It has a long, curving, beak-like snout and long, pointed ears, squared off at the ends. Its tail is straight and divided at the end (see MONSTER). The myth, in which Seth murders his brother Osiris, established him as a symbol of evil and violence. Seth was identified with a number of different animals. Thus images of the ritual killing of creatures like the CROCODILE, HIPPOPOTAMUS, ASS and, especially, ANTELOPE, symbolize Horus taking his revenge for the death of his father.

Seven Deadly Sins. The list of capital sins as we have it today was laid down in the 6th cent. by Gregory the Great.[69] The representation of individual sins as allegorical figures is common in medieval art, Lust and Avarice being the most popular. The group of seven occurs quite widely from the end of the Middle Ages and in the Renaissance, especially in painting, engravings and emblem books. Each figure may hold a shield bearing an attribute. All seven may have HORNS.

Pride. In medieval art, typically a rider thrown from his horse. The principal attributes of the female figure are LION, PEACOCK, EAGLE, MIRROR, TRUMPET. Three superimposed crowns are an anti-papist reference to the Pope's TIARA.

Avarice, or *Covetousness.* PURSE, KEY, BLINDFOLD, VULTURE, FALCON or other bird of prey, which may draw her chariot. Several Greek and Roman writers claim that the HEDGEHOG rolls on fallen fruit in order to gather it on its spines so that, according to Plutarch, 'it resembles a walking bunch of grapes'.[70] It therefore became an attribute of Gluttony and Avarice.

Lust. The uninhibited sexual behaviour of animals makes them the natural companions of Lust, thus: GOAT, BEAR (either may be her mount), PIG, BOAR, more rarely BULL and COCK, HARE or RABBIT (being so fecund), DOVE (borrowed from Aphrodite/Venus). She may hold a MIRROR or be surrounded by flames (the FIRES of passion). The mirror is sometimes held by an APE.

Envy. A hag. The SNAKE with its poisoned fangs is her attribute. She eats it, or gnaws her own entrails or a HEART. Like Medusa she may have snakes for hair. Other attributes: a snarling DOG, SCORPION, WHIP.

Anger. Usually represented as a wrathful figure, with a DAGGER or SWORD attacking another who is defenceless; or he is fixing three arrows together into his BOW. The allegorical female has a lion (see FOUR TEMPERAMENTS), occasionally a WOLF or bear. See also GESTURE.

Gluttony. Like Lust, one of the medieval 'sins of the flesh'; represented as a grossly fat man or woman, crowned with VINES, like DIONYSUS/BACCHUS, and holding a dish of fruit; sometimes riding a pig. Attributes include the hedgehog (see above), wolf (supposed to be voracious), bear (known from antiquity for its taste for honey).

Sloth. A moral rather than physical weakness; mental inactivity that leads to loss of creative inspiration or religious belief and to a state of melancholy, known as *acedia.* Sloth's attributes, however, mostly allude to the body, not the mind; ASS, OX or pig; SNAIL (contrasted with a BEEHIVE); playing CARDS, draughts-board.

Seven Liberal Arts. The basic subjects of a secular education in the Middle Ages, especially from the Carolingian Renaissance, consisting of a group of three, the Trivium (Grammar, Logic/Dialectic, Rhetoric) and a more advanced four, the Quadrivium (Geometry, Arithmetic, Astronomy, Music). Study of the Liberal Arts was a necessary preliminary to theology – they were called 'weapons against heretics'. They were set out in a treatise, dressed up as allegory, *The Marriage of Philology and Mercury*, by a 5th cent. grammarian, Martianus Capella, who was drawing on a much older, more widely based Roman source.[71] The arts are presented as seven bridesmaids at the wedding, each given appropriate attributes and each accompanied by an historical exemplar. They are seen in Romanesque and Gothic sculpture, sometimes paired with the seven THEOLOGICAL VIRTUES and CARDINAL VIRTUES. They are found widely in Renaissance art, especially Italian, with some additional attributes.

Grammar. A teacher, holding a WHIP; at her feet two pupils with BOOKS. From the 17th cent. she waters plants and may have a Latin inscription: 'Vox litterata et articulata debito modo pronunciata' – 'A literate and articulate tongue spoken in due manner'. Hist. ex.: Priscian or Donatus, both grammarians of late antiquity.

Logic. SNAKE, sometimes two, or SCORPION or, rarely, LIZARD. Ren. SCALES, FLOWERS or a flowering branch. Hist. ex.: Aristotle.

Rhetoric. BOOK, perhaps entitled 'Cicero', (not a scroll). Sometimes depicted as a martial figure with SWORD and SHIELD. Hist. ex.: Cicero.

Geometry. COMPASSES with which she may measure a GLOBE; also SET-SQUARE and ruler. Hist. ex.: Euclid.

Arithmetic. TABLET covered with figures, or ABACUS; ruler. Hist. ex.: Pythagoras.

Astronomy. Celestial GLOBE, though not usually clearly defined. COMPASSES, QUADRANT or sextant, armillary SPHERE. Hist. ext.: Ptolemy, Alexandrian astronomer.

Music. Various instruments, according to the period. Medieval: a chime of BELLS. Ren.: portative ORGAN, LUTE, viol, etc. Sometimes a SWAN, for its dying song.

See also PHILOSOPHY; FOUR TEMPERAMENTS.

Seven Treasures (Sk. *Sapta Ratna*; Ch. *Ch'i Pao*; Jap. *Shippo*). The attributes of a Universal Emperor of Indian legend 'whose rule extends to the shores of the four bounding oceans'.[72] He was designated Cakravartin, 'He who turns the Wheel', that is, the divine power that keeps the universe turning. The concept was applied to the BUDDHA at an early date. The Seven Treasures are the

WHEEL, ELEPHANT, HORSE, light-giving JEWEL, queen, treasurer (or military leader) and minister. The Cakravartin is first represented in Indian relief sculpture of the 2nd cent. BC, standing and surrounded by the Treasures. He raised his hand to the clouds causing golden coins to rain down, a symbol of the monarch as bestower of wealth. In Tibetan art the Seven Treasures often decorate the base of the Buddha's throne and, with the EIGHT LUCKY EMBLEMS, are placed round the circle of the MANDALA. See also VASE.

Shamash. Very old Mesopotamian sun-god known as Utu by the Sumerians. His main cult centres were at Larsa in the south of Sumer and at the Akkadian city of Sippar. A double temple founded by the Assyrians at Ashur in the mid-2nd mill. BC was dedicated to Shamash and the moon-god SIN. As a solar deity Shamash was all-seeing and supervised moral conduct on earth. At night, like the Egyptian sun-god, Re, he was judge of the dead. He is depicted on Assyrian cylinder seals in human form emerging at sunrise through heavenly DOORS that stand open on the eastern mountains. Rays shoot from his shoulders and arms. His distinguishing attribute is a serrated SAW. He may hold a rod-and-RING, or a MACE. He wears a horned cap (see HORN). He may be attended by two BULL-men or SCORPION-men. The HORSE was sacred to him in the neo-Assyrian period. In the same era he is represented in non-figurative form by the Mesopotamian type of solar disk (see SUN). On neo-Babylonian seals the disk surmounts a ZIGGURAT. He is also represented by the WINGED DISK, which may be supported by two bull-men. The CROSS, as an ancient representation of the sun, also probably denoted Shamash, at least from the Kassite period, when it was commonly worn by kings as an amulet.

Shiva. The gods with the greatest following among Hindus are Vishnu and Shiva. In their myths they are symbols of cosmic forces, creator and destroyer respectively, though Shiva eventually came to be worshipped as a benevolent, universal father. Together with BRAHMA they make a trinity often seen in Shiva-ite temples. Shiva has several roles, each with a distinctive iconography.

The worship of a Shiva-like god has deep roots. A deity very like him existed long before the arrival in India of the Aryan, Indo-European speaking peoples from Central Asia and their Vedic gods. His was a phallic fertility cult and may have involved human sacrifice. The god is represented on seals from the Indus Valley (3rd mill. BC) as a horned figure, possibly with three heads, seated in a yogic posture and ithyphallic. Plants growing from his head, together with the phallus, indicate a fertility deity. He is surrounded by wild animals. Shiva's epithet, 'Lord of Beasts', may be one link with the Indus Valley god, and possibly accounts for one of his attributes, an ANTELOPE.

The commonest object of worship in Shivaite temples is a phallus, or *lingam*. The oldest known examples date from the 2nd or 1st cent. BC. Shiva himself is incorporated in it, sometimes standing in a niche. The *lingam* often forms a composite image with the female vulva, or YONI, a symbolic union that expresses the god's creative energy. The figures of Shiva and his wife Parvati are represented together holding a *lingam* and *yoni* as attributes, or in a sexual embrace, the YAB-YUM. See also PHALLUS.

The old fertility god eventually joined the Vedic pantheon, thereby acquiring his present name. He became identified with a sky-god of the *Rig-Veda* called Rudra, one of whose epithets was 'Auspicious', or, in Sanskrit, *Shiva*. Rudra, the 'Howler', was the father of tempests, a destroyer whose arrows brought disease and death. Shiva's weapons, as a destroyer, are BOW and arrow, derived from Rudra, a rod surmounted by a TRIDENT, battle-AXE and flaming TORCH (or a bunch of flames). His third EYE, which shoots flames, is another instrument of destruction. From Rudra, who had a benign aspect as a healer, Shiva acquired his mount, the BULL called Nandin. From his pre-Aryan past Shiva has a human SKULL. It forms the top of his club, or is set in his hair, or he is garlanded with skulls (see also BONES). A single arrow from Shiva's bow destroyed the 'triple city' ruled by demon kings – another episode in the unending, symbolic struggle between gods and demons that runs through Hindu mythology (see also VISHNU). The three cities make up the entire universe: golden, which is heaven; silver, the air; iron, the earth.[73] Shiva is depicted standing in his great CHARIOT, bow in hand, having just loosed an arrow.

Shiva is the guardian deity of the Indian ascetic whose emaciated figure is portrayed sitting in a yogic pose before the god in his shrine. Shiva himself, as a teacher of yoga, has a ROSARY, sometimes a begging BOWL, or skull-cup, water-pot (VASE) and may be seated on a TIGER skin.

Shiva's best-known image is the *Nataraja*, or 'Lord of the Dance'. It is seen very widely in southern Indian bronzes (10th–12th cents. onwards), where the Tamil peoples had an ancient tradition of the dance as a religious ritual. It was originally a form of sympathetic magic intended to promote the growth of crops and was performed by many early peoples. Shiva's dance would therefore be entirely consistent with his ancient role as a fertility god, though its original function was eventually buried under layers of myth and symbolism. His body expresses lively movement with one leg raised. He should have four arms and should hold a DRUM and a spray of flames, or a torch. The drum's rhythm heralds the end of the cosmic age and the flames its final conflagration (see FIRE). His supporting foot treads on a prostrate DWARF, the Demon of Forgetfulness, a symbol of *maya*, the illusory world of our everyday perceptions. One right hand is in the *abhaya* pose (see MUDRA). The demon can take the form of an ELEPHANT, which Shiva slew and then flayed.[74] He then holds the skin in his upper pair of hands, or he dances within a kind of oval embrasure formed by the skin. He may then hold an elephant-GOAD and NOOSE, besides his other weapons. Shiva's hair, when dancing, is loose and flowing unlike his usual *jata-makuta* style (see HAIR). In either case, among the tresses may be seen, besides the skull, a CRESCENT moon, a tiny goddess, Ganga (see RIVER) and the flowers of the THORN-APPLE. The dance itself is said to show Shiva as the embodiment of cosmic energy, parts of his body symbolizing five different aspects: creation, or unfolding, preservation, destruction, *maya* that obscures the truth and Enlightenment that reveals it.

Elements of Shiva's cults and imagery were introduced into Buddhism, especially by the Vajrayana sect (see BUDDHA). The double aspect (calm and wrathful) of Tantric Buddhist deities reflects the god's dual identity as creator and destroyer. His weapons of destruction and the heads and skulls of his victims are a commonplace of the Buddhist art of Tibet, as are his female counterparts. (See further DEMON; DEVI; PADMASAMBHAVA. See also HEAD.)

Sibyl. The name of certain priestesses of APOLLO who uttered prophecies inspired by him. There was originally only one, the Erythraean Sibyl, but they eventually numbered twelve. Their oracles were recorded in the Sibylline Books, which were brought to Rome and consulted by the Senate in times of trouble. They were destroyed by fire in 83 BC. A new collection, compiled partly under Judaeo-Christian influence, was destroyed in the early 5th cent. AD. The Sibyls came to be regarded as pagan counterparts of the O.T. prophets and Christian influence is seen in their attributes. They appear together in medieval and later Christian art. The five Sibyls depicted by Michelangelo on the ceiling of the Sistine Chapel (marked (M) below) each have a book or scroll, but no other attribute.

Persian (M): LAMP, or lantern, SNAKE trodden underfoot.
Libyan (M): CANDLE, TORCH.
Erythraean (M): LILY of Annunciation.
Cumaean (M): BOWL.
Samian: CRADLE.
Cimmerian: CORNUCOPIA, CROSS.
European: SWORD.
Tiburtine: severed HAND.
Agrippine: WHIP.
Delphic (M): Crown of THORNS.
Hellespontic: CROSS, NAILS of Cross.
Phrygian: CROSS, FLAG (Banner of the Resurrection).

Sin. Akkadian name for the Mesopotamian moon-god, known in Sumer as Nanna or Nanna-Sin; a fairly rare example of a lunar deity who is male (the Japanese Susano-O is another). He was the son of ENLIL and father of Utu (SHAMASH) and Inanna (ISHTAR). Like Utu he was judge of the dead and decreed their fate. His oldest temple and its adjoining ZIGGURAT were built at Ur in the 23rd cent. BC. Later, he was worshipped at Harran (northern Syria) and at Ashur, in a double temple with Shamash. When represented in human form he is crowned with a CRESCENT moon and may stand in a crescent-shaped boat in which he crosses the heavens. The boat may also symbolize a journey, told in Sumerian myth,[75] which he made to Nippur with gifts to obtain his father's blessing. The myth may reflect an actual ceremony in which the god's image was transported to Nippur, the city of which Enlil was tutelary deity. The BULL and lion-headed GRIFFIN are sacred to Sin. His non-figurative form is a crescent, which is often seen beside the sun-disk of Shamash and the eight-pointed star of Ishtar.

Surya. Indian sun-god, one of several mentioned in the *Rig-Veda*, having features in common with Near-Eastern and classical solar deities. Like his Greek counterpart, Helios, his consort was the goddess of dawn. In Vedic texts he is associated with the HORSE, a solar animal. The earliest image of Surya, on coins from the last few centuries BC, takes the form of a radiant solar disk (see SUN). As an anthropomorphic deity he is represented on reliefs of the 2nd cent. BC driving a four-horse CHARIOT across the heavens. He may be accompanied by two female spirits, perhaps his wives, who banish the powers of darkness with BOW and arrow. Later, he may have a radiant HALO and WINGS, and hold a MACE and SWORD. As a standing figure he holds a LOTUS in each hand, the flower that opens at sunrise and closes at sunset. In north-west India Surya was specially venerated by rulers of the Kushan dynasty (late 1st to mid-3rd cents. AD), who came from central Asia. The god is depicted in the art of this region in the garb of the kings, especially as to their tall, thick boots.

Takara-Mono. Twenty-one 'precious things' carried in the Treasure Ship by the seven Japanese GODS OF HAPPINESS (see also BOAT). They are mainly symbols of worldly prosperity, several of Chinese origin, and are used widely as decorative motifs. The size and composition of the group vary but it commonly includes the following: the light-giving JEWEL, or *Tama* (one of the SEVEN TREASURES): HAMMER of Daikoku (one of the seven gods); *uchiwa* type of FAN; pair of SCROLLS or BOOKS; pair of RHINOCEROS horns (sometimes mistakenly called cloves); COINS (the last three are among the EIGHT TREASURES); an inexhaustible PURSE; KEYS to the store-room of the gods; cowrie SHELL, once used as money in India; vase holding spurs of CORAL; HAT, which, like Perseus' HELMET, made the wearer invisible; a lucky raincoat to protect against evil spirits; steelyard weights. The SACK of Hotei (another of the seven gods) is said to contain the Takara-mono.

Theological Virtues. The three virtues of FAITH, HOPE and CHARITY, first put together as a group by St Paul and mentioned several times in the Epistles.[76] They are very widely represented in Christian art from the Middle Ages onwards, usually as women with appropriate symbolic attributes. See also CARDINAL VIRTUES.

Thoth. Egyptian moon-god first worshipped in the form of an IBIS in the late pre-dynastic era, probably in the Delta region. Hermopolis (al-Ashmunayn) in the Nile Valley later became his main cult centre, where he merged with a local baboon deity. Thoth is therefore represented either as an ibis (or with the bird's head on a human body) or as a baboon (see APE). In the latter form he may, like another moon-god, KHONSU, be crowned with a CRESCENT and lunar disk. Thoth's primary role was god of writing and the patron of scribes. He is shown as a baboon enthroned above a scribe who sits cross-legged with an unrolled papyrus sheet on his lap and perhaps an ink-palette on his knee. He is also depicted, ibis-headed, in the well-known illustration in the *Book of the Dead* standing in the Hall of Judgement beside the SCALES, his brush poised to record the fate of the deceased. Or, as a baboon, he squats on the top of the scales. Alexandrian Greeks of Neoplatonist persuasion (3rd cent. AD) adopted Thoth, whom they called Hermes Trismegistus, as the imagined author of certain sacred books of mysticism and alchemy, making him the founder of an occult tradition which survived into the Renaissance. See also HARE; OSIRIS.

Three Fates (Gk. *Moirai*; Lat. *Parcae*). In Greek mythology, goddesses who were spinners of human destiny. The idea of a person's fate being spun was widely understood in ancient Europe and was of Indo-European origin. It appears also in the three Scandinavian female spirits, the Norns, who exercised the same arts. Hesiod[77] named the Greek goddesses Clotho, Lachesis and Atropos, the daughters of ZEUS/JUPITER. In the earliest Greek art they have no attributes. Later, Clotho, 'the spinner', has a spinning wheel (see SPINDLE, or in the Renaissance, a DISTAFF. Lachesis, 'the measurer', a measuring rod (see RING), or a GLOBE on which she writes, or (Ren.) holds a spindle. Atropos, 'she who cannot be turned', has a SCROLL, or sundial, or (Ren.) snips the thread of life with her SHEARS.

Three Friends (Ch. *San Yu*; Jap. *Sho-Chiku-Bai*). A group of three kinds of tree grown in China and widely popular in Chinese and Japanese decorative art. Together they stand for the hope of good fortune, a long life and the virtues to be expected from the well-bred. See further BAMBOO; PINE TREE; PLUM.

Three Graces (Gk. *Charites*; Lat. *Gratiae*). Graeco-Roman goddesses of beauty, grace and laughter, usually three in number. In mythology they have various parents. Hesiod makes them the daughters of ZEUS/JUPITER. Their names were Aglaea (radiance), Euphrosyne (mirth) and Thalia (revelry), and 'from their eyes as they glanced flowed love that unnerves the limbs'.[78] They were the attendants of various deities, especially, in later art, of APHRODITE/VENUS. In archaic art they have no attributes, but from the Renaissance onwards they take some from Venus, such as the ROSE, MYRTLE, APPLE, DICE. For the Stoic philosopher, Seneca, they symbolized aspects of generosity: the giving, receiving and returning of benefits or favours.[79] For Florentine humanists they stood for the three stages of love: beauty, arousing desire, bringing fulfilment; or they personified Chastity, Beauty and Love.

Three Monastic Vows, or Counsels of Perfection, are poverty, chastity and obedience, ideals that govern the conduct of Christian monastic communities. They are represented as human figures, usually female, with appropriate attributes. They are seen first in medieval art often accompanied by a corresponding vice. They seldom appear as a group, except in Franciscan painting. They are symbolized by the three knots in the girdle of the Franciscan friar.

Poverty, the voluntary renunciation of personal belongings, is a young woman, barefoot, her dress in tatters and patched. Francis of Assisi places a RING on her finger, a symbolic betrothal. Poverty, in the sense of indigence, was regarded as a vice and in secular art is represented as an old, haggard woman likewise barefoot and in rags. She reaches up with one hand that sprouts WINGS; the other is dragged down by a heavy STONE.

Chastity wears a VEIL, holds a PALM (recalling virgin martyrs), or a shield bearing a PHOENIX. She may also have a TOWER or SIEVE. She tramples on a SNAKE or BOAR, symbols of lust. In secular allegory she has a pair of DOVES denoting marital fidelity, or raises her shield to deflect Cupid's arrows.

Obedience, in Gothic art, is accompanied by an ASS with a MILLSTONE. Her shield bears a kneeling CAMEL. In the Renaissance she bears a YOKE. An accompanying figure, wearing a Jewish conical cap and in the act of striking a bishop, is Disobedience.

Three Sacred Relics. The regalia of the Japanese emperor and symbols of his divine sovereignty. They are SWORD, MIRROR and the COMMA-shaped jewels called *magatama*. Objects of this type were among many kinds once used in Shinto rituals as offerings to the gods. They were also kept as family heirlooms which passed down many generations and conferred magical powers on their owners. Those belonging to the emperor acquired a special sanctity, especially in the light of Shinto myths which ascribed (sometimes varying) divine origins to them.[80] The sword was found inside the body of a many-headed snake, slain by the ancient fertility god, Susano-O, after a terrible contest. He presented the sword to his sister, the sun-goddess Amaterasu, ancestress of the imperial family, to whom it descended. The mirror and jewels were hung on a tree to entice the sun-goddess from her cave (see further AMATERASU). Her spirit is present in the mirror, endowing it with great *kami* (*numen* or *mana*).

Trinity. More than one religion has recognized a group of three gods at its head. The Christian Trinity, the three-in-one consisting of Father, Son and Holy Ghost, was represented in its older forms entirely by symbols. Three entwined FISHES are found in the Roman catacombs. Three RINGS, or two TRIANGLES, interlocking, were common. The Father was sometimes represented as an EYE enclosed in a triangle or, especially from the 5th and 6th cents, as a HAND emerging from a cloud over the figure of Christ and a DOVE. The Father was not often represented in human form before the 12th cent. Thereafter he is typically enthroned and holds each end of the horizontal bar of the cross on which is Christ crucified. The dove hovers about Christ's head. Alternatively he holds a book inscribed A and ω, or Ω. He may have a triangular HALO. The Three Persons may all be represented in human form, each with a halo. See also BUDDHA, BUDDHISM; ENLIL; TRIUMPH – Eternity.

Triumph. In ancient Rome a festive procession in honour of a victorious general. He was borne through the city's streets on a triumphal car to the temple of Jupiter (ZEUS/J.) on the Capitoline Hill. He was preceded by magistrates and senators, the spoils of war, captives, and white bulls for sacrifice at the temple. Renaissance Italy revived the custom, celebrating not only military leaders and princes, but the pagan gods, heroes and poets of antiquity, etc. As a type of allegory the triumph became a very popular theme in Renaissance and Baroque painting, especially Italian. It was initially inspired by Petrach's set of verses, the *Trionfi*, which describes, in terms easy for artists to interpret, a sequence of allegorical figures. Each in turn is victorious over his or her predecessor. Thus Love is overcome by Chastity, who is followed by Death, Fame, Time and finally Eternity. They are typically represented thus:

Love. Cupid (EROS/C.) stands on his car shooting an arrow, or is BLINDFOLD. The car is drawn by GOATS or HORSES.

Chastity. Cupid kneels before her, blindfold, wings tied, bow broken. The Wise Virgins[81] may be present, one with a banner depicting an ERMINE. Drawn by UNICORNS.

Death. A SKELETON, sometimes cloaked, with SCYTHE. The dead and dying lie crushed under the chariot's wheels. Drawn by black OXEN.

Fame has WINGS. Attendants blow TRUMPETS. Historically famous people may accompany her. Drawn by ELEPHANTS, occasionally horses.

Time is FATHER TIME in person. Drawn by STAGS, fleet-footed like time.

Eternity. Often a Christian allegory. The car bears CHRIST or the TRINITY. Drawn by the APOCALYPTIC BEASTS, or angels.

Renaissance and later painting depicts the triumph of many classical gods and goddesses and other allegorical figures: see CHARIOT.

Twelve Months. The Labours of the Months, though wholly secular in character, are an integral part of Christian iconography. The medieval Church (with more than a hint of sophistry) taught that manual labour was not servitude but an act of liberation: 'It delivers man from the necessities to which his body is subject since the Fall'.[82] The twelve Labours have a special place in Romanesque and Gothic church sculpture, where they form a kind of pictorial calendar combined with themes like the FOUR SEASONS and the ZODIAC. They are found also in medieval psalters and Books of Hours and in 16th and 17th cent. tapestries. There are many variations of subject matter. The commonest, together with their zodiacal sign and, from the Renaissance, a pagan deity, are as follows:

January. A peasant felling trees or feasting at table; couples dancing.

Aquarius. Janus (see HEAD).

February. Grafting fruit trees. Fireside scene. Pisces. Venus and Cupid sailing in a strong wind.

March. Pruning vines, digging; shepherd playing lyre. Aries. Mars, god of war.

April. Training vines; youth crowned with flowers. Taurus. Jupiter as a garlanded bull abducting Europa.

May. Falconry; peasant scything, or resting in the shade. Gemini. Castor and Pollux drawing chariot of Venus, accompanied by Cupid.

June. Haymaker with scythe, or carrying hay. Cancer. Phaethon falling from the sky, nearly scorching the earth.

July. Peasant sharpening sickle, cutting corn, carrying sheaves, threshing. Leo. Hercules resting from his labours, holding an apple (from the Hesperides).

August. Harvesting, threshing, ploughing. Virgo. Ceres, crowned with corn, holding sheaf and sickle, on her chariot; Triptolemus, inventor of the plough, beside her.

September. Threshing; gathering and treading grapes. Casks of wine. Libra. Ceres, crowned with fruit, holding cornucopia of grapes, and scales.

October. Casking wine, sowing seed. Scorpio. Silenus and Satyrs, attendants of Bacchus, crowned with vine leaves, holding bunches of grapes.

November. Gathering wood, picking olives, sowing, tending pigs (for Christmas). Sagittarius. Nessus, a centaur, abducting Deianeira, wife of Hercules.

December. Digging; killing pigs, baking (for Christmas), feasting. Capricorn. Ariadne milks a goat to feed the infant Jupiter.

For the Chinese Twelve Terrestrial Branches, see CALENDAR.

Twelve Ornaments (Ch. *Shih-erh chang*). Symbolic motifs embroidered on the robes of Chinese emperors and government officials. Only the emperor's robe had all twelve. Officials had fewer according to their rank. (See also DRESS.) The ornaments are of great antiquity. Their original meaning is unknown. From early times they were associated with the principal seasonal sacrifices performed by the emperor every year on behalf of the people. It appears that all twelve symbols once had astronomical connotations that were relevant to the seasons. A Chinese classic, the *Shu Ching*, or *Book of Documents*,[83] quotes a legendary ruler, the Emperor Shun (late 3rd mill. BC), as saying the ornaments were symbols of the qualities required of a good king. This interpretation remained popular with later writers. Such virtues were central to the ethical teachings of Confucius (*c*. 551–479 BC). Early written texts compiled from ancient sources which included the *Shu Ching*, became known as the 'Confucian classics'. Their scholarly style became the model for later generations (see also FOUR TREASURES; FOUR ARTS).Confucianism was mainly a system of moral instruction, based on the classics, designed to promote good government.Its teaching was applicable to the emperor downwards. It included filial piety, the duties of sons to fathers (see JU-I).Its aim was to create an intellectual élite, to bring victory to good over evil and to balance the opposing forces of YIN AND YANG in society. The twelve ornaments are as follows:

SUN (a three-legged cock inside a red disk), MOON (with a white HARE pounding the elixir of immortality) and STARS (three, representing the handle of the Big Dipper), the sources of knowledge needed to rule wisely. The sun is *yang*, the active principle; the moon *yin*, the passive principle: the stars, the emperor's inexhaustible forgiveness and love.

MOUNTAIN: his constancy and firmness.

TWO DRAGONS: (ascending and descending): the *yin* and *yang*; his power to inspire his subjects with virtue.

PHEASANT: its colourful beauty a symbol of the shining example it was the emperor's duty to set.

Two ritual goblets (see VASE): symbols of purity and impartiality.

Water-weed (see WATER): female, *yin*, spirit of the waters.

FIRE (flames): male, *yang*, active zeal and love of virtue.

RICE or millet: plenty, which it is the emperor's duty to provide.

AXE: instrument of punishment, hence a symbol of justice.

FU (a homophone of 'forbid'): discernment of good and evil.

The Twelve Ornaments are found on state vestments until the end of the empire (1911–12) and are also seen on ceramics and other works of art.

Vairocana (Ch. *P'i-lu-she-na*; Jap. *Dai Nichi*). Head of a group of five 'Buddhas of Meditation', the so-called Dhyani-Buddhas. They were the product of later Buddhist teaching and were especially promoted by the Vajrayana sect in China, Japan and Tibet. The Dhyani-Buddhas are wholly transcendental and without any terrestrial connections, past or future. Between them, they reign over every part of the universe. Vairocana is 'Supreme Lord', the primordial or Adi-Buddha. He created the other four, together with the rest of the Buddhist pantheon, through the power of his meditation (see also BODHISATTVA: Samantabhadra). He embodies absolute truth and wisdom. He is regarded as identical with the First Person of the Buddhist Trinity, the 'Body of Essence' (see further BUDDHA).

The five often feature in the symbolic structure of STUPAS and pagodas. The statue of Vairocana is at the centre, representing Mt Meru, the cosmic MOUNTAIN, the symbol of absolute wisdom. The other four are each allocated a cardinal point of the COMPASS, where they watch over their quadrant of the heavens. They may occupy separate chapels or, as at Borobudur in Java, are placed on the exterior of the building. They are usually seated in the full lotus POSTURE. Their role is to overcome the vices of mankind that obstruct the path to Enlightenment, transmuting them into wisdom. They are distinguished by their gestures (MUDRAS), their mounts, attributes, and the vices with which they are associated (recalling the SEVEN DEADLY SINS).

Centre. Vairocana, *Vajra-mudra* (sometimes *Vitarka*), lion or dragon, WHEEL of the Law, hatred.

East. Akshobhya, *Bhumisparsha-m.*, elephant, THUNDERBOLT, wrath.

South. Ratnasambhava, *Varada-m.*, horse or lion, the 'wish-granting' JEWEL, avarice and pride.

West. Amitabha, *Dhyana-m.*, swan or peacock, LOTUS, lust.

North. Amoghasiddhi, *Abhaya-m.*, the eagle GARUDA, double-ended thunderbolt, envy.

In Japan Vairocana is known as Dai Nichi, the 'Great Sun', a fusion of Buddhist and Shinto deities. He is the central figure of the Buddhist pantheon and is also identified with AMATERASU. He may wear a crown displaying on the front five small Dhyani-Buddhas. He is also identified with a Japanese deity of fierce, Tantric appearance, known as Acala, or Fudo Myo-O. In this aspect he symbolizes the power to conquer the vices having, for this purpose, a flaming SWORD, encircled by a snake or dragon, and a NOOSE. He has a flaming, pointed AUREOLE. The Buddhas of Meditation were worshipped, especially by the Japanese, in the form of a MANDALA. Their images were replaced by a quincunx of different letters, which had the magical power to conjure the presence of the deities themselves. The letter A at the centre denoted Vairocana, the Adi-Buddha (see A).

Vanitas denotes emptiness, or the transient nature of earthly possessions. Many still-life paintings, especially 17th cent. Dutch and Flemish, consist of symbolic objects alluding to this theme. Thus: SKULL, the inevitability of death; HOURGLASS, CLOCK, a burning CANDLE, the inexorable passage of time; an overturned BOWL or similar vessel, emptiness; CROWN, SCEPTRE, GLOBE, JEWELS, PURSE, COINS, the power and possessions that death takes away; SWORD and other WEAPONS, a reminder that they afford no protection against death; FLOWERS with dew-drops, their short life; SHELL, emptiness, life having left it. Among Christian symbols, giving hope for the life hereafter, are WINE, BREAD, IVY, PELICAN, PHOENIX, BUTTERFLY, CRUCIFIX, ROSARY.

Victory. The Greek goddess Nike personified victory. She was messenger of the gods and frequently accompanied Zeus (z./JUPITER) and Athena (A./MINERVA). She descended to earth to crown the victor in war and in contests of athletics and poetry. She is widely represented in Greek sculpture, vase painting and on coins. Statues of Nike were erected in Greek cities to commemorate military victories. She has WINGS, except in Athens, where the citizens had her depicted wingless to prevent her flying away. Her garments flow in the wind and she wears a LAUREL crown. She may hold a PALM branch. A famous relief from the Athenian Acropolis depicts her fastening her SANDAL (Acropolis Mus.). The Romans identified Nike with their goddess Victoria, who had the same role. Images of the winged Victoria were a model for the angel in Christian art. She was revived in Renaissance art, retaining her principal classical attributes. She is seen bestowing a laurel crown or palm branch. In allegories of military conquest she is surrounded by, or stands on, a heap of WEAPONS, sometimes holding a SHIELD on which she is writing; a defeated enemy lies bound at her feet.

Virgin Mary. The mother of CHRIST. Over the centuries her devotional images have accumulated a very large number of attributes, most of them having some symbolic meaning. The images are of various kinds, illustrating different aspects of Marian dogma. Some symbols apply specifically to only one type of image. Those of general application include several flowers, in particular LILY, ROSE, VIOLET, IRIS, DAISY, COLUMBINE, FLEUR-DE-LIS. Also MYRTLE, OLIVE, CITRON, TREFOIL, TREE of Jesse, STARS. In pictures of the Virgin and Child, the infant Christ may hold an APPLE, ears of CORN with a VINE, POMEGRANATE, ORANGE, CHERRY, NUT, a bird, usually a GOLDFINCH. The Virgin of the 'Immaculate Conception', whom the Middle Ages identified with the Shulammite maiden of the O.T. *Song of Songs*, derives most of her attributes from that source: SUN, crescent MOON, halo of twelve STARS, MIRROR, FOUNTAIN, TOWER, a closed DOOR or gate, GIRDLE, sometimes with three knots, TREE of Jesse, Tree of Knowledge, PALM tree, CEDAR, OLIVE, a closed GARDEN. She treads underfoot a SNAKE or DRAGON. The Virgin enthroned as Queen of Heaven wears a CROWN, VEIL and holds orb and SCEPTRE. In association with the UNICORN she may sit in a closed garden and hold a mirror. A pomegranate tree may stand nearby. As Virgin of Sorrows her breast is pierced by seven SWORDS. As Virgin of Mercy she shelters the faithful under her CLOAK.

Virtues and Vices. The idea of representing abstract concepts as human figures probably began with the goddess Tyche in Hellenistic Greece (see FORTUNE). It was greatly developed in imperial Rome in the shape of numerous protective genii that surrounded the emperor. The Christian Church introduced the factor of good and evil. A 4th cent. Spanish poet and hymn-writer, Prudentius, in a work called the Fight for Man's Soul, or *Psychomachia*, describes a series of single combats between armed female warriors, Faith against Idolatry, Chastity against Lust, etc. It was a widely used source for the decoration of Romanesque churches. In Gothic art scenes of combat give way to static figures of Virtues treading Vices under their feet. By the end of the Middle Ages their number had greatly multiplied and the pairing of opposites was still widely maintained. Foremost among them are the seven that make up the THEOLOGICAL VIRTUES and CARDINAL VIRTUES, who may be paired with the SEVEN DEADLY SINS, or other vices.

Virtue and Vice themselves are personified in an allegory of Greek origin, popular in Renaissance and Baroque art and usually known as Hercules at the Crossroads.[84] Hercules, often portrayed in the likeness of the son of a noble family, sits and ponders a choice of paths, of duty or pleasure. Virtue, in the person of Minerva (ATHENA/M.), invites him to follow a narrow, stony way uphill where at the top stands the winged HORSE, Pegasus, symbol of Fame. Beside her a poet, LAUREL-crowned, records his deeds in a book. Above, Fame blows her TRUMPET and FATHER TIME looks on. Vice, on his other side, seductively half-naked, invites him down a broad, sunny road where nymphs are dallying by a pool. Her attributes suggest a wasted life and moral decay: playing CARDS, MASKS, PIPE and TAMBOURINE, while a rod and FETTERS give warning against wrong-doing.

Vishnu. Originally a relatively unimportant solar deity who became one of the supreme gods of the Hindu pantheon. Vishnu, BRAHMA and SHIVA make a trinity commonly seen together in Vishnavite temples. In consideration of his rank he is attended by lesser gods and goddesses and by *rishis*, the legendary Hindu sages. His varied iconography reflects a widespread tendency for him to be identified with other deities whose characteristics he absorbed. Some had animal forms which are embodied in his images. In the *Rig-Veda* Vishnu is creator of the universe, which he accomplishes by taking three great strides (Sk. *Trivikrama*), thereby measuring its extent.[85] His steps symbolize the SUN-god at sunrise, noon and sunset; alternatively, the three realms of the universe – earth, air and heaven. Vishnu as Trivikrama is represented in sculpture with one leg raised high, sometimes to the level of his head. Also present may be BRAHMA, who washes his other foot, and a DEMON, Bali, whom he conquered. His footprints are themselves objects of worship and are represented in his temples, decorated with his symbols (see FOOT). As a Vedic sun-god he also sets in motion a WHEEL, a sun-symbol of the turning year.[86]

Vishnu was identified with other aspects of creation. At the end of each cosmic cycle (see AGES OF THE WORLD) he devoured the universe and during the ensuing 'night of Brahma' was transformed into the primeval ocean (see

WATER). In that role he was known as Narayana, 'he who moves on the waters'. While he slept the world was restored to its original purity.[87] He is represented very widely from the 7th cent. reclining on the waters. His couch consists of the multiple coils of a great SNAKE, the cobra Ananta (the 'Infinite'). It is also called Shesha and symbolizes water. Ananta has seven or nine hooded heads which form a protective canopy for the god. A LOTUS grows from Vishnu's navel and in the flower sits the much smaller figure of Brahma. Among others present are Lakshmi, the wife of Vishnu, the earth-goddess Bhudevi, INDRA on an elephant and SHIVA on a bull. They are all smaller in scale.

Vishnu's most characteristic attributes are the conch-SHELL, DISK, CLUB and LOTUS, some of which he usually retains through his various changes of identity. He may have four or more arms, in which case two hands may be in the *abhaya* and *varada* poses (see MUDRA). His HAIR should be arranged in the *kirita-makuta* style but is sometimes the *jata-makuta*. He wears JEWELLERY, EAR-pendants and some form of Brahmanic SASH. If seated, his THRONE is the lotus or lion type. His mount is the wild goose, GARUDA. With the growth of his cult Vishnu's alternative forms, or 'incarnations' (Sk. *avatar*, descent), became very numerous as he assimilated local deities. By about the 11th cent. they had been reduced to a generally agreed corpus of ten, though individual examples are seen in sculpture of a much earlier date. In the myths the purpose of the *avatars* is to assist the god in his tasks of creating and guarding the universe, often from attack by demons. The images are mainly devotional figures in stone or bronze, rarely narrative.

1) *Fish*. Vishnu took the form of a fish to save mankind from a great flood. Stories of a flood are known worldwide, especially among the peoples of Asia. An early Hindu myth tells how Manu, the first man, was warned of its coming by a fish. He built a boat and was towed by the fish to safety on a mountain top until the waters subsided.[88] The story has marked parallels with Mesopotamian accounts in which the saviour was the god of fresh water, EA (who sometimes took the form of a fish). The latter was the source of the biblical story of Noah. Vishnu took over the role of fish much later, in the *Mahabharata* and the *Puranas*,[89] where he is known as Matsya (Sk. *fish*). He may be represented wholly as a fish, or human to the waist and fish-tailed below.

2) *Tortoise*. Vishnu, in his incarnation as Kurma (Sk. *tortoise*), takes part in the great symbolic enterprise of churning the ocean (see further MILK). The myth probably echoes some aspect of a tortoise-cult in primitive Indian folk-religion. Vishnu's association with it is developed in the *Mahabharata*. He is generally represented in human form from the waist up, his lower half being a tortoise.

3) *Boar*. Originally probably a non-Aryan sacrificial animal. Vishnu took the form of a boar, Varaha, in order to create the universe at the beginning of the cosmic cycle. There are several versions of the myth. He raised the earth from below the primeval waters, either on his tusk or using one hundred arms. It had been cast there by demons. Vishnu's deed symbolized the victory of the omnipotent creator over the powers of evil.[90] As Varaha, Vishnu may be wholly animal but more usually has a boar's head (crowned with the *jata-makuta* or *kirita-makuta*, as in other incarnations) on a human body. When seated he should occupy a lion-throne with his legs in the *lalitasana* POSTURE. He may be accompanied by Lakshmi and Bhudevi. In some texts the boar *avatar* is ascribed to Brahma.

4) *Man-Lion*. Vishnu became Narasimha, the man-lion, in order to overthrow another troublesome demon, Hiranyakashipu, whom Brahma had blessed with immunity from violent death. Narasimha's powers were greater. Being everywhere present in the universe, he sprang forth from a pillar in the demon's palace and tore him to pieces.[91] He has a lion's head on a human body. When seated, he occupies a lotus-throne, wearing a meditation BELT round the legs; alternatively he has a lion-throne and is in the *lalitasana* posture. He sometimes has seven-headed Ananta for a canopy. He may be seen using a sword to disembowel the demon who lies prostrate on his thigh.

5) *Dwarf*. The Vedic myth of Vishnu's three strides was amplified in later texts, once more involving demons. Their king, Bali, growing powerful, threatened the supremacy of the gods. Vishnu, disguised as a dwarf, Vamana, asked Bali to grant him all the space he could cover in three strides. Bali readily consented, whereupon Vishnu encompassed the whole universe. Bali and all his tribe were bound with rope and consigned to the Underworld.[92] Vishnu has human form, is youthful, of small stature but normal proportions. He holds a water-pot (see VASE) and UMBRELLA. sometimes a BOOK, the attributes, we are told, of a student of the *Vedas* or *Brahmanas*. He is alternatively represented as a hunchbacked, pot-bellied dwarf.

6) *Parashurama*, or 'Rama-with-an-axe', not the same as Prince Rama of the epics. He was a legendary warrior who avenged the death of his father (killed in a feud over a wish-granting cow) by declaring war on the ruling *Kshatriyas* (the warrior caste) whom he slew. Like many heroes of myth he was deified and came to be regarded as the incarnation of Vishnu.[93] There may be an historical element behind the story. Parashurama has human form and usually two hands, one of which holds an AXE. He wears Vishnu's usual body-ornaments.

7) *Rama*. Hero of the epic poem, the *Ramayana*, a mortal who became deified as an incarnation of Vishnu. In a famous episode Rama's wife, Sita, was abducted and held captive by a demon king, Ravana, in Sri Lanka. She was rescued by Rama with the help of an army of monkeys, led by Hanuman, who formed a bridge to the island (see APE). Ravana, a symbol of the world's evils, was slain by Rama's arrow which, having done the deed, flew miraculously back to its quiver.[94] Rama and Sita epitomize for Indians the ideal of married faithfulness. The figure of Rama holds a great BOW and sometimes an arrow, here symbolizing male prowess. He generally has Vishnu's adornments, with his hair in the *kirita-makuta* style. He is often accompanied by Hanuman, sometimes also by Sita, holding a flower, by his half-brothers Shatrughna, with a FLY-WHISK, and Lakshmana who has a large bow, like Rama's.

8) *Krishna*. Hero and pastoral cover were contrasting aspects of Krishna. Vishnu's incarnation, a late development in Krishna's mythology, is mostly applicable to the hero, in particular his overpowering of the serpent Kaliya. The serpent was banished, not killed. This was said to symbolize Vishnu protecting the universe by establishing a balance between the forces of conservation and destruction. The whole of creation, good and evil, was embodied in him, exemplified by the contrasting character of Ananta and Kaliya. (See further KRISHNA.)

9) *Buddha*. The view that the Buddha was an incarnation of Vishnu was not universally accepted and, when it was, the reasons were sometimes contradictory. According to orthodox Hinduism, Buddhism was heresy. In particular it taught,

like Jainism, that all life was inviolate. This was a denial of animal sacrifice that was at the heart of the teaching of the *Vedas*, the Hindus' oldest and most sacred literature. According to the *Vishnu Purana*[95] Vishnu took the form of Buddha, called the 'Deceiver', to persuade the demons (i.e. the sinful) to abandon the religion of the *Vedas*. Heresy would lead to their corruption and ultimate damnation and the victory of the gods of Hinduism. Later, with the decline of Buddhism in India, there was a move to bring heterodox sects within the sphere of Hinduism. The Buddhist temple at Gaya, in Bihar, built on the supposed site of Shakyamuni's Enlightenment under the bodhi tree, was re-dedicated to Vishnu and Shiva. It was now maintained that the *avatar* took place to demonstrate Vishnu's clemency towards all living things. The iconography of the Buddha was not influenced by Vishnuism.

10) *Kalkin*. The last *avatar* of Vishnu, when he will appear as a horse, amid the universal destruction that will occur at the end of the present Iron Age. (See further KALKIN; also HORSE.)

Yama. Hindu lord of the Underworld and judge of the dead, originally a beneficent deity mentioned in the *Vedas*.[96] He has counterparts in the West, like the Greek Minos, and it may be that his origins lay in that region. He is not widely represented in Indian art but comes into his own in Tibetan painting and bronzes as one of the gods of Tantric Buddhism. He is generally the ferocious type (see DEMON). He has a third EYE, long canines (see TOOTH) and a protruding TONGUE. His commonest weapons are a *khatvanga* SCEPTRE, TRIDENT, NOOSE and *karttrika* KNIFE. He may also wear a garland of SKULLS, hold a skull-cup (see BOWL) and have an erect PHALLUS. His mount is a black BULL. He is sometimes attended by two dancing SKELETONS, the Citipati. When in the YAB-YUM embrace the female represents his sister, Yami. As a temple guardian – a *dharmapala*, or defender of the faith – he faces the southern quadrant (see COMPASS). In China Yama is known as Yen-lo-Wang. He sits on the judgement seat sternly surveying the torments of sinners in hell. He is robed and wears the imperial CROWN. He may hold a MACE, but lacks the fearful attributes of his Tantric counterpart. An attendant demon holds up a MIRROR to the condemned, which reflects their coming fate. As a single figure his mount is a BUFFALO. Yama is known to the Japanese as Emma-O. He is not often represented and his imagery is mostly borrowed from China. He is seated, robed and wears a tiara. He holds a mace, or TABLET to record his judgements. He, too, may have an attendant with a mirror. Emma-O is commemorated at the summer Festival of the Dead. See also MANJUSHRI.

Zeus/Jupiter. The greatest of the Olympian gods of Greece. He ruled all other gods and mankind. His kingdom was the sky. All nature, including the weather, was under his command. Kings and princes received their power from him. He was the protector of families. Oaths were sworn in his name. In Rome a victorious general adopted the guise of Jupiter in his triumphal procession (see TRIUMPH). In a remoter age he was the divine father of the Indo-European peoples, called Dyaus Pita, which became Zeus Pater in Greek and Diovis Pater, shortened to Jupiter, in Latin. In the *Rig-Veda*[97] Dyaus foreshadows his classical role: he is god of heaven, personifies the sky, has a thunderbolt and is bringer of rain. The main cult centres of Zeus in Greece were at Dodona where his abode was an OAK tree and at Olympia in Elis where religious games were held in his honour. In these two contexts he may wear, respectively, a wreath of oak leaves, or of OLIVE. When his cult reached Crete he became identified with a local goat deity, from which arose the myth of Zeus as an infant being suckled by a goat, one of whose horns became the original CORNUCOPIA. It is sometimes his attribute. In Graeco-Roman art his principal attributes are the EAGLE and THUNDERBOLT of the sky-god. When enthroned he holds a SCEPTRE. In Greek vase painting the figure of ATHENA/MINERVA sometimes emerges from his head; or of DIONYSUS/BACCHUS from his thigh. He is widely represented in Greek and Roman antiquity and again after the end of the Middle Ages. See also ARCH; BODHISATTVA (Vajrapani); HAIR.

Zodiac. The belt of the celestial sphere corresponding to the sun's annual ecliptic. It is of great antiquity and is recognized by many peoples. It contains the sun, moon, all the known planets and the twelve constellations after which its divisions are named. The western zodiac, formulated by the Greeks, consists of: Aries, RAM; Taurus, BULL; Gemini, twins; Cancer, CRAB; Leo, LION; Virgo, virgin; Libra, SCALES; Scorpio, SCORPION; Sagittarius, archer; Capricornus, GOAT; Aquarius, water-carrier; Pisces, FISHES. As a symbol of the universe the signs surround the image of ZEUS/JUPITER, its supreme ruler, especially on coins of later antiquity; and of the sun-god MITHRAS. The robes of the priests of Mithras were decorated with the signs. In Christian art the zodiac symbolizes the universal extent of Christ's sovereignty. In medieval, especially Romanesque, sculpture it may be part of a broader scheme which includes the FOUR SEASONS and TWELVE MONTHS, often surrounding the figure of Christ. For the Chinese and Japanese zodiac, see CALENDAR.

Appendix

The Transcription of Chinese

There have been several systems for transcribing Chinese characters into the Roman alphabet. The system used in this book, known as Wade–Giles, was until recently the most widely adopted in Britain and the USA. It was devised by Sir Thomas Wade in 1859 and modified a little by H. A. Giles in 1912. In 1958 the Chinese authorities published a system called 'Pinyin zimu', which has advantages especially for teachers of Chinese. Pinyin is widely used nowadays for reference books and for labelling in museums. Nevertheless many basic books that are required by students and others (including the majority in the bibliography of this book) are only available in Wade–Giles. The following list shows the differences between the two systems, together with some examples.

Wade–Giles	Pinyin	Wade–Giles	Pinyin
ch (except if followed by i or ü)	zh	o (on its own or after h, k, k')	e
ch' (except if followed by i or u)	ch	o (after f, m, p, p' w)	o
chi	ji	o (after other consonants)	uo
ch'i	qi		
chih	zhi	p	b
ch'ih	chi	p'	p
chü	ju	ssu (sze)	si
ch'ü	qu	t	d
eh	e	t'	t
erh	er	ts	z
hs	x	ts'	c
i (as an initial or on its own)	yi	tzu	zi
		tz'u	ci
ieh	ie	u (after y)	ou
ien	ian	ü (after l, n)	ü
ih	i	ü	u
j	r	uei (after k, k')	ui
k	g	ung	ong
k'	k		

I Ching	*Yijing (Book of Changes)*	Taoism	Daoism
Han Hsiang Tzu	Han Xiangzi	T'ang	Tang (Dynasty)
Lan Ts'ai-ho	Lan Caihe	Chu	zhu (bamboo)
Pa kua	Ba gua (Eight Trigrams)	Ch'in	Qin (dynasty)
Chung	zhong (type of bell)	Chü	ju (chrysanthemum)
San Yu	San You (the three friends)	Yü	yu (jade)
Ho Hsien-ku	He Xiangu	Lao Tzu	Laozi

Notes and References

AITM: Ancient Indian Tradition and Mythology
SBB: Sacred Books of Buddhism
SBE: Sacred Books of the East

1: Abstract Signs

1 *Bhagavad Gita*, 10:32–3. See Bahm, A.J., Bombay, 1970.
2 Rev. 22:13, etc.
3 The *Nispanna-yogavali* by Mahapandita Abhayakaragupta. See Bhattacharyya, B., 1949, (English summary).
4 Wisdom of Solomon, 7:26.
5 Ezek. 9:4.
6 Giles, H.A., 1898, pp. 233–4. Jing-Nuan, Wu, 1991.
7 Shabaka Stone, British Mus., London.
8 Ps. 33:6–9.
9 Jing-Nuan, Wu, 1991.
10 Karlgren, Bernhard, 1950.

2: Animals

1 Prov. 6:6–8.
2 Sallust, *Bellum Jugurthinum*, 10.6.
3 See Boas, G., 1950, on Horapollo.
4 *Ramayana*, Bk V, canto 31ff (Griffith, R.T.H., 1915).
5 Num. 22:1–35.
6 See O'Flaherty, W.D., 1975, pp. 238–49. See also Rao, T.A.G., 1914–16, vol. 1, part 2, pp. 347–54.
7 Ovid, *Met.*, 2.836.
8 Ovid, *Fasti*, 5.385–6. *Achilleid*, 2.381–452.
9 Ripa, C., 1970, *s.v.* Elementi: Aria.
10 Pliny, *Nat. Hist.*, 8.33.
11 Homer, *Iliad*, 6.155–203.
12 Mark 14.66–72.
13 Called 'the drums of Chu-ko' after a famous Chinese general, Chu-ko Liang (AD 181–234) who set them up as alarm signals. See Giles, H.A., 1898, no. 459.
14 *Rig-Veda*. Rain-cloud cow is Prishni, see Griffith, R.T.H., 1920, 2.34.2, p. 301.
15 For Yoshitsune, see Joly, H.L., London, 1908, p. 409ff.
16 Joly, H.L., 1908, p. 146f.
17 Aristotle, *Historia Animalium*, 9.10.
18 Diodorus Siculus, 5.72. Pausanias, 2.17.4.
19 Kageyama, H., 1973, ch. 5.
20 Homer, *Ody.*, 12.6ff.
21 John 1.32.
22 Isa. 11.1–2.
23 On the imagery of early bronze vessels, see Yetts, W. P., 1912; Linduff, K.M., 1979, ch. 7; Rawson, J., 1987.
24 Sometimes called a serpent or snake, but usually represented as a typical Chinese dragon. See Davis, F. Hadland, 1913, pp. 28–30.
25 Philippi, D.L., 1969, 1.19.8–22, pp. 88–90; Chamberlain, B.H., 1932, p. 75.
26 Rev. 20.1–3.
27 Hesiod, *Theog.*, 820–80.
28 *Bhagavata Purana*, 10.15.47ff. See Dange, S.S., 1982, p. 170ff.
29 *Satapatha Brahama*, 6.1.1.10.
30 Werner, E.T.C., 1922, p. 76ff.
31 Hyginus, *Fabula*, 77.
32 Musée Guimet, Paris.
33 Alternatively, the son of the goddess Bhadramana, see van Buitenen, J.A.B., 1973, 1.(7).60.
34 See Zimmer, H., 1946, pp. 103–4.
35 Thomas, E.J., 1949, p. 32.
36 *Fo-Sho-Hing-Tsan-King: A Life of Buddha.* (transl.) Beal, S., Oxford, 1883 (SBE, vol. 19), pp. 246–9.
37 Apollonius of Rhodes, *Argonautica*, (transl.) Seaton, R.C., 1912, 4.123–81.
38 Werner, E.T.C., 1932, p. 255ff.
39 Matt. 25.32–3.
40 *Mahabharata*, 3.183–90., van Buitenen, J.A.B., 1973.
41 Livy, *History of Rome*, 5.47.
42 *Homeric Hymn to Aphrodite*, 218–38.
43 Exod. 10.1–20.
44 Pliny, *Nat. Hist.*, 7.2.
45 *Jataka*, Cowell, E.B., 1895–1907, 1913. Bk. 4, no. 316.
46 Hesiod, *Theog.*, 265–9.
47 Dante, *Divine Comedy* – Hell, canto 13.10–15.
48 See Rao, T.A.G., 1914–16, pp. 347–54.
49 Exod. 34.29.
50 Gen. 22.1–19.
51 *Rig-Veda*, Griffith, R.T.H., 1920, pp. 214–9, 1.162–3.
52 *Bhagavata Purana*, Skandha 5, ch. 18.6. (transl.) Tagare, G.V., 1978.
53 *Jataka*, Bk. 11, no. 460. (transl.) Cowell (note 45 above).
54 Or, in some versions a well of sea water, thus Apollodorus, 3.14.1.
55 2 Tim. 4.6–8.
56 Rev. 6. 1–8.
57 Gen. 4. 4–5.
58 Rev. 7. 9–17.
59 Judg. 14. 5–9.
60 Rev. 5.5.
61 1 Pet. 5.8.
62 Ovid, *Met.*, 8.152–73.
63 See Harrison, J.E., 1927, p. 119ff; Breuil, H., 1952, p. 170ff; Janson, H.W., 1962, ch. 1.
64 Ovid, *Met.*, 1.721–4.
65 Augustine, *City of God*, 21.4.
66 Pliny, *Nat. Hist.*, 10.2. (transl.) Rackham, H., 940, pp. 293–5.
67 Rao, T.A.G., 1914–16, vol. 2, Part 1, pp. 65–9. (Coomaraswamy, A.K., 1927, p. 39, has surely misread Rao?)
68 1 Kings 17.1–6.
69 Mount Mashu, where the sun-god, Shamash, rose. See also *Enuma Elish*, 'Epic of Creation', tablet 3: Dalley, S., 1989, pp. 245, 247.

70 Luke 10.19.
71 Homer, *Ody.,* 12.39ff, 158ff.
72 Faulkner, R.O., 1973, vol. 1, p. 72 (Spell 75) and note 9, p. 77 (Spell 76), p. 81 (Spell 78), etc. See also Hart, G., 1990, pp. 19–22.
73 *Ibid.*
74 Faulkner, R.O., 1985, ch. 87.
75 Wind, E., 1967, pp. 266–7.
76 *Rig-Veda*, Griffith, R.T.H., 1920, 1.32.1–15, pp. 43–5.
77 *Padma Purana*, 6.282.8–22a, 23b–52, 85–93. See also O'Flaherty, W.D., 1975, pp. 302–10.
78 *Vishnu Purana*, 1.4. (transl.) Macfie, J.M., 1926.
79 *Bhagavata Purana*, 10.17.2–12. (transl.) Tagare, G.V., 1978.
80 Apollodorus, 3.14.6.
81 Gen. 3.1–7.
82 Matt. 10.16.
83 *Liber de Infantia* ('Gospel of Pseudo-Matthew'), N.T. Apocrypha, ch. 27.
84 Apollodorus, (transl.) Frazer, J.G., 1921:3.5.8. According to Apollodorus the sphinx has 'a face of a woman, breast, feet and tail of a lion, and the wings of a bird'.
85 Ovid, *Met.,* 6.129–45.
86 Chamberlain, B.H., 1932, p. 170ff.
87 Matt. 27.48, etc.
88 Faulkner, R.O., 1985, ch. 86.
89 Hyginus, *Fabula*, 77.
90 Ovid, *Met.,* 2.367ff.
91 See Seckel, D., 1964, p. 264 and illus.
92 See Zimmer, H., 1946, p. 105.
93 Song of Songs, 4.15.
94 Waley, Arthur, 1954, p. 219.
95 Homer, *Ody.,* 11.576ff. Virgil, *Aeneid*, 6.595.
96 Jonah 1.15ff.
97 Matt. 12.40.
98 Ezek. 1.5–11.
99 Livy (*op. cit.*), 1.4.

3: Artefacts

1   Heb. 6.18–19.
2   Nut is invoked throughout the Pyramid Texts; her heavenly arch protects the king. See Faulkner, R.O., 1969, no. 782, etc.
3   Lev. 8:2, 26, 31; Deut.26:2, 4, 10, etc.
4   John 6.1–13, etc.
5   Exod. 28.31–55.
6   Matt. 14.22–3.
7   Rev. 5.1ff.
8   Homer, *Ody.,* Bk 21, *passim.*
9   Thomas, E.J., 1949, p. 48.
10 *Mahabharata*, 8.24.3–44 etc. See also O'Flaherty, W.D., 1975, p. 126ff.
11 The *Kinvad* (or *Kinvar*) bridge, which miraculously widened to allow the righteous to cross it; described in a Pahlavi text, the *Dina-i Mainog-i Khirad*, 'Opinions of the Spirit of Wisdom'. See SBE, vol. 24, (transl.) West, E.W., Oxford, 1885, 2.115–26, pp. 17–19.
12 The Islamic equivalent of the *Kinvad* bridge was called *Al Sirat.*
13 Luke 2.21–39.
14 Ps. 141.2.
15 Mark 14.23.
16 See note 10.
17 Mark 12.13–17.
18 Matt. 17.24–7.
19 Matt. 27.3–5.
20 Exod. 2.3.
21 Apollodorus, 2.6.3.
22 Portraits of Ch'in Ch'iung (6th–7th cents. AD) and Wei-ch'ih Kung, or Yu (AD 585–658), are sometimes painted on the entrance doors of official residences as symbolic guardians.
23 Ripa, C., 1970, *s.v.* Matrimonio.
24 Tertullian, *de Baptismo* (*Patrologia Latina*), 1. col. 1198.
25 Rev. 22.1–2.
26 Originally made of strips of white and blue cloth; later of paper. See Philippi, D.L., 1969, 1.17.11, p. 83; also Aston, W.G., 1956, vol. 1, p. 44, note 1.
27 Rev. 5.8.
28 Gen. 3.8–24.
29 John 20.14–18.
30 Matt. 16.18–19.
31 Rev. 20.1–3.
32 Gen. 22.1–19.
33 Ovid, *Met.,* 8.169–73; Plutarch, *Parallel Lives,* 1.19.
34 Faulkner, R.O., 1969, nos. 389, 468, 472, 479, 971–80, etc.
35 Gen. 28.10–22.
36 Matt. 25.1–13.
37 John 19.34.
38 Diodorus Siculus, 3.58–9. Hyginus, *Fabula*, 165.
39 Exod. 37.17–24.
40 See Sachs, C., *The History of Musical Instruments*, New York, 1940, p. 168; also Jennings, W., *The Confucian Analects*, London (undated), p. 167.
41 Homer, *Ody.,* 8. 266–365.
42 Faulkner, R.O., 1985, ch. 155.
43 *Rig-Veda*, Griffith, R.T.H., 1926, 10.5.6., p. 387.
44 Judg. 16.26–31.
45 Diodorus Siculus, 3.58–9. Hyginus, *Fabula*, 165.
46 *Bhagavata Purana*. For the pastoral Krishna see Tagare, G.V., 1978, Sk. 10, ch. 21, *passim.*
47 Philippi, D.L., 1969, 1.17.23, p. 85; also Aston, W.G., 1956, vol. 1, p. 45, also note 2.
48 Homer, *Ody.,* 10.1ff.
49 Plutarch, *Parallel Lives*, (transl.) Perrin, B. (Loeb), 1914: 'Theseus', 22, pp. 45–7.
50 Ascension of Isaiah (N.T. Apocrypha), ch. 1–5.
51 Rev.10.1–11.
52 Hesiod, *Theog.,* 147–92.
53 Rev. 7.2ff.
54 Acts of Thomas (N.T. Apocrypha), ch. 17.
55 Hesiod, *Theog.,* 147–92.
56 Pliny, *Nat. Hist.,* 28.12.
57 Gen. 3.23.
58 John 20.15.
59 Philippi, D.L., 1969, 1.3.2–3, p. 49; also Aston, W.G., 1956, vol. 1, pp. 11 and note 1. pp. 12ff.
60 Luke 10.38–42.
61 The Seven Sorrows are: 1) The prophecy of Simeon, Luke 2.34–5; 2) The Flight into Egypt, Matt. 2.13–15; 3) Dispute with the Doctors,

Luke 2.41–51; 4) Road to Calvary, Matt. 27.32, etc.; 5) Crucifixion, Matt. 27.33–56, etc.; 6) Descent from the Cross, Matt. 27.57–8; 7) Ascension, Acts 1.9–12.

62 Rev. 1.16.
63 John 18.10–11.
64 Exod. 32.15–16.
65 Rao, T.A.G., 1914–16, vol. 1, part 1, pp. 19–21.
    Saunders, E. Dale, 1960.
66 John 18.3.
67 1 Sam. 2.12–14.
68 Rev. 8.1ff.
69 Faulkner, R.O., 1985, ch. 156.
70 Tacitus, *Annales*, 3.1–2.
71 Exod. 2.1–10.
72 Matt. 3.13–17.
73 *Mahabharata*, see van Buitenen, J.A.B., 1973: 1(5)15.10ff.
74 Luke 7.37–8.
75 Mark 16.1.
76 Ovid, *Met.,* 4.765–86.
77 Hyginus, *Fabulae,* 33, 62.
78 Ezek. 1.16.
79 Coomaraswamy, A.K., 1972, p. 25.
80 Coomaraswamy, A.K., 1972, p. 27.
81 Herodotus, 1.199.
82 Ripa, C., 1970, *s.v.* Obedienza. Suave = sweet, the quality of Obedience.
83 Gen. 11.1–9.

4: Earth and Sky

1   Virgil, *Aeneid*, 2.756–67.
2   Acts 2.1–4.
3   Shakespeare, *Ant. and Cleop.* 4.8.28.
4   Yetts, W. P., 1912, pp. 1–5.
5   Exod. 19.9–16.
6   Philippi, D.L., 1969, 1.17.9, p. 82; also Aston, W.G., 1956, vol. 1, pp. 38 (and note 1), 49 (and note 1), 184.
7   Rev. 12.1.
8   Judg. 6.36–40.
9   Coomaraswamy, A.K., 1927, pp. 22, 61 (note 3). See also Coomaraswamy, 1972, pp. 9–10 and Pl. I–II (Figs. 1–4).
10 See Faulkner, R.O., 1973, the 'winding lakes of fire', vol. 1, p. 265 (Spell 335, pt. 2), p. 270 (Spell 336).
11 Exod. 3.1–6.
12 Exod. 14.24.
13 Exod. 19.18.
14 Acts 2.1–4.
15 Josephus, *Jewish Antiquities*, 2.9.7.
16 Dan. 3.15–27.
17 Apollodorus 2.5.11.
18 Exod. 32.1–20.
19 Rao, T.A.G., 1916, vol. 1, part 1 (Description of Terms), pp. 31–2.
20 Faulkner, R.O., 1969, no. 199.
21 Faulkner, R.O., 1985, ch. 149.
22 From the *Shuo Wen* by Hsu Shen (d. ? AD 120). See Giles, H.A., 1898, no. 787.
23 Acts 1.9–11.
24 Aston, W.G., 1956, vol. 1, pp. 27, 28 and notes 1 and 2.
25 Strabo, *Geographica*, 9.3.
26 Gen. 9.13–14.
27 Gen. 2.10–14.
28 See Kramer, S.N., 1963, pp. 153–5. Compare Dalley, S., 1989, pp. 154ff and note 11.
29 Hyginus, *Fabula*, 107.
30 *Ramayana*, bk. 1, canto 44, (Griffith, R.T.H., 1915). See also Zimmer, H., 1946, pp. 63, 112, 117ff; Coomaraswamy, A.K., 1927, pp. 102–5.
31 Dante, *Divine Comedy* – Hell, canto 14, 115–20; also Milton, *Paradise Lost*, 2.575–81.
32 Faulkner, R. O., 1973: see note 10 above.
33 Exod. 17.1–7.
34 Acts 5. 14–16.
35 Matt. 2.2–9.
36 Rev. 22.16.
37 Faulkner, R.O., 1969, no. 341 (and note 6), 929, 935.
38 Werner, E.T.C., 1922, pp. 73–4 (Chih Nu).
39 See MacDonell, A.A., 1905, p. 77.
40 *Rig-Veda*, Griffith, R.T.H., 1926, 1.154.1–6, p. 207.
41 Mal. 4.2.
42 Rev. 12.1.
43 *Rig-Veda*, Griffith, R.T.H., 1926, 10.129.1–3, p. 575.
44 *Vishnu Purana*, 1.4. (transl.) Wilson, H.H., 1961, p. 24ff.
45 *Padma Purana*, (transl.) Deshpande, N.A., Delhi, 1991 (AITM, vol. 47), part 9, pp. 3172–3.
46 Coomaraswamy, A.K., 1972, p. 17ff.
47 See Dalley, S., 1989, p. 233ff.
48 Gen. 1: 2.1–4.
49 Faulkner, R.O., 1969, no. 199.
50 Exod. 14.9–31.
51 Gen. 7: 8.1–19.
52 Pliny, *Nat. Hist.*, 4.35; and 8.
53 Homer, *Iliad*, 14.201.
54 Faulkner, R. O., 1973, vol. 1, p. 88 (Spell 83).

5: Human Body and Dress

1   Herodotus, 4.189.
2   Ezek. 1.15–28.
3   *Rig-Veda, passim*. On Agni as the first Angiras, see 1.1.6 and 1.31.1–2; also Griffith, R. T. H., 1920: vol. 1, pp. 1 and 40. See also O'Flaherty, W.D., 1975, p. 26.
4   See Rawson, P., 1973, p. 124ff.
5   Josephus, *Jewish Antiquities*, 2.9.7.
6   See SBE, vol. 5, a Pahlavi text, the *Bundahi*, ('original creation'), (transl.) West, E.W., Oxford 1880, 1.1–28 (pp. 3–10), 3.1–27 (pp. 15–20), 6–9, *passim* (pp. 25–31), etc.
7   *Vishnu Purana*, 1.4. See Wilson, H.H., 1961, p. 36.
8   *Vishnu Purana*, 1.20. See Wilson, H.H., 1961, p. 119.
9   John 18.10.
10 Graves, R., 1955, no. 56.
11 *Rig-Veda*, Griffith, R.T.H., 1920, 1.154.1–6, p. 207.
12 Acts 1.9–12.
13 Judg. 16.4–20.
14 *Taittiriya Samhita*, 7.4.9., (transl.) Keith, A.B., 1914.
15 Matt. 27.25–6, etc.
16 Luke 24.28–32.
17 See Zimmer, H., 1946, pp. 180–4.

18 *Mahabharata*, see van Buitenen, J.A.B., 1973: 3(37)213:1ff.
19 Mark 6.28.
20 Matt. 2.16.
21 Saxl, F., 1957, p. 58ff.
22 Diodorus Siculus, *Bibl. Hist.*, 4.9.
23 *Mahabharata*, see van Buitenen, J.A.B., 1973: 1(5)15.10ff.
24 Exod. 34.29.
25 Job 41.1ff.
26 Thomas, E.J., 1949, pp. 74–5.
27 Clement of Alexandria, *An Exhortation to the Greeks*, ch. 4.
28 Ps. 85.10.
29 Exod. 3.5–6.
30 See Rao, T.A.G., 1914, vol. 1, part 1, pp. 22, 111, etc; also Zimmer, H., 1946, p. 183 (note).
31 Matt. 27.57–60.
32 For the legend of Psyche, see Apuleius, *Metamorphoses*, or *The Golden Ass*. (transl.) Adlington, W., (Loeb), 1915: 4.28ff., p. 185.
33 Faulkner, R.O., 1969, no. 1652.
34 Faulkner, R.O., 1969, no. 199.
35 John 9.1–7.
36 *Saddharma-Pundarika: The Lotus of the True Law*, (transl.) Kern, H., Oxford, 1884 (SBE, vol. 21), pp. 7, 393.
37 Gen. 24.65.
38 Gen. 32.22–32.

6: Plants

1 Num. 17.1–8.
2 Ovid, *Met.*, 10.708–39.
3 Song of Songs 5.15.
4 See Joly, H. L., 1908, p. 171; also Edmunds, W. H., 1934, p. 135.
5 See Graves, R., 1955, no. 7b.
6 Theophrastus, *Inquiry into Plants*, 9.9.3.
7 One of the 'bitter herbs': Exod. 12.8.
8 Luke 1.26–38.
9 Ovid, *Fasti*, 5.251ff.
10 Song of Songs 4.12.
11 Jonah 4.6–11.
12 Num. 13.17–29.
13 Theocritus, *Idylls*, 19.
14 Matt. 3.4.
15 Ovid, *Met.*, 10.162–219.
16 Ps. 51.7.
17 Theophrastus, *Inquiry into Plants*, 3.18.9.
18 *Rig-Veda*, 6.16.13; 7.33.11, Griffith, R.T.H., 1920, p. 571; 1926, p. 36.
19 See 'Earth and Sky' note 45, above.
20 Ovid, *Met.*, 4.206ff.
21 Zech. 1.8–11.
22 Ovid, *Met.*, 3.339ff.
23 Lev. 8.10–13.
24 1 Sam. 16.1–13.
25 Danthine, H., 1937, *passim*.
26 Hesiod, *Homeric Hymn to Demeter*, 370–4.
27 Waddell, L. A., 1895, p. 99.
28 Plutarch, *Moralia*, 138(d).
29 Ovid, *Met.*, 1.689–713.
30 Theophrastus, *Inquiry into Plants*, 4.2.1–3.
31 Faulkner, R.O., 1985, ch. 109.
32 Gen. 3.18.
33 *Summa Theologica*, 2.2.q.164.2.0.
34 Exod. 3.1–10.

35 Proclus, 'Sermon on the Theotokos'; see *Patrologia Graeca*, 65.661–88.
36 Song of Songs 2.2.
37 Mark 15.16–20.
38 Faulkner, R.O., 1985, p. 70 and ch. 63A.
39 *Rig-Veda*, Griffith, R.T.H., 1926, 10.81.4, p. 497.
40 Gen. 3.22.
41 *Rig-Veda*, 10. 138.2. See Griffith, R.T.H., 1926 (vol. 2), p. 584 and note 2.
42 Hesiod, *Theog.*, 212–15; 333–5.
43 Isa. 11.1–3.
44 Exod. 17.1–7.
45 John 6.1–13.
46 John 11.1–44.
47 Num. 17.1–11.
48 Homer, *Ody.*, 10.359.
49 Homer, *Ody.*, 5.47–8.
50 Ps. 137.1–2.
51 Num. 13.17-29; Isa. 63.1–6.

Collectives

1 See further Zimmer, H., 1946, p. 13ff.
2 Hesiod, *Work and Days*, 109–201.
3 Ovid, *Met.*, 1.89–150.
4 Ripa, C., 1970, pp. 136–8.
5 *Rig-Veda*, Griffith, R.T.H., 1926, 10.51.1–9, pp. 453–4 and notes.
6 *Ibid.*
7 Philippi, D.L., 1969, 1.17.1–25, pp. 81–6; also Aston, W.G., 1956, vol. 1, pp. 41–9.
8 Ezek. 1.9–10.
9 Rev. 4.6–8.
10 Visser, M. W. de, 1923.
11 *Lawbook of Manu*, 1.5.5. See Pal, Radhabinod, *The History of Hindu Law*, Calcutta, 1958, pp. 227–36.
12 *Vishnu Purana*, 1.4.3–11, 25-9, 45–9. Wilson, H.H., 1961, pp. 26–7.
13 *Rig-Veda*, 6.16.13; 7.33.11. See Griffith, R.T.H., 1920 (vol. 1), p. 571 and 1926 (vol. 2), p. 36.
14 Yetts, W.P., 1912, p. 21, Fig. XIII.
15 Matt. 25.35–7.
16 John 10.14.
17 John 15.1–6.
18 Rev. 22.16.
19 'Gilgamesh and the Land of the Living'; see Dalley, S., 1989, pp. 67–77.
20 'Gilgamesh and the Bull of Heaven', *ibid.* 1989, pp. 80–83.
21 *Ibid*, pp. 252–5, note 20.
22 1 Sam. 17.34–6.
23 1 Sam. 16.12–13.
24 *Homeric Hymn to Demeter*, 2.
25 See O'Flaherty, W.D., 1975, pp. 238–49. See also Rao, T.A.G., 1914–16, vol. 1, part 2, pp. 347–54.
26 Ovid, *Met.*, 3.310–12.
27 Ovid, *Met.*, 3.597–691.
28 Kramer, S.N., 1963, pp. 171–83.
29 *Ibid.*, 1963, pp. 147ff.
30 *Ibid.*, 1963, pp. 120ff.
31 Hesiod, *Theog.*, 121–2.
32 Hesiod, *Theog.*, 133–87.
33 Albricus, *Liber ymaginum deorum*, *c.* 12th cent.
34 Homer, *Iliad*, 15.18–21.

35 See *The Golden Legend*, by Jacob of Voragine (*c*. 1230–*c*. 1298).

36 Ripa, C., 1970, pp. 332–9.

37 Isa. 6.6–7.

38 Ezek. 1.16.

39 Dan. ch. 6 and 'Apocryphal Additions to Dan.', vv. 23–42.

40 Hesiod, *Theog.*, 901–3.

41 *Brihaddharma Purana*, 2.60.1–4, 7–97, 106(b)–8. See also O'Flaherty, W. D., 1975, pp. 262–9.

42 *Brahmanda Purana*, 2.3.42.1–5. (transl.) Tagare, G.V., Delhi, 1983. (AITM, vol. 23). Also *Brahma-vairata Purana*, (transl.) Sen, R.N., SBH. vol. 24, part 1, 'Ganesha-Khanda', ch. 43, p. 88. See also Dowson, J., London, 1968, p. 107.

43 *Vayu Purana*, 2.36.74–86. (transl.) Tagare, G.V., 1988.

44 *Bhagavata Purana*, 10.17.2–12; 10.16.4–32, 54–67, (transl.) Sanyal, J.M., 1930–4.

45 Faulkner, R.O., 1969, *passim*.

46 *Homeric Hymn to Demeter*, 40–53.

47 Ovid, *Met.*, 1.668–721.

48 *Rig-Veda*, 10.124.1–9. See Griffith, R.T.H., 1926 (vol. 2), pp. 570–1.

49 See Dalley, S., 1989, p. 156ff.

50 Matt. 3.4.

51 John 1.29,36.

52 *Vishnu Purana*, 4.24. See Wilson, H.H., 1961, pp. 388–9.

53 *Mahabharata*, see van Buitenen, J.A.B., 1973, 3(37)213.1ff.

54 *Bhagavata Purana*, see Tagare, G.V., 1978, Skandha 10, ch. 17.2–12.

55 *Ibid.*, Sk. 10, ch. 8.28–30.

56 *Ibid.*, Sk.10, ch. 22.1–27.

57 *Ibid.*, Sk.10, ch. 8.34–45.

58 *Ibid.*, Sk.12, ch. 11.4–24.

59 *Digha Nikaya*. See Rhys Davids, T. W. and Estlin Carpenter, J., (eds Pali Text Soc.), vol. 3, p. 76. (Not translated.)

60 Exod. 17.1–7.

61 Exod. 34.29.

62 Plutarch, *Moralia*, 'Isis and Osiris', 5.1.

63 Hesiod, *Theog.*, 902.

64 Gen. 8.10–11.

65 Ovid, *Met.*, 4.765–86.

66 Ovid, *Met.*, 4.665–739.

67 Mark 14.66–72.

68 Boethius, *Consolations.* (transl.) Stewart, H.F., (Loeb), 1918, 1.1, pp. 131–2.

69 Gregory I, Pope, 'the Great', *Moralia in Job*, 31.45.

70 Plutarch, *de Solertia Animalium*, 16.

71 See further Mâle, E., 1984, pp. 79–91.

72 *Mahasudassana Sutta*, 1.10–48, (transl.) Rhys Davids, T.W., (SBE, vol. 11), 1881, pp. 251–9.

73 *Mahabharata*, 8.24.3–44. See Artefacts, note 10, above.

74 Rao, T.A.G., 1916, vol. 2, part 1, p. 150. *Kurma Purana*, part 2, Adhyaya 5 (Shlokas 47), ch. 5, ed. Gupta, A.S., 1972, various translators, pp. 309–14.

75 Ferrara, A.J., *Nanna-Suen's Journey to Nippur*, Rome, 1973 (doctoral thesis).

76 1 Cor. 13.13.

77 Hesiod, *Theog.*, 904–6.

78 *Ibid.*, 907–11.

79 Seneca, *De Beneficiis*, 1.3.2.

80 See Aston, W. G., 1956, vol. 1, pp. 41–5.

81 Matt. 25.1–13.

82 Vincent of Beauvais, *Speculum Doctrinale*, 1.9.

83 See Dickinson, G. and Wrigglesworth, L., 1990, *passim*.

84 Xenophon, *Memorabilia*, 2.1.22ff.

85 *Rig-Veda*, Griffith, R.T.H., 1920, 1.154.1–6, p. 207.

86 *Ibid.*, 1.155.6, vol. 1, p. 208.

87 *Matsya Purana*, 167.13–25; part 2, pp. 130–1. (Same edn. as note 89 below.)

88 *Satapatha Brahmana*, 1.8.1.1–6. See O'Flaherty, W. D., 1975, pp. 179–84.

89 *Matsya Purana*, 1.9–33; 2.1–19. (Sacred Books of the Aryans), (transl.) various (ed. Akhtar, J.D.), Delhi, 1972, pp. 4–7.

90 *Vishnu Purana*, 1.4. See Wilson, H.H., 1961, pp. 26, 27 (and note 6), 28–9.

91 *Padma Purana* (transl.), Deshpande, N. A., Delhi, 1988.

92 *Vayu Purana*, 2.36.74–86. See Tagare, G.V., 1988.

93 Rao, T.A.G., 1914–16, vol. 1, part 1, pp. 181–6.

94 *Ramayana*, bk. 6, canto 110. See Griffith, R.T.H., 1915.

95 *Vishnu Purana*, 3.17. See Wilson H.H., 1961, pp. 269–70: the 'Deceiver' is called 'an illusory form' by Wilson. See also 3.18, *passim*, on Buddhism and Jainism as heresies.

96 *Rig-Veda*, 10.7.1–2; 10.10.1–14. See Griffith, R.T.H., 1926 (vol. 2), pp. 391–4.

97 *Rig-Veda*, Griffith, R.T.H., 1920, 1926, *passim*; see index to both vols.

Bibliography

ALLEN, M.R., *Japanese Art Motives*, Chicago, 1917.

ASTON, W.G. (transl.), *Nihongi: Chronicles of Japan from the Earliest Times to AD 697* (2 vols.), London, 1956.

BACHHOFER, L., *A Short History of Chinese Art*, New York, 1946.

BAHM, A.J. (transl.), *Bhagavad Gita*, Bombay, 1970.

BALL, KATHERINE, M., *Decorative Motives of Oriental Art*, London, 1927.

BANERJEA, J.N., *The Development of Hindu Iconography*, Calcutta, 1956.

BASHAM, A.L., *The Wonder that was India*, London, 1954.

BEHLING, L., *Die Pflanze in der mittelalterlichen Tafelmalerei*, Weimar, 1957.

BHATTACHARYYA, B., *The Indian Buddhist Iconography*, London, 1924.

———, (transl.) *Nispanna-yogavali*, Calcutta, 1949.

BLACK, J. and GREEN, A., *Gods, Demons and Symbols of Ancient Mesopotamia*, London, 1992.

BOAS, G., *The Hieroglyphics of Horapollo* (Bollingen Series 23), Princeton, 1950; rev. edn. 1993.

BREUIL, H., *Four Hundred Centuries of Cave Art*, Montignac, 1952.

BUDGE, E.A.W., *The Book of the Dead*, London, 1928 (2nd rev. edn.).

BUHOT, JEAN, *Chinese and Japanese Art*, New York, 1967.

BULLING, A., *The Decoration of Mirrors of the Han Period*, Ascona, 1960.

CHAMBERLAIN, B.H., *Kojiki, or Records of Ancient Matters*, Trans. of the Asiatic Soc. of Japan, vol. x, supplement, Tokyo, 1932.

CHAVANNES, EDOUARD, *Mission Archéologique dans la Chine septentrionale*, 1909–15.

CLARK, R.T. RUNDLE, *Myth and Symbol in Ancient Egypt*, London, 1959.

COOMARASWAMY, A.K., *History of Indian and Indonesian Art*, New York, 1927.

———, *Elements of Buddhist Iconography*, New Delhi, 1972.

COPELAND, C., *Tankas from the Koelz Collection*, Michigan, 1980.

CORT, L.A. and STUART, J., *Joined Colours: Decoration and Meaning in Chinese Porcelain* (exhib. cat.), Washington D.C., 1993.

COWELL, E.B. (transl.), *Buddhist Mahayana Sutras* (SBE. no. 49), Oxford, 1894.

———, (transl.), *Jataka* (6 vols. + index), Cambridge, 1895–1907, 1913.

CUMONT, F., *The Mysteries of Mithra*, Chicago, 1903.

———, *Recherches sur le symbolisme funéraire des Romains*, Paris, 1942.

D'ALVIELLA, G., *The Migration of Symbols*, Brussels, 1884.

DALLEY, S., *Myths from Mesopotamia*, Oxford, 1989.

DANTHINE, H., *Le palmier-dattier et les arbres sacrés*, Paris, 1937.

DAVIS, F. HADLAND, *Myths and Legends of Japan*, Singapore, 1913.

DICKINSON, G. and WRIGGLESWORTH, L., *Imperial Wardrobe*, London, 1990.

DIDRON, A.N., *Christian Iconography* (transl., Millington, E.J.), London, 1851.

DORSON, R.M., *Folk Legends of Japan*, Rutland, Vermont, 1962.

DOWSON, J., *Classical Dictionary of Hindu Mythology*, London, 1968.

EBERHARD, WOLFRAM, *A Dictionary of Chinese Symbols*, London, 1986.

EDMUNDS, W.H., *Pointers and Clues to the Subjects of Chinese and Japanese Art*, London, 1934.

FAULKNER, R.O. (transl.), *The Ancient Egyptian Pyramid Texts*, Oxford, 1969.

———, *The Ancient Egyptian Coffin Texts* (3 vols.), Warminster, 1973.

———, *The Ancient Egyptian Book of the Dead*, London, 1985 (rev. edn.).

FERGUSON, G., *Signs and Symbols in Christian Art*, New York, 1954.

FRANKFORT, H., *Cylinder Seals, A Documentary Essay on the Art and Religion of the Ancient Near East*, London, 1939.

———, *The Art and Architecture of the Ancient Orient*, Harmondsworth, 1970 (4th rev. edn.).

FRAZER, J.G. (transl.), Apollodorus (Loeb), 1921.

GETTY, A., *The Gods of Northern Buddhism*, Oxford, 1914.

GILES, H.A., *A Chinese Biographical Dictionary*, London, 1898.

GOMBRICH, E.H., *Symbolic Images: Studies in the Art of the Renaissance*, London, 1972.

GORDON, A.K., *The Iconography of Tibetan Lamaism*, New York, 1939.

———, *Tibetan Religious Art*, New York, 1952.

GRAVES, R., *The Greek Myths*, Harmondsworth, 1955.

GRIFFITH, R.T.H. (transl.), *The Ramayan*, Benares, 1915.

———, *The Hymns of the Rig-Veda*, (2 vols.), Benares, 1920, 1926.

HAIG, E., *The Floral Symbolism of the Great Masters*, London, 1913.

HALL, J., *Dictionary of Subjects and Symbols in Art*, London, 1979 (rev. edn.).

HANSFORD, S. HOWARD, *A Glossary of Chinese Art and Archaeology*, London, 1961 (rev. edn.).

HARRISON, J.E., *Themis*, Cambridge, 1927 (rev. edn.).

HART, G., *Egyptian Gods and Goddesses*, London, 1986.

———, *Egyptian Myths*, London, 1990.

HOOK, B. (ed.), *The Cambridge Encyclopaedia of China*, 1982.

HUGHES, R., *Heaven and Hell in Western Art*, London, 1968.

JAMESON, A.B., *Sacred and Legendary Art*, London, 1848.

———, *Legends of the Monastic Orders*, London, 1850.

————, *Legends of the Madonna*, London, 1852.
————, *History of Our Lord*, London, 1864.
JANSON, H.W., *A History of Art*, London, 1962.
JING-NUAN, WU (transl.), *Yi Jing (I Ching), The Book of Changes*, Hawaii, 1991.
JOLY, H.L., *Legend in Japanese Art*, London, 1908.
JOUVEAU-DUBREUIL, G., *Iconography of Southern India*, Paris, 1937.
KAFTAL, G., *The Saints in Italian Art* (3 vols.), Florence, 1965–85.
KAGEYAMA, HARUKI, *The Arts of Shinto* (transl. Christine Guth), New York, 1973.
KARLGREN, BERNHARD (transl.), *Book of Documents (Shu Ching)*, Stockholm, 1950.
————, (transl.), *The Book of Odes (Shih Ching)*, Stockholm, 1950.
KATZENELLENBOGEN, A., *Allegories of the Virtues and Vices in Medieval Art* (Warburg Institute Studies, vol. 10), London, 1939.
KEITH, A.B. (transl.), *Taittiriya Samhita*, Harvard Oriental Series, 1914.
KIRSCHBAUM, E., *Lexikon der Christlichen Ikonographie*, Freiburg im Breisgau, 1968–72.
KNIPPING, B., *De Iconografie van de Contra-Reformatie in de Nederlanden*, Hilversum, 1939–40.
KRAMER, S.N., *From the Tablets of Sumer*, New York, 1956, reprinted as *History begins at Sumer*, 1959.
————, *The Sumerians: their History, Culture and Character*, Chicago, 1963.
KUNSTLE, K., *Ikonographie der Christlichen Kunst*, Freiburg, 1926–8.
LEGGE, J., *The Chinese Classics* (5 vols. as 4), Hong Kong (rep.), 1961.
LICHTEIM, M., *Ancient Egyptian Literature*, (3 vols), Calif. U.P., 1973–80.
LIEBERT, G., *Iconographic Dictionary of the Indian Religions*, Delhi, 1986 (rev. edn.).
LINDUFF, K.M., *Tradition, Phase and Style of Shang and Chou Bronze Vessels*, New York/London, 1979 (rev. edn)
LOEHR, MAX, *Buddhist Thought and Imagery*, Harvard, 1961.
————, *Chinese Art: Symbols and Images*, Catalogue of an exhibition at Wellesley College, Mass., 1967.
LURKER, M., *The Gods and Symbols of Ancient Egypt*, London, 1980.
LYALL, L.A., *Book of Meng-tseu*, London, 1932.
MACDONELL, ARTHUR, A., *A History of Sanskrit Literature*, London, 1905.
MACFIE, J.M. (transl.), *The Vishnu Purana*, (2 vols.), Madras, 1926.
MALCOLM, M., *Thangka Art*, catalogue of an exhibition at the Doris Wiener Gallery, New York, 1974.
MALE, E., *L'art réligieux de la fin du XVIe siècle, du XVIIe siècle et du XVIIIe siècle*, Paris, 1951.
————, *Religious Art in France: the Twelfth Century*, Princeton (Bollingen Series 90: i), 1978 (rev. edn.).
————, *Ibid, The Thirteenth Century*, (Boll. 90: ii), 1984.
————, *Ibid, The Late Middle Ages*, (Boll. 90: iii), 1986.
MARLE, R. VAN, *Iconographie de l'art profane au moyen age et à la Renaissance*, The Hague, 1931.
MITCHELL, A.G., *Hindu Gods and Goddesses*, London, 1982.
MUNSTERBERG, H., *The Folk Arts of Japan*, Tokyo, 1959.
NIHARA-RANJANA, R., *Brahmanical Gods in Burma: a Chapter of Indian Art and Iconography*, Calcutta, 1932.
O'FLAHERTY, W.D., *Hindu Myths*, Harmondsworth, 1975.
OLSON, E., *Tantric Buddhist Art*, New York, 1974.
PANOFSKY, E., *Studies in Iconology*, New York, 1939.
————, *Early Netherlandish Painting: its Origins and Character*, Cambridge, (Mass.), 1953.
————, *Meaning in the Visual Arts*, New York, 1957.
PARROT, A., *Sumer*, London, 1960.
————, *Nineveh and Babylon*, London, 1961.
PETIT, K., *Le monde des symboles dans l'art de la Chine*, Brussels, 1981.
PHILIPPI, D.L. (transl.), *Kojiki*, Princeton, 1969.
PIGLER, A., *Barockthemen*, Budapest, 1956.
PRITCHARD, J.B., *Ancient Near Eastern Texts*, Princeton, 1955.
RAO, T.A.G., *Elements of Hindu Iconography* (4 vols.), Madras, 1914–16.
RAWSON, JESSICA (ed.), various contributors, *The British Museum Book of Chinese Art*, London, 1992.
————, *Chinese Bronzes: Art and Ritual*, London, 1987.
RAWSON, PHILIP, *The Art of Tantra*, London, 1973.
REAU, L., *Iconographie de l'art chrétien*, (6 vols.), Paris, 1957.
RHIE, M.M. and THURMAN, R.A.F., *Wisdom and Compassion: the Sacred Art of Tibet*, catalogue of an exhibition at the Royal Academy of Arts, London, 1992.
RIPA, C., *Iconologia*, Rome, 1603 (illus. edn.); reprinted New York, 1970.
ROERICH, G., *Tibetan Paintings*, Paris, 1925.
SANYAL, J.M. (transl.), *Bhagavata Purana*, Calcutta, 1930–34.
SARASVATI, S.S.P. and VIDYALANKAR (transl.), *Rig-Veda*, (10 vols.), New Delhi, 1977–82.
SAUNDERS, E.D., *Mudra: a Study of Symbolic Gestures in Japanese Buddhist Sculpture*, New York, 1960.
SAXL, F., *Lectures* (Warburg Institute), London, 1957.
SCHILLER, GERTRUD, *Iconography of Christian Art*, London, 1971–2.
SEATON, R.C. (transl.), *Argonautica* (Loeb), 1912.
SECKEL, DIETRICH, *The Art of Buddhism*, London, 1964.
SEN, R.N. (transl.), *Brahma-vairata Purana*, (SBH. vol. 24), 1920.
STROMMENGER, E., *The Art of Mesopotamia*, London, 1964.
SULLIVAN, M., *An Introduction to Chinese Art*, London, 1961.
TAGARE, G.V. (transl.), *Bhagavata Purana*, Delhi, 1978.
————, *Brahmanda Purana*, Delhi, 1983.
————, *Vayu Purana*, Delhi, 1988.

TERVARENT, GUY de, *Attributs et symboles dans l'art profane, 1460–1600*, Geneva, 1958.

THOMAS, E.J., *The Life of Buddha as Legend and History*, London (rev. edn.), 1949.

VAN BUITENEN, J.A.B. (transl.), *Mahabharata* (2 vols.), Chicago, 1973.

VAN BUREN, E.D., *The Sacred Marriage,* Rome, 1932.

———, *The Flowering Vase*, Berlin, 1933.

———, *Symbols of the Gods in Mesopotamian Art*, Rome, 1945.

VAN LAARHOVEN, J., *De beeldtaal van de christelijke kunst. Geschiedenis van de iconografie*, Nijmegen, 1992.

VINYCOMB, J., *Fictitious and Symbolic Creatures in Art*, London, 1906.

VISSER, M.W. de., *Arhats in China and Japan*, Berlin, 1923.

VOLKER, T., *The Animal in Far Eastern Art*, Leiden, 1950.

VUILLEUMIER, B., *Symbolism of Chinese Imperial Robes*, London, 1939.

WADDELL, L.A., *The Buddhism of Tibet, or Lamaism*, London, 1895.

WALEY, ARTHUR (transl.), *The Book of Songs (Shih Ching)*, London, 1954 (rev. edn.).

WERNER, E.T.C., *Myths and Legends of China*, London, 1922.

WILHELM, RICHARD, *Book of Changes (I Ching)*, London, 1951.

WILLIAMS, C.A.S., *Outlines of Chinese Symbolism and Art Motives*, Shanghai, 1941 (rev. edn.).

WILSON, H.H. (transl.), *Vishnu Purana*, Calcutta, 1961 (3rd edn.).

WIND, E., *Pagan Mysteries in the Renaissance*, Harmondsworth, 1967.

WINTERNITZ, E., *Musical Instruments and their Symbolism in Western Art*, London, 1967.

YETTS, W.P., *Symbolism in Chinese Art*, The China Society, 1912.

ZIMMER, H., *Myths and Symbols in Indian Art and Civilization*, Princeton, 1946.

Chronological Tables

EGYPT

BC mid-4th cent.– c. 3100	Predynastic Period.	Worship of Mother-Goddess. Local gods worshipped in animal and plant form.
c. 3100–2613	Early Dynastic, or Archaic Period (1st–3rd Dynasties).	Union of kingdoms of Upper and Lower Egypt (1st Dyn.). Pharaoh becomes the incarnation of Horus. First pyramid built (3rd Dyn.). Anthropomorphic gods.
c. 2613–2181	Old Kingdom (4th–6th Dyn.).	Pyramid Texts (end of 5th Dyn., through 6th Dyn.).
c. 2181–2133	First Intermediate Period (7th–10th Dyn.).	Early Coffin Texts. Doctrine of the Judgement of the Dead formulated. Osiris the pre-eminent god of the dead.
c. 2133–1786	Middle Kingdom (11th–12th Dyn.).	Later Coffin Texts. Growth of the cult of Amun.
c. 1786–1567	Second Intermediate Period (13th–17th Dyn.).	Hyksos invasion and rule (15th–17th Dyn.) accompanied by infiltration of Syrian gods.
c. 1567–1085	New Kingdom (18th–20th Dyn.).	First *Book of the Dead* papyri (mid-18th Dyn.). Amun becomes supreme national deity. Reign of Tutankhamun (19th Dyn.).
c. 1085–343	Late Dynastic Period (21st–30th Dyn.).	Veneration of sacred animals; catacombs for Apis bulls built at Sakkara (26th Dyn.). Persian domination (27th Dyn.).
323	Conquest by Alexander the Great.	
323–30	Ptolemaic (Hellenistic) Period.	Cult of Graeco–Egyptian deity, Serapis, introduced by Ptolemy I. Cult of Isis spreads to Greece and Rome.
30 BC–AD 395	Egypt a Roman Province.	Founding of Coptic Church. First Christian hermits in the Theban desert (early 4th cent.).

MESOPOTAMIA

c. 4000–3100 BC	Uruk (Warka) Period.	Uruk the capital of Sumer. Invention of writing by the Sumerians, *c.* 3400 BC.
c. 3100–2390	Early Dynastic Period.	First city states. Gilgamesh the legendary king of Sumer. Oldest known cylinder seals.
c. 2390–2210	Akkadian Empire.	Founded by Sargon 'the Great'.
2168–2050	Third Dynasty of Ur.	Developments in architecture: ziggurats and temples.
2073–1819	Isin and Larsa Kingdoms.	
1950–1651	Old Babylonian Period.	Code of Hammurabi, king of Babylon (1848–1806).
1651–1157	Kassite (Middle Babylonian) Period.	'Kudurru' (boundary stones) and brick reliefs the characteristic monuments.
1500–1350	Mitannian Kingdom (northern Mesopotamia).	The 'sacred tree' becomes the most popular motif on cylinder seals.
1350–1000	Middle Assyrian Period.	The rise of the city of Ashur. Prominence of fabulous monsters on cylinder seals.
883–612	Neo-Assyrian Empire.	Subjugation of Egypt. Relief sculpture now a flourishing art, as in the palace of Ashurnasirpal II at Nimrud (Br. Mus., etc).
625–539	Neo-Babylonian Empire.	Nebuchadnezzar II rebuilds Babylon, 604–562 BC.
538	Achaemenid Persia. Cyrus captures Babylon.	
332	Alexander the Great takes Babylon.	
126 BC–AD 227	Arsacid (Parthian) Empire.	
226–651	Sassanian Empire.	
636	The coming of Islam.	

INDIA

c. 2500–1500 BC	Indus Valley civilization (the Harappa culture).	Stamp seals depicting a 'horned god' and sacred animals.
c. 1750–1500	Indus Valley peoples conquered by Aryan (Indo-European) tribesmen.	
c. 1200		The *Rig-Veda* hymns first written down (previously handed down orally).
c. 900–700		Composition of the *Brahmanas*.
c. 700		Composition of the *Upanishads*.
From 600		Vedic gods represented as symbols on coins.
c. 563–*c.* 483	Gautama Shakyamuni, the Buddha.	
c. 540	Birth of Vardhamana Mahavira, founder of Jainism.	
327–5	Invasion of Alexander the Great.	
c. 324–187	Maurya Dynasty.	
c. 273–232	Ashoka, Emperor of India, promotes Buddhism as the state religion.	First stupas built at Sanchi and Bharhut. 'Ashoka' pillars.
2nd cent. BC		Earliest textual records of images of Hindu gods in human form.
0–*c.* AD 100	Mahayana Buddhism fully developed.	
200 BC–AD 200		Composition of the *Ramayana*.
300 BC–AD 300		Composition of the *Mahabharata*.
1st–2nd cents.		First known images of Buddha in human form in Mathura and Gandhara.
2nd–5th cents.		Flowering of Gandharan art, much influenced by Rome.
320–*c.* 540	Gupta Empire.	
From 400s		Classical Gupta sculpture in Mathura and Sarnath, lasting until *c.* 750.
6th cent.	Development of Vajrayana Buddhism.	

From 1192	Islamic conquests of northern India.	Hindu and Buddhist monasteries and temples destroyed; Buddhism almost extinguished in the north.
1310	Mysore conquered by Islam. Muslim rulers dominate northern India until 18th cent.	In southern India, Shivaite Hinduism remains the predominant religion. Here, Vishnavite worship and imagery revived in the 14th cent.
17th cent.		Development of Rajput painting, popularizing Krishna.

CHINA
Pinyin in brackets

Early Dynasties		
Shang	*c.* 1500–1050 BC	The casting of ritual bronze vessels. Divination by 'oracle bones'. Development of written language. Ritual jade objects in use since Neolithic times.
Chou (Zhou)		Confucius (*c.* 551–479 BC).
Western	1050–771 BC	
Eastern	771–475 BC	
The Warring States	475–221 BC	
Imperial China		
Ch'in (Qin)	221–207 BC	Political unification of China.
Han		Revival of learning and establishment of classical literature.
W. Han	206 BC–AD 9	
Hsin (Xin)	AD 9–25	
E. Han	AD 25–220	First evidence of Buddhist communities, AD 65. Paper gradually replaces bamboo strips and silks for writing.
Three kingdoms		Warfare between the kingdoms inspired a great popular literature of romantic heroism.
Shu	221–263	
Wei	220–265	
Wu	222–280	
The Six Dynasties	263–589	Fa-hsien (Fa Xian), pilgrim monk, travels to India and Indonesia (*c.* 399) collecting Buddhist texts.
Northern Dynasties	386–581	Development of Buddhist sculpture, 5th–6th cent.
Sui	589–618	
T'ang (Tang)	618–906	Thriving period for all the arts under a stable dynasty.
The Five Dynasties	907–960	
Sung (Song)	960–1279	Imperial patronage of painting and other arts.
Yüan (Yuan)	1279–1368	
Ming	1368–1644	Progress of porcelain manufacture and decoration.
Ch'ing (Qing), or Manchu	1644–1911	
Republican	1912–	

JAPAN

4th–7th cents AD	Tumulus (Kofun) period.	Ritual objects from 6th cent. tombs (mirror, *magatama*, etc).
4th cent.	Earliest cultural influences from Korea and China, including writing.	
4th–5th cents.	Confucian and Taoist ideologies reach Japan.	
400	Probably earliest sporadic contact with Buddhism.	
585–7	Emperor Yomei accepts Buddhism.	Pairing of Buddhist and Shinto deities begins.
646–784	Nara period.	Great age of sculpture; Buddhist art under T'ang (Chinese) influence.
712		*Kojiki* (Records of Ancient matters.).
720		*Nihongi* (or *Nihon shoki*) (Chronicles of Japan.).
8th cent.	Rise of Shinto cults at sacred mountains: Hachiman, Sanno and Kumano.	
768	Shrine of Kasuga cult established under Mt Mikasu.	
794–1185	Heian period.	Development of wooden images in Shinto shrines (oldest extant examples 859–77).
11th cent.	Zao Gongen cult (Mt Kimpu).	
13th cent.		*Yamato-e* school of painting (oldest extant 13th cent.).
1185–1568		Amalgamation of Buddhist and Shinto deities reaches its peak.
1615–1868	Tokugawa period (Edo). Renaissance of Confucianism and Shintoism.	Lacquer, textiles and *netsuke* flourish.
1868	Official separation of Buddhism and Shintoism.	

TIBET

AD 638	Buddhism introduced into Tibet in the reign of Songtsen Gampo by his two wives (Chinese and Nepalese), both ardent Buddhists.	
640s		First Buddhist temples built at Llasa to house sacred statues brought by the royal wives.
747	Padmasambhava, Indian monk, comes to Tibet. Founder of Lamaism, and the Red Cap sect: his doctrines Tantric. Santarakshita (705–62), first abbot of Samyai, a Tantric teacher.	First Lamaist monastery built at Samyai in the reign of Trisong Detsen (c. 755–97).
826–c. 900	Persecution and decline of Lamaist Buddhism in central Tibet.	
1026	Atisha Dipamkara (c. 980–1058), Indian Buddhist priest and writer, comes to Tibet. Founds the Kadampa sect.	Revival of sculpture and wall-painting from the 11th cent. in western and central Tibet, mainly derived from Kashmiri sources. Development of *tangka* paintings.
1040–1123	Mila-Repa, the 'cotton-clad', Tibetan mendicant sage, poet, founder of the reformist Mahamudra school of Lamaism.	
1253	Conquest of eastern Tibet by Kublai Khan, who became a Lamaist convert.	
1357–1419	Tsong-kha-pa, writer, reformer, founder of the Yellow Cap sect, which remains the principal Lamaist sect. Its head is the Dalai Lama. Developing links with China.	Artistic renaissance accompanying the founding of monasteries. Growth of monumental bronze sculpture.
c. 1546	Mongol invasion of northern Tibet.	
1645	Potala palace, Llasa, residence of the Dalai Lamas, begun by Mongol prince, Gusri Khan.	Evolution of so-called 'black tangkas' in second half of 17th cent., which became a national Tibetan style.
1720	Civil war; Tibet finally brought under Chinese rule.	Destruction of many monasteries by Chinese troops.

THE WEST

BC *c.* 2000–1700	Middle Minoan, or 'Proto-palatial' period in Crete.	The first palaces built at Knossos, Phaestos, Mallia. Painted pottery, seal impressions.
c. 1400	Rise of Mycenaean empire.	
13th cent.	Greece invaded by northern Achaeans.	
c. 810–730		Composition of the *Iliad* and *Odyssey*.
8th cent.	Rise of Etruscans in central Italy.	
c. 700		Hesiod.
510	Foundation of the Roman republic.	
5th cent.	Golden Age of Greek civilization.	Building of Athens under Pericles.
c. 500–417		Pheidias.
356–323	Alexander the Great.	
205		Worship of Cybele, Mother-Goddess, introduced to Rome.
70–19		Virgil.
43 BC–AD 17		Ovid.
27 BC–AD 14	Augustus (Octavian) (b. 63 BC), first Roman emperor.	Deification of Roman emperors.
13 BC		Founding of the Altar of Peace (*Ara Pacis Augustae*) at Rome.
8 or 7 BC	Birth of Jesus.	
3rd cent. AD		First non-figurative Christian art.
313	Constantine the Great grants freedom of worship to Christians.	
330	East Roman, or Byzantine, Empire established, its capital Constantinople.	Use of mosaic in Byzantine churches.
726–843		Prohibition of religious images in Byzantine churches.
800	Charlemagne crowned Holy Roman Emperor.	
768–814		Carolingian renaissance.

910	Founding of Cluny abbey, Burgundy.	Growth of pilgrimage.
Mid-11th to end of 12th cent.		Romanesque art and architecture, much influenced by Cluny.
1095–1204	First Crusade	
1170–1221	Dominic	Art of the Dominican Order.
1181/2–1226	Francis of Assisi	Art of the Franciscan Order.
Mid-12th to 15th cent.		Gothic art and architecture. Flowering of monumental sculpture.
Mid-14th cent.	The Black Death	Themes of death and judgement in art.
1377–1446		Brunelleschi. First Renaissance architecture in Italy. Painting and sculpture promoted by new lay patronage.
1483–1546	Martin Luther	
1509–64	John Calvin	
1545–63	Council of Trent	New departures in Christian iconography – the Baroque period.
17th cent.		Revival of symbolic still-life in the Protestant North – 'vanitas' painting.
mid-18th cent.		Revival of the Graeco-Roman themes in French art – the neo-classical movement, a reaction against Catholic Baroque.
18th-early 19th cent.		Protestant iconoclasm, especially in France (exacerbated by the French Revolution), Germany and the Netherlands.

Index

234